LITERARY CULTURE AND TRANSLATION

Literary Culture and Translation

New Aspects of Comparative Literature

edited by

DOROTHY M. FIGUEIRA
CHANDRA MOHAN

PRIMUS BOOKS
An imprint of Ratna Sagar P. Ltd.
Virat Bhavan
Mukherjee Nagar Commercial Complex
Delhi 110 009

Offices at CHENNAI LUCKNOW
AGRA AHMEDABAD BENGALURU COIMBATORE DEHRADUN GUWAHATI
HYDERABAD JAIPUR JALANDHAR KANPUR KOCHI KOLKATA MADURAI
MUMBAI PATNA RANCHI VARANASI

First published 2017

ISBN: 978-93-84082-51-2 (hardback)
ISBN: 978-93-84092-73-3 (POD)
ISBN: 978-93-84092-76-4 (e-book)

Published by Primus Books

Lasertypeset in Bembo by Shine Graphics
Amar Colony, East Gokalpur, Delhi 110 094

Printed and bound in India by Replika Press Pvt. Ltd.

Contents

Preface

'COMPARATIVE LITERATURE is not only legitimate: now, as often as not, ours is the first violin that sets the tone for the rest of the Orchestra. Our conclusions have become other people's assumptions' (Saussy 2006: 3). This assessment of our discipline by one of its foremost practitioners, Haun Saussy, conveys the multiple rhythms and the varied sounds which play harmoniously together. This harmony is what makes the splendid music of Comparative Literature and contributes to its continued relevance in literary and cultural studies today.

Comparative Literary Studies in India and elsewhere has made many new and fresh contributions in several important areas of the Humanities and Social Sciences during the long span of twenty-five years since I edited the *Aspects of Comparative Literature* in 1989. Even at that time during his visit to India, the eminent scholar Henry Remak in his foreword to the book had written: 'Diversity in point of view and lusty dissent demonstrate that Comparative Literature in India is alive, well and kicking' (1989: vii).

Since then, much water has flown into the Indian and Atlantic Oceans and the Arabian Sea. Along with this ebb and flow have come new fragrant breezes. Comparative Literature seems to have attained maturity and Translation Studies is in the process of gaining acceptance as a discipline in Indian, South Asian, East Asian, European, South American and North American universities. In India, a remarkable change has occurred in the recent past that has strengthened the academic status and recognition accorded to the study of Comparative Literature. In addition to the already existing courses in the state universities, several newly opened central universities in India introduced Comparative Literature and Translation Studies either as a separate discipline or as part of another literature discipline, e.g. English or an Indian language Literature: Hindi, Gujarati, Bengali, Malayalam, etc. At the time when the first edition of this book was published, the University Grants Commission of India had just introduced the NET (National Eligibility Test) in the subject of

Comparative Literature. This provision supplied the much required impetus of formal recognition to Comparative Literature as a discipline and continues to do so today.

The practice of Comparative Literature in India has found a valuable resource in the discipline of translation. Translation between Indian languages has a tradition reaching back hundreds of years. Languages such as Persian, Arabic, Chinese and Tibetan (not to mention English, German and French) have actively contributed towards the growth of literary studies in India. The focus is quickly shifting from a hegemonic notion of what Roman Jakobson called 'interlingual translation' and moving towards incorporating inter-semiotic translation in a big way. Thus, translating for the audio-visual media (subtitling, etc.) and the study of the same is on its way to constituting an important part of the Translation Studies modules. Moreover, Comparative Indian Translation has long viewed the act of translation itself as an important constituent within larger loci of cultural exchange. Thus, how Shakespeare and Molière have been translated and received in the different Indian *bhashas* constitutes an important area of critical inquiry within Comparative Literature syllabi in Indian universities. Molière's *L'Amour Médecin*, for instance, inspired Girishchandra Ghosh, one of Bengal's greatest playwrights. The latter adapted the French play into Bangla, by and large retaining the plot, but situating the events in a colonial Bengali context. Thus, contemporary politics of nationalism and the concomitant commercialization of nationalism itself are all new elements that work their way into the text and give it a fresh lease on life. Hence, Translation Studies is a closely allied area which we address in this present volume.

The contours of translation which became sources of inspiration for the students of Comparative Indian Literature include a good number of ancient masterpieces. These include Dara Shikoh's translation of the *Upanishads* from Sanskrit to Persian titled as *Sirr-i-Astrar* or *Sirr-i-Akbar*, Charles Wilkins's translation of the *Bhagavad Gita* (1785), Sir William Jones's translation of *Abhijnanasakuntalam* (1789), Horace Hayman Wilson's translation of *Meghaduta* (1813), all these classics were translated from Sanskrit to English. Another translation work of merit includes *The Principal Upanishads* by Purohit Swami in association with W.B. Yeats in the mid-1930s.

Translation as a discipline has gained greater visibility during the past decades all over the world. In India, it has emerged both as a discipline and a vocation which is unlike other sites where translation has acquired respectable ground. With the emergence of a new literary condition in India, translators have come forward as major negotiators between linguistic and cultural clusters. They have to choose their text with greater care and consideration now than before, and decide on their translational strategy with greater caution since the text they produce is liable to be appropriated further. In India, this appropriation is taking place in the best possible way in the domain of Comparative Studies where it is gaining greater ground at a faster pace and becoming an authentic literary engagement. With the increasing number of texts available in translation today and with the slow but steady emergence of Comparative Studies in India, the prospects of both translation as a vocation and Comparative Literature as a discipline have grown quite considerably. In a major way, the new Indian literary scenario is being redefined, disciplines are being re-contextualized, and texts and authors are being relocated. Now, such authors who received no attention earlier are under critical focus. Similarly, texts are being translated now which did not receive any attention previously. With the coming of the peripheral to the centre, literary dynamics have changed and parameters of reception have undergone major transformation. Even though translation and Comparative Studies have always gone hand in hand, this is the time when both have re-organized themselves as major concerns of the literary and the non-literary reader simultaneously. This is a time of new prospects and perspectives in Translation Studies all over the world but more so in India, where the multilingual and multicultural nature of the Indian nation determines the literary scenario in a substantial manner.

It is now a well realized and an acknowledged fact that interdisciplinarity has become an area of study and research in Comparative Literature Studies programmes. It has particular relevance to India which is a multilingual society with highly diverse cultural traditions interacting and co-existing in a dynamic state of dialogue with other disciplines. Let me deliberate upon this important point in a little detail. The concept of interdisciplinarity and pluralism has been part of the Indian psyche from time immemorial. The *Taittiriya Upanishad* speaks of the discovery of *Mahas*, which was considered to be the conscious-will, the creative energy of the whole universe. It has come to us as a perception of unity. The noted aesthetician Kireet Joshi states that this concept, if studied in depth, provides the foundation for promoting interdisciplinarity among the various domains of knowledge that are understood in India as departments of the universe considered as a whole. It also implies the synthesis of the old and the new, the East and the West (cited in Singh 2013: ix). As far back as 400 BC the eminent theoretician Sushrute proclaimed that we should not come to a conclusion or decision by studying just one discipline. He makes clear his belief gleaned from experience in the following *shloka*:

> *Ekam Shastram adhiyano na vidya shastra nischayam*
> *Tasmat bahushrutah shastram biyaniyach chikitsaha.*
>
> —*Sushruta Samhita, Sutra Stham,*
> Chapter IV, *Shloka* 7, *Prabhasriya* Adhyaya (Singh 2013: ix)

Thus, the tradition of interrelational integrated study of the subject from different perspectives in Indian scholarship provides a viable and sound grounding for initiating comparative and interdisciplinary studies in Indian universities. It is, therefore, imperative that we in India study literature in a comparative framework to understand the nuances of the multiple strands that make up the core areas of our literatures. In a globalized world, where the Indian diaspora has access to the best of the world's fiction, poetry, drama, films and theory, we cannot remain insular and isolated from the global community of readers and writers. And indeed, Indian literature written in English and Indian writing translated into English have now made their mark beyond the borders of India. It is against this context that this volume is being reissued with new essays and case studies that reflect the vitality and vigour of Comparative Literature in India.

This process has taken various forms and has manifested itself in pedagogical reformulations both in the Indian context and in the West. Among other things, Comparative Literature has responded to this with alacrity. While the focus of Comparative Literature in India initially was admittedly on an archival level (in conformity with what was traditionally identified as the literary), the contours of our discipline have undergone certain changes in India over the last several decades. For example, the Department of Comparative Literature at Jadavpur University, confidently states that it has been teaching Niccolò Machiavelli's *Il Principe* (The Prince) since the late 1970s. This text is also part of the syllabus in many departments of Politics, Political Science and International Relations. By incorporating such a text in its curriculum, Comparative Literature gives it an 'afterlife' as it were. Can political treatises and historical documents be read as 'literature'? Or, indeed, what does 'literature' really mean to us today? These are questions that have been thrown up afresh by current practices in Comparative Literature in India. We note for instance that the B.A. course in Comparative Literature at Jadavpur University even teaches Hergé's *Tintin in the Congo* as a prescribed text.

It is aptly argued that an attempt to teach a text like *Tintin* obviously entails engaging with the historical context of the mid-twentieth century to understand the ambience within which Hergé was working. It is imperative to understand the tropes of colonialism and orientalism that were in circulation at that time. An understanding of Africa leads to a more nuanced understanding of Hergé's rather stereotypical depiction of black Africa in this comic book, which is said to border on racism.

Likewise, there are other disciplinary borders that end up getting breached when one reads a comic book like *Tintin* as a 'text' in the Comparative Literature classroom in India. There is an obvious engagement with art history and graphic technique that is called for. In such instances, practitioners of Comparative Literature need to master the skills and training of other arts and disciplinary contexts. An understanding of the differences between Hergé's early style of art and the *ligne claire* (or clear line) style he was to employ in his later works is essential in doing justice to the challenge of teaching such an unconventional text in the Indian university classroom.

Finally, the inclusion of such texts has a lasting and very important significance in the light of the prospects of Comparative Literature in the face of threats from the unformed and largely monolingual practices of Cultural/Culture Studies. With Comparative Literature striking this difficult balance in India between literary and non-literary texts, the entire project of Cultural Studies becomes problematic—one is left asking how it would be relevant in an age when Comparative Literature itself is fast reinventing itself along these lines. Again, Comparative Literature scholars in India have been undertaking projects that border on other disciplines that are not considered literary in the traditional sense. One notes, for example, work on researching, translating and anthologizing cultures of nationalism, translation and solidarity in the South Asian context, between Asia and Africa, as demonstrated in the papers.

Dorothy M. Figueira played the leading role in the preparation of this volume. She edited the contributions for consistency in style and language. She helped structure the thematic foci of these contributions from some of the most distinguished international scholars in the field. The essays collected here deal with pertinent concerns emerging from recent debates in comparative literary analysis and Translation Studies. We also examine the impact of our discipline on study of the Humanities in general. We worked with the sole objective of making this volume a useful resource for scholars, researchers and students in the discipline in India and abroad.

We are indeed grateful to all the eminent scholars who agreed to contribute their work. We would like to thank them for their patient cooperation especially through the long and meticulous editorial process.

New Delhi CHANDRA MOHAN

REFERENCES

Remak, Henry H.H., 'Foreword', in *Aspects of Comparative Literature: Current Approaches*, ed. Chandra Mohan, New Delhi: India Publishers & Distributors, 1989.

Saussy, Haun, ed., *Comparative Literature in an Age of Globalization: The 2004 ACLA Report on the State of the Discipline*, Baltimore: Johns Hopkins University Press, 2006.

Singh, A.K., *Towards Interdisciplinarity*, New Delhi: Creative Books, 2013.

Introduction

IN THE THIRTY-FIVE years since Chandra Mohan published *Aspects of Comparative Literature* much has changed in the field. To begin with, one of his Western-based compatriots had declared the death of the discipline (Spivak 2003). Perhaps, she was only looking in her near vicinity because at the very moment that she was offering her fatal diagnosis to a grieving (or jubilant) Western audience, Comparative Literature was growing by leaps and bounds in India. Perhaps, for this self-appointed spokesperson for the Indian other, it is simply that what happens in the West primarily matters. Certainly, departments of Comparative Literature in the US have been downsized and even absorbed into English Departments, as the emphasis on language training (always weak in America) declined and new theories and brands of criticism that did not demand Comparative Literature's linguistic breadth or methodology took precedence. Indeed, Comparative Literature also suffered attrition due to a paradigm shift towards Cultural Studies. But, to say that the discipline was 'dead', when it was thriving in Europe, developing in South America and Africa, and exploding in Asia (India, China, Japan, and Korea) was simply not true. While American Comparative Literature programmes were being reconfigured as foreign languages and literature programmes, absorbed (sometimes along with other programmes such as Slavic or Classics departments), morphing into Cultural Studies, or simply becoming something called 'Literature', half a dozen new Comparative Literature programmes cropped up in India in recently established and well-funded central universities located across the country. Not only would the new Comparative Literature programme be often the *first* humanities department founded in these universities, sometimes it was established in lieu of an English department! The prioritization of Comparative Literature was due to the fact that this discipline now meant something quite significant in the Indian context.

Gone were the days when Jadavpur University (Kolkata) provided the unique model of what Comparative Literature entailed in India. It prioritized Bengali literature and Western theoretical trends. It really was a product of Bengali institutions and its founding critics, who trained in the American Midwest, developed the programme along the model of Comparative Literature Departments one found in large land-grant state universities there. Because it was post-Nehruvian India, one studied Russian in addition to English, French and German. Also of interest were American New Criticism, British Marxist theory and whatever 'cutting-edge' Anglo-continental theory had come into vogue. In the new Indian Comparative Literature departments that have recently come into being, however, something quite unique has developed. While English Literature (with a smattering of French and German) and American, British and French theory have held their prestige, Indian Comparative Literature now follows a paradigm of its own making. The literatures compared today are as much domestic or internal to India or the Indian subcontinent as directed toward the West. The theory now studied focuses more on schools of thought deemed more pertinent to the Indian situation (colonial discourse analysis, postmodernism, Indian expressions of psychoanalytic theory, feminism, etc.).

These new Indian Comparative Literature programmes teach the literature of the state in which they are located, whatever European or African literatures they can field; and the literatures of other Indian *bhashas*. The tripartite emphasis of western Comparative Literature (traditionally English, French, and German) is now replaced, for example, by Malayalam, English, and Hindi. The new Indian Comparative Literature programmes also emphasize Translation Studies, thus, offering their students not only the skills needed to be scholars and teachers, but also the opportunity to develop as translators. While Translation Studies is devalued in many Comparative Literature programmes in the US (with the exception of Princeton), in India, it provides a principal focus. Comparative Literature programmes in India tend to compare internally and study (and occasionally speak for) their own minority communities, most significantly the Dalits and Adivasis. In this respect, Comparative Literature programmes in India differ from those in US universities which seem to be in constant need of new 'others' or minorities groups on whose behalf they wish to speak (traditional American ethnic minorities as well as 'newer' minority populations such as Gay, Lesbian, and Transgendered Studies, Male Studies, Disability Studies, Fat Studies, etc.). Contrary to Spivak's prognosis, the discipline is not dead but alive and kicking, if one looks at India in its present actuality and not as a fossilized object on a specimen tray to be 'presented' and marketed to Western readers. This volume seeks to give an overview of how the discipline of Comparative Literature is flourishing in India and elsewhere.

We have invited comparatists from India and abroad to contribute to this discussion, begun in 1989 with Chandra Mohan's ground-breaking volume, *Aspects of Comparative Literature*. We felt that three seminal essays from that volume warranted reissue today (Das, Trivedi and Fokkema). To these essays, we have compiled a volume that seeks to address the current concerns of the discipline.

The volume is broken down into four sections. Part I deals with some old and new aspects of Comparative Literature. We open with the late Sisir Kumar Das's essay from the original volume. In this essay, Das looks at how literature extends beyond language. He shows that the Greek notion of *syncresis,* so pivotal to our endeavour, is not found in the ancient Sanskrit or Tamil literatures. Das makes the important point that we should all keep in mind when we think of an Indian Comparative Literature: The initial Indian literary context studied its own traditions. In another essay from the original *Aspects*, the late Douwe Fokkema broaches the epistemological issues involved in cross-cultural comparative work. He questions the legitimacy of the comparative method, a topic that is ever-more-pressing as the field's necessity is called into question by Cultural Studies and World Literature. The moral issues involved in what we do are often absent from discussions of the newer paradigms.

In his provocative essay, Jüri Talvet speaks as both a poet and a critic. He calls for a symbiosis of Comparative Literature and World Literature. Based in Estonia, Talvet sees an urgent need for dialogue between the comparative and national literature departments. He presents an overview of Comparative Literature and World Literature in pre- and post-independence Estonia in order to broach the larger concern of the fate of minor literatures and the problems involved in canon formation, concerns not lost on Indian comparatists. Part I concludes with Haun Saussy's examination of the European discourse on political order that brings together the profession of medicine and the organization of the body politic. In the work of Rudolf Virchow, Saussy sees a model for the comparatist's discipline, particularly in Virchow's summons to translate, mediate and metaphorize through interdisciplinarity.

Part II continues to address concerns pertinent to India and elsewhere. Gerald Gillespie offers an outsider's perspective on Indian Comparative Literature. He sees in the Indian model not only one standard Comparative Literature awareness, but a global consciousness, which he attributes to India's continual involvement with the international community of scholars through the ICLA and the effect that Cultural Studies and World Literature have exerted on the field. Gillespie views the World Literature concept of Comparative Literature as a threat to India since it will have a negative effect on India's study of foreign languages. Indian Comparative Literature should maintain a commitment to the study of non-Indian languages in addition to cherishing its regional mission and promoting the studies of the literature in these local regions. This admonition not to follow too closely the paradigms of the West is echoed by Eugene Eoyang who problematizes the very conception of the West by examining the concept of ethnotypes, which he shows are never as universal as they pretend to be. Eoyang revisits the issue of cultural relativism, which is so pertinent to the discipline and a topic discussed throughout the volume.

We next proceed with several larger essays discussing the evolution of Comparative Literature in three theatres of its operation: the United States, France, and India. Dorothy M. Figueira charts the development of American Comparative Literature from its inception in the post-World War II era through its developments as identity studies, multiculturalism, postcolonialsim and most recently, World Literature. This essay parallels the contribution of Anne Tomiche, who gives us an overview of the institutionalization of Comparative Literature in France. Tomiche provides a history of what is compared and how the idea of comparison has changed over time. She looks at the foundational grounds of French Comparative Literature in myth studies, image studies and reception theory. Tomiche also provides the reader with a comprehensive bibliography of Comparative Literature scholarship. Next, we move to the Indian context with Sayantan Dasgupta's examination of the trajectory of Comparative Literature in India. Dasgupta examines an important (and often overlooked) fifty-year old essay by Buddhadeva Bose, the poet, scholar, writer and founder of the Comparative Literature programme at Jadavpur University. Dasgupta focuses on Indian Comparative Literature's symbiotic relationship with classical and modern Indian literatures, its relationship with Western literatures and its emphasis on the national literature of each individual department's location.

Ipshita Chanda then questions what is at stake in Comparative Literature in general and as it is practised in India. She addresses the current situation of the discipline and asks how Indian Comparative Literature differs from what is done in English departments. She notes that the multilingualism that stymies the discipline elsewhere is completely rational for Comparative Literature in India. She touches upon Indian Comparative Literature's current interest in domestic comparison, but laments how very little work is done on the relationship between Indian Literature's and Comparative Literature's methodology. In this respect, she sees Indian Comparative Literature as ill-prepared for the challenges it faces in the future. Is Indian Comparative Literature going to devolve into Cultural Studies with texts? Chanda asks whether Comparative Literature in India should be any different than anywhere else and concludes that Indian literatures can *only* be understood comparatively. This focus on the unique set of issues involved in defining an Indian form of Comparative Literature is then taken up by Subha Chakraborty Dasgupta in her discussion of the role of oratures in the Indian context. Dasgupta is concerned with the destiny of marginalized groups, languages, and voices. In order to talk about margins and centres, a popular topic in the discipline these days, Dasgupta's case study of oratures calls these very theoretical issues into question. She examines the characteristics, interrelatedness, and the manner in which oratures are marginalized in print cultures. Specifically and geographically situating this particular genre is more fruitful than theoretical notions of positionality.

Part III deals with a central issue in Comparative Literature and a topic of particular importance in Indian Comparative Literature: Translation Theory. Indra Nath Choudhuri introduces the topic by highlighting the need for a workable theory of translation in a polyglot country such as India. He shows how Sanskrit literature offers numerous models to develop such a theory, since Sanskrit writers did translate from the *bhashas* into Sanskrit. Choudhuri ties this Sanskritic tradition to a series of modern theoretical concerns. E.V. Ramakrishnan continues this discussion on how translation as a field of inquiry is not treated with the importance it merits. Like the previous essay, he too goes back to the Sanskrit sources and particularly Sheldon Pollock's notion of the vernaculars and critiques the trend to seek in the Indian tradition for translation practices along the lines of the European Enlightenment. He advocates for Indian Translation Studies to focus on living speech communities rather than the degree to which Sanskrit is reproduced in translation endeavours. He views the Indologist's approach to translation as similar to that of the Orientalists, freezing India into a timeless frame where everything desirable comes from the classical past. He laments how this neo-Orientalist discourse is now legitimized by its new clothing in literary theoretical garb. Indian Comparative Literature can step in here and free Translations Studies from Anglo-American paradigms and ground it in the practices of Indian regional languages.

Jasbir Jain returns to basics and asks us why we like to read comparatively. She emphasizes that Comparative Literature serves specific aims in India. As a discipline, it acknowledges India's plurality and its dependence on translation. Comparative Literature in India becomes problematic, however, when it seeks to fit a mold that is not of its own making. Jain calls for Indian comparatists to use the theoretical approaches that suit India's unique situation, in particular, the necessity and limitations of translation.

Anisur Rahman follows this discussion of the unique status of Translation Studies in India with an analysis of the translational drift as a site for debates on race and history. He structures his analysis on an analogy between translation and architecture. Assumpta Camps examines the work of transcultural authors. In particular, she looks at the challenges they have to negotiate with the dominant culture through translation. Sukrita Paul Kumar then examines the notion of India as the Other, in post-Partition literature through a series of authors and looks at how geography is defined politically.

The volume concludes with a series of case studies in Part IV. Harish Trivedi writes an Afterword to his article reprinted here from the original *Aspects* on the Urdu and Hindi Premchand. He revisits this essay as a way of opening the discussion on how the discipline has developed in the intervening decades. Like other contributors to this volume, he pinpoints postcolonial criticism and World Literature as posing threats to the well-being of the field.

Ganesh Devy reflects on what the loss of indigenous languages means for India today. He investigates the role of the oral versus the written in the fate of a language's survival, noting that orality has always been a topic problematized in Indian literature. He characterizes a script's relationship to a language's perceived value and survival in India as akin to aphasia. Marc Maufort moves beyond the confines of India and the genres of fiction and poetry to look at how Comparative Literature's methodology—particularly its openness to a non-Eurocentric focus—can enhance our understanding of indigenous playwriting in Canada, Australia and New Zealand.

The essay by Sieghild Bogumil-Nötz on Calvino's *If on a winter's night a traveller* concludes the volume. Bogumil-Nötz picks up the discussion of methodology and the current ethical discussion in Comparative Literature since its inception through the paradigm shift to Cultural Studies and World Literature. She sees these debates not only as central to the health and future of the field, but as reflections of the issues facing all readers today. These essays collected here address issues of disciplinary identity and challenges facing the field of Comparative Studies in the present and the future. They investigate the symbiotic relationship between Comparative Literature and other related fields of scholarship. In addition, several essays offer excurses into comparative analysis. The volume as a whole was conceived as resuming a discussion that began in 1989 with *Aspects*. Toward that end, we invited several scholars who were involved in that initial discussion (Gillespie, Mohan, Devy, Kumar, Choudhuri, and Trivedi) to voice their present-day concerns with the discipline. We have also attempted to show how the discipline has burgeoned in India by inviting contributions from a new generation of Indian comparatists and their international colleagues who through CLAI and ICLA have over the intervening years entered into dialogue and discussed the parameters of the discipline. Indian comparatists and their international colleagues all address key concerns that animate Comparative Literature today and, in these pages, they have sought to elucidate how they practice their craft.

University of Georgia DOROTHY M. FIGUEIRA

PART I

Aspects of Comparative Literature

1

Comparative Literature in India: A Historical Perspective

Sisir Kumar Das

LONG BEFORE comparative studies of literature emerged as a formal academic discipline, many scholars felt the inadequacy of the framework within which individual literatures were studied. Many of them realized that literatures did not evolve in isolation from one another and the study of a single literature more often than not obliged one to look beyond one's own language and literary tradition. The necessity for a wider perspective involving more than one language and one literary tradition was felt in different periods of history whenever two literatures came into contact. There have been many occasions in every civilized society when different cultures and different literary traditions came into close contact with one another, and all such occasions did pose a challenge. One can think of the Romans coming in contact with Greek literature, the Medieval Christian Europe with the Pagan Europe, Persian with Arabic, Japanese with Chinese and Indian with the literatures of Europe. All these contacts have resulted in certain changes, at times marginal, and at times quite profound and pervasive, in the literary activities of the people involved and have necessitated an enlargement of a critical perspective. One realizes that diversities of literature do not necessarily prevent one from discovering deeper affinities between them. The necessity for the study of literatures in relation to one another, which is the basis of Comparative Literature today, was felt very strongly not only in the nineteenth century but some of its regulating concepts appeared even earlier, albeit in an embryonic form.

We do not find anything comparable to the method of *Sunkrisis* (or comparative method) so popular among the Romans, in Indian literary criticism, though Sanskrit and ancient Tamil, languages belonging to

* This essay first appeared in *Aspects of Comparative Literature: Current Approaches*, 1989.

two different families, came into contact. Neither the ancient scholars of Sanskrit literature nor the scholars of ancient Tamil studied their literature in relation to one another. Nor did they raise the question of influence or impact of one literature on the other. The scholars of Sanskrit, however, studied Sanskrit along with Prakrit literatures. In classical Sanskrit plays, several Prakrits have been used in the dialogues of different characters. The kings and the priests speak Sanskrit, the women the Sauraseni Prakrit, the people of the working class the Magadhi, and the songs are invariably in the Maharashtri. This reflects, no doubt, the multilingualism of the society and the functional hierarchy of these languages, but also an idea of literature that could be written in more than one language. Some scholars have argued that the various Prakrits used in Sanskrit dramatic texts were actually mutually comprehensible class dialects, functionally similar to the role of dialects in modern plays and novels, which add distinct socio-linguistic dimensions to the characters. The mutual comprehensibility between the Prakrits to a varying degree and Sanskrit notwithstanding, the separate status of the Prakrit languages vis-à-vis Sanskrit is beyond doubt. They are different languages, different in their sound system and grammar, and they belong to a different stage of linguistic history of the Sanskritic languages. That the ancient Indian writers could use more than one language within one text without qualms, and the ancient critics found that practice normal enough, is itself evidence of a view of literature that extends beyond one language. The Buddhists and the Jains produced a literature in more than one language. But instead of dividing them in terms of the language employed in them, they viewed them as parts of one single literary corpus unified by one religious vision.

One must admit, however, that the early Indian scholars thought that the linguistic differences between Sanskrit and Prakrit only reflected two stages of evolution of the same language, they were otherwise linked by a common cultural heritage and their literatures were dominated by the same set of literary canons. In all probability, the Prakrit literature that flourished in southern India maintained a close relation with folk traditions as well as with ancient Tamil literature. George L. Hart in his *The Relations between Tamil and Classical Sanskrit* (1976) has tried to argue that the *Gatha Sattasai,* an anthology of poems in the Maharastri Prakrit (compiled some time between AD 200 and AD 800) has some connection with Tamil literature. Whatever the worth of such assumptions, the Indian scholars of the ancient period never tried to discover any relation between the Sanskrit and the Tamilian literary traditions.

In our medieval period, various literatures written in different languages came into close contact particularly with those languages spoken in neighbouring areas. Most of these literatures shared a common Sanskrit heritage and were exposed to Arabic and Persian influences in varying degrees. The medieval Indian scholar naturally studied his own literature with reference to Sanskrit but rarely thought about the interrelationship between the Indian literatures produced in younger languages like Telugu or Malayalam, Marathi or Gujarati, Punjabi or Sindhi. Some of the popular sayings current in different parts of the country reflect the common readers' understanding of the relationship between texts written in different languages, or between poets separated by time and distance. For example, the saying in Andhra Pradesh—Vilvamangal was reborn as Jayadeva, Jayadeva as Narayanatirtha, and Narayanatirtha as Ksettreya—speaks volumes about the common readers' attempt to discover the connections between four poets of different regions and of different times. We are not certain about the date of Vilvamangal. Popular tradition places him in the ninth century, though many scholars think he lived in the twelfth. We are not absolutely sure whether he came after Jayadeva, a twelfth-century poet, or not. But the similarities between the *Srikishna Karnamritam* of Vilvamangal and the *Gitagovindam* of Jayadeva, both written in Sanskrit, are indeed striking. Narayanatirtha and Ksettreya, both seventeenth-century poets, wrote in Sanskrit as well as in Telugu. And both of them had remarkable similarities with Vilvamangal and Jayadeva in respect to the spirit of their poems and treatment of themes.

Links between texts can be established through evidence. Similarities, while often mere coincidence can be shown to have an intertextual basis. The comparatist tries to build a framework within which similarities can be studied and appreciated. The medieval Indian reader almost intuitively felt the existence of links between the texts written in different languages and having a common theme or ideological backdrop, though he failed to construct any critical apparatus to study them. The interactions between neighbouring literatures, however, continued throughout the medieval period resulting in the growth of new genres and themes, and occasionally, styles. One of the interesting proofs of such interactions between two languages is found in the growth of a style known as Manipravalam. It was an attempt, and a successful one, towards the creation of a hybrid style composed of Sanskrit and Malayalam. Such a hybrid poetic language is found in Tamil and Telugu as well, but it was only in Malayalam that Manipravahm developed into a rich body of literature and critics had to take notice of this phenomenon created by the interaction between two languages belonging to two different linguistic families. The fourteenth-century text *Lilatilakam*, written in Sanskrit, deals with grammar and rhetorical devices of the Manipravahm. It is the first work in Indian criticism analysing a literary phenomenon, which cannot be adequately understood without involving two languages and two literatures.

Another artificial language, Brajabuli, extensively used in sixteenth-century Bengali poetry, and to some extent in Assamese and Oriya, was a hybridization of Maithili, the language in which Vidyapati wrote, and Bengali/Assamese/Oriya. Such stylistic experiments went beyond the linguistic boundaries of any particular literature and called for a more flexible critical framework.

With the introduction of Persian in Indian letters, its influence on various Indian literatures became more and more apparent. With respect to themes, forms and style, Persian began infiltrating Sindhi, Punjabi and Bengali through translations and adaptations of Persian texts. A new langauge, Urdu, emerged out of the interaction between Persian and Khariboli, a form of Hindi, and grew into a supple and sophisticated instrument of literary expression by the end of the seventeenth century. Many great Urdu poets not only borrowed themes and motifs from Persian and grafted them onto this new Indian language but imported a considerable number of poetic forms and metrical structures. Some of them were also welcomed into other Indian literatures. An appreciation of Urdu literature and an understanding of its growth will remain incomplete without reference to its intimate and fruitful relation with the great Perso-Arabic literary tradition. Treatises on Urdu rhetoric and metrics reflect this awareness. Had Indian literatures formed a regular part of the academic curriculum of the medieval period, this awareness would have certainly taken the shape of a critical framework, focusing on the study of literatures and deemphasizing the distinctions between languages and geography. In the nineteenth century, when the literatures of modern India were finally thought to be proper subjects of study in our academic institutions, they were compartmentalized according to their linguistic affiliations and a false impression about their autonomy had developed in the minds of many intellectuals.

However, the nineteenth century was also the period when a sense of inadequacy had begun to be felt about the insularity of literary studies not only in Europe, but also in India. The discovery of Sanskrit by European scholars gave a tremendous impetus to the growth of comparative linguistics, and later comparative religion and mythology. Even eight years before Sir William Jones talked about the Sanskrit language bearing a strange affinity to both Greek and Latin, in his famous inaugural speech at the Asiatic Society of Bengal in 1784, his friend N.B. Halhed was astonished to find the similitude of Sanskrit with Persian and Arabic, and Greek and Latin. In his *Code of Gentoo Law* (1786) Halhed talks of remarkable affinities between India and Europe at various levels. The initial excitement at the discovery of similarities between different languages, myths, and religious thought made the Orientalists think of certain universals, and they continued to look for archetypes in cultures with great enthusiasm, thus creating a climate congenial for the growth of Comparative Literature.

Warren Hastings, the first Governor-General of India, in his introduction to Charles Wilkins's translation of the *Gita* (1785) into English pleaded for a comparative study of the *Gita* and European works of great merit. 'I should not fear' he wrote, 'to place, in opposition to the best French version of the most admired passages of *Iliad* or *Odyssey*, or the 1st and 6th books of our own Milton, highly as I venerate the latter, the English translation of the *Mahabharata*' (Hastings 1785: 10). Hardly any Indian of that time was aware of this statement but it certainly created an impact on those for whom it was written. In the Fort William College, which was established in 1800 for the general education of the young civil servants, many British scholars were exposed to Oriental literatures, and some of them raised interesting questions relating to the problems of inter-literary relationships and divergent literary cultures. T. Macan, a student at the college, who proposed to translate the Persian poem *Shahnamah*, observed that

> the laws of composition by which the Poets of Europe have been generally guided since works of Homer became generally known, have never been established or recognised in the Eastern world and consequently the rules of criticism founded upon these laws are wholly unapplicable to the writings of Firdoosse. Of his merits indeed a fair estimate can be formed only by his countrymen or the inhabitants of those other Eastern nations to whom the language, customs, and laws of the ancient Persians are comparatively familiar, and such it may be safely affirmed that he is admired, esteemed and venerated in a degree not unsurpassed by the most ardent lovers of Homer and Virgil. (Qtd. in Das 1978: 113)

The familiarity with Eastern literatures created certain critical problems for Western readers particularly those believing in the infallibility of Western critical canons. They either dismissed oriental literatures as necessarily inferior or pleaded for a different set of canons for their evaluation. But there were some who felt the necessity for a new poetics that would accommodate works of art of diverse nature, rooted in different cultures. Lord Minto, commenting upon the English reading of the *Meghadutam* by the famous nineteenth-century British Sanskritist H.H. Wilson wrote:

> The work of Kaleedas unfolded now for the first time to such distant generations as our own displays this uniformity in the characters and genius of our race which

seems to write at once the most remote of regions of time and space, and which always gratifies the human mind to discern through the superficial varieties in which some slight difference of external or even intellectual fashions may disguise it. In Kaleedas we find poetical design, a poetical description of Nature, in all her forms, moral and material, poetical imagery, poetical inventions, just and natural feeling, with all the finer and keener sensibilities of the human heart. In these great and immutable features we recognize in Kaleedas, the fellow and kinsman of the great masters of ancient and modem Poetry. (Qtd. in Das 1978: 114)

This is one of the most significant pronouncements on the universality of letters defending the study of literature as a manifestation of the unifying spirit of human creativity. This statement was made in 1806 long before Goethe thought of the possibility of a world literature. And one must remember that Saint-Beuve made a similar statement about fifty-four years later when the term 'Comparative Literature' had been already coined by Matthew Arnold in English, and the French term *Littérature Comparée,* first used by Villemain in 1829, was fairly well established. Saint-Beuve wrote: 'Homer, as always and everywhere should be first, like a god, but behind him, like a procession of the three wise kings of the East, would be seen the three great poets, the three Homers, so long ignored by us, who wrote epics for the use of the old people of Asia, the poets Valmiki, Vyasa of the Hindus, and Firdousi of the Persians, in the domain of taste; it is well to know that such men exist and not to divide the human race' (1938: 130). An assumption of the basic unity of the human race was certainly one of the main factors in the growth of comparative studies of religion and mythology, and at the time, scholars in their anxiousness to vindicate the universality of spirit overlooked the importance of the diversity of human institutions and cultures. There were scholars, of course, who appreciated the value of diversity and the 'differentness' of cultures without any prejudice. The visitor at the Fort William College in a lecture in 1806, for example, observed that the Bengali version of *Aeneid,* translated by a student of that college, would 'set before the native scholars of these provinces present or to come, that model of epic genius and Augustan taste' and in future the Indian writers would choose between the Western model and the Oriental one. Indeed, knowledge of literatures, other than one's own, does present different models for literary works and a new world of experience. The novelty of that world is as important as the realization of the unity of the human race.

With the spread of English education and with the growth of an English-educated community in India, there also grew a new critical awareness, which prompted Indian scholars to evaluate their own emerging literatures, and in some cases the ancient texts written in

Sanskrit or Tamil, with reference to English literature, in particular, and European literature, in general. The initiative came from European scholars, many of whom could not pronounce any critical judgement on Indian literature without taking recourse to European literature. Albrecht Weber, for example, talked of a possible influence of the *Iliad* on the *Ramayana* as well as of a Greek influence on Sanskrit plays.[5] Similarly, G.U. Pope in the introduction to his English translation of the Tamil classic *Kural* (1886) pointed out the resemblance between the Tamil couplets and the gnomic poetry of Greece, not only in respect to their epigrammatic wit and brevity, but also in their themes and sentiments. He found in the style of the *Kural* 'some thing of the same kind' that is found in Greek epigrams, Martial, and the Latin elegiac verses. There is a beauty in the periodic character of the Tamil construction in many of these verses that reminds the reader of the happiest efforts of Propertius (1958: xxii). In the preface to his celebrated edition of *Tiruvacakam* (1908) Pope pleaded with Tamil scholars to study the anthologies of religious verses available in English, only to share his conviction that 'no literature can stand alone'.

The belief that every literature is not only distinctive but should be studied in isolation persists among many scholars. One of the problems that kept the Roman critics busy, soon after Latin came in contact with Greek, was that of *contamination*. The word is derived from the verb *contaminare*, meaning to bring one thing in relation to another. This term was used to describe the practice of putting together scenes from the original Greek, or of borrowing heavily from another play. This is linked up with various problems of imitation, adaptation and influence. Terence defended his right to contaminate literature and appealed to the examples set by Navius and Flatus. The conflict of ideals between Terence and his opponents was actually about the measure of freedom with which Greek originals should be handled.

But it has another dimension as well. How 'pure' can a literature remain and how can one keep a literature free from the impact of other literatures. These questions were raised in India in the mid-nineteenth century by the makers of modern Indian literature, which drew heavily from European literature. In 1858, Michael Madhusudan Dutta wrote to one of his friends, 'Do you dislike Moore's poetry because it is full of orientalism? Byron's poetry for its Asiatic air, Carlyle's prose for its Germanism?' In 1874, Bankim Chandra Chatterjee defended 'imitation' in literature by citing instances from social and literary history. His spirited defence of imitation was not merely a justification of the actions of contemporary Bengali writers, but also of the creative spirit that refuses anything as alien in the process of expression. In the same way Michael Madhusudan Dutta's questions actually pleaded for a new critical model and a new methodology as opposed to the model sustained by the idea of the exclusiveness of national literatures.

While the Indian writers in the nineteenth century tore off the illusion of the exclusiveness of national literature, some critics tried to lay the foundations of comparative studies in literature. In his essay, 'Shakuntala Miranda, and Desdemona' (1873), Bankim Chandra Chatterjee tried to evolve a new critical framework within which literatures as distantly related as Sanskrit and English could be studied. The most significant outcome of this critical temper was the abolition of all nationalistic considerations in literary evaluation. The 'father of Hindu nationalism' had no hesitation in placing Shakespeare above Kalidasa, and comparing Vedic hymns with the nature poems of Byron and Shelley. In another essay entitled 'Uttiracharita' he compares the play of Bhavabhuti with some of the works of Shakespeare, and his comparison does not appear to be odious if only because of his insistence not on some accidental and superficial similarities, but on the generality of the literary process and literary techniques involving borrowing and transcreation. Similarly, in another essay, he compares *Kumarasambhava* with *Paradise Lost* to consider their respective treatment of the supernatural. Modern critics may have different opinions about the value of these essays, but what remains undisputed is the fact that Bankim Chandra wanted to give a new direction to our study of literature. He presented a new universe of literary discourse unfragmented by languages and nationalities. One can talk about a literary genre or a form or a text in terms of its distinctiveness with reference to other genres or forms or text, and finally construct a poetics, which will account for all forms of diversity.

The first person to plead eloquently for a comparative study of literature and that too as an academic discipline in India was Rabindranath Tagore. The newly established National Council of Education or Jatiya Siksa Parisad (1906), formed by some of the leading men of the time, to create a parallel system of education outside the University of Calcutta, invited Rabindranath in 1907 to speak on Comparative Literature. The title of Rabindranath's lecture in Bengali was *Visva-Sahitya* meaning world literature (*Sahitya*, 1907). It is interesting that Tagore used the English expression 'Comparative Literature' to explain what he meant by 'world literature', a term that immediately reminds one of the term *Weltliteratur* used by Goethe in 1827. This being the first pronouncement on Comparative Literature by an Indian writer, an abridged summary of the essay made by Buddhadeva Bose is reproduced here.

I have been called upon to discuss a subject to which you have given the English name Comparative Literature. Let me call it World Literature in Bengali.

If we want to understand man as revealed in action, his motivation and his aims, then we must pursue his intentions through the whole of history. To take isolated instances, such as the reign of Akbar or Queen Elizabeth, to merely to satisfy curiosity. He who knows that Akbar and Elizabeth are only pretexts or occasions; the man, throughout the whole of history, is incessantly at work to fulfil his deepest purposes, and to unite himself with the All—it is he, I say, who will strive to see in history not the local and the individual, but the eternal and universal man. His pilgrimage will not end in observing other pilgrims, for he will behold the god whom all pilgrims are seeking.

Likewise, what really claims our attention in world literature is the way in which the soul of man expresses its joy through the written word and the forms which he chooses to give to his eternal being. Whether he portrays himself as a sick man or a voluntary or an ascetic—the impulse is always the same, and that is his joy in uniting himself with the world. It is in order to realize the truth of this relationship that we must enter the world of letters. It is absurd to think of literature as artificial; it is a world whose science no individual can ever master; as in the world of matter, its process of creation is perpetual, and yet in the heart of this ever-unfinished creation there is an ideal of stillness and completion. . . .

What I am trying to say amounts to this. Just as this earth is not the sum of patches of land belonging to different people, and to know the earth as such is sheer rusticity, so literature is not the mere total of works composed by different hands. Most of us, however, think of literature in what I have called the manner of the rustic. From this narrow provincialism we must free ourselves; we must strive to see the work of each other as a whole, that whole as a part of man's universal creativity, and that universal spirit in its manifestations through world literature. Now is the time to do so. (Bose 1959; Guha 1979)

When Tagore wrote this, Comparative Literature as an academic discipline was still in its infancy in Europe and America, and its introduction in universities was vehemently opposed by many eminent scholars. Even in the 1920s, Lane Cooper described 'Comparative Literature' as a 'bogus term' that makes 'neither sense nor syntax'. Moreover none of the British universities, which acted as models for Indian academic centres in the colonial days, thought highly of Comparative Literature as a worthy subject to be included in their literature faculties. Therefore, although many scholars of Indian literature responded to Tagore's call to free ourselves from the 'narrow provincialism' of literary scholarship, and some of them indeed made significant contribution towards the enlargement of our literary perspective, the first department of Comparative Literature came into existence in this country fifty years later in 1956 at Jadavpur University. It is indeed a pleasant coincidence that the National Council of Education, where Tagore delivered his lecture on Comparative Literature, is the ancestor of Jadavpur University.

Tagore's equation of Comparative Literature with World Literature is not accepted by many. But even if one intends to maintain a distinction between the two, there are, as Buddhadeva Bose points out, 'large areas where the two overlap, in intention if not in scope'. The main point is that Comparative Literature, whatever be its scope, is expected to study several literatures together. The syllabus of Comparative Literature at Jadavpur University concentrated on, to use the words of Buddhadeva Bose, the first professor of the department at that university, 'the most intense moments in Western literature, from antiquity to the present times' along with 'the living literature and the classical tradition of the native soil.' This department has certainly presented a new model of teaching literature and literary scholarship in India but various socio-economic factions, in addition to general resistance from single literature disciplines, have curtailed the spread of this discipline to any other university till today. However, a growing sense of inadequacy about existing single-literature disciplines prompted many Indian scholars to identify a new area of literary scholarship.

The search for a new area, however, began in the second decade of this century. Sir Asutosh Mukherjee, at whose initiative the first department of modern Indian languages in this country was established in 1919, thought that courses exclusively devoted to any one Indian literature would be unwise and academically unsound. The same year in his presidential address to the Howrah Bangiya Sahitya Sammelan he wanted Bengali scholars to look beyond Bengali and study other Indian literatures. 'We shall have to think of ways,' he said, 'by means of which Bengal, Bihar, Orissa, Madras, Gujarat, Rajputana, and Punjab can all be weaved into one garland, and can all be assembled on the same shore of the ocean of literature'. As his idea of Jatiya Sahitya (national literature) went beyond individual languages and literature, so did his plan of Indian language study in Indian universities. His idea of Jatiya Sahitya did not emerge merely from a political consciousness and nationalistic demand. It was a reflection of his scholarly concern about the content and direction of the study of Indian literature at the highest level. It was only later that linguistic chauvinism and academic complacency narrowed the scope of the study of Indian literature, and separate departments of Indian literatures without any relation to one another became the norm in Indian universities. Almost about the same time as Sir Asutosh was building up the department of Modem Indian Languages in the University of Calcutta, Sri Aurobindo wrote a series of articles entitled Indian literature (*Arya*, 1919). This is perhaps the first attempt by an Indian scholar to view Indian literature as an expression of the Indian mind. The multiplicity of languages did not deter him in viewing Indian literature as one complete whole. Perhaps criticizing the orientalists' obsession with Sanskrit, which prevented them from developing a complete view of Indian literature, Sri Aurobindo, continued,

> Nor is it in the Sanskrit tongue alone that the Indian mind has done high and beautiful and perfect things, though it couched in that language the large part of its most prominent and formative and grandest creations. It would be necessary for a complete estimate to take into account as well the Buddhistic literature in Pali and the poetic literature, here opulent, there more scanty in production, of about a dozen Sanskritic and Dravidian tongues. The whole has almost a continental effect and does not fall so far short in the quantity of its really lasting things and equals in its things of best excellence the work of ancient and medieval and modern Europe.

The idea of an Indian literature was mooted by Sarojini Naidu in her presidential address at the first All India Writers' Conference organized by the Indian PEN in 1945. 'India is one and indivisible. While her children speak with many tongues' declared Sarojini Naidu, 'they can only speak with one undivided heart.' This very idea of the unity of Indian literature was reiterated by S. Radhakrishnan when he wrote 'Indian literature is one though written in many languages.' Several scholars such as V.K. Gokak (1957), Suniti Kumar Chatterji (1963), Nagendra (1959) and the newly founded Sahitya Akademi tried to present the view of indivisibility in Indian literature and the basis of a common heritage, analysable in terms of themes and movements and ideas, of all the Indian languages. These efforts by many distinguished scholars and writers, however, did not have much impact on the literature programmes in our universities. The Bengali Department of Calcutta University did include courses on English Romantic poetry and selections from Sanskrit literature in its Bengali M.A. programme, and called them 'Comparative Literature', as early as 1958-9, but no one thought of a full-fledged programme of Comparative Literature or Indian literature. One of the recommendations of the seminar on Indian literature organized by the Indian Institute of Advanced Study in 1970 was 'the acceptance or the reality' of the 'common denominator of Indian literature' which can give 'a wide base and healthy orientation to the study of the various Indian languages and literatures' (Podder 1972). Four years later the department of Modern Indian Languages,

University of Delhi, under the leadership of Professor R.K. Das Gupta started a post-MA course in Indian Literature, which came to be known as 'Comparative Indian Literature'. Since then the term Comparative Indian Literature has gained currency nationwide, and several language departments in different universities in this country have started courses on Comparative Indian Literature as part of their literature programmes. Several seminars on Comparative Indian Literature have been organized since 1976 and debates in all those seminars have inevitably centred around the question of Comparative Literature as an academic discipline and its relation with the existing single literature departments. The debate is not of nomenclature, Comparative Literature or Comparative Indian Literature, but of the identification of the area of literary study. The Western scholars of Comparative Literature have made major European literatures as their area of study, even when they are aware of the existence of many great literatures outside the Western world. Eurocentricism may not be the only explanation for this trend. It is a question of feasibility, a question of limited competence. Comparative Literature provides a methodology, a wider perspective and a more catholic attitude to study several literatures together. If the Indian scholar feels obliged to concentrate on the various literatures within a geographical limit or literatures bound by certain cultural affinities, it is not necessarily because of any political or cultural isolationism. He is free to make European or African literatures, or Asian literatures a part of his scholarly universe provided he has the competence and the facilities. Indian literatures provide the natural basis of a comparative study, if only because it is his *own literature*—he understands it better than any other literature. Comparative Indian Literature is not merely a search for a national literature counteracting the search for a universal literature, which is the professed aim of the study of Comparative Literature. It is not an exercise in discovering the abstract universals of literature. Comparative Literature must deal with literatures in their concreteness, and hence, the study of Indian Literature together is but a part of the comparative literary studies as an academic discipline. The future of Comparative Literature in this country will naturally be directed towards an intensive study of various Indian literatures in the main, but as long as it realizes that its texts and contexts are Indian, its methodology comparative, and its main subject is literature, it will serve the cause of Comparative Literature.

REFERENCES

Arya, Aurobindo (1919), in *The Foundations of Indian Culture* (1953), New York: Sri Aurobindo Library, Pondicherry: Sri Aurobindo Ashram, 1971.

Bose, B., 'Comparative Literature in India', *Yearbook of Comparative and General Literature*, 8 (1959). Repr. in *Contribution to Comparative Literature: Germany and India*, ed. Naresh Guha, Kolkata: Jadavpur University, 1979, pp. 85–99.

Chatterji, S.K., *Languages and Literature of Modern India*, Calcutta: Bengal Publishers, 1963.

Das, S.K., *Sahibs and Munshis, An Account of the College of Fort William*, Calcutta: Papyrus Publishing House, 1978.

Gokak, V.K., ed., *Literatures in Modern Indian Languages*, New Delhi: D.K. Publisher, 1957.

Hart, George L., *The Relations between Tamil and Classical Sanskrit*, Wiesbaden: Harrassowitz, 1976.

Hastings, W., 'Introduction', in *The Bhagavat-Geeta or Dialogues of Krishna and Arjuna*, tr. C. Wilkins, London, Bangalore: The Wesleyan Mission Press, 1847.

Nagendra, ed., *Indian Literature*, Agra: Lakshmi Narain Agarwal, 1959.

Podder, A., ed., *Indian Literature*, Simla: IIAS, 1972.

Pope, G.U., *Kural*, New Delhi: Asian Educational Services, 1997.

Saint-Beuve, Charles Augustin, *What is Classic?*, tr. E. Lee, Cambridge: Harvard Classics, 1938.

Weber, A., *The History of Indian Literature*, tr. J. Mann and T. Zachariae, London: Kegan Paul, Trench, Trübner & Co., 1882.

2

Towards a Methodology in Intercultural Studies

D.W. Fokkema

THE TOPIC of cultural relativism implies a number of very complicated but at the same time challenging problems. I will first briefly discuss some of the entanglements we encounter while confronting the important question of 'Cultural Relativism and Literary Value'. I will then turn to some epistemological issues in the cross-cultural study of literature, to a discussion of method and its legitimation, and finally, to the problem of evaluation.

We often come across a view firmly expressed in some such terms as these: 'The days of cultural complacency are over. No more can we be content with a self-ascertained sense of cultural superiority.'[1] These words suggest that the discussion of cultural relativism has a moral basis. Feelings of cultural superiority are supposed to be bad. Modern life calls for a particular action: *we should* learn to understand other cultures. My immediate reaction is to say that I agree with this moral dictum, but I also want to emphasize that it indeed is a moral exhortation, an exhortation based on an ethical—and perhaps also political—value judgement. The call for getting rid of cultural superiority feelings issues from a value judgement, which by definition cannot be universally valid. There is no compelling logic, which tells us that cultural complacency is false and cultural relativism is right. At most, we may say that in a certain context, cultural complacency is bad and cultural relativism good. Cultural relativism, 'is not a method of research, even less a theory: it refers to a moral stance which may influence the scholar in his selection of research methods and theoretical positions' (Fokkema, 1984: 239). This explains the entanglement we are in—we wish to have an intellectual and academic discussion, we wish to develop the means for increasing

* This essay first appeared in *Aspects of Comparative Literature: Current Approaches*, 1989.

our knowledge of literature, including literature in distant cultures, but we start out from a moral position. Can we keep the two apart? In other words, is it possible to distinguish between knowledge and valuation?

I believe we can, and I would suggest that for clarity's sake, the distinction should be made. Following Nicholas Rescher (1969), we may describe a value judgement as being motivated by the interest of a subject who is to act or has acted, and therefore, as a proposition that in principle is not universally valid. Propositions expressing empirical knowledge, however, do not imply action and are not necessarily linked to subjective interests; they are propositions, which in principle are universally valid. Therefore, it is worthwhile to bring this sort of knowledge together in publications, which receive a wide distribution, e.g. encyclopedias. Value judgements can be found in other media, such as literature and the arts, and in literary criticism. I cannot but conclude that not only philosophers but almost anybody can make a distinction between the presence of a thing and the value of a thing. We are all familiar with the possibility that two people agree about the presence of a thing but at the same time disagree over its value. In practical life (e.g. in any marketplace) people know how to distinguish between facts and values. In scholarly discussions, we may meet with complications but also have the instruments (such as precise language) to overcome these complications and to work on the basis that a distinction can be made between propositions concerning facts and those concerning values. The distinction to be made does not exclude the possibility that one and the same person may switch easily from the one kind of proposition to the other and back. It is perfectly defensible that our discussion of intercultural studies has a moral impulse. What is indefensible is to let our moral impulse interfere with the rules of analytical argument or scientific exploration. There are more complications, such as the richness and variety of the various vibrant cultures studied, with their various distinct traditions, that make it almost impossible to speak of one Indian culture, except if we admit a considerable amount of simplification. This also poses a methodological problem. Are we to postulate one Indian culture? And if we want to do so, how do we proceed from its manifold manifestations to the one abstract notion of one Indian culture? The same applies to other cultures, of course, including European culture.

In scholarly discussions, however, it is not possible to avoid certain simplifications. But as long as we know *that* and *how* we are simplifying, we still may reach some valid results—what can be called 'controlled simplification' (Fokkema 1964: 249). Those who are afraid of any simplification are bound to identify themselves with the complex totality of their object of investigation—a text, for instance—but will not be able to talk about it except by repeating the words mentioned in that text. I am not convinced that the mere repetition of an object of investigation is capable of adding anything to our knowledge. I would rather venture that simplification—the recording of a text by means of an external analytical instrument—is a basic condition for acquiring knowledge. In my view, additional knowledge can be acquired only if it can be matched with knowledge that we already possess. New data must be made amenable to connect with data that are already in our memory. But new data which are completely disconnected to knowledge that we possess cannot be assimilated. This is what both didactics and neurology have taught us.

In cannot help conclude on the one hand, that the rejection of all simplification necessarily leads towards complete identification, implying mechanical repetition or mystical silence. Yet, the acquisition of new knowledge depends on controlled simplification, on carefully designed analytical instruments, or simply on very precise questions, which emanate from older knowledge that we—however tentatively—possess. Controlled simplification requires precise linguistic expression and provides a basis for thoughtful dialogue. For example, when I have misunderstood a text from another culture and have given expression to my interpretation, I can be corrected by others who phrase their critical comments, and so on.

LEGITIMATIONS OF METHOD

The question of the methodology of intercultural studies is a key point of analysis. Before going into the problem of method, it is necessary to say a word on the difference between intercultural and intracultural studies—the study of literature originating in different cultures and the study of literature produced within the boundaries of one culture.

First, the notion of the extension of a culture is problematic. The term 'culture' can be variously applied. One may say that each nation, class, or person has his or her own culture. Within the context of this essay, I would propose to reserve the term 'culture' for large, primarily geographical zones coinciding with continents or, for that matter, subcontinents. As a consequence, it is warranted to speak of Indian culture, European culture, Chinese culture, Latin American culture, etc. Intercultural studies would comprise, among other things, the comparative study of literature across cultural boundaries.

If we assume that we vaguely know to what these abstractions of Indian, European, Chinese cultures refer, there is still the question as to what extent the comparative study of literature *within* one cultural zone differs from the comparative study of literature across the boundaries of cultural zones. In both cases, there is a distance between the researcher and his/her object of investigation. The distance may be large, both in intracultural studies and intercultural studies. European scholars studying the work of Chaucer or Chrétien de Troyes must bridge an enormous historical distance, as well as a cultural distance, which is certainly not smaller than the distance they have to cover when studying more or less contemporary writers who have lived at a considerable geographical distance, such as Rabindranath Tagore or Kawabata. The cultural distance between the researcher and the object of examination can be enhanced by historical, geographical and social factors. It is not at all self-evident that the cultural distance between a researcher and the object under examination is larger in the case of intercultural studies than in intracultural studies. What is more important, even if this were the case, is that the difference between a large and a small cultural distance is only a matter of degree, Jan Mukarovsky suggested several years ago when he claimed that in principle there was no difference between interliterary and intraliterary comparison (Ďurišin 1974: 94). Whether the cultural distance to their object is large or small, researchers must apply analytical instruments, ask questions and search for answers, which are bound to simplify or even distort the material under examination. In short, they will begin a dialogue, which will be continued by other scholars, some of them living in another cultural zone.

Why do we attach value to cross-cultural dialogue in scholarly matters? The answer to that question is simple. In the empirical study of literature we have the pretension to produce statements that are universally valid. Therefore, we want to defend our views across cultural boundaries and welcome criticism from scholars educated in quite different cultural surroundings. Claude Lévi-Strauss (1978: 19) was certainly right in postulating that 'the human mind is everywhere one and the same and that it has the same capacities', although we may wonder whether this can be true without exception, or how this important statement can be tested. As a postulate it is the preliminary condition of intellectual debate across cultural boundaries.

All research—also in the field of literature—may begin with vague intuitions or speculations that will then go through a stage of conceptualization, in order to finally produce propositions, which can be tested and, if they have withstood pertinent criticism, can be held to be tentatively true. I subscribe to Karl Popper's view that, in principle, there is *one method* in scientific research. The term 'scientific', if applied to the sphere of the humanities, is somewhat problematic in English (though not in German, Russian, Hebrew or Dutch). But this is less bothersome than the much more important problem of how propositions can be tested, which amounts to questioning the legitimation of judgements on the correctness or validity of so-called scientific propositions.

There are, of course, complications here—arguments advanced by sociologists of knowledge, or postmodern philosophers such as Jean-François Lyotard (1979). Nevertheless, if we wish to have scholarly discussions across national and cultural boundaries, we need common standards for distinguishing between correct and false, between valid and invalid propositions. The question then is: What are our criteria of scientific validity? We need to solve that epistemological problem if we want to be taken seriously by our colleagues in and outside the humanities. If we do not go into this epistemological problem, we will run the risk of falling victim to any new fashionable trend that may arise. Indeed, it is embarrassing to see that after short intervals of ten or twenty years our discipline seems to enter a totally new paradigm—after positivism we saw the rise of New Criticism and Structuralism, which were succeeded by Deconstruction and Poststructuralism, and these again seem now to be replaced by a New Historicism. What we need in our discipline is the continuity of reliable results. The empirical study of literature aims to produce such results, i.e. propositions, which can be tested and if they have withstood sustained criticism, are added to the stock of provisionally accepted hypotheses. It is a serious weakness that apart from the accumulation of simple facts in biographies and encyclopedias, literary studies lacks continuity. Each new generation feels the urge to produce new concepts of literature, new theories of literature. To some extent, criticism of the results of earlier research is of course necessary, but is it necessary to start time and again from scratch?

It seems that there are three main criteria for judging scientific propositions. First, there is the well-known view that a scientific proposition is correct and valid if it corresponds with the empirical facts it purports to describe. The proposition is legitimized by the criterion of *correspondence* with the facts. Second, a proposition can be considered valid on the basis of it being in agreement with theories that are held to be correct. Here the proposition is legitimized by the criterion of *coherence* with accepted theories. Third, a proposition can be considered valid on the basis of agreement among a particular community of scholars. Now the proposition is legitimized by the criterion of *consensus* (Rescher 1973; Kriz 1985: 8).

Things become rather complicated, however, when we realize that, as a rule, none of these three criteria alone is sufficient to legitimize scientific propositions. They are operative in conjunction, although usually one of them is emphasized in particular. For a long time, the correspondence criterion was held to be a sufficient means for establishing the validity of scientific propositions. However, in recent discussions regarding the possibility of testing the correspondence of propositions with empirical facts, it has been pointed out that there is no such thing as direct, naive observation, and that there is a tension between the idea of a mental frame guiding the researcher's observations and the desirability that facts also should be recognized even if they do not fit into the pre-existing mental frame. My compatriot and colleague J.J.A. Mooij (1979) discussed the issue several years ago. In recent publications, the import of the mental frame or guiding theoretical conceptions has been more emphasized than the significance of direct observations. For instance, Siegfried Schmidt, whose theories are professedly empirical, seeks support in the coherence of theoretical conceptions that are subscribed by a community of researchers, and therefore, are called 'intersubjective', rather than in the direct observation of facts (Schmidt 1980: 6–7; cf. Finke 1982: 108–16). In fact, Schmidt emphasizes both the coherence and the consensus criteria. One or two out of the three major kinds of legitimation may be pushed into the foreground, but one could argue that we get close to optimal legitimation only if all three kinds of legitimation apply. Such an argument will probably seek support in social practice. When looking for certainty, people highly estimate an appeal to facts, as well as to coherence and consensus.

In my view, an appeal to either empirical facts alone or a coherent theoretical system subscribed by a community of scholars cannot be convincing. If one would maintain—in spite of Gombrich's argument (quoted in Finke 1982: 111)—that it is possible to observe isolated facts, one would have to admit that, as soon as these facts are related to each other, an element of interpretation is introduced based on concepts of causality and the theoretical positions accepted by a particular community. The naive reliance on so-called facts alone does not result in valid propositions. It is equally impossible to rely exclusively on the criteria of intersubjectivity or coherence with established theories. For reasons of self-interest or indolence, or other reasons, a community of scholars may wish to protect itself against criticism. If there is to be progress in scientific research, criticism must be heard and new facts investigated. Therefore, the possibility of an open discussion is a precondition of scientific research.

There is more to say on the triangle of correspondence, coherence and consensus by which the validity of scientific propositions is ascertained. In certain disciplines one of these forms of legitimation is deemed more adequate, and therefore, more popular, than in others. In experimental physics, the criterion of correspondence with observed facts is rather important. Theoretical physics, however, relies very much on the criterion of coherence with established theories. In the humanities, intersubjectivity or consensus among a community of scholars has often been considered sufficient legitimation. However, as argued above, the other criteria cannot be ignored. The experimental physicist cannot ignore the criterion of theoretical coherence, nor can the theoretical physicist refuse to take notice of the one or two successful experiments in his field. Likewise, the student of literature cannot rely on consensus alone. The New Critics and Structuralists who did so entered a blind alley without being aware of it. Again it is important to emphasize that scientific propositions are stronger and have a greater survival when they are supported by all three possible kinds of legitimation.

The findings of literary scholars may become more reliable and as a result, the study of literature may acquire greater continuity, if scientific propositions about literature and literary communication are supported not only by consensus, but also by correspondence with empirical facts and by coherence with accepted theories. And if this ideal cannot be immediately put into practice, the relative validity of our propositions can be established by the degree to which the criteria of correspondence, coherence and consensus each have been respected. The validity of our propositions in the field of literary studies can be expressed in the degree to which they are supported by empirical research, theoretical coherence and, backing by a community of scholars.

In order to avoid the inadmissible protection of tentative scientific propositions, the wall separating the humanities and the social sciences must be torn down. Intersubjectivity is different from consensus within a cenacle, and, in order to prevent the immunization of intersubjectively held beliefs, the testing of scientific propositions must have an interdisciplinary dimension (Schmidt 1980: 2–3). The observations of the literature student on stylistics, aesthetic experience, or social relations among writers and readers should be open to criticism by linguists, psychologists and sociologists, respectively. When these observations have withstood possible criticism from the perspective of other disciplines, they can be used by scholars working in these other disciplines and can contribute to our general knowledge of society. *Intersubjective* testing will liberate literary studies from the image of being based on personal convictions. *Interdisciplinary* testing goes one step further; it will—from various points of view—separate reliable from unreliable results, and make the reliable findings accessible to the general public. As such, it extends the range of intersubjective testing and relieves literary studies from its image of elitist isolation. Finally, *intercultural* testing—the worldwide testing of results which too long have remained within the boundaries of one culture—may provide the pretension of universal validity with a basis. Intercultural testing may emancipate literary studies from its possible ethnocentric bias. As a result, the range of intersubjectivity will attain global dimensions.

THE CHOICE OF ANALYTICAL INSTRUMENTS

Admittedly, the preceding observations have the character of a prolegomena. In my view, any research begins with a problem or question, whether simple or complex, and if the research that is planned is to have scientific value, it must be related to problems that are in discussion, but which have remained unsolved so far. Such problems are considered to be scientifically relevant.

One way of connecting with current research is to investigate aspects of literary communication, such as those distinguished by Felix Vodicka (1942) and Roman Jakobson (1960). This can be specified as research with regard to (a) the production of texts with a literary intention—anywhere in this world, (b) the literary reception—anywhere in this world—of texts irrespective of whether or not these texts have been produced with a literary intention, (c) the distribution of texts intended for literary reception—including the distribution outside the cultural zone where they were produced, (d) the analysis of texts, which by particular segments of the reading public—wherever in this world—have been received as literature, and (e) the codes which can be construed to function as an explanation of how the understanding of texts accepted as literature by a particular reading public—again, wherever they may live—is possible (cf. Fokkema 1987). This is not only a comprehensive but also very ambitious programme. I mention it to show that we may construe an object of truly global magnitude, transcending cultural boundaries. In fact, it is a programme sufficient to satisfy the scientific curiosity of large teams of scholars in many places in the world.

It may be more attractive to stake out a less comprehensive problem, for instance, the comparison of explicit poetics, i.e. the comments of writers on their own literary production in various cultural zones. An Arabic poet has compared a poem with a tent. An old Chinese treatise on poetry characterized it as a tissue or texture. In the Persian tradition, the poem is a storehouse of secrets (Idema 1983). Would the conclusion be warranted that in several Asian traditions the literary text has been conceived of as a 'construction'—for a tent, a tissue and a storehouse are constructions—precisely as was emphasized later by the Russian Formalists? One remembers Jurij Tynjanov's definition of literature 'as a language construction which is experienced as a construction' (1924: 406–7). My enumeration of metaphors of poetry, however, was rather selective. I ignored the comparison of the poem with a precious stone, a golden coin, sugar, honey, etc. And yet it would be interesting to bring the metaphors of poetry in various traditions together and to analyse them perhaps not with the aim to discover one or two common semantic features, but to understand the differences between the literary traditions of the various cultural zones.

A recurrent problem in intercultural studies is the question of which corpus of texts—both oral and written—should be examined. Of course, the problem occurs in intracultural research as well, where the extension of the literary domain is quite an issue, but in the comparison between literary traditions in different cultures there is a confusingly large range of options. It seems that the farther we go back in history, the greater is the chance that literature is conceived of as being equal to all texts that have been handed down by tradition. This seems to apply at least to China where in *The Literary Mind and the Carving of Dragons* (*Wenxin dialong*), written in the early sixth century, all sorts of genres are discussed which at present, also in China, are no longer considered to belong to literature—such as the treaty, the epitaph, the philosophical argument and the declaration of war (cf. Liu Hsieh 1959). Here, we see a historical development from an early concept of literature comprising many different kinds of texts to a modern concept of literature accommodating a less wide range of genres. Perhaps, the historical development from a broader concept of literature to a narrower one is a universal phenomenon, applicable also to Indian literature.

The different range of literary concepts in different cultures and at different times is a complicating factor in intercultural research. However, it is a difficulty that can be overcome and indeed can be reduced to harmless proportions if one is aware of it. Perhaps one of the most interesting research topics nowadays is the question of how the domain of literature has been staked out, and which factors have determined the shape of the literary system. In the modern Western tradition, the idea that literature is a precarious product of convention and innovation has found considerable support. Supposedly, the text must induce both recognition and surprise. It must be relevant to the life-world of the reader, and it must allow for a new outlook on things. The ideal combination of relevance and innovation leads to the aesthetic or literary reception of a text. This means that the definition of literature cannot be given in the abstract, but must refer to a specific communication situation and a specific reader—for it is the reader who is to judge whether he or she considers a text relevant and innovative. Both relevance and innovation are relative concepts, shifting with the position, knowledge, interest and emotional constitution of the perceiver.

In modern reception theory, these notions have been elaborated and the findings of reception theory may be interesting also for scholars outside the European tradition. Also in Indian poetics, the role of the erudite reader or critic—the *sahṛdaya* or *rasika*—has been emphasized. It is not certain whether the function of *sahṛdaya*, in fact, points to a concept of literature that respects the judgement of the addressee. In any case, the examination of the function of the *sahṛdaya* and other forms of literary criticism, in Indian and other traditions, may bring us closer to an understanding of the workings of the literary system in various cultural zones.

Value Judgements

In the preceding argument, although I have emphasized the perspective of the universal validity of propositions, now I wish to focus on propositions of subjective, restricted validity, i.e. value judgements. I believe that the value judgement with regard to texts is very much linked to the necessity of protecting oneself against being overwhelmed and paralysed by the constant flow of information. If we have a sense of purpose and want to use our time well, we must distinguish between information, which we like or can use, and information, which is merely superfluous or even an obstacle. Our selection of texts will be guided by the purpose we have in mind, or by criteria related to that purpose. It is evident that no two people may necessarily have the same goals, neither in practical life nor in literary studies. Therefore, it would be wrong to force one another to adopt the same criteria in selecting literature for our own use or for educational purposes.

Also each person lives in a different circumstance. Each of us has a different past and a different cultural tradition, and our goals may be different. It follows that one may prefer to read and teach literary texts, which are not necessarily the same as the ones that another person may select. It may be interesting from a comparative point of view, however, to learn what an individual's preferred text corpus is, and which criteria are employed in selecting it. As long as we are speaking of personal preferences, there is, in principle, complete freedom in selecting the texts we wish to read.

Things are different, however, when we talk of literary canons. A canon of literature is a selection of well-known texts, which we consider valuable, and therefore, use in teaching and for literary criticism (Fokkema 1986: 246). Canons used in teaching will be the product of a compromise between people who have decided to adopt certain educational goals—goals that may vary as they are linked to different ideological, political, philosophical and religious worldviews. Usually, one does not design a canon from scratch. There are canons around, and the problem rather is how to adjust existing canons to the challenge of new developments.

It appears that adjustment of a canon is bound to occur if there is a considerable difference between the knowledge transmitted by the canon and the knowledge needed and available in non-canonized texts. A discrepancy between a canon, which cannot serve social and personal needs, on the one hand, and a set of non-canonized texts, which answers those needs on the other, will in the long run inevitably lead to a change or adjustment of the canon, to the effect that the texts that are providing an answer will be included in the new canon. In this perspective, it is a function of the canon to offer models for problem solving. A change in historical consciousness, such as the one which occurred in Europe in the eighteenth century, led to new problems, and thus, to a new canon. A change in social consciousness, such as manifested in the present awareness of living in a multiracial society as well as in a period of feminist emancipation, undoubtedly will lead—and to a certain extent has already led—to the adjustment and expansion of the canon (Riesz 1985; Gilbert and Gubar 1985).

Continued secularization, the introduction of universal suffrage and parliamentary democracy, increasing awareness of the equality of all human beings without regard to race or sex have created the need for a reshuffling of existing canons. At the same time, our knowledge of the world, even of the universe, has grown enormously. It would be no surprise if our attitude towards canons and canon-formation would become more flexible and tolerant, leading towards a situation in which almost every teacher would feel free to design his or her own canon. This would make our canons not less, but more interesting.

One of the future tasks of the comparatist may be the comparative examination of various canons of world literature in different cultural zones. But in such a cross-cultural study we have left the problem of evaluation behind us and turned again toward an examination of the literary system in different parts of the world, which is perhaps where we should begin our investigation, since it will provide us with knowledge about the potentialities and effects of literature. Let us hope that on the basis of that sort of knowledge we will become good critics, reliable *sahaṛdayas*.

NOTE

1. Quoted from the letter of invitation to the Jadavpur seminar on 'Cultural Relativism, 1987'.

REFERENCES

Ďurišin, D., *Sources and Systematics of Comparative Literature*, Bratislava: Comenius University, 1974.

Finke, P., *Konstuktiver Funktionalismus: Die wissenschaftstheoretische Basis einer empirischen Theorie der Literatur*, Braunschweig und Wiesbaden: Vieweg, 1982.

Fokkema, D., 'Cultural Relativism Reconsidered: Comparatist Literature and Intercultural Relations', in *Douze cas d'interaction culturelle dans Europe ancienne et l'Orient proche ou lointain*, Paris: UNESCO, 1984, pp. 239–58.

———, 'The Canon as an Instrument for Problem Solving', in *Sensus Communis. Contemporary Trends in Comparative Literature*, ed. Riesz et al., Tubingen: Narr, 1986, pp. 245–54.

———, 'On the Reliability of Literary Studies', *Poetics Today*, vol. 9, no. 3, 1988, pp. 529–43.

Gilbert, S.M. and S. Gubar, *The Norton Anthology by Women: The Tradition in English*, New York: W.W. Norton, 1985.

Idema, W.L., ed., *Oe vorsten van het woord: Teksten over dichterschap en poezie uit Oosterse tradities*, Amsterdam: Mcalenhoff, 1983.

Jakobson, R., 'Linguistics and Poetics', in *Style in Language*, ed. T.A. Sebeok, New York: Technology Press, 1960, pp. 350–78.

Kriz, J., 'Wie empirisch ist die Empirie', *SPIEL*, vol. 4, no. 1, 1985, pp. 7–40.

Lévi-Strauss, C., *Myth and Meaning*, London: Routledge and Kegan Paul, 1978.

Liu, H., *The Literary Mind and the Carving of Dragons*, tr. V. Yu-chung Shih, New York: Columbia University Press, 1959.

Lyotard, J-F., *La Condition postmoderne: Rapport sur le savoir*, Paris: Minuit, 1979.

Mooij, J.J.A., 'The Nature and Function of Literary Theories', *Poetics Today*, vol. 1, no. 2, 1979, pp. 111–35.

Rescher, N., *Introduction to Value Theory*, Englewood Cliffs, NJ: Prentice Hall, 1969.

———, *The Coherence Theory of Truth*, Oxford: Clarendon Press, 1973.

Riesz, J., 'Afrikanische "Klassiker": Zur Herausbildung eines Kanons der modernen afrikanischen Erzahl-Literatur', *Universitas*, vol. 40, 1985, pp. 31–42.

Riesz, J., P. Boerner and B. Scholz, eds., *Sensus Communis. Contemporary Trends in Comparative Literature*, Tubingen: Narr, 1986.

Schmidt, S.J., *Grundriss der empirischen Literaturwissenschaft, Der gesellschaftlichen Handlungsbereich der Literatur*, Braunschweig and Wiesbaden: Vieweg, 1980.

Sebeok, T.A., ed., *Style in Language*, New York: Technology Press of the MIT, 1960.

Striedter, J., ed., *Texts der russischen Formalisten*, Munich: I. Fink, 1969.

Tynjanov, J., 'Das literarische Faktum', in *Texts der russischen Formalisten*, ed. Striedter, Munich: I. Fink, 1969, pp. 393–431.

Vodicka, F., 'Die Literaturgechichte, ihre Probleme und Aufgaben', in *Die Struktur der literarischen Entwicklung*, ed. Vodicka, Munich: I Fink, 1976, pp. 30–86.

———, ed., *Die Struktur der literarischen Entwicklung*, Munich: I Fink, 1976.

3

Comparative Literature and World Literature: Towards a Symbiotic Coexistence

Jüri Talvet

ONE OF THE postulates of my article is that Comparative Literature has really never enjoyed a pivotal or central position in the broad field of literary studies. At the same time, however, specialized studies of separate literary traditions, indispensable, central, and pivotal as they are and have been (at least as considered from different national points of view), have not been able to fill lacunae in our understanding of literary creation as a broader cultural phenomenon influencing (though often 'invisibly') the world view and axiological attitudes of entire societies and vast communities of people. Nor has literary theory, adequately filled the void. It oscillates between two extremes, from formal theories to sociological approaches, neither of which sufficiently explains the essence of a literary work or a literary phenomenon in the broader intercultural context. Moreover, there is a rapidly growing tendency in literary theory to become an exclusive self-meditation, a discipline for its own sake, with little if any contact with historical processes and developments taking place in the world.

Besides these discrepancies between national literatures and world/comparative literature, literary creation and criticism of 'centres' and 'peripheries', major and smaller nations, literary creation and literary science, there recently seems to be a schism emerging between world literature and comparative literature. On the one hand, there is a pragmatic approach (visible above all in the recent books by David Damrosch) of teaching under the label of world literature all those works that are available in English translation, have become part of Anglophone literature, and have gained acceptance in criticism and literary scholarship of major Western countries, the US and Great Britain above all. On the other hand, such a pragmatic approach has been criticized by another wing of influential comparatists (Dorothy Figueira, Gerald E. Gillespie), for whom 'world literature' taught and researched in the framework of English Studies entails a serious simplification and self-restriction of the field of comparative literature.

For my part, developing some of my own ideas expressed in my book *A Call for Cultural Symbiosis* (2005) and in my article '*Edaphos* and *Episteme* of Comparative Literature' (2005: 46–56), as well as the ideas of the Tartu cultural philosopher Yuri M. Lotman, especially in his 'semiospheric' period (with his last book *Culture and Explosion*, 1992), I will propose a symbiotic approach, aimed at reconciling these oppositions and establishing a dialogue that would strengthen the position of comparative as well as world literature in the wider arena of the humanities. The interaction of both is urgently needed, to overcome fragmentation between different parts of literary and cultural research and the widespread mechanical application of theories to arbitrarily selected, isolated literary phenomena, with little, if any, relevance for the spiritual, mental and social processes occurring in the world.

Furthermore, once world literature and comparative literature have been reconciled, there is an urgent need to establish a fruitful dialogue between comparatists and scholars specialized in national literatures. There is nothing ready, definite and finished in the canon of world literature, nor in the canon of national literatures. It is the task for comparatists especially to aid national literatures scholars by providing them with the comparative context of a wider spectrum such as European literature or world literature. In this, scholars of traditional 'centres' and 'peripheries' should establish a steady dialogue, provide new insights for the study of national literatures and keep open to new and old works and authors. By following this direction, we are likely to contribute to the renovation of the world's spiritual fundament, a challenge poorly met in our days by the hard sciences and those softer sciences that mechanically copy their methods. In the following discussion, I pose a series of questions and make a few observations on these concerns.

ABOUT TERMINOLOGY. WHAT DID 'FOREIGN LITERATURE' (*ЗАРУБЕЖНАЯ ЛИТЕРАТУРА*) MEAN IN THE FORMER SOVIET UNION?

Comparative Literature and World Literature (henceforth CL and WL) are concepts that date back to the nineteenth century. The introduction by Johann Wolfgang Goethe in 1827 of the term *Weltliteratur* is often taken as the starting point of further conceptualization of the phenomenon. At the beginning of the twenty-first century, it reappears, especially in the

US where a new pragmatic approach to the canon of WL has emerged. In contrast, CL, although initially germinated in Central and Eastern Europe, has gained recognition as a field of research worldwide. Although the 'death' of CL has been repeatedly declared by spokespersons narrowly specialized in fashionable trends in humanities (Li Xia 2011: 6), the International Comparative Literature Association (ICLA) still remains one of the largest world organizations devoted to literary and cultural research in the West. In some Asian countries, notably in China, CL, is gathering new energy (ibid.: 6–7). In Central and East European countries (Slovenia, Slovakia, Romania, Lithuania, among others) important activity in CL has developed recently at a number of universities. In the following discussion, my intention is not to revise the existing history of CL and WL, but rather to meditate on its institutional scholarly configurations.

While a formal signifier should not determine the content of a field, it is quite certain that in the case of CL it does, even to a greater extent than one might presuppose. I started teaching Western literary history at Tartu University in the mid-1970s. During most of that period, the curriculum of nearly all universities of the former Soviet Union, was called *зарубежная литература*. It literally meant all literature produced outside the borders of the SU. Literature created in Russian and other languages of the SU were never included under this rubric. In practice, the curriculum (a uniform course established by programmes prepared and confirmed by Moscow) included predominantly the canon of Western literature, with some selections from Eastern European literatures. Classical Greek and Roman literature was taught apart from *зарубежная литература*, while Oriental literatures were taught only at some few universities or institutes in major centres such as Moscow and Leningrad (St. Petersburg). Russian literature was taught extensively, but as a special subject. Thus, Yuri M. Lotman, the world-famous semiotic philosopher, worked for most of his life in Tartu University as the chaired professor of Russian literature. At the same time Estonian literature was taught separately and comprehensively only to students of Estonian philology.

The canon of Western literature taught to all students of philology (regardless of their specialization) included all major authors and their work from the Middle Ages through the nineteenth century. In modern (twentieth century) *зарубежная литература*, there were substantial omissions, since a number of Western authors generally labelled as 'modernists' were declared 'decadent'. Even if a short characterization of their works was provided, it had to emphasize their negative features and be in line with the Marxist interpretation. In fact, students could not really read much of these works, since translations into the languages of the SU were severely limited. (For an eloquent review of how *зарубежная литература* fared in Soviet Latvia, see Eglāja-Kristsone 2012.)

The whole process of the reception of Western literature in the former SU—a major research area and challenge for comparatists—is still overwhelmingly unexplored. To draw any far-fetching conclusions on the basis of only one or two language areas of the SU would be misleading. Suffice it to say that only a few examples from Estonian literature entered into discussion. Thus it was not until the second year of Gorbachev's *perestroika* that a major volume assembling Kafka's three novels was published in Estonia. Surprisingly enough, however, a volume of Kafka's short stories (including *Die Verwandlung*) appeared in Estonian translation as 'early' as in 1962 and Kafka's grimmest novel, *Der Prozess* (including the large essay 'Kafka' by the French Marxist philosopher Roger Garaudy!), was published in 1966. The first two collections of Jorge Luis Borges's intellectual-fantastical stories were translated into Estonian in 1972 and 1976, well before the Argentine writer's work was translated into Russian. So, it was not the rule that all Western literature translated into other languages of the SU had to be preceded obligatorily by translation in Russian.

FROM *ЗАРУБЕЖНАЯ ЛИТЕРАТУРА* TO WORLD LITERATURE AND COMPARATIVE LITERATURE

To return to the question of terminology, towards the end of the 1980s under increasingly more liberal conditions, Tartu University decided to replace the designation, *зарубежная литература* or *väliskirjandus* ('foreign literature'—which was the Estonian adaptation of the Russian term) with a new and bolder signifier, *maailmakirjandus* ('world literature'). The aim of this shift was to abolish the restrictive borders that formerly had kept the literatures created by the nations of the SU apart from the rest of WL. Naturally, as our staff was limited to only a few professors, we continued to teach courses on major phenomena and authors of Western literature.

When Estonia's political independence as a state was re-established in the beginning of the 1990s and our international contacts with Western countries suddenly began to flourish both academically and institutionally, we started to use in correspondence written in English the term 'comparative literature', as the closest international term applicable to our activity. I doubt if at that time any other university in the world, beside Tartu, had a chair of WL. But the denomination of

CL fully described the main direction of our activity in literary research. In 1994, we founded our Estonian Association of Comparative Literature, as a collective member of the ICLA. Our scholars started to take part in the activities led by the ICLA, while at the same time we introduced changes in teaching our Western literature courses. We tried to shift our emphasis to literature as an intercultural phenomenon. The same focus was introduced in new high school and university textbooks of WL. Chapters were no longer organized according to the national-linguistic categories (thus, presenting separately overviews of English, French, German, Spanish and other literatures, as it had been the overwhelming practice in the study and teaching of 'foreign literature' in the SU). Instead, there were chapters on European Renaissance and Baroque poetry, the Enlightenment and Romantic novel (with its different subspecies), symbolist and early modernist poetry, naturalistic and realistic prose fiction, the great modernist breakthroughs and experiments beginning with WWI, etc. The distinctive feature of this reconfiguration was that all these phenomena came to be viewed and characterized comparatively, transcending national-linguistic borders.

We thus introduced a hybridization of CL and WL. We teach general courses of a comparative Western literary-historical canon. It is not an exaggeration to say that these courses, because of literature's multifunctional core-role in the societal and moral self-consciousness of all communities, also necessitates the teaching of Western cultural history. We are fully aware that we cannot teach everything and we are not able to go into minute analytical detail in these overview courses. We do, however, make an effort to complement these courses with more specialized seminars, in which a comparative methodology is followed as much as possible.

MEN OF SCIENCE IN NEED OF THE HUMANITIES

Our academic programmes at Tartu University are far from perfect. Yet, over recent years, I have been able to observe that our courses in WL/CL are attended not only by those students for whom they are compulsory, but also by students specializing in philosophy, semiotics, history, psychology, and even in hard sciences such as biology and physics. In other words, it seems that these young people feel the need to complement their specialization with cultural knowledge they cannot get in their own major fields of interest.

Also, the general trend in Western universities has recently been to focus on interdisciplinary studies, which actually just means making the humanities look more like the sciences, i.e. saturating them with elements from the technological sciences. This tendency seems to have played itself out, since it was in large part artificially constructed and contrary to the inherent nature of various fields involved. It did not take into account the special moral and spiritual role the humanities have always played in society. Why do we fail to envision institutionally confronting a radically different challenge, especially in a time when the present global crisis can no longer remain hidden, namely that individuals workings in the hard sciences and technology are in need of moral and spiritual support that can only be provided by reactivated humanities?

Why cannot departments of comparative and world literature become the core units providing courses in comparative world cultural history for all university students, regardless of their specialization? It is a great challenge that would presuppose a special preparation and expansion of the CL and WL teaching staff. However, the benefit of reforming the social and moral conscience of young people and future scholars would be incomparably greater than any material investments that such a radical reform might require.

VERGLEICHENDE LITERATURWISSENCHAFT, COMPARATIVE LITERATURE AND *LITTÉRATURE COMPARÉE*

More needs to be said about the use of the terms CL and WL. Quite early on, ambiguous yet significant nuances appeared in the denomination of the activities of literary comparatists in large cultural-linguistic areas. English 'comparative' has its closest equivalent in Russian where the corresponding term is *sravnitel'nyi*. The German *vergleichende* also has a slightly different nuance. In all three languages, however, the adjective applies to a subject that has set out to compare objects. English-language culture has until recently refused to acknowledge literary research as a form of scientific activity. As the subject's complement is missing, 'comparative literature' sounds in English extremely liberal and unscientific. It is not very clear what is meant by 'literature'. Does it belong to the researched object or the researching subject? Or both at the same time? Germans and Russians have eliminated this ambiguity by introducing the word 'science' or 'research': it is respectively *vergleichende Literaturwissenschaft*, *сравнительное литературоведение*. In contrast, three most popular Romance languages have moved the emphasis of CL to the object. In French, Spanish and Italian, the field is respectively: *littérature comparée*, *literatura comparada*, and *letteratura comparata*. It is clearly defined as literature, which is compared or treated comparatively. Thus, the field is implicitly contrasted with other types of literary research in which the object can be treated in isolation from other objects.

Maybe, these problems of terminology were less apparent in the past. However, in view of the strong present-day trend to make the humanities look more like science, the signifier of CL/WL can easily fail to fully describe the discipline's identity. If in its denomination the accent is placed on science, as in German, Russian and, under their direct influence, also in my native Estonian (*võrdlev kirjandusteadus*), then one may ask how can such science be differentiated from any other theoretical discourse applied to literature? In fact, any particular current of abstract thinking with which literature is treated can apply the principle of comparison. One can without any problems apply the term comparative to other fields: why not 'comparative semiotics', 'comparative translation studies', 'comparative philosophy', 'comparative psychology', 'comparative narratology', 'comparative epistemology', etc.? Indeed, the label 'comparative', in imitation of CL has been already introduced in various fields, such as 'comparative political sciences' or 'comparative economics', among others.

'Comparative' has not at all lost a certain attractiveness as an academic term. The problem in the field of literature pedagogy is that 'comparative literary science' is rivalled institutionally by '(general) literary theory'. As theory is an inalienable part of most hard sciences, one may ask if 'comparative literary science' cannot be regarded just as a part of the theory of literature? Defined as a kind of science, does it need autonomy at all? Indeed, at a number of European universities, particularly in several universities in Spain, the theory of literature and CL form a conjoint unit, department, or institute. As far as I know, within these units, the theory of literature significantly outweighs CL. Some more fashionable aspects of CL (thus, literature's relations with other arts) are sporadically taught, but the fundamental task of CL, viewed as teaching and research literary phenomena in the transnational and trans-linguistic context of world culture and WL, has generally been neglected.

THE *EDAPHOS* OF COMPARATIVE LITERATURE

To avoid the above-mentioned ambiguities of interpretation, the application of a signifier with an emphasis on the field or the *edaphos* (ground, soil), as applied in Romance languages, would probably solve the above-mentioned dilemmas. If a university department is called 'French Literature' or 'Estonian Literature', it is obvious to anyone that in these departments French and Estonian literatures are taught and researched.

Yet the attribute *comparée* (which indeed cannot be applied to all languages beyond the Romance languages with an equal facility) leaves a margin for ambiguity. Why cannot the research and study of a national literature apply a comparative approach? What makes then CL differ from French or Estonian literature? Besides, in the recent years, apparently under the influence of CL and WL, increasingly comparative elements have been introduced into the research and teaching of national literatures.

Some twenty years ago, Stockholm University assembled all literary research and teaching in a 'department of literature'. It assembled the teaching and research staff dedicated to Swedish as well as world (foreign) and comparative literature. It also combined literary history and theory. In my opinion, such a structural unit is what is needed: an academic centre providing the possibility to study literature in its widest possible context and at the same time offer a detailed treatment of literary phenomena as a substantial factor of national culture, in its linguistic, social dimensions.

At present, the respective department at Stockholm University has been renamed as the 'department of literature and history of ideas'. It is not my purpose here to criticize my Swedish colleagues for the apparent redundancy in their department's name. Besides, I know all too well that most academic restructuring at universities has its origin in people engaged in bureaucratic power plays, rather than in serious research and teaching. I just mentioned the Swedish case as an example of a general trend at European and Western universities to diminish the role of the humanities by introducing elements of fragmentation. Behind the nobly-looking directive of 'interdisciplinary' research, there is a transparent strategy to undermine the autonomy of the humanities and to turn them into a kind of a beggarly appendix to the 'real' or 'hard' sciences.

FUTURE UNIVERSITY DEPARTMENTS DEALING WITH THE HISTORY OF SENSIBILITY, PASSION, AND LOVE?

The above-mentioned combination 'literature and history of ideas' could well be expanded. Why not establish a 'department of literature and the history of sensibility, passion and love'? Does anybody seriously think that great world literature has less to do with passions and love than with reasoning and ideas? The greatness of literature as a form of artistic creation lies in its multilayered essence. Literature epitomizes symbiotic creation in the arts. It is at the same time philosophy, psychology, history, anthropology, sociology, aesthetics, ethics, linguistics, etc. Unless we intentionally narrow its perspectives and reduce its significance by imposing on it formally or sociologically biased research and pedagogy, literature is itself thoroughly interdisciplinary.

Literature has the enormous capacity to influence the conscience of entire societies. It works by means of sensual images and, as such, is capable of entering both our waking and dream consciousness. Today's public media, manipulated as they are by economic and political strategies, seek to drive literature away from the social arena because great literature, by its socially and morally critical attitudes, threatens a world driven overwhelmingly by masculinist and consumerist ideology. In the past, literature represented the voice of the 'other' (woman, socially, and racially subjugated people) and counterbalanced the reason-based linear vision of progress and profit, the cornerstones of Western male ideology.

Literary criticism and the philosophy of literature have their main task and responsibility in explicating literature as a historical and social phenomenon. The central position of both CL and WL is defined by their object, which cannot be isolated or narrowly envisioned. The term CL was not specifically mentioned by Goethe or other Romantic German writer-philosophers. WL, however, could only have emerged from the essential philosophical relatedness of 'self' and 'other', or 'own' and 'alien'. There is a spiritual openness to the world of creation in its totality, characterized by its breadth, amplitude, and diversity. WL basically means establishing a canon of authors and works of world literature. CL, as the root element in this process, has a key role in maintaining the openness of the canon and grounding its discourse in serious research and (re-)interpretation. It would be utterly mistaken to try and establish a WL canon for the future, definitively determine works belonging to WL, or works fated to remain exiled in the remote obscurity of a national literature. Clearly all national practices of teaching WL depend strongly on the accessibility of literary texts in translation, on the quality of the translations, and on the linguistic capabilities of the individual students and scholars. Teaching and researching in WL demand a tentative canon, with nothing definite or closed.

IDENTIFYING TASKS OF COMPARATIVE LITERATURE

CL has often been called interdisciplinary. Indeed, comparing works in different fields of the arts, their motivations, philosophies, and creative principles can be quite fruitful. However, I am still convinced that the main purpose of CL should remain literature itself. It is a vast field, including all possible inter-literary, as well as intra-literary and intracultural processes. For me, CL means first and foremost the study of literary works and phenomena in contexts. It transcends (but in no case abandons!) a determined national-linguistic area of culture.

I would especially emphasize the responsibility of CL scholars with regard to research in the reception of WL (its existing active and passive canons as well as its potential canon). It is absolutely obvious that such research cannot be carried out by scholars who define themselves exclusively as specialists of a national literature. Here, the identity of a CL scholar can be appreciated. He/she should be well versed in broad intercultural processes, on the one hand, and a given national-literature and culture, on the other hand. The linguistic knowledge of a CL scholar cannot be limitless, but a certain fluency in several languages beyond one's mother tongue is, however, a prerequisite.

Translation history forms a special chapter in the reception (intercultural transmission) process and requires even more specific linguistic preparation. For successfully coping with these tasks, national, CL and WL scholars should develop their skills.

In the diachronic perspective of CL, it would hardly be possible to conceive and achieve a perfect literary history. No international team of scholars can sufficiently understand the needs of every culture involved. At their best, collectively written literary histories are compilations of fragments of national literary histories. Every talented literary scholar has his/her own style and it is not always possible to form a team comprising of equally mature and capable scholars. It is relatively easy to track literary history as the history of ideas. Such a history, however, would represent only a kind of 'extra-history', something developing on the surface of time. To apply the ideas of the Spanish writer and philosopher Miguel de Unamuno, this 'extra-history', a hidden 'intra-history', expands, full of human passions and existential tragedy.

To grasp literature's varied narratives that combine 'extra-histories' with 'intra-histories', a CL scholar should be imbued with a special sensibility. It is not by accident that at the height of one of Europe's greatest creative 'explosions' in literature and, at the same time, of the emergence of WL, the most productive thinkers on literature were writers themselves. If deprived of such sensibility, literary scholarship can easily err in undervaluing important core-segments of literary creation, such as poetry and lyrical poetry. Naturally, every literary history bears the footprints of its own time. However, to turn the predominant perceptual-aesthetic attitudes of *one's own* time or *one's own* ideology into an exclusive platform for a literary history would obviously lead to a great distortion of the creative reality.

Who creates the canon of WL? I am far from admitting the claim of Roland Barthes and others about the omnipotence of critics, but it is true that the most capable thinkers on literature, individuals who dialogue with the work of talented writers, are probably in the forefront of those who have historically established literary canons, including those of WL. Their efforts are complemented by the hard work of many translators. Then, these texts are adopted in high school and university curricula, while scholarly research and critical discussion is taken up into academic journals and trade periodicals.

In former times, the visual media, especially TV, played an important role. However, the whole process was happenstance and absolutely unpredictable. Also and quite often, 'exterior' factors (such as literary prizes or personal events) enhanced a writer's chance of being consecrated in either the passive or the active canon of WL. Certainly, writers working in major internationally widespread languages have a great advantage over writers in minority languages who are often fated to occupy only a place in the secondary category of canons, those of national literatures. This is an especially important issue not only for my own geographical region, but also for India.

THE ACTIVE WL CANON

What do I mean by the active canon of WL? The writers belonging to the active canon of WL are those whose work, has become a more or less permanent object of international discussion. Not only critics and scholars of a specific national culture discuss it, but the discourse about their work transcends the national-linguistic cultural space as well as the circles of specialized scholars. Their work has been widely translated, so that the widest possible international reading public has access to it.

Among the authors whose place in WL canon has been organized (at least since Romanticism) we find Shakespeare, Goethe, Molière, Boccaccio, and Cervantes. A lot depends on the genre in which an author's major work has been written. I do not possess precise data to confirm such a claim, but my impression is that Boccaccio's *Decameron* is by far more widely known and discussed in the world's CL and WL curricula than Dante Alighieri's *Commedia* or Petrarch's *Il canzoniere*. It is simply because prose fiction can more easily than poetry be transferred from one linguistic-national space to another, especially the variety employing end-rhymes and meter.

As for those WL authors who temporarily may have been obliged to 'withdraw' from the canon, I would mention certain great Spanish writers of the Baroque era, such as Pedro Calderón de la Barca, Tirso de Molina or Francisco de Quevedo. They were well known to Goethe, the Schlegels and other Romantics who established the WL canon in its basic contours, as we know it today. Subsequently, the 'classics' of WL have geographically shifted from Germany to France and then to the US. In France, Molière's *Don Juan* has overshadowed the original (and by no means inferior) Spanish Don Juan, portrayed in *El burlador de Sevilla y convidado de piedra* by Tirso de Molina. Molière created his *Don Juan* in prose, while Tirso de Molina's play was written (as Spanish 'Golden Age' drama in general) in a variety of metrical forms, all employing end-rhymes.

Ideological differences may have also influenced the international reception process. As far as I have been able to observe, even if the work of Calderón has generated interest in England and France, it did not attract a wider theatre public there. It has not engendered much discussion beyond the circle of specialized scholars, or *hispanistas*. Lord Byron knew well the work of Francisco de Quevedo, but I doubt if an average successful British writer of today has ever even heard about that Spanish master of existential poetry and satire, in both prose and verse. It has to be admitted, however, that to translate Quevedo's grotesque imagery is quite challenging for any writer.

As twentieth-century Anglo-America and France have been in the forefront in canonizing WL authors, little knowledge of the Spanish classics has spread to the eastern part of the world. Shakespeare, Goethe, and Ibsen have all enjoyed considerable success among literati in contemporary China, Japan, and Korea (cf. Yip 2012, Tam 2012), whereas sixteenth- and seventeenth-century Spanish literature is still almost unknown in these countries. Nevertheless, I am convinced that, given time and some happy coincidence of reception, great works of WL will be reintegrated in the canon. Talented new translators, especially writers and poets, may well play a substantial role in this resurgence. There is an urgent need for new and more flexible translations.

THE PASSIVE WL CANON

The 'passive' canon of WL is comprised of translations belonging to WL, which have been 'pushed' aside, no longer residing on the exclusive 'inside' of their culture of origin. In other words they are seldom discussed by international scholars outside their determined linguistic-national culture. If ever they have been included in international WL anthologies, it is because articles have been written on them by specialized scholars from other national literatures, rather than by CL researchers. Even today, the world does not have a sufficient number of well-prepared CL scholars. Thus, the analyses of 'peripheral' literature by some CL scholars belonging to 'centric' areas, appear quite superficial (Virk 2010).

As an example of a major work belonging to the passive canon of WL, I would mention the epic by Friedrich Reinhold Kreutzwald, *Kalevipoeg* (1861). On the whole, one could probably find a short article about Kreutzwald and/or his epic in most multi-volume WL encyclopaedias. For example, there is an article about Kreutzwald in volume 5 of the German *Brockhaus*, while the 3-volume *Kleines literarisches Lexikon*, even if failing to appreciate duly Kreutzwald as a poet and author, at least briefly mentions *Kalevipoeg* in volume 1.

Consecrated in Estonia as our 'national epic', Kreutzwald's masterpiece has been translated in its full form into thirteen languages, the latest being a second translation into English (2011) and a Hindi translation (2012). Still, it is obvious that the epic has not yet become an object of international discussion. Its inclusion in the active WL canon has been inhibited by Estonia's own literary scholarship, which until recently viewed the epic as exclusively Estonian, rather than informed by some wider world and European context of epic poetry. Thus, a folklore-centred approach to *Kalevipoeg* has prevailed, preventing the work's treatment as a European philosophical masterpiece in the genre of lyric-epics, in many ways comparable to Goethe's *Faust.*

THE POTENTIAL WL CANON

Finally, with regard to what I would call the potential canon of WL, it is formed by the world's majority literatures. Most writers do not orient their work to the massive public, adapt it to fashionable (and profitable) topics, or strive to be visible outside their own national-linguistic area. This point is especially true for those who create their work in the great majority of languages beyond the traditional 'centric' Western languages, which besides being spoken by extended communities are also taught at schools and universities throughout the world. Though Chinese, Russian, Arabic and many other languages belonging to the eastern part of the globe are spoken by tens and hundreds of millions of people, they still have a relatively modest role in international cultural communication. The translation process that ideally should facilitate access to the works of talented writers working in languages other than English, French, German, Spanish, (and maybe) Portuguese and Italian, is often biased by simple commercial factors.

The greatest injustice in the field of WL is done to poets. Not only is it hard to translate poetic works, it is by no means easier to find publishers for poetry, especially translated poetry. Far more than prose translation, rendering poetry in another medium entails tremendous risks. Quite probably a CL scholar who does not know the language in which a poem has been created, would not dare submit the work to a closer analysis. (Luckily, cultural transfer is a much broader phenomenon. It does not preclude, for instance, some Western writers from seeking inspiration in oriental language translations. Goethe did not know Persian and García Lorca did not know Arabic, yet both created their respective 'divans'.)

My example of a potential writer for the WL canon is my compatriot, the poet Juhan Liiv (1864–1913). In recent years, I have dealt intensively with his work. I find creative originality in his philosophic-lyrical imagery that can not be found in the works of any other European or Western poet adapted to a mainstream or fashionable poetic trend of his/her time. There is a brief mention of Liiv in the multi-volume *Brockhaus*, but he does not appear in the *Kleines literarisches Lexikon*. There is indeed little reason why Liiv's work should have entered the canon of WL. Kreutzwald's *Kalevipoeg* was originally published in Estonian, with a parallel translation in German, thus having from the very beginning a wonderful accessibility outside vernacular Estonian. Liiv, who spent his life in dire poverty and in 1893 fell mentally ill, did not manage to publish any poetry of his own selection during his lifetime. His canon in Estonia was established posthumously by some younger writers, such as Friedebert Tuglas who before WWII published two monographs on Liiv's life and work (1914, 1927), as well as two major selections of Liiv's poetry (1919, 1926). Tuglas considered Liiv's poetry a creative miracle that would be impossible to translate into other languages.

Thanks to Tuglas, Liiv has been celebrated as one of Estonia's all-time great poets. Efforts to translate his poetry have, however, been scant. As independent books, translated poetic selections of his poetry appeared only in Russian (Tallinn 1933; Moscow 1962) and Esperanto (Tallinn, 1980), that is, in languages, which are limited in their intercultural scope. Liiv seems to be destined to remain exclusively in his own national canon, without any hope of being admitted to WL. During the period of his mental illness (a kind of schizophrenia), Liiv imagined himself to be the son of the Russian tsar Alexander II and the Estonian poetess Lydia Koidula. At the same time, he saw himself as the heir to the Polish throne. He dreamed of going to Warsaw, in order to be welcomed by the Poles as their king. In reality, he never even crossed the Estonian border. However, history remains open to surprises and unexpected turns. Despite the prophetic visions in his poetry, Liiv could probably not have imagined that a hundred years after his death English translations of his poems would be published in several influential US poetry magazines (thus, in *Poetry*, *Rowboat*) and thereafter would be discussed in various influential poetry blogs on the internet.

Liiv never had a typing-machine. He left all his manuscripts to posterity in scribbled handwriting. A first small bilingual Estonian-English selection of his poetry was published in Estonia in 2007, while a substantially renewed and enlarged bilingual selection appeared in Canada in 2013, a century after his death. It seems that, contrary to all gloomy predictions from 'inside' Estonia, Liiv's work is gradually emerging and being recognized in the wider world. If CL ever manages to defend and strengthen its place in global academic culture, one hopes that our Juhan Liiv is only one of the many writers whose work will in the future enrich and adorn the canon of WL.

REFERENCES

Damrosch, David, *What Is World Literature?*, Princeton: Princeton University Press, 2003.

———, 'World Literature in a Postcanonical, Hypercanonical Age', in *Comparative Literature in the Age of Globalization*, ed. H. Saussy, Baltimore: The Johns Hopkins University Press, 2006, pp. 43–53.

Eglāja-Kristsone, Eva, 'Filtered Through Iron Curtain: Soviet Methodology towards a Canon of World (Foreign) Literature and the Latvian Case', in *Interlitteraria: World Literature and National Literatures*, Tartu University Press, 2012, pp. 342–52.

Figueira, Dorothy, 'The Brahmanization of Theory: Commodity Fetishism and False Consciousness', in *Interlitteraria: History of Literature as a Factor of a National and Supranational Literary Canon*, vol. 10, no. 1, Tartu: Tartu University Press, 2005, pp. 10–31.

———, 'Comparative Literature and the Origins of World Literature in National Literatures', in *Interlitteraria: World Literature and National Literatures*, vol. 17, no. 1, Tartu: Tartu University Press, 2012, pp. 10–17.

Juvan, Marko, 'World Literature in Carniola: Transfer of Romantic Cosmopolitanism and the Making of National Literature', in *Interlitteraria: World Literature and National Literatures*, Tartu University Press, 2012, pp. 28–50.

Li Xia, 'The Precarious Future of the "Humanities Enterprise" in the Digital Information Millennium', in *Interlitteraria: World Literature and National Literatures*, vol. 16, no. 1, Tartu: Tartu University Press, 2011, pp. 20–38.

Лотман, Ю. М., *Культура и взрыв*. Москва: Прогресс, 1992.

Лотман, Ю. М., О семиосфере.—*Труды по знакоьм системам*, 17, Tartu: Tartu University Press, 1984, pp. 5–23.

Spiridon, Monica, 'Literary Studies at the Crossroads: The Strategies of Co-optation', *Interlitteraria: World Literature and National Literatures*, vol. 14, no. 1, Tartu: Tartu University Press, 2009, pp. 41–49.

Talvet, Jüri, *A Call for Cultural Symbiosis*, Toronto: Guernica, 2005.

———, '*Edaphos* and *Episteme* of Comparative Literature', in *Interlitteraria*, vol. 10, Tartu: Tartu University Press, 2005, pp. 46–56.

———, 'The Author and Artistic Creativity', *Primerjalna Književnost*, vol. 32, 2009, pp. 169–80.

Tam, Kwok-kan, 'Chineseness in Recreating Ibsen: Peer Gynt in China and Its Adaptations', in *Interlitteraria: World Literature and National Literatures*, Tartu University Press, 2012, pp. 268–81.

Terian, Andrei, 'Reading World Literature: Elliptical or Hyperbolic? The Case of Second-World National Literatures', in *Interlitteraria: World Literature and National Literatures*, Tartu University Press, 2012, pp. 18–27.

Virk, Tomo, 'Romanticism as a Literary-historiographical Project', in *Interlitteraria: World Literature and National Literatures*, vol. 15, no. 2, *History of Literature as a Factor of a National and Supranational Literary Canon*, Tartu: Tartu University Press, 2010, pp. 545–70.

Yip, Terry, 'World Literature and Cultural Transformation in Modern Chinese Literature', in *Interlitteraria: World Literature and National Literatures*, Tartu University Press, 2012, pp. 51–65.

4

Doctoring the State

Haun Saussy

THE YEAR 1848 was one of failed revolutions. But it was also a time of intense political creativity. In some countries, it was the occasion for new 'peoples' to invent themselves and their cultural identity, whilst claiming sovereign rights. In France, the insurgent left started from the proposition that the Revolution of 1789 had not gone far enough, that it had overturned a throne but had not accomplished the sort of fundamental change in the order of things that would prevent the return of kings, emperors, and tyrants—since, after all, they had returned and prospered in Napoleonic and post-Napoleonic Europe. Industrialization and its counterpart, the labour movement, predisposed the revolutionaries of 1848 to think that the change to be instituted this time around would have to do not with the law or political structures, but with property regimes. Industry would be nationalized. Even charity had to be rethought on a basis of equality.[1] And 1848 was the year of the Communist Manifesto, a very big proclamation issued by a very small party that basked in its self-description as 'the spectre haunting Europe' (Marx and Engels 1848). Due to the later prominence of Marxist parties, we often forget that the attention of the world in 1848 was focused on other revolutionaries and reformers: Proudhon, Blanqui, Saint-Simon, Ozanam, Schoelcher, Lamartine, Victor Hugo, etc. Inequality was on everyone's mind, but characterizing it, measuring it and remedying it took a variety of forms.

The revolutionary impulse even reached bureaucratic, hierarchical, militaristic Prussia. In the summer of 1848, a young medical doctor and civil servant named Rudolf Virchow wrote in the editorial column of

* This essay was first written for the 2014 De Carle Visiting Professorship at the University of Otago, Dunedin, New Zealand. I am grateful to Professors Jacob Edmond and Christine Prentice for the invitation.

a journal he had just founded, called *Medical Reform*, some words that were to become famous: 'The reform of medicine is necessitated, not for the sake of the doctors, but for that of the sick. . . . Doctors are the natural attorneys of the poor (*die natürlichen Anwälte der Armen*), and the social question falls, to a significant degree, within their jurisdiction' (Virchow 1848: 2). These words are often cited in writings on public health (a discipline of which Virchow has a claim to be one of the founders). They do not particularly show Virchow stepping out of line. His argument appears to be framed, rather, in terms of professional competence and of the ethics of vicarious decision-making, two conditions that doctors have in common with attorneys—it is built into the nature of their work that they should often be acting on behalf of people who are not able to devise cures or plead cases themselves. In Prussia, moreover, both lawyers and doctors had to receive commissions from the state before they could exercise their professions. A few years earlier, when Immanuel Kant had claimed the authority to think and publish as he pleased, the polemic in which he laid out his right to intellectual freedom, *The Conflict of the Faculties*, accepted as just and natural that the state should dictate the content of medical, legal and religious teaching, just not that it had any business meddling with philosophy (Kant 1992). Inasmuch as the state monitored medicine and law and had a concern that the licensed professionals in these fields should perform within authorized guidelines, the state could in all legality restrict the exponents of those fields to statutorily defined services. Kant found the intellectual authority of the state inapplicable only to the work of the philosophical faculty whose job was the application of reason to any and all subjects, whatever the outcome might be. Virchow, in calling for a reform of medical practice together with greater independence of physicians, and in announcing that the sphere of medicine naturally extended to 'the social question', could be seen as speaking as much on behalf of the state in its role as guarantor of the quality of medical services as on behalf of doctors and patients.

Virchow, however, had more to say, and this would put him in a different position in regard to state authority. He had just returned from observing the consequences of a typhus epidemic in Upper Silesia, an area populated mainly by Polish-speaking mine workers. Poorly housed and fed, exhausted from overwork, and unable to claim the advantages of German-speaking Prussian citizens, the Silesian typhus victims died in higher proportions than other sufferers from the same disease. Virchow's later editorials draw the conclusions: medicine is not just about diagnoses and cures, it must also have to do with food, housing, the regulation of work hours and salary, if medicine's concern is to protect people from disease. (Though Virchow was already well-known as a pathologist and experimentalist, germ theory was not yet known in 1848 and not available to explain the propagation of epidemic disease; hence the emphasis on living conditions.) Given the difference in morbidity and mortality rates between the poor and the better-off, a difference that Virchow's Silesian tour had made impossible to ignore, it was absurd to think that the practice of medicine was not a political matter. Virchow's judgement on the Prussian government of the time was surprisingly harsh:

> When the state, for any reasons whatsoever (whether these stem from Heaven or from everyday life) allows its citizens to lapse into conditions in which they *must* starve to death, it ceases legally to be a state.
>
> (Wenn der Staat es zulässt, dass durch irgend welche Vorgänge sei es des Himmels, oder des täglichen Lebens Bürger in die Lage gebracht werden, verhungern zu *müssen*, so hört er rechtlich auf, Staat zu sein.) (Virchow 1990; emphasis original.)

'It ceases legally to be a state': this was an extraordinary thing to say in the Prussia of the 1840s. Now you might think that this utterance is adequately explained as something a very angry and disappointed young doctor might say in that dizzying summer of 1848. But Virchow is engaging here in a long-standing debate on the essence and definition of the state, much of which had been going on around him in Berlin over the previous decades. Hegel had recently described the state in terms that would make such a judgement inconceivable, especially on the part of a minor servant of that same state.

> The state is the actuality of the ethical Idea. It is ethical mind *qua* the substantial will manifest and revealed to itself, knowing and thinking itself, accomplishing what it knows and in so far as it knows it. . . . [The state's] substantial unity is an absolute unmoved end in itself, in which freedom comes into its supreme right. On the other hand this final end has supreme right against the individual, whose supreme duty is to be a member of the state. (Hegel 1952: pars 257–8, pp. 155–6)

Against this deification of the state (Hegel's annotation to paragraph 258 helpfully adds: 'The march of God in the world, that is what the state is'), Virchow speaks as if medicine, taking note of the state's failure to be a state, had joined forces with Thomas Hobbes. Indeed, Virchow continues his accusation by saying that the state that lets its citizens starve 'legalizes theft (i.e. self-help) and deprives itself of any moral ground to guarantee the security of persons or property' (*er legalisirt den Diebstahl (die Selbsthülfe) und beraubt sich jedes sittlichen Grundes, die Sicherheit der Personen oder des Eigenthums zu wahren*). Some two hundred years earlier, in the famous Chapter 13 ('Of the Natural Condition of Mankind, as Concerning their Felicity and Misery') of *Leviathan*, Hobbes had speculated that all governments had originated from the need of primitive people to band together for mutual security. Faced with 'that condition which is called war; and such a war as is of every man against every man', our ancestors entered into associations that grew and differentiated into states (Hobbes [1651] 1909: 94). Virchow seems to add to Hobbes here. Hobbes had considered our natural enemies to be only other humans. Virchow thinks of disease and starvation as enemies of mankind which the state is bound to resist on behalf of its subjects. The defensive power of the state is automatically triggered by those ills, just as the social contract demands that the parties thereto give each other assistance against the bands of wild humans that are liable to rob, enslave or kill them. Whenever the state fails in its mission of protection, Virchow says, 'it ceases legally to be a state', as if government had lapsed into the condition of nature when, to quote Hobbes again, 'nothing can be unjust. The notions of right and wrong, justice and injustice, have there no place. Where there is no common power, there is no law; where no law, no injustice' (98). Virchow says that it does not matter whether the emergency of epidemic or famine comes from the heavens or from human action. It is an existential problem for the democratic state, which Virchow defines as 'desiring the welfare of all citizens, since it acknowledges the equal rights of all'. He adds, 'Since the state stands for or exists as the ethical entity of a group of individuals all having equal rights ... it implies the solidarity of obligation' (Virchow 1990: 1: 15).

Defining the state—its responsibilities and its legal conditions of existence—through its readiness to confront its medical responsibilities was something entirely new, and should, if this innovation is rightly assigned to Virchow, give him a place among the political theorists and not just among the heroes of public health. It is certainly not a generalization derived from observing the behaviour of actually existing states. These have always been quite cavalier about ordering their citizens to sacrifice themselves on the battlefield, in the workshop and in the marketplace for its own greater glory; indeed the power to command such obedience has always been the greater part of that glory. Although Germany began, partly at Virchow's urging (for he was by then a senator), to have a national health insurance scheme in the 1880s, the welfare state in Europe is a child of the two World Wars, and mostly of the second, with a highly irregular rate of implementation in different countries. The United States provided Medicaid for the poor in the 1960s and only since 2013 has the nation had the skeleton of a national health-insurance programme still awaiting fulfilment and hotly resisted in some quarters. Atul Gawande (2009) has written about the strategic moment that came for passing universal healthcare legislation in those Western countries that now have it, and about why letting the moment pass digs a channel that is hard to get out of.

The resentment expressed toward universal health care cannot entirely be explained by the fear that it will cost too much and burden the state, clog the economy and leave the citizens prisoners of an endlessly rising bill for ever more complex and expensive services. There is also a theory of human nature at work—a theory written out in detail already in 1792 by Wilhelm von Humboldt, an observer of both the French revolutionaries' willingness to subordinate everything to the popular will and of the technocratic authoritarianism of his own Prussia.

A medical metaphor is one of the argumentative resources of the version of libertarianism framed in *On the Limits of State Action,* an essay written and circulated by Humboldt in 1792 but not published until 1851. (Some may think libertarianism was first codified in philosophy by Robert Nozick in the 1970s. This was not so.) Humboldt starts from a broad humanistic claim that 'the true end of Man, or that which is prescribed by the eternal and immutable dictates of reason, and not suggested by vague and transient desires, is the highest and most harmonious development of his powers to a complete and consistent whole' (von Humboldt 1854: 11). In consequence, 'any State interference in private affairs, not directly implying violence done to individual rights, should be absolutely condemned'. The only job of the state is that of a referee invited to keep us from trampling on one another's rights. It does not itself create or confer any rights. Humboldt is dismissive of

> the entire efforts of the State to elevate the positive welfare of the nation; of its solicitude for the population of the country, and the subsistence of its inhabitants ... in short, of every political institution designed to preserve or augment the physical welfare of the nation.... Now all such institutions, I maintain, are positively hurtful in their consequences, and wholly irreconcilable with a true system of polity. (21)

This has become a familiar tune: 'state action is always vicious; private initiative is always in the right'. Humboldt elaborates on the well-intentioned damage that he thinks public benevolence will always inflict:

'to view their agency in the most favourable light, States like those to which we refer too often resemble the physician, who only retards the death of his patient in nourishing his disease. Before there were physicians, only health and death were known' (27). So, to follow the steps of Humboldt's analogy, the state is a physician, and physicians are bunglers; away with them then, let us live in the clear stark alternative of health and death. This style of thinking relishes absolutes and subscribes to the magical thinking that if the troublesome in-between of sickness and therapy is removed, all those who are not dead, that is, alive, will automatically be healthy. The doctor, for Humboldt, is the natural attorney, not of the poor, but of poverty and sickness themselves.

One of the changes that had crept into the world between 1792 and 1848 was the collection and interpretation of statistics. Adolphe Quételet's *Social Statistics*, first published in 1832, formally initiated this field, although close record-keeping was a feature of both the Napoleonic armies and of the utilitarianism of Bentham and Mill.[2] Statistics made it harder to bandy about absolutes like health and death. Virchow is an up-to-date user of surveys and percentages. 'In a single year 10% of the population of the Pless district died, 6.48% of starvation combined with the [typhus] epidemic, and according to official figures, 1.3% solely of starvation. In 8 months in the district of Rubnik, 14.3% of the population were affected by typhus, of whom 20.46% died' (Virchow 2006: 2102–5). With such numbers, health and death no longer stand in such stark contrast. Now it is the difference between a greater and a lesser fatality rate that draws the professional's attention. The 'patient' with whom public health is concerned—a collectivity—becomes tangible through such numbers. The degree to which a population was affected by hunger or contagion could be more precisely ascertained; comparisons could be drawn between groups differently situated; it became possible to issue predictions about what 'the average man' was likely to do. The state becomes the aggregate of its people, who are now perceivable not as allegory, as genealogy or as representative types, but as a collection of numerical levels rising and falling over time. The object of public health—and of modern governing techniques—is inconceivable without statistical collections.

No doctor wins definitive victories. Virchow would have been proud enough to lower the fatality rate through improvements in living conditions in the districts he surveyed—an entirely relative and temporary victory. Nonetheless, the leverage of technique upon conditions affecting populations leads Virchow to imply a different conception of political life. He frames the state, not as a minimal constraint designed to liberate our personal energies (that would be Humboldt), nor as a leviathan entitled to grind our bones to make his bread (that would be Hegel), nor as a powerful conglomeration of rights and interests that may incidentally be led to invest in a greater or lesser degree of comfort for its citizens, as a matter of incidental policy and whim (that would be the post-war consensus in wealthy Europe). Rather, he derives the state's very right to existence from its success at protecting the citizens from the risks of starvation and disease. Consistent with this protective agenda, Virchow's imagined state, as described in other of his writings, will forswear capital punishment and war (Virchow 1985: 17–18). Both, after all, destroy citizens' lives, and that in itself should delegitimate the state.

Medicine as policy, we might call it by shorthand. But no sooner are the words out of our mouths than we think of the uses of medical expertise and medical rhetoric in the service of powerful states. It has not typically been peaceful or glorious. There have always been doctors ready to diagnose, medicate, hospitalize, amputate, sterilize, euthanize or simply to use their authority to terrify people who were for one reason or another outside the lines. Susan Sontag's essay *Illness as Metaphor* explores the connotations of diseases, in particular tuberculosis and cancer, and reserves special mistrust for the rhetorical invocation of cancer. To say that 'X is a cancer upon the body politic' legitimizes extreme treatments—everything short of collective suicide, it seems—and so that analogy is a favourite of those who would rule with an iron fist, declaring that narcotics, or Jews, or labour unions, or whatever the *bête noire* of the moment is, must be dealt with, and quickly, and with overwhelming force (Sontag 1990). But in that kind of relation of medicine to politics, politics had the upper hand, and medicine was simply a means for politics to express itself, a handle by which it got pragmatic purchase on the bodies of individuals. If the same ends could have been accomplished by telegraphy or Morris dancing, the politicians would have used them. Virchow's version of the relation is a deep revision, one in which the doctor is using politics and the state for curative ends. Where the state fails to serve those ends, the doctor discards it, or declares it legally void. There is something more in this than the usual agenda of public health programming, budgeting and providing.

In performing this inversion of the usual 'politics as medicine, medicine as politics' relationship, Virchow was engaging with a constellation of ideas as old as Plato, and never resolved. What is the place of medicine in a political order? At the centre? Off to the side? On the top? Down among the masses? The difficulty of defining the relation has to do with the fact that the two things being related, medicine and politics can never be defined in wholly distinct ways. They are always in each other's pockets, and perhaps it took a medical doctor with a strong sense of injustice to reorder their relationship in the way he found most consistent with justice.

In Book One of Plato's *Republic*, a group of Athenians are talking about justice, how to recognize it, how to define it, whether it is possible in this world or not. Polemarchus holds to an old-fashioned idea of dealing justly: 'that the meaning of justice is to benefit one's friends and harm one's enemies'. This is not going to be good enough for Socrates. To benefit one's friends is well and good, but no one is truly just who chooses to harm others, even enemies. That is rather the behaviour of the unjust man. 'For it has been made clear to us,' says Socrates, summarizing an earlier discussion, 'that in no case is it just to harm anyone. . . . Very well, since it has been made clear that this too is not justice and the just, what else is there that we might say justice to be?'

Now Thrasymachus, even while we were conversing, [says Socrates as narrator] had been trying several times to break in and lay hold of the discussion but he was restrained by those who sat by him who wished to hear the argument out. But when we came to a pause after I had said this, he couldn't any longer hold his peace. But gathering himself up like a wild beast he hurled himself upon us as if he would tear us to bits. . . . [Thrasymachus said:] 'What balderdash is this that you have been talking, and why do you simple-simons truckle and give way to one another? . . . Hearken and hear then. I affirm that the just is nothing else than the advantage of the stronger'. (Plato 1971: 336b ff.)

Socrates then goes to work on Thrasymachus. He makes him first admit that sometimes the strong act against their own better judgement and make mistakes that result in injustice being done even to themselves—thus, there must be some kind of art of ruling, an art in which some are more skilled than others, and those skilled in this art might be the just. 'And is it not also true,' says Socrates,

that the art naturally exists for this, to discover and provide for each his advantage? . . . Just as if . . . you should ask me whether it is enough for the body to be the body or whether it stands in need of something else, I would reply, 'By all means it stands in need. That is the reason why the art of medicine has now been invented, because the body is defective and such defect is unsatisfactory. To provide for this, then, what is advantageous, that is the end for which the art was devised'. (341b–e)

Thus, Socrates injects into the discussion the idea of a beneficent use of power, for which medicine is his example. Thrasymachus a little hastily accepts this idea, presumably because it gives some advantage and power to the stronger, as his definition of justice had demanded.

[Socrates:] 'Then medicine does not consider the advantage of medicine but of the body?'

[Thrasymachus:] 'Yes.'

[Socrates:] 'Nor horsemanship of horsemanship but of horses, nor does any art look out for itself—for it has no need—but for that of which it is the art. And surely, Thrasymachus, the arts do hold rule and are stronger than that of which they are the arts.'

By 'that of which they are the arts', Socrates means the domain on which they practice. For medicine, that would be the defective human body; for public health, the public envisioned as an aggregate of such bodies.

'Then no art considers or enjoins the advantage of the stronger but every art considers the advantage of the weaker which is ruled by it'.

This too [Thrasymachus] was finally brought to admit though he tried to contest it.

[Socrates:] 'Can we deny, then, that neither does any physician insofar as he is a physician seek or enjoin the advantage of the physician but that of the patient? For we have agreed that the physician, precisely speaking, is a ruler and governor of bodies and not a money-maker....'

[Then Thrasymachus burst out:] 'You think that the shepherds and the neatherds are considering the good of the sheep and cattle and fatten and tend them with anything else in view than the good of their masters and themselves. And by the same token you seem to suppose that the rulers in our cities, I mean the real rulers, differ at all in their thoughts of the governed from a man's attitude toward his sheep or that they think of anything else night and day than the sources of their own profit. . . . Thus, Socrates, injustice on a sufficiently large scale is a stronger, freer, and more masterful thing than justice, and, as I said in the beginning, it is the advantage of the stronger that is the just, while the unjust is what profits a man's self and is for his advantage (343d).

In Plato's *Republic*, medicine was one of the analogies—along with horsemanship and seafaring—that allowed Socrates to get a tighter grasp on what justice is: it is the exertion 'by the stronger' of an art that benefits those who submit to it. After having been briefly tempted by this account, Thrasymachus, in the end, has to throw out the idea of an art or technique and come back to the sheer power discrepancy and non-community of interests between sheep and shepherd that define his picture of the justice of the stronger. Thrasymachus knows what it means to act 'on behalf' of the sheep and cattle: it is to keep them in good enough condition to serve the purposes of the owners until the time of slaughter or sale. Here at least there is no ethical ambiguity about serving another's and one's own interest. Plato, having used Thrasymachus as a mouthpiece for a view he intended to combat, lets him go, and we hear little more of him in the five later books of the dialogue; but outside Plato's works, Thrasymachus is far from having rested his case.

We may identify Thrasymachus with all actually existing governments. Leo Strauss saw in Thrasymachus' thesis 'the thesis of the city itself' (1978: 75). And the consensus of posterity is to identify Socrates with philosophy, or with the ideal of the philosopher-king, the person who combines the art of truth-seeking with the power to accomplish the ends of justice. But what is the exact discipline which Socrates is practising when he refers to medicine? It is not medicine, of course: he is not curing any diseases. If it is philosophy, or justice, then that art is another instance of 'the stronger' and the art of medicine is for a time its domain: medicine is here 'the weaker', in the very terms of the analogy between medicine and the body. Justice is the medicine of which medicine is the defective body; the bodies on which medicine acts are at a double remove from the highest 'art', that of justice. And indeed, once medicine has served Socrates as an analogy for the operation of justice in the state, is he not also putting aside the analogy as having served its illustrative purpose? Could not seafaring or furniture-making or other crafts have performed the same work for Socrates' purposes? Is Socrates not treating medicine as something that exists for the benefit of his political argument, and not allowing medicine to speak in its own behalf or to do what it can on behalf of the sick? Indeed, in the later books of the *Republic*, the verdict on medicine is largely a negative one: medicine must be regulated by philosophy, and it is the philosophers, the specialists in the good of the city, who decide which citizens are deserving of medical care and which ones should be left to die without it (*Republic* 407e, 410a). Once medicine has served Socrates to legitimate the discipline whose concern is justice in the state, it becomes quite obviously a mere instrument of state purposes, including a form of eugenics (see Levin 2014: 115–39).

This further development within Plato's dialectic allows us to sharpen our statement of the difference between the two instances of the analogy between politics and medicine. In *Republic,* section 341, Socrates is not conscious of, or not concerned with, the fact that the provision of medicine is something that states actually do regulate, distribute or command in various ways. Even in ancient Athens, the state was involved in the cult of Aesculapius, among other healing institutions (see Mitchell-Boyask 2008). In *Republic,* section 407, medicine is merely a means for the state to maintain its strength. Virchow, on the other hand, cannot make a medical metaphor for governance without alluding to the pragmatic mutual imbrication of state and healthcare. And with Virchow, the medicine/justice relation is not to be put aside once it has served to point us on the road to justice. Medicine serves as the criterion for political legitimacy: it goes all the way up the logical chain. There is no point at which, for him, politics takes over, as an art distinct from healing. If justice is to be reached, this will happen through the provision of medicine itself, not by another set of deductions bearing an analogy to medicine. It would not be enough to say that medicine is a metaphor in *The Republic* and a literal thing in Virchow's article; the difference is rather in the way the term 'medicine' serves as test and trigger of other concepts.

Where the two instances of the analogy coincide is in their use of the threat of brutality to orient the concepts of medicine and politics toward a compromise in therapeutic governance. Thrasymachus opens up a properly bestial account of human communities ('the good of the sheep and cattle'), only to be beaten back by the metaphorical power of medicine to bring about the human good; Virchow points to the imminent dissolution of all social bonds in a Hobbesian anarchy as the fruit of a social policy that is not dominated by concern to preserve life.

On the showing of this series of episodes in a 2500-year conversation, medical matters are not technical questions to be solved by specialists, nor is the relation of state to medicine just an instrumental one, as if the question were how to get political backing for medical projects or the inverse. Medicine, in some way, founds the category of politics. It involves issues of justice and language and philosophy which stand logically prior to the constitution of medicine and politics as separate domains. It is as if we can't think about social organization without thinking about medicine. And this is reasonable, because human beings are physical people—defective bodies, as Socrates recognized—and we need to be maintained in health, fed, kept in a suitable environment, or none of our speculations about justice will come to anything. Biological, social and economic conditions enable our agency, however much we may like to imagine ourselves as accountable only to our own freedom. (As an extreme case, consider the individuals orbiting around our planet in the

International Space Station. Their biological existence is maintained, at great cost, by resources dedicated to space programmes by sovereign states. They are 'state-supported' to a degree unapproached by any other natural, artificial or institutional object; where they reside, the 'state of nature' is entirely unfriendly to their existence.)

Socrates and Virchow are engaging, to use an anachronistic term, in interdisciplinarity, in which I see the future (the hope and risk) of comparative literary studies. They extract models and terms from one domain of professional competence and put them to work in another domain. They are not simply claiming that to be a good doctor is the same thing as to be a good ruler, or that having been recognized as the former entitles you to act as the latter: that would actually be a formula for the subsumption of disciplines, in this instance the engulfing of politics by medicine. What makes their analogy work, by which I mean what makes it produce new intellectual fruits and unsettle some of the usual routines in the previously existing disciplines, is the risky, dialogical nature of its combination, the way it subjects politics to the test of medical virtue and medicine to the test of political virtue. Interdisciplinarity, we also learn from this pair of examples, always involves a struggle for precedence. Which science will emerge from the dialogue having successfully reformulated the other? Socrates used medicine as a means of reformulating the current idea of justice, making it into a craft with a correlative field of application and normative constraints (he put off, however, the moment at which he would call on politics to redefine medicine), and Virchow used the lack of medical concern to symptomatize a failure of state legitimacy, thus defining, though negatively, the state through identification of its normative ends with those of medical treatment. Such redefinitions do not, as a rule, emerge naturally from the disciplines being combined, but only from their confrontation. Indeed, one (negative) test of the utility of an interdisciplinary argument is whether it reduces to the claims of one of the disciplines.[3]

Mixed metaphors are endemic to the kind of interdisciplinarity I am advocating. Indeed, this train of thought would lead us to view disciplinary purity with the strongest skepticism. Against Virchow's interweaving of medical and political language, consider the specialist reactions of the managers of the East India Company, as narrated by Sir Amartya Sen.

When a famine was developing in Gujerat in 1812, the Governor of Bombay turned down a proposal for moving food into the affected areas by asserting the advisability of leaving such matters to the market mechanism, quoting 'the celebrated author of the *Wealth of Nations*'. Warren Hastings, who had tackled a famine in Bengal in 1783–4 by using public channels for moving food into the region, was rapped on the knuckles by Colonel Baird-Smith for not having understood his Adam Smith. . . . This basically non-interventionist famine policy in India lasted late into the nineteenth century, changing only around the last quarter of it. (Sen 1981: 160)

Refusing to aid famine victims because that would compromise Smithian economic doctrine, the executives of the Company showed a specialist reflex. The needs of those who were short of food, unfortunately, corresponded to a methodological blind spot in the application of Smith's model. 'Adam Smith's proposition is, in fact, concerned with efficiency in meeting a market demand, but it says nothing on meeting a need that has not been translated into effective demand because of a lack of market-based entitlement and shortage of purchasing power' (161). I take the word 'translated' here as a summons to us interdisciplinarians to translate, mediate, make tangible, metaphorize and metaphrasize the 'externalities' of the disciplines by confronting them with one another, and not to assume too quickly that because one discipline has a solution to a problem, that that was, therefore, the problem that needed solving. Perhaps with its interest in enabling communication among specialist languages, and despite its being, most likely, 'master of none', comparative literature can play a role in the enrichment of discourse going well beyond the specialism currently known as 'literature'.

NOTES

1. One leader in this enterprise was the comparatist Frédéric Ozanam. See Maurice Agulhon (1976: 210–22) and Pierre Brunel (2000: 287–305).
2. See Bahmueller (1981). For Foucault (2004), the shift from a society of discipline to one of security occurs over the whole of the eighteenth century. On controversies surrounding the initial adoption of statistics to guide policy, see Supiot (2015: 119–49).
3. For an example, see 'Introduction: The Right to Claim Rights' in Saussy (2010: 2–3).

REFERENCES

Agulhon, Maurice, *Les Quarante-huitards*, Paris: Gallimard, 1976, pp. 210–22.

Bahmueller, Charles F., *The National Charity Company: Jeremy Bentham's Silent Revolution*, Berkeley: University of California Press, 1981.

Brunel, Pierre, 'Frédéric Ozanam (1813–1853) et l'enseignement des littératures étrangères', *Revue de littérature comparée*, vol. 74, 2000, pp. 287–305.

Foucault, Michel, *Sécurité, territoire, population: Cours au Collège de France, 1977–1978*, Paris: Gallimard, 2004.

Gawande, Atul, 'Getting There From Here', *The New Yorker*, 26 January 2009.

Hegel, G.W.F., *The Philosophy of Right*, tr. T.M. Knox, Oxford: Clarendon Press, 1952.

Hobbes, Thomas (1909), *Leviathan*, 1651; repr., Oxford: OUP, 1909, p. 94.

Humboldt, Wilhelm von, *Ideen zu einem Versuch, die Grenzen der Wirksamkeit des Staatszubestimmen*, tr. Joseph Coulthard, *The Sphere and Duties of Government*, London: John Chapman, 1854, p. 11, <oll.libertyfund.org/title/589>.

Kant, Immanuel, *The Conflict of the Faculties*, tr. Mary J. Gregor, Lincoln: University of Nebraska Press, 1992; *Der Streit der Fakultäten*, 1798.

Levin, Susan B., *Plato's Rivalry with Medicine: A Struggle and its Dissolution*, Oxford: OUP, 2014.

Marx, Karl and Friedrich Engels, *Manifest der KommunistischenPartei*, London: Bildungs-Gesellschaft der Arbeiter, 1848; English translation available at <https://www.marxists.org/archive/marx/works/1848/communist-manifesto/index.htm>, accessed 4 September 2015.

Mitchell-Boyask, Robin, *Plague and the Athenian Imagination: Drama, History, and the Cult of Asclepius*, Cambridge: CUP, 2008.

Plato (1961), Republic, tr. Paul Shorey in the Collected Dialogues of Plato, Including the Letters, ed. Edith Hamilton and Huntington Cairus, Princeton: Princeton University Press.

Saussy, Haun, ed., *Partner to the Poor: A Paul Farmer Reader*, Berkeley: University of California Press, 2010.

Sen, Amartya, *Poverty and Famines*, Oxford: OUP, 1981.

Sontag, Susan, *Illness as Metaphor* [1978] *and AIDS and its Metaphors*, New York: Doubleday, 1990.

Strauss, Leo, *The City and Man*; repr., Chicago: University of Chicago Press, 1978 [1964].

Supiot, Alain, *La Gouvernance par les nombres*, Paris: Fayard, 2015.

Virchow, Rudolf, 'Was die *medicinische Reform* will', *Die medicinische Reform*, vol. 1, 10 July 1848, p. 2. Also available through Hathi Trust: <http://catalog.hathitrust.org/Record/011569975>, accessed 4 September 2015.

Virchow, Rudolf, *Collected Essays on Public Health and Epidemiology*, tr. L.J. Rather, Canton, Mass.: Science History Publications, 1990, 1: 15; *Die Medicinische Reform*, vol. 5, 4 August 1848, p. 22.

Virchow, *Collected Essays on Public Health and Epidemiology*, pp. 17–18.

PART II

India and Elsewhere

5

Nation, Region, Culture, and Civilization: India in a World Context

Gerald E.P. Gillespie

LITERATURE IS studied in a myriad of contexts and approaches. However, whether dealing with works in a specific language stream and local culture, or in multiple language streams, or on a cross-cultural or interdisciplinary basis, we remain constrained in our practice by natural limits. There is no magic formula that opens the literary and artistic expression of the world to us. As a researcher who deals mainly with the literatures, arts and cultural histories of Western Europe and the New World, I shall attempt to sketch from an outsider's perspective the situation of Indian comparative studies as we enter the second decade of the twenty-first century. This task involves juxtaposing two unwieldy complexes of developments. One subject matter is the uneven flow of different kinds and stages of theory and the practice of Comparative Literature (CL) which one finds in various geocultural territories, and in the successive and cumulative 'generations' of persons who self-identify as practitioners of CL in these territories and/or internationally. Another subject matter is the multifaceted reality that a new standard or level of awareness has emerged independent of any single major territory. This new awareness exists as a collective achievement of international CL, as distinct from any single local variety, but it is clearly and objectively present today on the global plane. For purely pragmatic reasons I will employ a 'general systems' approach that regards all belief systems (religions, philosophies, political and social doctrines, theorizing about literature and the arts, various codes in the arts, etc.) to be elements in the repertories of various cultures, but considers such reportorial elements possessing no dogmatic value for international CL, even though many elements in these various repertories may serve efficaciously as heuristic tools in particular instances.

It would be useful to review a few of the basic ideas that helped shape CL when scholars mainly from Europe and North America refounded it in 1954 in the immediate aftermath of World War II, under French law, on a global scale. Starting from the initial congress at Venice in 1955, the newly created Association Internationale de Littérature Comparée/International Comparative Literature Association (AILC/ICLA) succeeded in establishing a regular pattern of holding triennial international congresses, the venue of which eventually moved beyond sites in Europe and North America to Africa, Asia and South America as well. In parallel, the ICLA Executive Committee, with the heads of its various research committees, maintained the routine of meeting annually in conjunction with a conference sponsored by a national academy, a regional association of CL, or a leading university. In addition, the various research groups constituted under ICLA aegis have been meeting according to their own independent patterns in international and regional conferences around the globe for half a century. In combination, these several hundred meetings of all sizes to date have contributed cumulatively to a newer general global consciousness of what a many-faceted CL can achieve. One among the restart cohort, Henry Remak, described the potential complex range for CL in a famous opening paragraph to an essay on this question first published in 1961.[1]

I was privileged to participate in one of the grand gatherings of the ICLA Executive Council in India in 1990, and in the fascinating conference held afterwards jointly with the Sahitya Akademi. From this collaboration derived the collective volume *Narrative: A Seminar* (1994). Our Indian colleagues had already held a major symposium at the Indian Institute of Advanced Study in Shimla in 1987 on the vast topic 'Comparative Literature: Theory and Practice', the proceedings of which appeared in 1990. Thus, it is legitimate to mark the end of the 1980s as the axial moment when the CL movement in India established itself through the efforts of a remarkable pioneer generation that included figures such as Amiya Dev, Sisir Kumar Das, Chandra Mohan and Gurbhagat Singh. They addressed many of the issues to which I shall return, viewing them from a contemporary vantage point. In essence, Indian scholars felt the pull of competing attractions, just as had European scholars in the 1950s, 1960s and 1970s. The question in those earlier decades for the then overwhelming majority of practising comparatists was whether CL was yet ready and able to reach beyond the field's original main homelands (Europe and North America) and accomplish serious work involving non-Eurocentric cultures, or whether the bulk of scholars should concentrate on Europe and the established Eurocentric immigrant nations in the Americas and elsewhere. The comparable question in India around 1990 was whether the extant cadres of home-grown comparatists should or could, at least in the near future, undertake a dual mission: on the one hand, seek to cope with the profusion of cultures within the great Indic basin and/or, on the other hand, devote extensive energies to the enormous body of cultures and several major distinct civilizations in the world, so as not to fall behind in the already evident movement toward a global level of comparative studies.

Especially in Europe and in North America, awareness of the complicated nature of cultural traditions and of their interactions past and present, and predictable in the future, led to the establishment of two distinct terms around the middle of the twentieth century. General Literature (GL) designated all the activities in which one engages in reading or hearing works that have originated in the local language stream or have been adapted into it in translation, and includes the theorizing done in that framework. Comparative Literature (CL) designated cross-cultural studies, including those that were simultaneously interdisciplinary, using the texts of different cultures in the original languages and construing the values and semiotics of the various cultures in their specific contexts as well as in larger contexts, such as regional and international. Naturally, there were many blends of CL and GL, and many academic departments and learned societies and some scholarly journals chose to incorporate both of these terms in their official names (e.g. the Institut für Allgemeine und Vergleichende Literaturwissenschaft at the Free University of Berlin, the Sociedad Española de Literatura General y Comparada, the *Yearbook of Comparative and General Literature* published at Indiana University, etc.). There was a strong sense that GL and CL were closely related though each represented a distinct kind of focalization. Occasionally, GL might be used as the official name to represent the totality of both CL and GL, and their interactions (e.g. Algemene Literatuurwetenschap, at Utrecht University), or conversely CL would serve for encompassing both GL and CL endeavours (e.g. the Department of Comparative Literature, at Stanford University). Likewise, a local department, institute, or programme might opt to emphasize the role of theory by making it a key term in the official name. The term World Literature (WL) was not widely employed in such names during the twentieth century, the most prominent example being the Gorki Institute of World Literature in Moscow. In debates of the 1960s, some notable Marxist theoreticians favoured trying first to define some universally operant 'laws' of culture to guide comparative studies, before embarking on detailed examination of works in actual literary systems, and they preferred the designation WL.

In contrast, a preponderant number of scholars from Western countries favoured grappling immediately with sets of works and literary systems using a variety of hermeneutic approaches, under the banner of CL.

The rise of so-called 'Cultural Studies' in the 1970s and 1980s, notably in the Americas, but soon in other geocultural zones, led to the coining of further programme names, such as 'Comparative Literature and Culture', which tended to substitute for what formerly was subsumed under Comparative and General Literature, although a closer analysis of these entities reveals that many had, or today still have, a scant or effectively no CL component. (On these larger evolutionary features, see Gillespie 2005.) More recently, originating from the United States of America and principally spawned out of departments of English, but soon turning up in other countries, is the so-called World Literature (WL). As would be expected, new coinages of programme names containing this term already abound today. Upon closer analysis WL appears to be an attempt to recycle GL under a new garb in response to the decline in American high school and college training in foreign languages and the consequent diminishment of advanced capacity for cross-cultural or interdisciplinary study. WL sounds 'grander' and appeals to educational administrators as a supposedly 'new' approach that is not parochial. Thus, it will also appeal to universities in a number of countries where powerful departments of English currently flourish and can rapidly import WL as a means of securing their predominance locally. Simultaneously, especially in Eurocentric institutions, the availability of WL as a cheaper immediate option will impede striving to attain the more difficult goal of introducing deeper study of non-European works. World Literature also offers a convenient cover under which to promote the hiring of 'token' ethnic representatives in the local American or European social framework, rather than building teams of qualified scholars in 'foreign' literatures and cultures regardless of their ethnic background and for the sole sake of the important subject matters. (On these topics, see Gillespie and Figueira 2013.)

'New-style WL' (at best a disguised version of GL) thus, can serve both the locally dominant 'national' literature departments and the imported Anglo-American studies groups as a means to maintain political clout and the curricular status quo. It can also opportunely 'colonize' and 'co-opt' existing CL programmes and foreign literature programmes and lower their horizon of expectations. In a country like the United States of America or the United Kingdom, an English department can deprive neighbouring foreign language departments of important contact with students by co-opting literature courses taught in translation, which these respective foreign language groups might otherwise offer as gateways to the study of works in the original languages. Educational institutions can also 'dumb down' established CL programmes by using WL as the excuse for not providing a richer assortment of offerings from other cultures, subject matters which ideally should be presented by dedicated experts in those foreign cultures. The spread of English as the major global *lingua franca* allows Anglophone scholars, if they so choose, to pose as experts in 'comparative studies' worldwide without possessing any serious CL expertise. In all too many cases, unqualified persons from minority segments of a population can readily be tempted to exploit the pretext of 'political correctness' and ally themselves with the old élite by 'representing' a social group, instead of being encouraged to master and teach some difficult complex of materials. Participation in CL as a teacher or researcher ordinarily is already limited by the sterner demands of learning beyond the GL framework. In practical terms, the appellation 'comparatist', which once meant that one had mastered some at least partial command of a wider range of cultural knowledge, as well as possessed 'literacy' in theoretical propositions, may today no longer be a reliable indicator in many places. Hence, when an aspiring programme of CL is pulled in the direction of contemporary WL in an institution of higher education almost anywhere in the world, CL is probably in danger of ceasing to be CL by a significant measure. Below, I shall consider the possible deleterious impact this kind of new-style WL intrusion can have in India because of India's special characteristics.

It is self-evident that the concept of 'nation' is a very weak reed on which to posit any generalization today. Serious practitioners of CL must be very careful in invoking the word and are duty-bound to define the specific context in each particular case. In our contemporary world we have 'nations' in a wide variety of sizes, shapes, populations and historical credentials. They range from small islands or enclaves, over several medium-sized entities, to larger ones, and indeed to very huge polities, sub-continental or continental in scope (e.g. Brazil, USA, Russia, India, etc.). Anyone familiar with the history of the two World Wars knows that dozens of countries today are the result of the packaging and repackaging of former colonial territories. The (often unstable) configurations loosely called 'nations' range from a congeries of intermixed tribal areas without any genuine national sentiment grouped inside some inherited postcolonial boundary to a consolidation of the parts of a great civilization as in the case of India. We are still witnessing the break-up of unions created by the Great Powers, as for example in the case of the now defunct Yugoslavia. Some nations are effectively monoglot, even if they happen to share the main local language with other nations (as England does with Australia, Scotland, etc.); or have a scattering of smaller languages (for example, Tanzania has well over a hundred indigenous languages but uses two international languages, English and Swahili, for official purposes); some nations have a few principal languages (for example, Canada has two main languages, Belgium has three, Spain and Switzerland each have four); and some boast a plethora of active tongues acknowledged as 'national' (e.g. India, South Africa). There are anomalies rooted in local history (for example, Luxembourg's majority native language is German, but it uses French and Dutch officially and English extensively for pragmatic reasons). The configuration of languages, sociolects, and dialects of a given nation may have an important bearing for any GL and/or CL inquiry. Even mere *synchronic* understanding of any polity that styles itself a 'nation' is woefully deficient (although some kinds of 'structuralist' analysis have sought to ignore the problem). Only the *diachronic* understanding of a 'nation's' status and constitution is truly adequate as a starting point, before one looks into the nature of the culture, cultures, and sub-cultures which it houses and which in some instances, it may share with other nations, or one or more regions. In addition, a particular CL investigation may need to distinguish precisely what is *not* shared or what kinds of sharing have been submerged. Sharing can occur through borrowings and lendings over the course of time, or through the effects of diasporas and migrations, as well as conquests, and other systemic interferences. A serious international CL comprehends the dynamics in cultural systems and their literatures, and it accepts varieties of metamorphosis as well as variability and constancy in all domains.

Indian colleagues have been keenly aware of the reality that their 'nation' in its modern incarnation is in great measure the product of past attempts by a now withdrawn, declining, overseas imperial people, the British, as well as by several other overseas colonial powers on a lesser scale, to rule the disparate parts that now constitute India. In many ways it is perplexing for the variegated population to belong not merely to a 'nation' but to a sub-continental 'region', which can readily be seen in analogy to Europe as a whole. Once we consider the historical depth of the roots and processes that went into the making of both Europe and India, we also encounter the reality that there is an Indic 'civilization' persisting over several millennia that bears formalistic analogy to European civilization. In a seminal book, the Western comparatist and Japanologist Earl Miner (1990) has underscored the importance of recognizing the separate ontological pathways of great civilizations and the incongruity among their differing literary codes and aesthetics prior to any global convergences in the modern era. The impact of Indian religions and philosophies on other parts of Asia and the Near East is an enormous subject matter. Not negligible with regard to the modern period is the influence of the Indian cultural experience as it has surfaced in Western literature, art and thought. Likewise, the origins of aspects of Indian cultures, because of important 'interferences' in the course of time (e.g. Indo-European migrations, Muslim invasions, Western colonial episodes, etc.), constitute an absorbing subject matter. Thus, the job of constructing pan-Indic studies is similar to pursuing pan-European studies, with the obvious major exception that in the past five centuries, several European nations have spawned a remarkable set of independent immigrant nations today. When I consider the enormity of the range of phenomena to consider, my opinion as an outsider is unequivocal. There is nothing dishonourable in being a Europeanist or an Indologist, in the sense of a CL scholar whose main endeavor is to research extensively across internal dividing lines and through strata in these regions and their peripheries, rather than to expand such inquiries trans-regionally on a larger scale. In recognition of the cultural dimensions, which evade or transcend 'national' frontiers, a large number of European scholars and other 'extra-territorial' Europeanists have recently created a regional cross-cultural association, the Réseau Européen d'Études Littéraires Comparées/European Network for Comparative Literature Studies (REELC/ENCLS), to supplement and complement the several excellent 'national' associations of CL in Europe and a number of ICLA research committees dedicated to Europe as a whole, to regions of Europe, and to offshoots of colonialism. Both intra- and trans-regional studies are worthy when we consider the complicated situation of polyglot modern India with its rich history.

However, as in the United States, there is an inherent problem that arises for India because today both of these sub-continental nations have the advantage of possessing as a principal language, the global *lingua franca*: English. This situation sometimes tempts English departments in India as in America to co-opt materials from other departments and programmes concerned with culture and, in effect, to repress the intellectually (and for many, also socially) desirable expansion of studies on a global level. Having English as a common denominator is an accident of history, and of course it would be futile to ignore the utility of this privileged position. But nowadays it may mislead English departments in India to adopt the widespread and shallow American notion of WL. In the worst case, adoption of WL may constitute a deliberate means to block a more sophisticated pursuit of deeper expertise undertaken in the large set of necessary programmes in foreign languages and literatures on which CL depends, or in some instances Anglicists and Americanists in India may be unconscious of the likely repercussions, of the fact they may actually be impeding sounder academic development. CL is simply more demanding. There is no escaping the reality that CL is an elitist enterprise (Gillespie 2003). It is a faux pas to denounce it as such. It is a naturally higher level of analysis and synthesis that the world situation in the modern age has evoked. Today there are hundreds of millions of persons who work and roam around the globe, and who are aware that they may or must interact with their fellow internationalists in particular ways, in various contexts, while they live on a different local footing within their own home culture. It is not surprising that the desire for culture identity often leads to resistance to shallow and synthetic forms of globalism (Gillespie 2004). It is equally true that the attempt on the part of smaller cultures to imitate the politically inspired arrangements in the USA called 'multiculturalism' leads to deleterious strains and losses in the majority culture. These can be severe because the local circumstances are not comparable to the cultural history and situations of huge immigrant nations like the USA or Brazil (Gillespie 1995) or because there is misunderstanding of the limits of cultural relativism and of probable negative outcomes to arbitrary interventions in local cultures (Gillespie 1997).

The cosmopolitan strata of various societies are, nonetheless, realities equally worthy of CL's attention as are social classes and ethnic identities within particular societies. If authors are interested in them, all these phenomena will be reflected in works of literature. Both locally and beyond their home grounds, untold millions of persons have multiple identities. As a Eurocentric comparatist, I see a reciprocal challenge that has evolved in the European and Indian 'regions' or 'systems'. Just as European CL in the future should strive to maintain a pan-European capacity, yet also expand its capacity in other systems, likewise should Indian CL cherish its own regional mission and nurture an appreciation of local cultures, but also defend and promote studies of cultural systems and major civilizations in other regions. Very few scholars will wish or be able to encompass both tasks, at least not widely; a division of labour is the more realistic pathway. Contemporary international CL is indeed beholden to a number of individuals who have taken up this bigger mission, because having a greater number of trans-regional experts is a necessary step in overcoming many of the false generalizations that are unwittingly picked up by students around the world from the ideologically charged GL repertory of countries like the USA, via the *lingua franca*. Colleagues located at institutions in Asia will inevitably have to sort through the useful as against the merely faddish imitators of 'foreign' (i.e. Western) themes as supposedly glamorous. A more sophisticated CL will enhance the ability of students everywhere to grasp propositions as elements of cultural repertories, and therefore, be in a sounder position to make better informed decisions about values. The heightening of genetic and formal knowledge on the part of serious CL practitioners will eventually foster more reliable 'value judgements'.

Some comparatists can do indispensable work based on deep expertise mediating among phenomena in the contexts of several local cultures and their histories (e.g. Bengali and British, or Bengali and Hindi, or Urdu, French and Swedish, etc.) and others may explore wider relationships (e.g. Indic civilization reaching into China or Southeast Asia, or trans-Atlantic interchanges between Latin America and Europe, etc.). There are some great, inspired authors in the modern period who have felt the imperative of exhibiting the world level of interaction and complexity, for example, Thomas Mann in *Der Zauberberg* (*The Magic Mountain*, 1924), and some comparatists will attempt to emulate the lesson in scholarship. I have not focused here on the primary questions of poetics and aesthetics, of genres and modes, of the relationships among the arts, of authorship and readership, worldviews, and so forth, but rather have stressed certain sociological angles, which have a bearing on comparative studies. By no means do I wish to imply that nowadays the fundamental aspects of literature and literary experience should occupy a secondary place in our thoughts. I am merely accepting the fact that literary studies, including the realm of CL, have gone through an extended episode of virtual merger with the so-called *sciences humaines*. Comparative Literature itself will and can never override or abolish the function of the local critic imbedded in a particular culture who (like the best readers) reacts to works of literature out of the totality of his or her personal background and experience. The same proposition holds for critics whose main position is within some particular framework of Indian society, or as part of the diaspora, or as acculturated to another system, or as total foreigners attracted to India and its cultural diversity. India like Europe qualifies as what a scholar like Erhard Schüttpelz (2009) has described as a 'partial world system', a major distinct area of civilization of *longue durée* already in place before the forces of convergence in our contemporary era accelerated certain kinds of cultural mixture and homogenization. The comparatist Yue Daiyun elegantly evoked the Chinese world in her contribution (1990) to the Shimla conference of 1989, in the course of explaining the prospects for our field in China in the immediate aftermath of the foundation of the Chinese Comparative Literature Association. Of course, as Earl Miner explained, the Indic partial world system will not match up with the Chinese system or others, nor should India match up neatly with any other major system. Instead of seeking artificial common denominators and imposing pseudo-scientific tenets, Indian comparatists will be better served by gravitating towards any compelling subject matters anywhere in the world that attract their interests because of their content and expression. As a network of multiple crossroads, contemporary international CL is certainly one of the best places to meet kindred souls.

NOTE

1. Remak's opening statement in his essay 'Comparative Literature: Its Definition and Function': 'Comparative Literature is the study of literature beyond the confines of one particular country, and the study of the relationship between literature on the one hand and other areas of knowledge and belief, such as the arts (e.g. painting, sculpture, architecture, music), philosophy, history, the social sciences, religion, etc., on the other. In brief, it is the comparison of one literature with another or others, and the comparison of literature with other spheres of human expression'.

REFERENCES

Dev, A. and S.K. Das, eds., *Comparative Literature: Theory and Practice*, New Delhi: Sahitya Akademi, Allied Publishers, 1989.

Dev, A., ed., *Narrative: A Seminar*, New Delhi: Sahitya Akademi, 1994.

Gillespie, G., 'Newer Trends of Comparative Studies in the West', in *Aspects of Comparative Literature: Current Approaches*, ed. Chandra Mohan, New Delhi: India Publishers & Distributors, 1989, pp. 17–34.

———, 'Rhinoceros, Unicorn, or Chimera?—A Polysystemic View of Possible Kinds of Comparative Literature in the New Century', *Journal of Intercultural Studies*, vol. 19, 1992, pp. 14–21.

———, 'Auf den multikulturellen Irrwegen der amerikanischen Komparatistik: Kontrast und Mahnbild für ein junges Europa', in *Weltliteratur heute*, ed. M. Schmeling, Würzburg: Königshausen & Neumann, 1995, pp. 85–99.

———, 'The Significance and Limits of Cultural Relativism', in *Cultural Dialogue and Misreading*, ed. M. Lee and M. Hua, Sydney: Wild Peony Press, 1997, pp. 3–10.

———, 'Comparative Literary History as an Elitist Metanarrative', *Neohelicon*, vol. 30, no. 2, 2003, pp. 59–64.

———, 'The Conflict between Synthetic Globalism and the Desire for Cultural Identity', in *Cybernetic Ghosts: Literature in the Age of Theory and Technology*, ed. Dorothy Figueira, Provo, Utah: International Comparative Literature Association, 2004, pp. 91–8.

———, 'Literary Studies: General and Comparative', *Neohelicon*, vol. 32, no. 2, 2005, pp. 337–41.

Gillespie, G. and Dorothy Figueira, 'Der vermeintlich "neue" Weltliteraturbegriff als Restaurierung kultureller Beschränktheit', in *Kultur/Poetik*, vol. 13, no. 3, 2013, pp. 1–8.

Miner, E., *Comparative Poetics: An Intercultural Essay on Theories of Literature*, Princeton: Princeton University Press, 1990.

Mohan, C., ed., *Aspects of Comparative Literature: Current Approaches*, New Delhi: India Publishers and Distributors, 1989.

Remak, H.H.H., 'Comparative Literature: Its Definition and Function', in *Comparative Literature: Method and Perspective*, ed. Newton Phelps Schnallknecht and Horst Frenz (rev. edn.), Carbondale and Edwardsburg: University of Southern Illinois Press, 1971.

Schüttpelz, E., 'Weltliteratur in der Perspektive einer Longue Durée I: Fünf Zeitschichten der Globalisierung', in *Wider den Kulturzwang: Migration, Kulturalisierung und Weltliteratur*, ed. E. Özkan, D. Kimmich und A. Werberger, Bielefeld, 2009, pp. 335–56.

Yue, D., 'Prospects of Chinese Comparative Literature', in *Comparative Literature: Theory and Practice*, ed. A. Dev and S.K. Das, New Delhi: Sahitya Akademi, 1989, pp. 370–80.

6

The West in the World: Subliminal and Paradigmatic 'Westernizations'

Eugene Chen Eoyang

THE LITERATURE on 'Westernization' is voluminous, and this study is not intended to add to what is, by now, already copious scholarship on the subject. What I wish to explore in this essay are the hidden and subliminal biases that complicate the notion of 'westernization', and inevitably skew the use of the words 'West' and 'Westernization' in favour of white, Caucasian culture.

My first concern is with the word 'West'/'west' alternately offered in caps or lower case. The appearance of 'west' in lower case implies that 'west' is generic and universal when the word refers to European and North American culture. It is not: the 'West' is what the 'West' calls itself: it is not generic.

In Chinese, for example, 'west' refers to India, which, from the 'Western' point of view is decidedly 'Eastern'. The Chinese novel, 西游記 (*The Journey to the West*), is not about a trek to Europe or the Americas, but to India. In Japan, the notion of a country to the west would immediately conjure up China, not Great Britain or the United States. A 'Western' country, however, is definitively a country in Europe or North America.

But there is another sense in which the direction west cannot be treated as if it were universally determinative. While it is true that the notion of 'west' connotes 'sunset' in most cultures (German: '*Abendland*', Latin: '*occidentere*'), it is not reliable as an absolute designator of place. The American West is east of Japan and China, and there is, unlike 'north' and 'south', no place on earth beyond which one could not find a place more 'west'. In other words, there is no 'East Pole', and there is no 'West Pole'. When one uses the word 'West' or 'Western' to denote Europe or North America, one is using a Western 'ethnotope', i.e. a cultural premise (made in the West) which is erroneously assumed to be universal. A particular European bias exists in the terms 'Near East' and 'Far East', which makes sense from Paris or London, but not from San Francisco or Vancouver.

Nor, despite common conceptions, are the directions 'west' and 'east' neutral. Whether admitted or not, there is a widespread assumption that 'West' is 'best' and 'East' is 'least'. The irony is that this misconception may be found in so-called 'non-Western' countries. In Japan, particularly in the Meiji Period, the West was elevated to the first rank. In an article on the novelist Haruki Murakami, Roland Kelts has written, quoting Motoyuki Shibata, 'a translator, scholar, and professor at Tokyo University': 'Early [Japanese] translators and readers ... approached life and literature with a rigid racial hierarchy, with the Caucasians at the top, the Japanese in the middle, and the remaining ethnicities and colors at the bottom. Anything written by whites from the West was deemed inherently superior, just because Japanese looked up to them' (2013).[1]

Even without the explicit acknowledgement of Western superiority, the West assumes priority by imposing its chronology onto the world's history. The way the world reckons time is decidedly millennial, and Christian. There are alternative chronologies—the millennial year 2000 is year 5760 in the Hebrew Calendar, and in traditional Hebrew, the twenty-first century is the fifty-eighth century. Anno Domini 2000 would be Anno Hegirae 1421 in the Muslim calendar. The year 2000 in the Christian calendar is the year 5101 in the Kaliyuga calendar; either 2544 in the Buddha Nirvana calendar, or 2543 in the Buddhist Era of the Thai solar calendar; 1407 in the Bengali calendar, or 1362 in the Burmese calendar. The Chinese calendar would have begun in 2697 BC, so AD 2000 would be 4697 to Chinese historians. The oldest calendar in the world, the Egyptian, appears to have begun in 4236 BCE, and the year 2000 would have been 6236 according to the ancient Egyptians.

If the arbitrariness of dating systems is considered trivial in importance, may I remind the reader of the furor and the obsessive confusion of the Y2K dilemma that plagued every country using IBM computers or their clones prior to the year 2000. The cost of that concern, and the steps to prepare for it have been estimated to be more than US$100 billion, and led, at least in the US, to 'Millennium Mania' or the TEOTWAWKI ('The End of the World As We Know It') phenomenon ('Y2K: Much Ado About Nothing', 2013). Arbitrary conventions can lead to tangible consequences. Mostly biased in favour of the West—in this case based on the Christian calendar—they have been blithely accepted as universal premises. The use of ethnotopes in a globalized world involves costs that are far from trivial.

Salient time periods or as I have called them, *Zeitanschauungen* (which, as an analogue to *Weltanschauungen* indicate how one views time as opposed to how one views the world) have decided effects on our perspective. I wonder how many New Yorkers, excited as they are in watching the lighted ball descend at the stroke of midnight in Times Square at the beginning of every New Year, are even remotely aware that in the twenty-three other time zones in the world, the New Year has already arrived or has yet to arrive. The descent of the ball at One Times Square is touted as 'a global tradition', not merely a ritual of the East Coast in the United States. The 'magic moment' of the New Year in Times Square is yet another 'ethnotope', something assumed to be universal, which it is not. Of course, it is ironic that the new millennium was widely celebrated on 1 January 2000, when it should have been celebrated a year later, on 1 January 2001, as the US Naval Observatory, the Royal Greenwich Observatory, the Library of Congress, the National Institute of Standards of Science and Technology, as well as the World Almanac, all insisted (Chadwick 2005). I leave aside the basic error of the Christian calendar, which purports to be based on the birth of Christ marking its beginning. Few seem to be bothered about celebrating the 'birth of Christ' on December 25 on a calendar that claims to start with 'the birth of Christ', which would have marked the birth, presumably, as January 1. Some experts estimate, furthermore, that Jesus was actually born four years into the calendar that is based on his birth.

One's mindset can be shaped indelibly by one's *Zeitanschauung*: for most corporations, the salient time frame is the annual quarter (three months), by which their performance and the performances of their CEOs are evaluated. Christians tend to think in terms of millennia, while Buddhists invoke *kalpas* (the shortest denomination of which is 4.3 billion years). *Zeitanschauungen* also determine the ontology of sports—the key time-period in US basketball, for example, is now a second, or a fraction of a second, on which the outcome of many an exciting game is decided, whereas the key time-period in a cricket match, in contrast, is days.

One's judgement will differ if one is deciding the outcome in a few seconds, or a few hours, days, months, years, decades, centuries, millennia or *kalpas*. Let us consider the extinction of species. If viewed from the *Zeitanschauung* of decades, years or centuries, it might be reasonable to campaign for the preservation of every species on earth. If viewed from the perspective of *kalpas*, one might recognize that the extinction of species is part of the evolutionary process, that is, if species did not go extinct, new species would not emerge—as *homo sapiens* did when the dinosaurs became extinct.

Certain hidden assumptions underlie cultural biases. The notion of 'human rights', for example, often touted as a universal entitlement, may be subject to different interpretations, depending on whether one defines 'human' as an individual or the collective. Do 'human rights' privilege the individual (as they do in the West) or the collective (as they might in the East)? In the US, it is clear that 'human rights' means 'individual rights'. In Asia, the rights of the family, even those of the 'human family', may take precedence over the rights of the individual—the branch of the (family) tree more important than any (individual) leaf. If the species is to survive, it could be that the interests of the collective may be more crucial than the interests of the individual. This notion may not be unfamiliar to followers of the utilitarianism of Jeremy Bentham and John Stuart Mill and the concept of 'the greater good'. To insist on one version of 'human rights' globally is to impose one's own interpretation of 'human rights' on others. The pernicious effect of subliminal Westernization is that it promulgates a Western ethnotope throughout the world. It is as if the entire world had to witness the coming of the New Year through the perspective of a New Yorker.

Perhaps the most concerted belief in the superiority of the West prevailed in the late Ottoman Empire and the beginning of the Turkish republic in 1923. 'The civilian clothing reform of 1829, which replaced the turban with the fez', Kader Konuk writes, 'indicated the Ottoman equation of Westernization with modernization' (2010: 7). When the Ottoman Empire was overturned by Kemal Atatürk, this attitude toward the West was unchanged as 'Atatürk believed that modernization necessitated Westernization' (Konuk 2010: 8). Of course, whatever the official policy, the reality, as Nergis Ertürk reminds us in his *Grammatology and Literary Modernity in Turkey*, was more complex.

There are, in fact, different versions of the West in Westernization. Sometimes, 'Westernization' means 'Eurocentric'. The terms 'Near East' and 'Far East', as I have already pointed out, reflect a Eurocentric perspective. Sometimes, Westernization reflects a Northern Hemisphere bias, as in the case of another ethnotope: 'clockwise' and 'counterclockwise', terms which have been universally adopted, but which derive from the way the shadow moves around the sundial—in the *northern* part of the world. Certain Northern Hemispheric traditions—Christmas in winter, Easter in the spring—are, of course, reversed in the Southern Hemisphere, where Christmas occurs in the summer, and Easter in the autumn. The Northern Hemisphere bias may be also seen in the first fifty years of the Nobel Laureates for Literature, during which all but one (Gabriela Mistral from Chile in 1945) came from the Northern Hemisphere. In the next

50 years, eleven winners of the Nobel Prize for Literature came from below the equator (Eoyang 2012: 100).

There is a subtle and unnoticed 'ethnotope' even in the definition of the word 'world'. Goethe's notion of *Welt* was truly cosmopolitan, and he included Asia as well as Europe. Africa, the Western Hemisphere and Australia were generally considered uncivilized (or barely civilized) in that era, and scarcely warranted consideration. Gorki's Institute of World Literature concentrated, in fact, on the literatures in Europe outside of Russia. There was little concern with Africa, Asia, or South America. Its scope extended to the Mediterranean, but not eastward toward Asia. The attack by Fedayev in 1947 on the Gorki Institute of World Literature, however politically motivated, centred on the Institute's heavily Eurocentric bias. 'Fadeev expressed dismay that 'all matters of literary education for young people at the Gorky Institute of World Literature, as well as at the Moscow and Leningrad Universities, are headed by parrots of Veselovskii and his blind apologists'. The Institute was denounced for subscribing to 'the Western school of philological and literary scholars' (Azadovskii and Egorov 2002: 71).

More recently, the Indologist Sergei Serebriany, in a paper entitled 'On the Eurocentrism of Comparative Literary Studies: An Outsider's View from post-Soviet Moscow', wrote, 'I just gave vent to my discontent with those conditions under which I had to do my research at the ... Gorky Institute of World Literature from 1970 up to 1992'. Serebriany reports: 'I found it more and more difficult to reconcile my conscience as a scholar ... with the norms of literary studies which prevailed at that Institute' (Serebriany 2012: 63).

In the US, the *Norton Anthology of World Masterpieces* made its ethnotopic use of the word 'world' explicit, when it declared, as late as 1979, in its fourth edition, that '*World Masterpieces* is an anthology of Western literature'. (Mack 1979; Eoyang 2012: 84–94). The statement is true of the volume it describes, but one cannot accept the imputation that *all* the masterpieces of literature in the world are Western, or the assumption that one is justified in titling a collection *World Masterpieces* when it includes only works from the West. In the preface, the Norton editors justify their practice with the following rationale, that: 'The Literatures of the Far East have been omitted, on the ground that the principal aim of a course on world literature is to bring American students into living contact with their own Western tradition, and that this aim cannot be adequately realized in a single course if they must also be introduced to a very different tradition, one requiring extended treatment to be correctly understood' (Mack 1979: xvii). What the rationale defends relates to limitations of time and background on the part of the students, but it offers no justification for equating 'the Western tradition' with 'the world'. Nor was this rationale cited when subsequent editions did include selections from the literatures of the 'Far East'.

There is a model of Westernization as the only way to modernize, which confuses the issue. The whole notion of developed and developing countries embodies implicitly the assumption that the West is the apex of development, certainly as far as technology is concerned. Few if any can conceive of modernization without Westernization. The consequence of that impression is that one must accept the historical development of the West as paradigmatic for all cultures. It also implies that the East is backward and retarded when compared to the West (the euphemism is 'developing').

The prevailing view of Western history provides a template, whether we are aware of it or not, of the way we assume that all cultures develop. This is perhaps the reason why the divisions in the *Norton Anthologies* were so restrictive and so ill-suited in accommodating works outside the Western tradition. In not every culture does Romanticism follow Neoclassicism. Nor do Enlightenment writers in the rest of the world always appear in the eighteenth century, and 'high modernism' may not always follow an expansionist imperialist phase in cultures outside the West. The expansionist Ottoman Empire peaked in the sixteenth century, not the nineteenth, when the British Empire flourished; the Mughal Empire prevailed in India from the sixteenth to the eighteenth centuries. Neither the Ottoman nor the Mughal Empires appear to have been immediately succeeded by a 'modernist' phase. Not every culture passed through the Dark Ages in the first five centuries of the first millennium, or emerged from a medieval period in the fourteenth and fifteenth centuries. The 'Middle Ages' in the West encompass a period that was anything but benighted in China. The Tang Period (618–906), is perhaps the most brilliant and enlightened segment of Chinese history. The arts flourished in the Byzantine Empire from 476 to 1453, which corresponds to a less than glorious phase of European history. The late Middle Ages in Europe pales in comparison to the Song Period in China (960–1279), which introduced such 'modern' technologies as paper currency, the compass and moveable type.

The bias in the terms 'West' and 'Western' is not always one-sided. As much as it predisposes some in its favour (especially, but not exclusively, in the West), it also antagonizes a significant portion of the Third World who view anything Western as a taint on one's cultural authenticity. The case of Gao Xingjian, the winner of the Nobel Prize for Literature in

2000, is an interesting example of global ambivalence. As a French citizen of Chinese descent, he is admired by some for his familiarity with French culture, but also vilified in China for not being sufficiently 'Chinese' and considered as overly Westernized. Nor does the demonization of Westernization always originate from the indigenous peoples. Stephen Owen, an American Sinologist, has criticized the poetry of Bei Dao for not being sufficiently 'Chinese' (Owen 1990; Eoyang 2012: 89–91). But, surely the bias in either direction is unfair and unjust. To be Westernized should constitute neither an advantage nor a disadvantage in the perspective of posterity.

The ethnocentricity of the West is nowhere more apparent than in the widespread use of the term, 'non-Western', which reflects a concept of the self and the world as 'the West' and 'the Rest', and emphasizes the distinction of what is 'West' and what is not 'West'. But to define something by what it is not, is not to see the thing for itself. The phrase 'non-Western' assumes that: (1) 'Western' as a term is unambiguous and determinate; and (2) the term adequately designates 'other' cultures. What it does designate is the perspective that equates cultures outside the West with being unknown, and that their most salient trait is that they are not 'Western'. But Asians and Africans do not conceive of themselves as 'non-Western'. In fact, one could argue that the term 'non-Western' points to a null-category, a term that 'non-Westerners' would not recognize as a category which includes them. (The term 'Third World' is a slightly less ethnocentric appellation.) While there are many words for 'foreign' in Asian languages, I am not aware of any widespread use of the word 'non-Asian'. What *is* used is a translation of 'Western', which, as I have pointed out, is a Western self-designation. The Chinese do have a term, 'non-Han', but it does not refer to the cultures outside of China, but rather to the indigenous people in China not of the Han race.[2]

One is reminded of the early American tourists to China, who were appalled by the lack of sanitation, the abject poverty in some areas and the inconvenience for Westerners who did not speak Chinese. They returned with a decidedly negative image of China because it was not the United States. What these tourists saw was that China is not the United States, but what they did not see was what China is, no matter how it compares to the US. Of course, as China becomes more Westernized and more modern, American tourists are less appalled by what they see there. They are amused and reassured to find Kentucky Fried Chicken and McDonalds dotting the Chinese landscape. This perception merely reinforces the ethnocentricity of their perspective, which privileges a likeness to US culture as a basis for a positive judgement of a foreign culture. Other cultures cannot be understood merely as an index of their differences from Western culture. Unless one understands a different culture on its own terms, based on its own values (which may differ from the fundamental values of Western civilization), they cannot be understood at all. This phenomenon may be seen in the missionary experience of China in the nineteenth century, when the Chinese were viewed as heathens, as non-Christians, rather than as polytheistic and syncretic devotees, concurrently, of Confucianism, Buddhism and Daoism.

Nowadays, when one thinks of the West, the predominant language is indisputably English. There is an unwritten rule that the discourse of international conferences must be in English. This is sometimes justified by the conviction that 'English is the world's language'. This statement, widely cited, is, however, not strictly true. First, 'English is not the world's language', as one Japanese businessman observed, 'It is broken English that is the world's language'. His comment points to one of the unintended consequences of the use of English at international conferences. Those whose native language is not English are severely disadvantaged in presenting their research in a global setting. The result is that scholars who may be brilliant in their fields and impressive in their own language must come across in (broken) English as inarticulate and unintelligent (the shibboleth of ignorant Americans reflects this: 'If you're so smart, why don't you speak English'!). The logical inference here is that unless one presents oneself well in English at international conferences, one cannot be intelligent. (This phenomenon is less pronounced in the sciences, where the insights offered involve mathematical expressions and formulae that do not require fluency in English to comprehend.) If languages are, as many maintain, not semantically or gesturally equivalent, the exclusive use of English narrows the scope of discourse, and precludes insights more accessible in other languages. George Steiner put it this way: 'Each and every window in the house of languages opens on to a different landscape and temporality, to a different spectrum of perceived and classified experience' (1995: 10). The reliance at international conferences on English exclusively impoverishes the nature of the discourse, and compromises the quality of the intellectual exchange.

There is a second reason why the statement 'English is the world's language' is wrong, if not misleading. While it may not be true that English is the world's language, it is unarguably true that English is the world's *second* language. More people speak or use English as a second language today than any other. The requirement that English be used at international conferences means that local researchers who wish to report on their research cannot use their own language to present their results. The injunction results in an injustice as well as an impropriety. Only those who are proficient in English are allowed to be comfortable with the medium of presentation at international conferences.

The problem occurs when English is required as the only medium of discourse. Given modern technology, however, it is possible to offer concurrent alternatives to an audience with different language competencies. I discount (1) simultaneous translation, which is impractical, first, because it is extremely difficult, and second, because the necessary qualified personnel may not always be available at conference venues; (2) consecutive interpretation, which is time-consuming and arduous, cutting by at least half the time available for presentation. It is inefficient for the monolingual audience for whom half the presentation is incomprehensible, and tedious for the bilingual audience because it presents everything twice. What I propose, at least for plenary presentations, is that the speaker should be allowed to use whatever language s/he is most comfortable in, as long as s/he provides the conference with a translation in English that can be projected on a screen concurrently with the presentation, so that the audience can understand the proceedings, either aurally (if they understand the language the speaker is using) or visually (by reading the English translation as the speaker is making his/her presentation. The practice is akin to the widespread use of 'super titles' at operas). The bilingual audience can choose either to hear or to read the presentation. Depending on the resources of the conference organizers or the speaker, the reverse can also be arranged—translations of plenary presentations into the local language can be projected on the screen while the speaker makes his/her presentation in English.

In other words, one exploits the fact that English is the world's second language, more likely than any other to provide the broadest possible access for presentations in different languages. With the emergence of China and its massive population, and the growing interest in the Chinese language around the world, it may not be too far off when speakers of English who have not studied Chinese may be grateful for access through the world's second language to a translation of the proceedings that one can read while the presentation is being made in Chinese.

We are now in the second decade of a new (Western) century, at the end of which, according to many prognosticators, the hegemony of English and the West may be at an end, or at least declining. We would be, therefore, well advised to examine carefully the subtle and unrecognized 'Westernizations' that skew and constrain our discourse.

NOTE

1. A recent movie about an anti-capitalist eco-terrorist group is titled 'The East'; in the movie, and in its slogan, 'the East is everywhere', the East is clearly depicted as other, and sinister.

REFERENCES

Azadovskii, K. and B. Egorov, 'From Anti-Westernism to Anti-Semitism', *Journal of Cold War Studies*, vol. 4, no. 1, 2002, pp. 66–80.

Chadwick, I., 'Blame the madness on Dennis the Short'. 2005, (Online Essay) <http://www.ianchadwick.com/essays/madness.html>.

Ertürk, N., *Grammatology and Literary Modernity in Turkey*, New York: OUP, 2011.

Eoyang, E., *The Promise and Premise of Creativity: Why Comparative Literature Matters*, New York: Continuum, 2012.

Kelts, R., 'Lost in Translation?', *New York Times*, 2013. (Online) May 9. Retrieved from <http://www.newyorker.com/online/blogs/books/2013/05/lost-in-translation.html>.

Konuk, K., *East-West Mimesis: Auerbach in Turkey*, Stanford: Stanford University Press, 2010.

Mack, M., General Editor, *The Norton Anthology of World Masterpieces*, 4th edn., New York: Norton, 1979.

Owen, S., 'What is World Poetry?', *The New Republic*, vol. 203, no. 21, pp. 28–32, 1990.

Serebriany, S., 'Comparative Literature and Post-colonial Studies: An Outsider's View from Post-Soviet Moscow'. (Online) In *Building Bridges between India and Russia: A Festschrift for Prof. J.P. Dimri*, Kolkata: Power Publishers, 2012, pp. 63–82, Retrieved from <http://www.academia.edu/2263612Comparative_literature_and_postcolonial_studies_an_outsiders_view_from_post-Soviet_Moscow>.

Steiner, G., *What is Comparative Literature?: An Inaugural Lecture Delivered before the University of Oxford, on 11 October 1994*, Oxford: Clarendon Press, 1995.

'Y2K: Much Ado About Nothing?' (Online Video) Retrieved from <http://www.nytimes.com/video/2013/05/27/booming/100000002243885/y2k-much-ado-about-nothing.html>.

7

Comparative Literature in the United States

Dorothy M. Figueira

COMPARATIVE LITERATURE

I DID NOT COME to Comparative Literature through some direct path.[1] I question whether anyone 'chooses' to become a Comparative Literature scholar. One accedes to this discipline by detours. A colleague of mine once opined that she thought comparatists were people with comparative lives. There is much truth in this assertion. In the United States, Comparative Literature is primarily a post-World-War II phenomenon developing with the arrival of scholars escaping totalitarian regimes. These refugees found themselves in America with language skills and in need of employment. Comparative Literature, a field that had already existed in Europe, was a nascent discipline in the States. It flourished with the arrival of these immigrants to our shores.

In the US, Comparative Literature programmes were usually embedded in French Departments, since they were more numerous than other national language departments and most of the new immigrant scholars had competency in French. Since Nazi refugees and, later on, Eastern Europeans fleeing the Soviets were often francophone in addition to their own native languages and the classical philological training they would have received in the European system, they had the requisite linguistic skills to work in multiple idioms. Due to this influx of European scholars, Comparative Literature in American universities tended to follow the model established in France (*Littérature comparée*) and in Germany (*Vergleichende Literaturwissenschaft*). By definition, it compared (usually in terms of theme, genre, style, or period) two or more *texts* from *different* languages or cultural groups. From the 1940s through the 1970s, this basic definition held. In the 1980s, however, the notion of what constituted a text became open to question. It was an era when notions of high and low culture were coming under scrutiny. Why, it was asked, should only higher forms of cultural production be worthy of analysis? Were there not lower, popular art forms worthy of critical assessment? These were the days when a humanist could equally well specialize in the European novel as in Madonna's music videos. Both were texts and certainly the latter was more easily consumed. Scholars inevitably sought to push the limits of textuality. In the State University of New York (SUNY) where I held my first job, one could find not only the distinguished professor of music videos, but there was another professor whose textuality of choice consisted of Jazz LP liner notes and *Penthouse*'s Letters to the Editor. For the first (but definitely not the last time) theoretical and pedagogical rationales were used by tenured faculty to justify their teaching whatever they wished, regardless of the benefits their students might accrue from such idiosyncratic ventures.

'Language' was also a term open to interpretation. Also in the early 80s, there were some discussions as to what constituted a language. Could we count sign language? Yes, it was a language, it was argued, but it did not have a literature and thus, although it might fulfil the foreign language requirement, could not satisfy a literature requirement and, by extension, there was no criticism written in sign language! But then again, it was a language of disability. Was it discriminatory not to accept it as a foreign language? Was not musical notation also a language? In this instance, there was a literature (the Western musical tradition). Could not the ability to read music constitute knowledge of a foreign language? What about American, British and Irish English? Should they not be considered as separate languages and literatures? We might laugh today, but these very cases were petitioned when I taught on the SUNY faculty in the late 1980s. Under the guise of theoretical and pedagogical debates, such discussions bear witness to the dumbing down of the curriculum and erosion of scholarly standards during these years.

Once the value of actual texts had been called into question in Comparative Literature programmes, theory seemed to assume an exaggerated role. Naturally, there were those departments that held to traditional standards and continued to teach traditional texts (even if literature now expanded its definition to include comics, cinema, and music videos). But, there were also departments focusing primarily on theory. Some programmes tried to do both. Often the two foci clashed. One was either in the camp of the virtuous (texts or theory) or under the sway of evil forces (texts or theory). Students were sometimes put in the middle of such confrontations and forced to decide which camp warranted their allegiance and this choice often came at a heavy price (which professor would deign to support you on the job market, write letters on your behalf, and promote you to colleagues who were hiring).

Another development occurred around the same time. Earlier, it was required that students coming into Comparative Literature have some familiarity with literature and know some languages. With the de-emphasis on language learning and a shift in how languages were taught, there were fewer students capable of reading texts in foreign languages, let alone two or three languages and literatures. Part of this problem was that language acquisition became more tied to conversational skills. When I studied French or German in college, we learned the language through the literature. So, after a few years, one could read, write a bit, speak a bit and had some knowledge of a language's canon of literature. With the shift from such courses to conversational language classes, the student could read and speak, but knew nothing about a given culture's literature. In conversation-focused courses, students read comics for slang, studied advertisements for cultural knowledge, and listened to television commercials for pronunciation.

The 1970s were also a time in America when general requirements were dropped from many curricula. I graduated from an elite women's college never having taken a hard science, a social science, or math class. It is no surprise then that language acquisition and literature requirements also disappeared from programmes of study. Furthermore, the de-emphasis in language training also coincided with the introduction of new disciplines with rather diffuse offerings. These two developments made it possible for students to graduate from even good schools in the US having learned very little. So, one could encounter in certain Comparative Literature graduate programmes students with an undergraduate major in psychology or Women's Studies with neither language nor literature training. I was able to segue into Comparative Literature after majoring in religion and graduate degrees in theology because I had learned several languages sufficiently to do scholarship (and hence knew some literature) and had read enough philosophy to be able to glide into those trends in theory that were philosophically inflected. So when I was first confronted with Derrida, I knew there had been a Heidegger, Husserl and Jaspers that preceded him. I knew what structuralism was before I needed to grapple with post-structuralism. Many of my fellow students were not so fortunate, especially those who majored in certain 'new' fields which were content-light and ideology-heavy. They were ill-prepared for graduate work. In Europe and India, no such problem could occur, since the curricula are more standardized and substance-light disciplines are not so prevalent. Moreover, in Europe and India, students studying Comparative Literature know several languages. I doubt very much that a student who has never studied any literature and knows no secondary language would find themselves in a Comparative Literature programme in India or Europe.

With all its own problems, Comparative Literature was also prey to the issues besieging other disciplines in the humanities, particularly English. At some point in the early 90s, English Departments in the US were undergoing a crisis of their own. It had become increasingly difficult for them to place students in jobs and there were fewer and fewer new things to say about the canon of English, Commonwealth and American literature. Then, English Departments realized that their students would perhaps be more marketable if they could also sell themselves as continental theory scholars. They might have been a bit envious of the expertise of comparatists and other national literature scholars who know some theory and had read it in the original language rather than excerpted passages anthologized in handbooks. In the face of budget cuts and downsizing, all humanities programmes had to strategize and English Departments were no exception. They came up with the brilliant idea of wresting the teaching of theory from Comparative Literature. Because of their size and resources, they sometimes succeeded to the extent that they even swallowed up Comparative Literature programmes in the process. English Departments now had enough material to teach, topics for dissertations and areas in which to market their students. Flush with their success, they then looked around to see what else they might colonize. English Departments then discovered the world. At roughly the same time, national literature scholars also discovered themselves as topics of inquiry. To understand how this shift in focus could occur, we must first retrace the genesis of identity studies in American institutions.

MULTICULTURALISM

In the early 1970s, we saw the emergence of Black Studies and Women's Studies Programmes, devised to represent the experience and cultural production of then underrepresented Blacks and women in academe. One important thing to note is that these programmes were usually staffed with African-Americans and women respectively. The representation of underrepresented groups expanded over time to include other minorities (Hispanic, Native-American) and hyphenated ethnicities (Asian-Americans). Identity Studies was thus born as a discipline. It often entered the curriculum under the rubric of multiculturalism and was supported by a theoretical superstructure devised to justify its inclusion. Multiculturalism was, therefore, ab initio, institutionalized in the United States as a bureaucratic structure purporting to foster minority rights. It was marketed as an outgrowth of the movement in the 1980s on American campuses to revamp the canon. It claimed to open the canon and the university up to subalterns, exiles, and others. Ideally, it sought to facilitate dead white authors being supplanted by authors from underrepresented groups (writing in English) in the curricula and deadwood white male professors being supplanted by women and minorities in the classroom. This latter goal succeeded in the hiring of significant numbers of white women. It succeeded to a far lesser degree in the recruitment of Blacks, Hispanics and Native Americans. Nevertheless, multiculturalism claimed to re-envision the world from a decolonizing and anti-racist perspective.

Although multiculturalism theoretically claimed to attack Eurocentrism rather than Euro-Americans, some critics were not convinced. Some found it questionable that multiculturalism *assumed* that certain people might do well in academe studying themselves rather than translating difference (Gitlin 1995: 208–9), studying cultures that were not their own 'heritage', or working in fields where they were truly unrepresented (such as the hard sciences). A Stanford University student, when asked during that university's debates over canon revision about studying important non-Western trends, such as Japanese capitalism or Islamic fundamentalism, responded: 'Who gives a damn about those things? I want to study myself' (San Juan 1995: 230–1). Multiculturalism thus contributed to the further balkanization of minorities in American academe, a process that, since the inception of Affirmative Acton in the 1970s, was well under way. Minorities could enter American academe, but were managed, that is, directed toward fields that showcased their ethnicity, so universities could use one minority placement to make two political statements: show their commitment both to diversity hiring and flaunt their promotion of minority studies. It was only uppity minority members like myself who dared to specialize in something they were not genetically predisposed to find interesting! How many times was I asked during job interviews if my specialization was liberation theology, rather than Hinduism, just because the interviewer could not pronounce my name! The sad truth was that some multiculturalists who in theory saw themselves as border-crossers or even 'cultural workers' (Giroux 1992: 21), in practice defined 'alterity' in quite narrow terms. Minorities were welcome into the ivory towers of American universities when they limited themselves to those fields that were defined for them as apt (acceptable) areas of specialization and did not really threaten the power structure or how 'the Other' was being packaged and marketed by university administrators.

As it is practiced in American institutions today, multiculturalism presupposes two basic ideas. First, it recognizes that American history is not solely reflected in the activities of one race (white), one language group (English), one ethnicity (Anglo-Saxon) or one religion (Christianity). It quite correctly claims that African-Americans, Latinos, Asian-Americans, Native-Americans and others have made central contributions to American culture. It does not *act* on this presupposition by contextualizing the American ethnic experience within the source culture in any substantive manner. Acknowledging difference is all that matters. Actually learning about the different source languages or cultures is not necessary because multiculturalism takes for granted that beneath the differences among Americans are some underlying principles and values that bring us together. This theory of diversity presupposes and requires the notion of the assimilationist 'common' culture and fosters a social order founded on the principle of unity in multiplicity (San Juan 1995: 223). It revisions the image of America as a melting pot into America as a salad that is now not only colourful and beautiful, but more easily consumable. This transformation begs the question: 'Who is the consumer?' (Davis 996: 45).

Multiculturalism functions not just as an epistemological phenomenon. The consumption of multiculturalism within the university replicates that of corporate-level structures, since universities are also corporations (Lubiano 1996: 70). We can, therefore, compare multicultural educational practices to corporate diversity management initiatives that derive from the assumption that racially and ethnically diverse groups need to be managed and controlled in ways to contain conflict and fortify power relations.[2] The corporate model of disciplining diversity as a strategy for more control of workers (Davis 1996: 41) does not attempt to assimilate diversity into the dominant culture. Rather, it digests unassimilated diversity with the same results as if homogeneity prevailed. The control problem with this model is that the cultures of multiculturalism are not the same and cannot be so easily consumed by the dominant white culture. Nor do substitutions to the menu work: Africans are not really the same as African-Americans. Indians cannot be swapped out for Mexicans. Nevertheless, multiculturalism purports to include representatives of neglected groups, even if they are not the traditionally discriminated groups, and offer an alibi for liberal reform that may not, in fact, exist.

In this effort, the educational system has manifestly entered the important promotional work of encouraging recognition, tolerance, pluralism, and diversity as rearguard control (Cruz 1996: 32). Under this format, multiculturalism serves as an institution's strategic response to a perceived deterioration of progressive policies, Civil Rights gains, and changes in demographics.[3] Toward this same goal of teaching tolerance, institutional offices of diversity, workshops at teachers' conventions, publisher's marketing sessions, and curricula in primary and secondary schools throughout America now all target 'cultural diversity' and multicultural literacy as prime directives. It is important to notice that the very real aims of Affirmative Actions might get lost in this shuffle. This might even be the desired aim of such initiatives.

Multiculturalism was initially presented as an alternative to the civilizational model made popular by Samuel Huntington in *The Clash of Civilizations and Remaking the World Order* (1996) and others.[4] It was Huntington's thesis that the West is losing ground and that non-Western civilizations are expanding economically, militarily, and politically by exploiting Western modernization as well as their own indigenous traditions.[5] The non-West culls what the West can offer in terms of technology while at the same time reaffirming the values inherent in and traditional to their own cultures (Huntington 1996: 20). Huntington claimed that it is just this type of re-indigenizaton that was needed in the West to bring about a similar resurgence of its civilization, but it was impeded by movements (such as multiculturalism) that encouraged immigrants from other civilizations to reject assimilation. While it is not the place here to refute Huntington's rather Tocquevillian thesis, I would like to highlight how his civilizational model, an inclusive idea that there exists a set of cultural values, is presented as the antithesis of multiculturalism's institutional practice of recognition that purports to be equally inclusionary.

Proponents of multiculturalism portray it as a necessary antidote to the vision of the world order offered by Huntington. In fact, multiculturalism should be promoted as a crucially needed agenda of 'progressive humanism' (Palumbo-Liu 2002: 126–7), an offshoot of 1970s activism, Third World consciousness, antiwar politics, the rise of the New Left, and the burgeoning Feminist, Gay, and Lesbian Movements (Palumbo-Liu 2002: 116–17). It is in such rhetoric that we find the not-too subtle *glissement* from the pedagogical to the political, from the gestural to the realm of the real. Multiculturalism should be championed as a form of cultural Affirmative Action (O'Brian and Little 1990). It should not concern us if, in the very years that multiculturalism flourished as a pedagogy, statistical evidence shows that the numbers of minorities in American universities plummeted (Figueira 2008).

Stanley Fish, one of the few theorists who did not accepted the master narrative of multiculturalism as a pedagogy of inclusion,[6] dismissed it as an ultimately incoherent concept (Fish 1997: 338).[7] Other critics were equally dismissive in their assessment of multiculturalism's role within university politics. Slavoj Žižek characterized it as an experience of the Other deprived of its Otherness.[8] Wahneema Lubiano condemned multiculturalism's cult of recognition as an empty abstraction used by administrators to take the political heat off institutions for their failure to diversify (Lubiano 1996: 68). Institutional recognition flourishes as a programme while it weakens as a reality (Jacoby 1994b: 124), since students are still held to Euro-American values for education and life success (Guerrero 1996: 61). Studying the Other in multiculturalism's thoroughly appropriated and diluted fashion ensures that the continued domination of Euro-centric knowledge remains unchallenged. Multiculturalism is then nothing more than subterfuge for business as usual. One can bring Native-American Studies, for example, onto campuses as a 'polite pseudo-intellectual vehicle to provide the appearance of ethnic diversity'. However, Native American cultural production is not presented in any in-depth manner where it might be able to offer an alternative to Euro-centrism and its institutions. It is taught in such a diluted and uninformed manner that it ends up only providing validation to supposed insights and conclusions of Euro-American academia (Guerrero 1996: 56).

The simple fact is that not only conservative think-tanks and champions of the Western canon criticized the institutionalization of multiculturalism. Minority critics and students made their voices heard. At the University of Texas, Chicano students expressed their uneasiness regarding multiculturalism. They viewed is as a bland, catch-all phrase connected with diversified reading lists or required courses on non-Western cultures. They perceived it as a means of thwarting a head-on confrontation that should take place over institutional racism (San Juan 1995: 224). Their perception was valid. As an imposition of some form of recognition, multiculturalism is inherently a form of control (Essed 1991: 210). Does not the process of liberalizing the canon by simple addition of minority literature betoken tokenization (Pratt 1994: 59)? If non-White materials are perceived as 'add-ons' to White structures, they never address the centrality and dominance of the latter or institutional and structural determinants of inequality (Gordon and Newfield 1996: 79, 87). Multiculturalism should question old definitions of knowledge and disciplines as defined by a Western canon of texts. Ultimately, difference should make a difference (Davis 1996: 48). Satisfied with bracketing the Other, multiculturalism glosses over ever-present problems of a political, legal, and economic nature within academe. Nevertheless, in American universities, large portions of the world are packaged under the umbrella of multiculturalism and the fairly inclusive rubric of postcolonial literature. Such pedagogies feed American monolingual arrogance and cultural isolationism.

POSTCOLONIALISM

As in the case of multiculturalism, Postcolonialism also claims to engage the Other. It shares with multiculturalism many of the same deficiencies and brings its own set of critical problems, the first being that its practitioners never formed a consensus as to what constituted reading a text from a postcolonial perspective or what differentiated a postcolonial text from a non-postcolonial text. Postcolonialism is generally deeply concerned with the location of the theorist. Yet, it never adequately seems to address the location of the term 'postcoloniality', its ahistoricity and its universalizing deployments (Shohat 1992: 99). Somehow, claiming that postcolonial criticism 'covers all the cultures affected by the imperial process from the moment of colonization to the present day' (Ashcroft, Griffiths and Tiffin 1989: 2) or that it 'foregrounds a politics of opposition and struggle' (Mishra and Hodges 1991: 399) sufficed. Postcolonial theory never seemed to define what was actually being done with what body of works.

An essentialism beset discussions of postcoloniality from its arrival on the critical scene in the 1980s in the wake of Edward Said's *Orientalism* (1978). As time went on, it seemed that no society was not postcolonial and, while lip-service was paid to the special and distinctive regional characteristics of the cultures and literatures under investigation, it was thought that, as in the case of multiculturalism, there was some common experience they all shared rooted in the time when 'they all emerged from the experience of colonization and asserted themselves by foregrounding the tension with imperial power' (Ashcroft, Griffiths and Tiffin 1989: 2) and that condition could now be called postcoloniality. Like multiculturalism, postcolonial criticism did not demand significant linguistic skills.

There was also something 'prematurely congratulatory' (McClintock 1992: 87) about postcolonial criticism's claim to speak in terms of intervention and resistance when, as a project, it engaged in no political or social reality but functioned exclusively in a rhetorical manner. The postcolonial archive consisted of a handful of endlessly recycled articles by a small group of theorists and a limited body of published texts in English and French, as if these were totally representative of the postcolonial situation. With the exception of Spivak's Mahasweta Devi, vernacular texts that *might not* deal with colonialism or did not fit the master narrative of oppression this theory promoted did not enter into discussion. Postcolonial critics claimed acuity with regard to the intricacies of their readings (Sunder Rajan 1997: 603–5), yet their ignorance of key aspects in the narrative they sought to deconstruct often led to gross distortions. These mistakes were usually not given any significance or even acknowledged because overriding importance was assigned primarily to the critical theorizing.

In fact, the critic's location and the master narrative of hegemonic violence often eclipsed the national historical situation and exegetical context altogether. Because little reference was made to culturally specific details, the discourse of postcoloniality can even be seen to mimic colonial thinking, since postcolonial theory while claiming to problematize the binaries of Western historicism, still orders the globe according to the single binary of the colonial and the postcolonial (McClintock 1992: 85). In this manner, the multitudinous cultures of the world are marked and marketed in postcolonial theory with their geopolitical distinctions telescoped into invisibility (McClintock 1992: 86). One colonial experience (like one multicultural experience) resembles another. Stripped of cultural specificity postcolonial prognoses have little to do with the Third-World reality. Relying on the experience of modern colonialism, the critic divides history into manageable and isolated segments, while at the same time arguing against the false homogenization of Orientalist projects (Bahri 1995: 52). A contextual and fragmentary analyses are accepted out of a deep cynicism regarding the Other as a fossilized object of clinical experimentation. Indiscriminately embracing the Other levels out the various competing Others. All postcolonial experiences are the same, since their actuality is never taken seriously. Thus, the unfortunate Fredric Jameson had to be taken to task for assuming that all Third-World narratives functioned in the same way as national allegories. What is really important is that the Other always be perceived as correct, regardless of differences and histories, in order to fulfil the postcolonial critic's desire for a pure otherness in all of its pristine luminosity (Chow 1995: 45). Postcolonial criticism thus exhibits an uncritical primitivism that privileges non-Western culture and glories in its presumptive, eventual—and always revolutionary—resurgence (Clark 1996: 44).

Like multiculturalism, postcolonial criticism relies in great measure on the notion that some heritage of systems limits the reader. Our present condition, although seemingly benign, imposes an existential limit and theory alone can liberate us from systemic constraints (Fluck 1996: 216). Curiously missing from both multiculturalism and postcolonial criticism is any serious questioning of how the text's appearance as a network of hegemonic or subversive gestures suits the state of literary theoretical professionalization or how theory allows individuals cut off from any effective social action and buoyed by their security as academic professionals to claim solidarity with the disenfranchised. This alienation from *real* powerlessness (like the academic Marxist's guilt vis-à-vis the worker) can then be compensated for by a posture of powerlessness vis-à-vis representation. The result of such a critical stance is that it allows a privileged class of academics the opportunity to forge a wide-ranging identification with the marginalized Other.

It is noteworthy that postcolonial criticism found urgent currency in the First World, whereas fewer ripples resonated in the ex-colonialized worlds of South Asia, Africa or satellites of the former Soviet Union. The predominance of critical contestants in Euro-American centres reflects how much this brand of theory was Euro-centric and culture bound (Clark 1996: 24). The posturing and positioning of postcolonial critics did not, however, go unquestioned. Benita Parry accused them of exorbitation in their self-appointed roles and their suppression of native voices (1994: 172). Arif Dirlik (1997: 343) and Rajeshwari Sunder Rajan (1997: 598) cited postcolonial theorists' disengagements from significant issues of neo-colonialism and their continual retreats into rarefied forms of postmodern abstraction. Dirlik even saw postcolonialism's emergence as a form of global capitalism where critics, commanding high salaries in the First World, presume to be existentially connected to continuing problems of Third-World social, political and cultural domination. Since Spivak's subalterns were theoretically mute, she could effectively co-opt their voice. In the process, she created the need for a theorist (Spivak herself) who will determine the discourse of the victimized. This is, indeed, a slippery game. But, for the postcolonial critics, notions of voicelessness and absence served to licence the neglect of any texts ('archives', 'voices', and 'spaces') that contradicted the theoretical script.

At work here was the age-old problem of the engaged intellectual and the pretense that academic criticism can function as a political act and 'textual culture' can displace 'activist culture' (Ahmad 1). Regardless of their own socio-economic status and privileges, the postcolonial critic (like the multicultural critic before him/her) speaks as/for minorities and as representatives for minority communities and their victimization. They function as 'victims in proxy' (Bahri 1995: 73). This role is rarely seriously challenged. Spivak voiced, on occasion, concern that some critics might lack the objectivity to conceptualize their *Dasein*, as if by projection she was absolved of accruing any blame herself. But this strategy of projection, utilized with such aplomb by Said to mask a multitude of sins, does not change the fact that victimization by proxy represents a tendency of false consciousness all too prevalent in post-structuralist literary criticism.

In reality, multiculturalism and postcolonialism as modes of recognition only offer the illusion of victory over racism, because they do not address the issue of who has the power to determine what courses are taught and what requirements are established (San Juan 1995: 224–25). They do, however, beg the question: who really benefits from the identity industry? This is the central question for me. It is very clear who benefited from the construction of India in postcolonial criticism, the privileged diasporic critic based in the West. At this juncture, one can safely claim that, contrary to their inflated aspirations, multiculturalism and postcolonial criticism do not guarantee equality of opportunity or access to resources for the disenfranchised. As theories and pedagogies of the Other, they do not clarify or liberate anyone. In fact, the case can be made that they provide a smokescreen for societal and institutional unwillingness to change the academic situation of minorities.

Yet, studies of the Other in American academe today continue to pride themselves on their focus on recognition, tolerance and acknowledgement of victimhood. The sense of empathy had always been a component of the initial programmes in identity studies, such as Black Studies and Women Studies; it was carried over into multiculturalism and postcolonialism. It was then expanded or transmogrified to other minoritized groups, finding expression in Queer Studies, Transgendered Studies, Handicapped Studies, Nomadology, Fat Studies, White Male Studies, LGBTQ Studies, etc. In many of these purported sub-disciplines, there are seldom any texts involved, or following a trend established by postcolonial studies, the canon consists of a discrete selection of theoretical articles. On the rare occasion when there is a text involved, one looks less at the actual text and more at the critics' experience of the text in terms of their subjectivity (as Queer, Fat, Transgendered, etc.). So literary criticism now needs no longer even talk about cultural products, but rather critics can talk exclusively about themselves. The critic can, in fact, become the text. Self-referentiality had always been present in theory and certain critics (like Spivak) took this tendency to great heights, but now it seems to be a significant main point of discussion. This trend has led us to the cult of the critic as the spokesperson for the globalized Other and disseminator of the world's literary production. In other words, this trend has brought us to World Literature.

WORLD LITERATURE

The new 'ism' of World Literature is actually not new at all, but very similar to the European construct of 'General Literature' which in the past formed a dyad with Comparative Literature, as in the *Journal of General and Comparative Literature* published by Indiana University. World Literature is nothing but a reformulation of Area Studies, a Cold War era Pentagon construction of managing the global situation that was discredited as racist, colonialist, and illegitimate a few decades ago. World Literature, like its Cold War and more recent precursors, also seeks to market the Other for commodification and consumption in the West. World Literature differs, of course, from Area Studies in that it is bankrolled by large publishing conglomerates churning out anthologies rather than the State Department. But it is similar to multiculturalism and postcolonial criticism in that it, according to its chief proponent in the US, David Damrosch, promotes recognition, equal opportunity, and tolerance (Damrosch 2011). However, the projects of World Literature, Area Studies, multiculturalism, and postcolonial criticism are remarkably the same: The West still interprets the rest.

This shift was possible because of the history I have outlined above and the radicalization of theory that occurred in the last three decades, where the literary paradigm shifted from the aesthetic to the political. First, one began to view literature as an outmoded form of cultural capital belonging to the bourgeoisie. Then, an important stage in this process of radicalization involved the rejection of the literary canon in favour of the cultural studies model. We have noted how dismantling the canon often had less to do with installing a more immediate and less conservative hierarchical format and more to do with establishing a new authority, grounded in ideology and seeking reification by identifying and marketing marginalized populations. We have also seen how, in the case of American universities, these commodity populations were packaged and marketed first under the rubric of multiculturalism and then under the umbrella of postcolonial literatures. In a new variation of this theme, they are now marketed as World Literature. These pedagogies all claimed to be bringing the literatures from the margins to the centre when, in fact, all they really did was allow critics from the centre to co-opt the margins.

These theories have focused on postmodernist concerns, such as hybridized and syncretic views of the modern world, rather than economic and political forces. The work of Baudrillard has been particularly influential in this regard, especially his notion that travel can be viewed as a spectacular form of amnesia. According to such a theory, any part of the world can be recreated or made to stand for another. In a world of third-order simulacra, encroaching pseudo-places merge to eliminate geographical or ethnic space entirely. This levelling out of the world has contributed to the aforementioned theoretical and pedagogical formulations of the margins, metaphorical spaces in which to dwell that are separate from the real space critics might inhabit. In this metaphorical space, critics can voice ideologies of subversion and rebellion that would be too unsettling, if voiced from their own actual space. Their delicate balancing acts stem from the paradox of academics inhabiting a space of bourgeois comfort, while needing at the same time to distance themselves from global capitalism. When critics appropriate the metaphorical space of the margin, they hope to exonerate themselves for all the benefits they receive from this same capitalism.

In this process, we find the meeting of incommensurables—a deep seated need for the experience of political engagement coming out of the 1960s meeting a 1990s need to be media savvy, to package and market intellectual capital. There is no small irony here, in how easily these two conceptual frameworks have melded. If the belief in criticism as a viable intervention is a relic of the 60s that has proven itself bankrupt (which I think it has), we might want to view all these purportedly cutting-edge pedagogies as ventures in socio-political impotence. Potency, when it exists, resides in the critic's relationship to colleagues as it is constructed through the coinage and use of jargon, but more importantly, in their collaborations with university administrators and publishers.

In American institutions today, intellectual endeavours are trumped by commercial potential. The marketing opportunities of new pedagogies and theories are twofold. First, there is marketing to and through university administrators who buy into the idea that an initiative such as World Literature (like postcolonial criticism and multiculturalism before it) provides the most advanced and 'logical' approach to the miasma of competing cultures and ethnicities. Of course, in such initiatives, engaging the global Other easily degenerates into the diversity of college catalogues and state- or corporate-managed United Colors of Benetton pluralism (Shohat and Stam 2003: 6). Though an initiative such as World Literature pretends to 'restructure' with supposedly radical responses to new socio-economic realities, it is really no different than the other attempts to engage the Other summarized here.

The practical reason for this packaging of alterity, whether it be a newly-minted World Literature departments, Multicultural or Postcolonial Studies programmes, is obvious: all these 'specializations' are relatively easy. They do not involve in-depth knowledge of another culture or demand learning foreign languages, skills that have fallen by the wayside among American students. In fact, one of the explicit reasons for World Literature, as formulated by Damrosch, is the difficulty of adequate language training eroding the competency of many Comparative Literature programmes. The inability to train students in languages and literatures derives from the aforementioned decline in learning and standards beginning in the 60s. World Literature's solution to these lower standards is to universalize them. Pedagogies such as multiculturalism, postcolonial criticism and now World Literature allow the Other to preserve its own heritage, as long as that heritage speaks English (Prashad 2000: 112). In the Internet age, when the globalization of English has contributed to diminishing the need to learn languages, the Other can in these formats be consumed 'on the cheap'. Furthermore, such pedagogies also feed American isolationism. As cosmetic celebrations of otherness and diversity, they in no way compromise American tendencies to cultural provincialism, triumphalism, or indifference to the world. Like Multicultural and Postcolonial Studies before it, World Literature allows students to taste other cultures without digesting them. The resounding global education that such pedagogies offer a literature student can consist of nothing more than snippets from endlessly recycled representative 'othered' authors writing or translated into the English language.

Within such pedagogical initiatives, there is little need to contextualize the foreign or ethnic experience or broaden its significance by drawing associations within the source culture that might extend knowledge beyond the master narrative that one has responsibly engaged the world. By thus appropriating the Other, pedagogies of alterity of which World Literature is the latest avatar, sanction a selectively ignorant exploration, ensuring a general failure of real engagement. Their deficiencies not only reveal ignorance but highlight the hubris of those who wish to speak for and hence co-opt the Other. They affect a respect for the Other as a reified object of cultural difference but only deliver a fragmented and watered-down vision. Moreover, I fear that the missionary zeal exhibited by some practitioners of these pedagogies actually deflects attention away from social issues such as discrimination, unequal access, and hierarchies of ethnic privilege that are far from being resolved (Huggan 2000: 126) in American academe today. What is insidious is that these pedagogies claim to offer the putative end of meta-narratives, while, in reality, they only offering a one-way street, with Anglophone culture as the one recognizing the non-Anglophone and often non-white culture. In order 'to be' or 'speak out', the non-white and/or non-Anglophone culture must seek legitimacy and recognition from Anglophone white culture and use the language of that culture to produce itself (Rizvi 1994: 63). Institutionalizing the study of alterity in such a format obscures issues of power and privilege. In fact, it sanctions a tokenistic approach to dealing with difference (Chow 2002: 113).

The recent revival of World Literature, like the earlier pedagogies of alterity, is conceptualized by many as having arisen in an attempt to uncover occluded and submerged identities and to liberate the repressed through the dissemination of peoples' histories. It shares their mission to recognize the contributions of neglected groups and offer a reform project heralding diversity and promoting progressive politics. By unmasking and repudiating inferential racism, all these pedagogies claim to redraw boundaries and affirm the authority of external cultures and internal colonies. However, the politics behind the installation of such pedagogies should be viewed in more critical terms, since class divisions and systemic inequalities remain intact. World Literature, like multiculturalism and postcolonial criticism, does not really challenge structures of power but rather promotes an ethos of recognition without questioning. Eurocentric definitions of knowledge. Like other pedagogies of alterity, World Literature ultimately offers stasis and consolidates power. Some critics, among whom I count myself, conceive the establishment of such identity studies as a strategy by an academic elite seeking to displace, diffuse, and thus intensify class, gender, and racial contradictions.

CONCLUSION

In a recent article, the Cuban-American critic Al López speculated on a possible encounter between the Cuban poet Jose Martí and Walt Whitman at a reception following a lecture on Abraham Lincoln by the American poet at Madison Square Theater in 1887. If Martí and Whitman did, in fact, speak, López notes that it would have been in English, although Martí could have dialogued in Spanish and French. Martí might have broached any number of interesting topics, since he was learned in the Classics and had advanced degrees in law and philosophy, was a renowned journalist, editor, novelist and playwright. Whitman, in contrast, was a cursory reader, perusing a dozen books as any time, reading a few pages here and there, seldom getting sufficiently interested in any volume to read it in its entirety, dipping into various genres and reading no language but English.

Although he never travelled beyond North America, it did not prevent him from envisioning the many places he evokes in 'Salut au Monde' through, as López notes 'his own mystical, abstracted vision of an America at once generalized and exceptional'. The world Whitman presented in this poem was populated by undifferentiated Others 'facilely reduced to "Camarados" in turn subsumed into his Hegelian vision of America as an ever-expanding end-of-History' (López 2011: 6).

Martí's considerably larger intellectual scope was grounded, as López notes, in 'a keen awareness of cultural and material difference' (López 2011: 7). While Whitman did not possess expertise in a broad range of subjects and disciplines, one certainly would not guess it from his poetry or its expansive and expansionist claims. Whitman had no scruples regarding his parochial vision or his provincial experience of the world. Certainly, none surface in poems such as 'Starting from Paumanok' where the American poet imagines himself 'sailing to other shores to annex the same, yet welcoming/ every new brother. Coming among the new Ones myself to be their companion/ and equal' without stopping to wonder how he proposes to accomplish this in English, or how his prospective new 'brothers' might feel about being 'welcomed' in their own homeland by some interloper (cited in López 2011: 7).

Whitman's inverted logic of welcoming new brothers as long as they speak English presents a crystallization of American exceptionalism that serves as an apt metaphor for what I see to be at work in recent formulations of World Literature. Martí's interdisciplinarity, in-depth knowledge of other cultures and languages, and awareness of cultural difference calls to mind Comparative Literature at its disciplinary best. I fear that Whitman's claims to annex the world reflects far more World Literature's rather baroque vision of a world to be consumed in English, the new academic imperial language, rather than in any other language of that world. It is ironic that one model was and is practiced in America by mainstream figures and the other model, by Hispanic renegades like Martí, López and myself.

In my recent book, *Otherwise Occupied*, I make the case that academic theories and pedagogies of the Other (identity studies, multiculturalism, postcolonial criticism, and now we might add World Literature) have been constructed and used in America to undermine Affirmative Action by influencing institutional policies for recruitment. Theoretical constructions of the Other have proliferated in direct proportion to the failure of statistical evidence to support the success claims of institutional diversity. In other words, they aid in masking the continued marginalization and containment of America's minorities within academe. They also dovetail very nicely with university marketing concerns. In the past, universities have occluded low numbers in diversity by establishing various ethnic studies programmes and peopling them with under-represented ethnics. Granted it was not an ideal situation. In fact, it was a balkanization of ethnics into fields for which they were deemed biologically and culturally suited. In other words, ethnics could enter the ivory tower only if they were willing to settle for studying themselves. Minorities were thus neutralized and contained in such placements. Now, with pedagogies focused on representing (and not necessarily studying in any real fashion) under-represented populations, universities need not even hire minorities. To quote Aijaz Ahmad, under the guise of studying colonialisms of the past we facilitate imperialisms of the present (Ahmad 1992: 222). Under the guise of promoting tolerance, pedagogies of alterity support the white power structure and the Third-World elites it subcontracts to further neutralize minorities in American academe.

I also suspect that the resurgence of interest in World Literature betokens an effort on the part of certain scholars to retool themselves now that other identity theories and pedagogies have proved themselves to be bankrupt. What better persona to adopt, in the age of multiculturalism and globalism, than that of a comparatist doing World Literature? Or better yet, why not adopt the posture of a World Literature scholar whose formation has been almost exclusively in English literature and who makes a career championing a brand of criticism that claims to engage a voiceless and under-represented world? Clearly, we should not take at face value academic projects that blithely claim to engage in a reform process, especially when the readings they offer still stem from a privileged perspective and its norms. We should rather interrogate what is behind gestures that promise to reinstall the standards of cultural and linguistic specificity to the discipline of Comparative Literature. Especially, if what they deliver is considerably less than what comparatists have known and practiced for decades without subtitles.

Certainly in a post-9/11 world, we should be able to admit that there is a failure to grasp the essential role played by source contexts and languages that has led to subsequent egregious failures of interpretation and understanding. The postmodern tendency to treat all literatures as a kind of meta-language that can be lifted out of their natural linguistic context and examined on the a-historical specimen tray of contemporary theory has proved to be woefully inadequate. What is urgently needed is not a continuation of these Lilliputian exercises but a commitment to understanding literature's connection to and elucidation of the socio-cultural context from which it springs. Identity is not simply a matter of positionality and these pedagogies do not present any means of recuperating sensibilities disintegrated by society and the labour market (San Juan 1992: 4). Such problems cannot be solved by university canon reform. The neutral shibboleths of difference and diversity cannot replace real-life suffering and struggle for survival and dignity (San Juan 1992: 138). The real concern is not just the texts that transmit the heritage of the humanities in order to preserve standards and promote excellence. Rather we should ask who defines the standards of excellence and whose interests are at stake? Who should articulate the purpose and meaning of a humanities education and how? In other words, who makes the tasty salad, who is meant to consume it, and what is its nutritional value? It is clear that in the twenty-first century students need to be able to experience and interrogate this totality of the world's literatures, not just the constricted and diluted product packaged and marketed by the self-serving managers of American academe.

Multiculturalism, postcolonial studies, and World Literature all seek to consume a levelled out group or population in English and according to Western epistemes. They all market an assimilationist common culture. While they claim to recognize the contributions of neglected groups and offer a reform project heralding diversity and promoting a progressive politics, in actuality they only honour diversity on a superficial level. They all share a co-optive strategy of canon revision as an ethos of recognition. Yet, they treat under-represented and minority literatures as add-ons with little care given to problematizing the Euro-Amero-centric perspective of their project or its definitions of knowledge. They deal in tokenism; their gestures of inclusion are illusory, since they do not in any way challenge dominant white structures of power and occlude the real failure on the part of American academe to diversify. With the world thus diluted, a Euro-Amero-centric vision continues to articulate the meaning of the humanities and define standards as well as validate the insights of Euro-American academe. As for the worldly collaborators in the World Literature anthologies, I cannot help but think of Ashis Nandy's metaphor of the gladiators bowing and paying homage to Caesar (Nandy 1983: xiv), in this case, the Western-based critic and/or editor. India has to decide whether it wants to participate in this performance, especially since it is in a position to do so much more with its command of languages, its ability to expand the canon with intra-Indian comparisons, and its rich indigenous theoretical tradition. How ironic it would be if, after postcolonial theory and all its talk of the margins, the centre, colonizing discourses and hegemonies, India were to fall prey to the new hegemony of World Literature!

NOTES

1. A version of this essay has appeared as 'Comparative Literature: Where Have We Been, Where Are We Now, Where Are We Going?' *Working Papers*, Jadavpur University 2011.
2. In fact, David Rieff has argued, the treasured catchphrases of multiculturalism—'cultural diversity', 'differences', the need to 'do away with boundaries'—resemble the stock phrases of the modern corporation: 'product diversification', 'the global world', and the 'boundary-less company' (Jacoby 1994: 123).
3. As a University of Wisconsin faculty committee expressed it, there is a general belief that an ethnocentric view pervades mainstream curricula and that they are restricted 'to the Euro-American experience.' Excluded and left invisible are the people of color whose labour and sacrifices have been and continue to be neglected (San Juan 1995: 225). Due to this situation, the committee claimed, American students have been made insensitive to and intolerant of cultural and ethnic difference.
4. In particular, see Joel Kotkin, *Tribes: How Race, Religion and Identity Determine Success in the New Global Economy* (1993); Robert D. Kaplan, *The End of the Earth* (1996); and Benjamin R. Barber, *Jihad vs. McWorld: How Globalism and Tribalism are Reshaping the World* (1995).
5. The civilizational model broadly claims that in the post-Cold-War world, conflicts will not be waged between nation states or along ideological grounds, such as capitalism opposing socialism. Rather, conflict will be based on what Huntington terms 'civilizational' grounds. Huntington divides the world up into a discrete group of civilizations: Sinic, Japanese, Western, Latin American, and possibly, African.
6. Fish identifies two forms of multiculturalism operating in American academe today: what he has termed the boutique as opposed to the strong version. Boutique multiculturalism establishes a superficial relationship, wherein students are encouraged to admire and recognize the legitimacy of traditions other than their own. They stop short of approving other cultures when some value at their core generates an act that offends the canons of civilized decency as they have been either declared or assumed. In other words, boutique multiculturalism embraces difference up to the point precisely where it matters most to committed members (Fish 1997: 378). Strong multiculturalism, in contrast, claims to accord a deep respect to all cultures at their core. Each has the right to form its own identity and nourish its own sense of what is rational and humane (Fish 1997: 389). For strong multiculturalists, the first principle is tolerance. Strong multiculturalism works to the point where a culture whose core values you are tolerating reveals itself to be intolerant. At this juncture, you can either stretch your toleration to expand to their intolerance or condemn their core intolerance and, therefore, no longer accord it respect. The strong multiculturalist usually opts for the latter choice in the name of the supra-universal. In short,

strong multiculturalism reveals itself to be not very strong after all. Essentially it is not very distinct from boutique multiculturalism, just a deeper instance of what boutique multiculturalism presents in a shallow form (Fish 1997: 383).

7. According to Fish, neither boutique nor strong multiculturalism comes to terms with difference (Fish 1997: 385), although their inabilities are asymmetrical. Boutique multiculturalism views the core values of cultures as overlays on a substratum of essential humanity and thus tolerates them without taking them seriously and seeing them as truly core (Fish 1997: 379). We are all essentially alike. Boutique multiculturalism also views difference in terms of matters of lifestyle. It honours diversity in its most superficial aspects, with a deeper loyalty given to some notion of its universal potential. Strong multiculturalism takes difference seriously as a general principle but cannot allow its imperatives full realization in political programmes since it would inevitably lead to the suppression of difference (Fish 1997: 386). In these competing notions of recognition, Fish questions where respect for the Other actually resides, in tolerating difference (and, thereby, 'disrespecting' it) or taking it seriously enough to oppose it (Fish 1997: 338).
8. The idealization of the Other in multiculturalism shows him/her dancing fascinating dances and having an ecologically sound holistic approach to reality, while practices like wife-beating remain out of sight (Žižek 2002: 11).

REFERENCES

Ahmad, Aijaz, *In Theory: Classes, Nations, Literatures*, London: Verso, 1992.

Appadurai, Arjun, *The Social Life of Things: Commodities in Cultural Perspective*, Cambridge: CUP, 1986.

Ashcroft, Bill, Gareth Griffiths and Helen Tiffin, *The Empire Writes Back: Theory and Practice in Post-Colonial Literatures*, London: Routledge, 1989.

Bahri, Deepika, 'Once More with Feeling: What is Postcolonialism?', *Ariel*, vol. 26, 1995, pp. 51–82.

Chow, Rey, 'The Fascist Longings in our Midst,' *Ariel*, vol. 26, 1995, pp. 23–50.

_____, 'Theory, Area Studies, Cultural Studies: Issues of Pedagogy in Multiculturalism', in *Learning Places: The Afterlives of Area Studies*, ed. Masao Miyoshi and H.D. Harootunian, Durham: Duke University Press, 2002, pp. 103–18.

Clark, John, 'On Two Books by Edward W. Said', *Jurnal Bicara Seni*, Universiti Sains Malaysia, June 1996, pp. 20–47.

Cruz, Jon, 'From Farce to Tragedy: Reflections on the Reification of Race at the Century's End', in *Mapping Multiculturalism*, ed. Avery F. Gordon and Christopher Newfield, Minneapolis: University Minnesota Press, 1996, pp. 19–39.

Damrosch, David, Keynote Address, American Comparative Literature Association, 2011.

Davis, Angela Y., 'Gender, Class, Multiculturalism', in *Mapping Multiculturalism*, ed. Avery F. Gordon and Christopher Newfield, Minneapolis: University Minnesota Press, 1996, pp. 40–8.

Dirlik, Arif, *Third World Criticism in the Age of Global Capitalism*, New York: Westview, 1997.

Essed, Philomena, *Understanding Everyday Racism: An Interdisciplinary Theory*, Newbury Park: Sage, 1991.

Figueira, Dorothy, *Otherwise Occupied: Pedagogies of Alterity and the Brahminization of Theory*, Albany: State University of New York Press, 2008.

Fish, Stanley, 'Boutique Multiculturalism or Why Liberals are Incapable of Thinking about Hate-Speech', *Critical Inquiry*, vol. 23, Winter, 1997, pp. 378–95.

Fluck, Winfried, 'Literature, Liberalism and the Current Cultural Radicalism', in *Why Literature Matters: Themes and Functions of Literature*, ed. Rüdiger Ahrens and Laurenz Volkmann, Heidelberg: C. Winter, 1996, pp. 211–34.

Giroux, Henry A., 'Post-Colonial Ruptures and Democratic Possibilities: Multiculturalism as an Anti-Racist Pedagogy', *Cultural Critique*, Spring 1992, pp. 5–39.

Gitlin, Todd, *The Twilight of Common Dreams: Why America is Wracked by Cultural Wars*, New York: Metropolitan Books, 1995.

Gordon, Avery F. and Christopher Newfield, eds., *Mapping Multiculturalism*, Minneapolis: University of Minnesota Press, 1966.

Guerrero, M. Annette Jaimes, 'American Indian Studies and Multiculturalism', in *Mapping Multiculturalism*, ed. Avery F. Gordon and Christopher Newfield, Minneapolis: University of Minnesota Press, 1996, pp. 49–63.

Guillory, John, *Cultural Capital: The Problem of Literary Canon Formation*, Chicago: University of Chicago Press, 1993.

Huggan, Graham, 'Exoticism, Ethnicity, and the Multicultural Fallacy,' in *'New' Exoticism: Changing Patterns in the Construction of Otherness*, ed. Isabel Santaolalla, Amsterdam: Rodopi, 2000, pp. 91–6.

Huntington, Samuel P., *The Clash of Civilizations and the Remaking of World Order*, New York: Simon and Schuster, 1996.

Hutcheon Linda and Marion Richmond, eds., *Other Solitudes: Canadian Multicultural Fictions*, Toronto: OUP, 1990.

Jacoby, Russell, 'The Myth of Multiculturalism', *New Left Review*, vol. 208, November–December 1994, pp. 121–6.

López, Alfred J., 'Translating Interdisciplinarity: Reading Martí Reading Whitman', *The Comparatist*, vol. 35, 2011, pp. 5–18.

Lubiano, Wahneema, 'Like Being Mugged by a Metaphor: Multiculturalism and State Narratives', in *Mapping Multiculturalism*, ed. Avery F. Gordon and Christopher Newfield, Minneapolis: University of Minnesota Press, 1996, pp. 64–75.

McClintock, Anne, 'The Angel of Progress', *Social Text*, vols. 31–32, 1992, pp. 84–97.

Mishra, Vijay and Bob Hodge, 'What is (Post)-colonialism?', *Textual Practice*, vol. 5, 1991, pp. 399–414.

Nandy, Ashis, *The Intimate Enemy: Loss and Recovery of Self under Colonialism*, Delhi: OUP, 1983.

O'Brian, Mark and Craig Little, eds., *Reimaging America: The Arts of Social Change*, Philadelphia: New Society Publications, 1990.

Palumbo-Liu, David, 'Multiculturalism Now: Civilization, National Identity, and Difference Before and After September 11th', *Boundary*, vol. 29, no. 2, 2002, pp. 109–27.

Parry, Benita, 'Resistance Theory/Theorizing Resistance of Two Cheers for Nativism', in *Colonial Discourse/Postcolonial Theory*, ed. Francis Barker, Peter Hulme and Margaret Iverson, Manchester: Manchester University Press, 1994, pp. 172–96.

Prashad, Vijay, *The Karma of Brown Folk*, Minneapolis: University of Minnesota Press, 2000.

Pratt, Mary Louise, 'Humanities for the Future: Reflections on the Western Culture Debate at Stanford', in *Falling into Theory: Conflicting Views on Reading Literature*, ed. David Richter, Boston: St. Martin's Press, 1994, pp. 55–63.

Rizvi, Fazal, 'The Arts, Education and the Politics of Multiculturalism', in *Culture, Difference and the Arts*, ed. Sneja Gunew and Fazal Rizvi, St. Leonards, Australia: Allen and Unwin, 1994, pp. 54–68.

Rockefeller, Steven C., 'Comment', in *Multiculturalism and 'The Politics of Recognition': An Essay*, ed. Charles Taylor and Amy Gutmann, Princeton: Princeton University Press, 1992, pp. 87–98.

San Juan, E(piphanio), *Racial Formations/Critical Transformations: Articulations of Power in Ethnic and Racial Studies in the United States*, Atlantic Highlands: Humanities Press, 1992.

_____, *Hegemony and Strategies of Transgression: Essays in Cultural Studies and Comparative Literature*, Albany: State University New York Press, 1995.

Shohat, Ella, 'Notes on the Post-Colonial', *Social Text*, vols. 31–32, 1992, pp. 99–113.

Shohat, Ella, and Robert Stam, eds., *Multiculturalism, Postcoloniality, and Transnational Media*, New Brunswick: Rutgers University Press, 2003.

Spivak, Gayatri, *Death of a Discipline*, New York: Columbia University Press, 2003.

Srivastava, Aruna, 'Postcolonialism and Its Discontents', *Ariel*, vol. 26, no. 1, January 1995, pp. 12–17.

Sunder Rajan, Rajeshwari, 'The Third World Academic in Other Places or, the Postcolonial Intellectual Revisited', *Critical Inquiry*, vol. 23, 1997, pp. 596–616.

Taylor, Charles, *Multiculturalism and 'The Politics of Recognition': An Essay*, ed. Charles Taylor and Amy Gutmann, Princeton: Princeton University Press, 1992.

_____, *Multiculturalism: Examining the Politics of Recognition*, Charles Taylor and Amy Gutmann, eds., Princeton: Princeton University Press, 1994.

Žižek, Slavoj, 'Multiculturalism or the Cultural Logic of Multinational Capitalism', *New Left Review*, vol. 225, September–October 1997, pp. 28–51.

8

Comparative Literature in France

Anne Tomiche

Even though the history of French Comparative Literature has been well-documented (see for example Brunel, Pichois, Rousseau; Chevrel; Pageaux), it is worth reviewing some of its key aspects as they pertain to the development of the discipline and its current configuration.

In 1878, Nietzsche called the nineteenth century the 'era of comparison' ('das Zeitalter der Vergleichung', *Menschliches, Allzumenschliches*, 1878, aphorism 23). Indeed, by the time the philosopher published *Human, All too Human*, the idea and the term 'comparison' had grown very popular in Europe and in France—with the development, for example, of comparative anatomy and comparative zoology (under the impulse of scientists such as Lamarck, Étienne Geoffroy de Saint-Hilaire, Georges Cuvier) or of comparative law (in the wake of Montesquieu's *De l'esprit des lois*), of comparative grammar (with Franz Bopp, Jacob and Wilhelm Grimm) or comparative geography (with Karl Ritter and then Oscar Peschel), or of comparative political sciences (with Alexis de Tocqueville, Karl Marx, Émile Durkheim or Max Weber). In this context, it is not surprising if, at the end of the nineteenth century, literary studies would also promote comparison as a methodological approach, and Ferdinand Brunetière would write: 'If it is indeed interesting to compare the platypus and the kangaroo, the exact same reasons, stemming from the need to know, and, in order to know better, to compare, make it just as interesting, or rather necessary to compare Shakespeare's drama and Racine's tragedy or the lyricism of Byron and that of Victor Hugo' ('S'il est intéressant de comparer l'ornithorynque et le kanguroo, les mêmes raisons, absolument les mêmes, tirées du besoin de connaître, et pour mieux connaître, de comparer, rendent également intéressante, ou plutôt nécessaire la comparaison du drame de Shakespeare avec la tragédie de Racine, ou du lyrisme de Byron avec celui de

Victor Hugo' (Brunetière 31; unless indicated otherwise, all translations are mine).

The first French textbook using the expression 'Comparative Literature' in its title is François Noël's 1804–1827 *Cours de littérature comparée*: the term 'comparative' may be present in this title, but the approach merely consists in a juxtaposition of volumes devoted to various literatures, French and foreign (*Leçons françaises de littérature et de morale* in 1804, followed by: *Leçons latines, Leçons anglaises, Leçons italiennes, Leçons grecques, Leçons allemandes* ...). Then, the term appeared again in Abel Villemain's 1828–1829 lectures at the Sorbonne, where he presented a literary 'comparative picture' ('tableau comparé'), focusing on the reciprocal influences of France and England on each other and the influence of France in Italy during the eighteenth century. A few years later, Jean-Jacques Ampère promoted what he called the 'comparative study of literature', which he developed in his inaugural lecture at the Sorbonne in 1832. Ampère examined the connections between medieval French literature and foreign literatures. In 1835, Philarète Chasles dedicated his inaugural lecture at the Parisian Athénée to 'la littérature étrangère comparée'. Even though the term 'comparative' is present in each of these instances, it is not used in a way that a French scholar in Comparative Literature would today use it because juxtaposition is privileged over confrontation, and because comparisons are merely suggested and sound impressionistic, rather than developed and argued. Several elements in this nineteenth century enthusiasm for literary comparisons are nevertheless worth emphasizing since they explain the direction French Comparative Literature took in the twentieth century.

The first element to be noted is that the term 'comparative' is, in fact, used to signal an interest for *foreign* (i.e. non-French) literatures. In the wake of German Romanticism, more specifically Friedrich Schlegel's interest in a 'European literary science' and Goethe's notion of *Weltliteratur*, nineteenth-century Europe called into question the exclusively national approach to the study of literature. The desire 'to compare', in France and in Europe, has to be understood as an awareness, stemming from socio-economical changes in literary production and reception (development of translations, increase in book circulation, opening of sections devoted to foreign criticism in literary journals), that literature cannot be understood in strictly national terms. In the very Franco-centred academic institution, throughout the nineteenth century, French literature gradually ceased being considered as constituting the whole of literature: at the university level, several chairs in 'foreign literature' (in the singular, more rarely in the plural—French literature constituted one unified entity and Foreign literature, i.e. all literatures outside of France, constituted another) were created, the first one at the Sorbonne in 1830, held by Claude Fauriel, other ones in 1838, in Rennes, held by Xavier Marmier, in Bordeaux, Montpellier, Lyon, and Strasbourg (see Espagne). The notion of 'foreign literature' thus testifies to an opening of the notion of 'literature', an opening that introduced a triangular configuration in the way the institution understood such a notion of literature—classical, French, foreign. French literature (which remained the central focus) needed to be related not only to Greek and Latin classical literatures (as it always had), but now also to foreign literature. As the institutional distinction became stronger between Comparative Literature and chairs in diversified and specialized foreign literatures (at the Collège de France, a chair in Slavic literature was created in 1840, the following year one in literature of Southern Europe and another in German literature were opened), the importance granted to the notion of 'foreigness' (*l'étranger*), i.e. to the confrontation with what is foreign, remained one of the defining elements of the discipline.

The change in official denomination—from 'littérature étrangère' to 'littérature comparée'—occurred at the beginning of the twentieth century. Institutionally, the first chair in Comparative Literature was created in Lyon in 1896, where Joseph Texte was appointed, followed by Fernand Baldensperger. A *charge de cours* in Comparative Literature was created at the Sorbonne in 1910 for Baldensperger, while another chair was created in Strasbourg in 1919 and then at the Sorbonne in 1925. Beginning in 1925, Paul Hazard held the first 'chair in the history of Comparative Literatures of Southern Europe and Latin America' ('chaire d'histoire des littératures comparées de l'Europe méridionale et de l'Amérique latine') at the Collège de France. In 1921, with Baldensperger, Hazard created the *Revue de littérature comparée*, and then a collection, the 'Bibliothèque de la Revue de littérature comparée' (which, by 1939, included more than 120 volumes). The *Revue de littérature comparée* has long been and still is the most important French scholarly journal in Comparative Literature.

The second element that might be stressed in this survey of the institutionalization of Comparative Literature in France is that the form first taken by this interest towards '*l'étranger*' has been the study of sources and influences, the study of 'factual' relations and exchanges. After dominating the field throughout the first half of the twentieth century, this approach, considered to be too directly causal, has been replaced by reception studies; a focus on 'cultural transfers' has replaced the emphasis previously placed on factual influences. In fact, as early in the twentieth century as in

Virginia Woolf's *To the Lighthouse* (1927), the study of influences is used to caricature the young scholar in Comparative Literature, Charles Tansley, whose thesis topic varies between 'the influence of something upon somebody' and 'the influence of somebody upon something'. Until the 1960s, the specificity of French comparative reception studies and, more generally, of French Comparative Literature can, however, be traced to French comparative literature's original emphasis on questions of sources, influences, and factual relations. Hence the form often taken by early comparative studies in France—'Victor Hugo et l'Espagne', 'Stendhal et l'Italie', 'Stendhal et l'Angleterre', 'Giraudoux et l'Allemagne', 'Balzac et le monde slave', 'Madame de Staël et la Suisse', 'Leopardi et la France', 'T.S. Eliot et la France', 'Les romantiques portugais et l'Allemagne' . . . or, when the preposition that indicates the comparative relation is not 'and', it is 'in': 'Marivaux en Allemagne', 'Boileau en Hollande', 'Michelet en Italie', 'La culture française en Russie', 'Le goût chinois en France' . . . . The introduction in the designation of the discipline of the adjective 'general' marks an evolution away from such exclusively binary topics and from an exclusive focus on influences and relations. This shift tended to include more general and global approaches to literary phenomena: in the early 1970s 'littérature générale et comparée' becomes the official designation of the discipline and the French Society of Comparative Literature, founded in 1956 under the name of *Société Nationale Française de Littérature Comparée*, became the *Société Française de Littérature Générale et Comparée* in 1973.

The third element that needs to be stressed is that the development of Comparative Literature as an academic discipline in France cannot be dissociated from the emergence and the development of the concept of *lettres modernes*, i.e. the study of literature considered less from the point of view of its relations to classical literature (*lettres classiques*) than from the point of view of its relations to modern languages. Historically speaking, it was the creation, in 1959, of the *agrégation de lettres modernes* with two examinations focusing specifically on Comparative Literature (as opposed to the *agrégation de lettres classiques*, with examinations in Greek and Latin) that gave Comparative Literature its strong institutional status in the curriculum. Because the *agrégation de lettres modernes*—the examination required to teach at the high school level and strongly recommended for teaching at the university level—includes two major examinations in Comparative Literature, one written and one oral, and because the entire curriculum of studies in literature is conceived as a preparation for the *agrégation*, Comparative Literature is a mandatory component for French literature students throughout their studies. Courses in Comparative

Literature on the undergraduate level—for the *licence*, which covers the first three years of studies—can be varied in terms of number and content. Depending on the institution, a Comparative Literature course may be mandatory in the first semester of the first year of undergraduate studies or it can be mandatory only in the second year. Comparative Literature courses usually tend to be organized around the study of literary genres (for example the picaresque novel, the fantastic, theatre during the Baroque, etc.), of literary myths (Faust, Oedipus, Phaedra, etc.), or they deal with the relations between literature and the other arts such as cinema, painting, or music. The goal of such courses at this level is to introduce students to the main currents of European and extra-European literature. Texts are studied in French translation, but some universities make it mandatory to also study one of the texts of the corpus in its original language. In terms of its presence in the undergraduate curriculum, Comparative Literature is thus present and established, even if the number of mandatory courses in the discipline is rather limited compared to the number of other courses required. Students interested in Comparative Literature can choose optional courses in the field. No university delivers a *licence* (the equivalent of a B.A.) in Comparative Literature. At best, Comparative Literature constitutes a *parcours* (a minor) within a *licence de lettres modernes*. For students in foreign languages, visual arts, art history, or other fields in the humanities, Comparative Literature can be optional courses, but the situation concerning the possibility and the number of such options varies from institution to institution.

At the level of the Master of Arts degree, students can specialize in Comparative Literature. The nature and the number of courses they have to take vary depending on the institution, but the comparative nature of their Master of Arts degree depends mainly on the subject of their thesis and on their supervisor. In terms of courses required to complete a Master of Arts degree, the importance given to specifically Comparative Literature courses varies, with each university offering a unique set of combinations. Some Master of Arts degrees are entirely comparative in focus and content while others offer only a comparative component. Besides the courses that a Master of Arts student must take, he/she also has to write two theses (one in the M.A. first year and another one in the second year, usually between 60 and 100 pages long). Some institutions have brought down the required number of theses to only one, defended at the end of the second year of master studies. These master's theses constitute a student's first serious piece of academic research and the second thesis often forms the basis for a doctoral dissertation. At the doctoral level, dissertations in Comparative Literature encompass a broad range of subjects and languages, examined either in a diachronic perspective or with a focus on a given period. A working knowledge of the languages represented within the chosen literary corpus is a requisite, as all the texts from the corpus must be quoted in the original language and analysis must be based on the original versions. After approximately four or five years, the student submits a dissertation of an average length of 350 to 700 pages, which is then defended in front of a panel of three to five professors.

In his contribution to the 2006 ACLA report on the state of the discipline in the United States, Haun Saussy wrote: 'Comparative literature . . . has never been better received in the American university. The premises and protocols characteristic of our discipline are now the daily currency of coursework, publishing, hiring, and coffee-shop discussion' (p. 3). Such a statement could not be truer in France today. Authors and critics who wrote in 'foreign languages' are indeed taught in departments of French; 'interdisciplinarity' is a keyword in most projects and grant proposals. Comparative teaching is present in a number of courses in departments other than those wearing the label of 'Comparative Literature'. For example, in a context of globalization and of a general decrease in the number of students enrolling in literature departments, the very recent past has seen the creation in many universities of world literature courses. These classes are meant to consist of courses in general education for students in literature but also attract students in other disciplines (psychology, education, history . . .). At the same time, though, as Saussy pointed out, 'this victory brings little in the way of tangible rewards to the discipline' (p. 4). Indeed, the above-mentioned world literature courses may be taught by teachers in Comparative Literature or they may not; and such courses are listed as 'transdisciplinary courses' rather than as courses in Comparative Literature. In fact, for Comparative Literature as a discipline, the difficulties and the dangers of such a paradoxical situation are high: they are institutional as well as intellectual, calling into question the very specificity of the discipline and of Comparative Literature programmes. From an institutional point of view, as long as the *agrégation de lettres modernes* remains, the presence and the status of Comparative Literature in the curriculum of French studies is probably not going to be at risk.

There are approximately 200 faculty members of Comparative Literature—both as *maîtres de conférence* and as *professeurs*—in France. *Maîtres de conférences* and *professeurs* are tenured positions, but *maîtres de conférence* have not taken the *habilitation à diriger des recherches*, which is required in order to supervise doctoral research. At the end of the

1980s, the *doctorat d'état* ceased to exist. In order to become a *maître de conférences*, one needs a *doctorat nouveau régime* while to become a *professeur* the *habilitation à diriger des recherches* is required. Non-tenured faculty (teaching assistants, adjunct faculty) are also likely to teach Comparative Literature courses. *Maîtres de conférence* and *professeurs* are called *enseignant-chercheurs*, meaning that they are both teachers and researchers. They most frequently conduct research in a research centre of their university. Most Comparative Literature research centres in France are not exclusively composed of Comparative Literature faculty but, rather, gather specialists in Comparative Literature, as well as in French or foreign literatures. Only a rather limited number of research centres, at large institutions, are entirely devoted to Comparative Literature. Research centres are evaluated every four or five years and the financial support they receive depends on this evaluation. Until recently, research centres were financially supported directly by the Ministère de l'Enseignement Supérieur. The situation has changed with a law, voted in 2007 and implemented gradually between 2008 and 2012. This law has granted so-called 'autonomy' to universities. University presidents and boards now have the power to use however they wish the funding given to their institution by the Ministry: they can, for example, decide not to renew positions, transfer a position from one discipline to another, and/or decide to give a research centre more or less funding based on the results of the evaluation. Consequently, the French academic system, wherein all universities used to be government-run, is changing as universities are now in the hands of the presidents and their boards. This shift in governance has also gone hand in hand with a decrease in governmental funding to the universities. The impact of this new system on the status of research, scholars, and teachers in Comparative Literature, as well as in other fields, cannot yet be fully measured. What is certain at this point, is that since the implementation of the law on governance an important number of French universities are undergoing financial difficulties and that all of them have implemented budgetary cuts at the various levels of research funding and teaching-lines.

In terms of organization, the discipline of Comparative Literature in France is represented and supported by the *Société Française de Littérature Générale et Comparée* (SFLGC), similar to the American Comparative Literature Association, the Comparative Literature Association of India, the Japanese Comparative Literature Association, etc. Since its creation in 1956, in Bordeaux where it held its first Conference, the SFLGC organizes a conference each year except when the International Association of Comparative Literature/Association Internationale de

Littérature Comparée (ICLA/AILC)—whose legal residence is in Paris—holds its triannual congress. These conferences are always attended by a large number of Comparative Literature specialists from France and abroad. In 2013, the SFLGC consisted of approximately 350 members and served as the official interlocutor with the government when dealing with matters pertaining to the discipline. The Association's website includes a directory of French Comparative Literature specialists, a list of Comparative Literature research centres, announcements of new publications in the field, calls for papers, etc., and a web-based library with selected articles on a diversity of issues relevant to the field such as, for example, on the notion of comparison in its relation to the discipline (Pageaux), the articulations between Comparative Literature, philosophy and psychoanalysis (Dumoulié), the relations between comparative studies and postcolonialism (Moura), between myth and fiction (Gély), between literature and science (Robineau-Weber), literature and history (McIntosch-Varjabédian; Ksiazenicer-Matheron) or literature and music (Berthommier; Finck; Picard). The SFLGC also publishes and distributes to all its members an internal quarterly—*Feuille d'Information Trimestrielle*, and a yearly edited volume in the collection *Poétiques comparatistes* (see Arnoux-Farnoux and Hermetet; Clavaron; Duprat and Lavocat; Gély; Montandon, *Littérature*; Parizet; Poulin; Tomiche and Zoberman). Each volume deals with one of the theoretical aspects of Comparative Literature in France and frames the field within an international context (for example, the relations between literature and anthropology, between literature and gendered identities, between culture and fiction).

Several more or less global assessments of the discipline have been published in the past twenty years—Yves Chevrel (see *L'Information littéraire* [1992]; *Comparative Literature World Wide* [1997]), the volumes edited by Sylvie Ballestra-Puech and Jean-Marc Moura (see *Le Comparatisme aujourd'hui* [1999]), by Jean Bessière and Daniel-Henri Pageaux (see *Perspectives comparatistes* [1999]), by Pascal Dethurens and Olivier Bonnerot (see *Fin d'un millénaire* [2000]), or the sixth edition of Yves Chevrel's *La Littérature comparée* (first published in 1989). To date, the SFLGC has published two reports describing the current status of the discipline. The first report was edited by Daniel-Henri Pageaux and served as a reference guide in France for many years (see Pageaux *La Recherche*). More recently, in the context of the celebration of its 50th anniversary the SFLGC organized another assessment that appeared in 2007 (see Tomiche *La Recherche*). Insofar as this report purports to draw a picture of the various areas of Comparative Literature both in a national context (how has this or that area of scholarship evolved within France?) and in an international perspective (what relations does this or that area of scholarship have with similar domains in other cultures?), it can be read in conjunction with the 2006 report published by the American Comparative Literature Association (see Saussy). What such a report showed and what remains true in 2013 is that next to certain territories, which have evolved but can be considered as 'founding territories' for the discipline in France, others have, more or less slowly, emerged to expand the frontiers of French Comparative Literature. All these territories, whether older or more recent, define their specificity either in terms of their object of study (the objects of myth studies are literary myths, those of translation studies are literary translations . . .) or in terms of their theoretical and methodological approach (historical poetics or the study of relations between literature and philosophy, to take only two examples, designate a specific approach to texts rather than a given object). Obviously the two kinds of definitions cannot be separated and comparative approaches should engage both the construction of their objects and their theoretical choices and assumptions.

With regard to the French tradition of Comparative Literature, three domains constitute the 'founding grounds' of the discipline: myth studies, image studies, and reception studies. Less prominent in the Anglo-American tradition than in the French tradition (with the exception of Northrop Frye and Theodor Ziolkowski), myth studies in France, and more specifically the study of Greek and Latin myths, owe their status to the historical importance of *lettres classiques* in literary studies and the manner in which French literature has traditionally been linked to the classical tradition, i.e. to Greek and Latin literature. As developed by and following Raymond Trousson's and Pierre Brunel's work, myth studies have long been considered a prominent area of study in French-language Comparative Literature. Myth studies also represent an important area of study in Swiss French (e.g. Heidmann; Steiner) and in Belgian French Comparative Literature (e.g. Couloubaritsis and Ost; Klimis). One of the most prominent representative in the field in France today, Véronique Gély distinguishes three directions of research on literary myths: (1) 'mytho-criticism' (*mythocritique*), which uses myths as critical and hermeneutic tools in order to read literary texts, and which operates on the assumption that myths pre-exist texts (see also Chauvin; Eissen and Engelibert), (2) studies devoted to specific myths or mythological figures (see for example Backès, *Oreste*; Ballestra-Puech; Dancourt; Foucrier), and (3) 'mytho-poetics' (*mythopoétique*), which, rather than consider myths to be exterior to texts, focuses on the question of how texts 'make' myths and how myths 'make' texts (see for example Brunel; Ballestra-Puech).

Two further areas of research, linked to myth studies even if they extend beyond the above-mentioned approaches, have developed in the past fifteen to twenty years. The domain pertaining to the investigation of the relations between literature and the Bible was initiated by Robert Couffignal in the late 1960s and then developed further by Danièle Chauvin. It covers today three types of approach: studies of Biblical myths (e.g. Hussher; Léonard-Roques; Parizet; Wajeman), the analysis of Biblical references or quotations in a given text (a type of approach that does not constitute a field of study in itself but is explored whenever there is a Biblical reference in a text), and the investigation of an author's relation to the Bible (see for example Couffignal on Apollinaire, Chauvin on Blake or Prigent on Huysmans). The second domain, related but not limited to myth studies, concerns the investigation of the Greek and Roman heritage, an investigation that can take several paths: the study of images of Antiquity either at a given moment in time or throughout several centuries (see for example David-de Palacio), the analysis of a writer's relation to the Latin language, the investigation of the evolution of a given literary genre since Antiquity (see for example Humbert-Mougin; Plazenet), or the exploration of the reception of a given work or of a given author from Antiquity to the present (see for example Backès, *L'Iliade*; Stead).

The second 'founding' domain in the French tradition of Comparative Literature is image studies (*imagologie*), going back to the work of Jean-Marie Carré (e.g. *Images d'Amérique*) and Marius-François Guyard (e.g. *Littérature comparée*), and then Michel Cadot (e.g. 'Les Études d'images') and Daniel-Henri Pageaux (e.g. *Littératures*). As defined by Pageaux, a literary image is 'a set of ideas concerning what is foreign, a set of ideas caught in a joint process of socialization and of becoming-literary' ('un ensemble d'idées sur l'étranger prises dans un processus de littérarisation mais aussi de socialisation') (*La Littérature* 60). The study of images thus understood does not aim at evaluating the more or less important degree of similarity between the image and the 'real', but aims at analysing the conditions of the production of such images and the distance between the culture that produces the image and the culture that is represented by it. This field of research has been explored by scholars including Jean-Marc Moura, Alain Montandon, Yves Clavaron, and Bertrand Westphal. Westphal develops studies in 'geo-criticism' (*géocritique*), i.e. image studies which focus on the representation of space rather than on the representation of humanity.

While image studies in France until recently focused on relations in the West or relations solely within Europe, Moura has opened the field to new geographic horizons including the image of the 'third world' in French contemporary literature and exoticism in Western literature. More recently, research programmes focusing on the relations East/West and on 'Orientalisms' have developed (see Yves Clavaron on modern and contemporary literature; Anne Duprat on pre-eighteenth century). Their work is relevant with regard to postcolonial studies, a field of research that already has a fairly long history in the United States, where it has developed since the late 1970s (with the work of, e.g. Edward W. Said, Gayatri Chakravorty Spivak, and Homi K. Bhabha, among others), but that started only more recently to develop in France, in the late 1990s, especially in the context of Francophone studies (see for example D'hulst and Moura; Bessière and Moura). Due to its history and political origins, the context of Francophone studies did not coincide with that of postcolonial studies as they developed in the United States—which explains, at least in part, why postcolonial studies took so long to reach France. Created by Onésime Reclus in 1880, at a time when the Empire was expanding and when the *Alliance française* was created in order to increase the French population in the colonies and spread the language, the term 'francophone' is historically part of the colonial enterprise. *Francophonie*, as an institutionalized notion, appears later, during the period of de-colonization, in the 1960s and can be interpreted as a means for France to compensate for the loss of the Empire. The political and ideological assumptions that govern the notion of *francophonie* rely on the mythical idea that French is universal and the language of human rights and of freedom. Because they insist on a specificity linked to France (areas colonized or de-colonized by France), because they focus the definition of the notion of *francophonie* on the question of language and because they consequently encompass very dissimilar areas (North Africa and the Carribeans) rather envision think historically the effects of colonialism and of its discursive power beyond linguistic and regional specificities of European colonization, Francophone studies have often been seen as an ultimate neocolonial enterprise. Recent research has nevertheless developed in order to rethink the possible relations between Francophone studies and postcolonial theory (see Fordsick and Murphy; Murdoch and Donadey).

The third 'founding' area of French Comparative Literature, reception studies, has developed in the wake of a long-standing tradition of studies in literary influences and has gradually replaced it. The term 'reception' entered French critical terminology in the 1970s, as a result of the introduction in France of Hans Robert Jauss's and Wolfgang Iser's work. While the 'French School' of reception studies, as developed by Yves

Chevrel (see for example *Œuvres*) and Claude de Grève, and more recently by Daniel Mortier or Anne-Rachel Hermetet, certainly owes much to the German school, the French school distinguishes itself from the Konstanz school in at least two respects: first, it considers real readers much more than implicit ones, thus relying on critical tools borrowed from such fields as the sociology of literature or the history of reading and second, it is less interested in a theoretical approach and in constructing theoretical models than in case studies. Against René Wellek's and Austin Warren's position in *Theory of Literature*, asserting that there is no methodological difference between a study devoted to Shakespeare in France and a study devoted to Shakespeare in eighteenth-century England, Chevrel argued for the specificity of the critical discourse elaborated on a foreign text. Such a position, which prevails today in French comparative reception studies, stems from the fact that critical discourses on foreign texts need to rely on a specific object, i.e. translations, which, in turn introduce a specific dimension absent from critical discourses on literary objects written in the same language as the critical discourse itself. While it has been for a long time only a privileged tool for reception studies, the analysis of translation and translated texts (*traductologie*) has become an autonomous field of investigation within Comparative Literature since the mid-1990s, and has developed in two directions: the investigation of the poetics of translation (be it the analysis of a number of different translations of a given text through time or the analysis of different translations of a text at a given moment in time) and the analysis of works by specific translators or of the role translation plays in works by specific writers (see for example Dayre, *L'Absolu*; D'hulst; Lombez; Marty; Oséki-Dépré). One of the most important works-in-progress to-date in the field consists of a series of volumes devoted to the history of translations written in French (see Chevrel and Masson).

Fields of studies that have developed more recently include the exploration of the relations among the various arts: relations between literature and music (see for example Backès *Musique*; Cannone; Claudon *La Musique*; Faivre-Dupaigre; Locatelli; Rallo-Ditche), literature and opera (Claudon, *Dictionnaire*; Picard; Rallo-Ditche *Opéras, Passions*), literature and painting or text and image (see for example Hénin; Labarthe-Postel; Wajeman), literature and cinema (see for example Cléder; Murcia), literature and dance (see for example Ducrey; Montandon *Sociopoétique*, *Écrire*), and literature and architecture (see for example Prungnaud). Studies concerned with 'literature and the other arts' have gradually taken more and more importance, especially since the 1986 Congress of the SFLGC that was devoted to the theme 'Art and Literature'. They are not exclusive to Comparative Literature since they are also explored by other disciplines such as visual arts, film studies, music studies, media studies, or studies in national literatures. The issue is, thus, that of the specifically comparative dimension brought to the study of these questions: such a dimension stems both from the corpus chosen (with the presence of several linguistic and cultural traditions) and from the method(s) used (with privilege given to broad spaces and long duration in order to confront diachronically, in large cultural and linguistic areas, the relations among the different forms of artistic expression). The fact that an interdisciplinary approach to the interactions between the arts may not be the exclusive territory of institutionally labelled 'comparatist' scholars testifies to the importance of discussing and re-defining the borders of the various territories that constitute the Humanities in France—territories that are institutionally very rigidly delineated—and of re-thinking the relation between the 'general', indeed 'global', dimension of such studies (be they comparative or not) and their more specialized dimension (whether it is comparatist or pertains to the study of French literatures or of other national literatures).

Another more recently developed domain engages research on children's literature and popular literature (mainstream novels, detective stories, science fiction, fantasy, etc. [see for example Ferré and Besson 'La littérature']). While research on children's literature has developed following Jean Perrot's and Isabelle Nières-Chevrel's work, this interest has gone hand in hand with an increase in the number of courses taught on subjects related to children's literature and, consequently, in the number of university positions allocated to teach such courses. Scholarship on detective novels, fantastic literature, or science fiction existed already in the 1990s (see for example Boyer; Bozetto; Mellier) and recent developments include work on Tolkien and the genre of fantasy (see for example Besson, *D'Asimov*, *La Fantasy*; Ferré), as well as a dialogue with Anglophone cultural studies (see for example Chalard-Fillaudeau). In that vein, the 2008 SFLGC conference was devoted to the investigation of the relations—convergences, as well as differences—between cultural studies in their Anglophone versions and the developing field in France that deals with popular culture and the investigation of frontier zones between 'high' and 'low' culture (see for example Leiva, Hubier, Chardin, Souiller). While in the foreword to his 1983 report, Pageaux announced a 'break-through' in two distinct areas of investigation, the first one focusing on the relations between literature and other artistic and cultural activities and the second one focusing on the study of domains 'bordering' literature (such as children's literature and popular literature), these two fields of scholarship can certainly no longer be considered 'break-throughs': today they are fully integrated in scholarly research and curricula.

Yet a further area of study that has developed in the last ten or fifteen years can be seen in the theoretical study of the relations between literature and other disciplines in the humanities and social sciences including philosophy, history, (cultural) anthropology, etc. Beyond the question of the philosophical or ideological dimension of a text or of a literary movement—a question which bears on the history of ideas (*histoire des idées* and *histoire des mentalités*) and that has a long tradition in French Comparative Literature (see for example Chardin; Chevrel, 'Littérature'; Souiller, *La Littérature baroque*, *Calderon*)—recent research explores relations between literature and philosophy (see for example Baron; Dumoulié; Manzari; Tomiche; Tomiche and Zard). Such relations are investigated in at least two complementary directions: the confrontation between philosophers (and philosophical systems) and writers (and literary representations and constructions)—for example Nietzsche and Artaud (e.g. Dumoulié), De Quincey and Kant (e.g. Dayre) or Nietzsche in France (e.g. Le Rider)—and the investigation of the literary dimension of philosophical writings or of the stakes of philosophical discourses on literature. If, owing to structuralism's rejection of the historical dimension of textuality, research on the articulations between literature and history did not constitute an important field of research until the beginning of the 1980s, it has since then developed considerably (e.g. Morel; Bouju; Coquio). Scholarship in this area has taken at least three directions: the investigation of the poetics of history (i.e. the investigation of the specifically literary means used to write history in relation and as opposed to the means of historiography), the confrontation between the way literary history constructs literary periods and the way general historiography divides history into periods, and a more sociological investigation of the inscription of literature within the historicized social field (i.e. the investigation of the relations between the symbolic field of literature and historical temporality and the investigation of the possibilities, for the actors of the literary field, to act upon history with specifically literary means). Many recent collected volumes edited by scholars in Comparative Literature have undertaken such analyses (see for example Bessière and Daros; Bessière and Sinopoli; Bouju; Bouju, Gefen, Hautcoeur, Macé; Coquio). The development of a critical dialogue between literature and anthropology has been and is crucial in the works of major figures in French Comparative Literature (see for example Daros; Montandon; Pageaux; Souiller). Recently, the relationship between literature and science has sparked the interest and attention of a number of scholars in Comparative Literature and research programmes have developed in that area (see for example Baron; Dahan-Gaïda; Weber). Similarly, research on fiction and fictionality has developed following the initiative of Françoise Lavocat's work. Borrowing for their theoretical and epistemological foundations in analytical philosophy and in the theories of possible worlds, Comparative Literature scholars interrogate the notion of fiction and its operating modalities (see for example Duprat and Lavocat).

What is striking in the evolution of Comparative Literature in France in the past fifteen years is that, while approaches such as post-colonial studies, gender studies, and cultural studies already have a long history in Anglophone scholarship, they have only recently received attention in France. The irony here lies in the importance that so-called 'French theory' had in the early developments of postcolonial and gender studies in the Anglophone world. But postcolonial approaches need to find their way in relation to Francophone studies; gender studies, if they have been very present in disciplines such as sociology since the late 1960s, have only become slowly integrated in literature departments in France; and cultural studies has met resistance from those arguing for the specificity of literary objects and for the need for literature departments to study literature. However, these different approaches are now clearly part of the current disciplinary reconfiguration of Comparative Literature in general. The long-standing tradition of image studies has opened up its canon, its objects and its inquires to encompass postcolonial concerns and approaches. Discussions of gender construction and representation are elaborated in a dialogue with American gender studies (i.e. from feminist studies to queer studies) (see for example Tomiche and Zoberman; Banoun, Tomiche and Zapata). Creating a dialogue between the French traditions of historical investigation (embodied by the École des Annales) and of historical and cultural anthropology on the one hand and Anglophone cultural studies on the other, French Comparative Literature is defining its own specific territory of *études culturelles* (see for example Leiva, Hubier, Chardin, Souiller). One of the specificities of the French approach to postcolonial, gender or cultural studies can be seen in its emphasis on the study of literature proper and in its assumption of the specificity of literary objects within the cultural field. Finally, in the double context of the growth of the European Union and the development of a globalized world, one of the issues at stake—politically and ideologically—within French comparative studies today is the articulation between the concept of world literature, a concept that such French Comparative

Literature specialists as René Étiemble already promoted in the early 1970s before it was promoted and discussed in the United States by David Damrosch, Rey Chow or Franco Moretti, and the concept of a European literature within the context of Comparative Literature (see for example Casanova; Chevrel, *Précis*; Didier; Souiller and Troubetzkoy; Tomiche, 'Littérature européenne'; Troubetzkoy).

REFERENCES

Arnoux-Farnoux, Lucile and Anne-Rachel Hermetet, eds., *Questions de réception*, Nîmes: Lucie Éditions pour SFLGC, 2009.

Backès, Jean-Louis, *Musique et littérature: Essai de poétique comparée*, Paris: PU de France, 1994.

———, *Oreste*, Paris: Bayard, 2005.

———, *L'Iliade d'Homère*, Paris: Gallimard, 2006.

Ballestra-Puech, Sylvie, *Les Parques: Essai sur les figures féminines du destin dans la littérature occidentale*, Toulouse: Éditions Interuniversitaires du Sud, 1999.

———, *Métamorphoses d'Arachné: L'Artiste en araignée dans la littérature occidentale*, Genève: Droz, 2006.

Ballestra-Puech, Sylvie and Jean-Marc Moura, eds., *Le Comparatisme aujourd'hui*, Lille: Presses de l'Université Charles-de-Gaulle Lille 3, 1999.

Banoun, Bernard, Anne Tomiche and Mónica Zapata, eds., *Fiction(s) du masculin: Discours et représentations des masculinités dans les littératures occidentales*, Paris: Classiques Garnier, 2014.

Baron, Christine, *La Pensée du dehors*, Paris: Harmattan, 2007.

———, *La Littérature et son autre*, Paris: Harmattan, 2008.

Bessière, Jean and Philippe Daros, eds., *Instaurer la mémoire*, Roma: Bulzoni, 2005.

Bessière, Jean and Jean-Marc Moura, eds., *Littératures postcoloniales et francophonie*, Paris: Honoré Champion, 2001.

Bessière, Jean and Daniel-Henri Pageaux, eds., *Perspectives comparatistes*, Paris: Honoré Champion, 1999.

Bessière, Jean and Franca Sinopoli, eds., *Histoire, mémoire, réécritures et relectures littéraires*, Roma: Bulzoni, 2005.

Besson, Anne, *D'Asimov à Tolkien: Cycles et séries dans la littérature de genre*, Paris: CNRS Éditions, 2004.

———, *La Fantasy*, Paris: Klincksieck, 2007.

Besson, Anne and Vincent Ferré, 'La littérature de grande diffusion', in *La Recherche en littérature générale et comparée en France en 2007: Bilans et perspectives*, ed. Anne Tomiche and Karl Zieger, Valenciennes: PU de Valenciennes, 2007.

Bouju, Emmanuel, ed., *L'Engagement littéraire*, Rennes: PU de Rennes, 2005.

Bouju, Emmanuel, Alexandre Gefen, Guiomar Hautcoeur, and Marielle Macé, eds., *Littérature et exemplarité*, Rennes: PU de Rennes, 2007.

Boyer, Michel-Alain, *La Paralittérature*, Paris: PU de France, 1992.

———, *Poétiques du roman d'aventure*, Nantes: Cécile Defaut, 2004.

Bozetto, Roger, *Le Fantastique dans tous ses états*, Aix-en-Provence: PU de Provence, 2001.

———, *Fantastique et mythologies modernes*, Aix-en-Provence: PU de Provence, 2007.

Brunel, Pierre, ed., *Mythes et littérature*, Paris: PU de Paris-Sorbonne, 1994.

———, ed., *L'Étude des mythes en littérature comparée: Bilans et perspectives de recherche*, Paris: PU de Paris-Sorbonne, 2005.

Brunel, Pierre, Claude Pichois and André-Michel Rousseau, *Qu'est-ce que la littérature comparée?*, Paris: Armand Colin, 1996.

Brunetière, Ferdinand, *L'Évolution des genres dans l'histoire de la littérature* [1890], 6th edn., 2 vols., Paris: Hachette, 1914.

Cadot, Michel, 'Les Études d'images', in *La Recherche en litterature générale et comparée en France: Aspects et problèms*, ed. Daniel-Henri Pageaux, Paris: Société Française de Littérature Générale et Comparée, 1983, pp. 71–86.

Cannone, Belinda, *Musique et littérature au XVIIIe siècle*, Paris: PU de France, 1998.

———, *Philosophies de la musique, 1752–1789*, Paris: Klincksieck, 1990.

Carré, Jean-Marie, *Images d'Amérique*, Lyon: H. Lardanchet, 1927.

Casanova, Pascale, *The World Republic of Letters* [1999], tr. M.B. DeBevoise, Cambridge: Harvard University Press, 2007.

Casasus, Gilbert and Sabine Haupt, eds., *Comparer? Vergleichen? Komparatistische Wissenschaften im Vergleich/La Comparaison dans les sciences*, Berlin: Lit, 2011.

Chalard-Fillaudeau, Anne, ed., *Études et sciences de la culture: Une résistance française?*, Special issue of *Revue d'Études Culturelles*, vol. 5, 2010.

Chardin, Philippe, *Le Roman de la conscience malheureuse*, Genève: Droz, 1992.

Chauvin, Danièle, *L'Œuvre de Blake: Apocalypse et transfiguration*, Grenoble: ELLUG, 1992.

———, ed., *Questions de mythocritique*, Paris: Imago, 2005.

Chevrel, Yves, *La Littérature comparée* [1989], 6th edn., Paris: PU de France, 2009.

———, 'Douze ans de travaux français en littérature générale et comparée (1981–1992): esquisse d'un bilan', *L'Information littéraire*, vol. 44, no. 4, 1992, pp. 3–12.

———, 'Littérature (générale) et comparée: La Situation de la France', in *Comparative Literature World Wide: Issues and Methods/La Littérature comparée dans le monde: Questions et methods*, ed. Tania Franco Carvalhal, Porto Alegre: L&PM Editores, 1997, pp. 53–79.

———, 'Littérature comparée et histoire des mentalités: Concurrence ou collaboration?' in *Comparative Literature Now: Theories and Practice/La Littérature comparée à l'heure actuelle: Théories et réalisation*, ed. Steven Tötösy de Zepetnek, Milan V. Dimić and Irene Sywenky, Paris: Honoré Champion, 1999, pp. 51–63.

———, ed., *Œuvres et Critiques*, Special issue of *Méthodologie des études de réception: Perspectives comparatistes*, vol. 11, no. 2, 1986, pp. 1–234.

———, 'Peut-on écrire une histoire de la littérature européenne?' in *Précis de littérature européenne*, ed. Béatrice Didier, Paris: PU de France, 1998, pp. 19–36.

Chevrel, Yves and Jean-Yves Masson, eds., *Histoire des traductions en langue française*, Lagrasse: Verdier. The first volume, devoted to the nineteenth century (1815–1914), edited by Yves Chevrel, Lieven D'hulst, and Christine Lombez came out in 2012.

Claudon, Francis, *Dictionnaire de l'opéra comique français*, Bern: Peter Lang, 1995.

———, *La Musique des Romantiques*, Paris: PU de France, 1992.

Clavaron, Yves, *Le Génie de l'Italie: Géographie littéraire de l'Italie à partir des littératures américaine, britannique et française 1890–1940*, Paris: Connaissances et Savoirs, 2006.

———, *Inde et Indochine: E.M. Forster et M. Duras au miroir de l'Asie*, Paris: Honoré Champion, 2001.

———, ed., *Études postcoloniales*, Nîmes: Lucie Éditions pour SFLGC, 2011.

Cléder, Jean, ed., 'Ce que le cinéma fait à la littérature (et réciproquement)', *Fabula: Littérature, Histoire, Théorie*, no. 2, 2006, <http://www.fabula.org/lht/2/>.

Coquio, Catherine, ed., *L'Histoire trouée: Négation et témoignage*, Nantes: Atalante, 2003.

———, ed., *Parler des camps, penser les génocides*, Paris: Albin Michel, 1999.

Couffignal, Robert, *L'Inspiration biblique dans l'œuvre de Guillaume Apollinaire*, Paris: Minard, 1966.

Couloubaritsis, Lambros and François Ost, eds., *Antigone et la résistance civile*, Bruxelles: Ousia, 2004.

Dahan-Gaïda, Laurence, *Musil. Savoir et fiction*, Vincennes: PU de Vincennes, 1994.

———, *Poétique de la science chez Botho Strauss*, Strasbourg: PU de Strasbourg, 2008.

Dancourt, Michèle, *Dédale et Icare: Métamorphoses d'un mythe*, Paris: CNRS Éditions, 2002.

Daros, Philippe, *L'Art comme action: Pour une approche anthropologique du fait littéraire*, Paris: Honoré Champion, 2012.

David-de Palacio, Marie-France, *Antiquité latine et décadence*, Paris: Honoré Champion, 2001.

———, *Reviviscences romaines: La Latinité au miroir de l'esprit fin-de-siècle*, Bern: Peter Lang, 2005.

Dayre, Eric, *L'Absolu comparé: Littérature et traduction*, Paris: Hermann, 2009.
———, *Les Proses du temps: Thomas De Quincey et la philosophie kantienne*, Paris: Honoré Champion, 2000.
Dethurens, Pascal and Olivier Bonnerot, eds., *Fin d'un millénaire: Rayonnement de la littérature comparée*, Strasbourg: PU de Strasbourg, 2000.
D'hulst, Lieven and Reine Meylaerts, *La Traduction dans les cultures plurilingues*, Arras: PU Artois, 2011.
D'hulst, Lieven and Jean-Marc Moura, eds., *Les Études littéraires francophones: État des lieux*, Lille: Presses de l'Université Charles-de-Gaulle Lille 3, 2000.
Didier, Béatrice, ed., *Précis de littérature européenne*, Paris: PU de France, 1998.
Ducrey, Guy, *Corps et graphies: Poétique de la danse et de la danseuse à la fin du XIXème siècle*, Paris: Honoré Champion, 1996.
———, *Tout pour les yeux: Littérature et spectacle autour de 1900*, Paris: PU de Paris Sorbonne, 2010.
Dumoulié, Camille, *Littérature et philosophie: Le gai savoir de la philosophie*, Paris: Armand Colin, 2002.
———, *Nietzsche et Artaud: Pour une éthique de la cruauté,* Paris: PU de France, 1992.
Duprat, Anne and Hédia Khadhar, eds., *Orient baroque/Orient classique: Variations du motif oriental dans les literatures d'Europe (XVIe-XVIIIe s.)*, Paris: Éditions Bouchène, 2010.
Duprat, Anne and Françoise Lavocat, eds., *Fictions et cultures*, Nîmes: Lucie Éditions pour SFLGC, 2010.
Duprat, Anne and Émilie Picherot, eds., *Récits d'Orient dans les littératures d'Europe (XVIe-XVIIe siècles)*, Paris: PU de Paris Sorbonne, 2008.
Eissen, Ariane and Jean-Paul Engélibert, eds., *La Dimension mythique de la littérature contemporaine*, Poitiers: La Licorne, 2000.
Espagne, Michel, *Le Paradigme de l'étranger: les chaires de littérature étrangère au XIXe siècle*, Paris: Éditions du Cerf, 1993.
Faivre-Dupaigre, Anne, *Poètes-musiciens: Cendrars, Mandelstam, Pasternak*, Rennes: PU de Rennes, 2006.
Ferré, Vincent, *Tolkien: Sur les rivages de la Terre du milieu*, Paris: Christian Bourgois, 2001.
———, ed., *Dictionnaire Tolkien*, Paris: CNRS Éditions, 2012.
Fordsick, Charles and David Murphy, eds., *Francophone Postcolonial Studies: A Critical Introduction*, London: Arnold, 2003.
Fordsick, Charles and David Murphy, eds., *Postcolonial Thought in the French-Speaking World*, Liverpool: Liverpool University Press, 2009.
Foucrier, Chantal, *Le Mythe littéraire de l'Atlantide (1800–1939)*, Grenoble: ELLUG, 2004.
Gély, Véronique, *La Nostalgie du moi: Écho dans la littérature européenne*, Paris: PU de France, 2000.
———, *L'Invention d'un mythe: Psyché: Allégorie et fiction du siècle de Platon au temps de La Fontaine*, Paris: Honoré Champion, 2006.

———, ed., *Enfance et fiction,* Nîmes: Lucie Éditions pour SFLGC, 2012.

Guyard, Marius-François, *La Littérature comparée* [1951], Paris: PU de France, 1978.

Heidmann, Ute, ed., *Poétiques comparées des mythes: De l'antiquité à la modernité,* Lausanne: Payot, 2003.

Hénin, Emmanuelle, *Ut pictura theatrum de la Renaissance italienne au classicisme,* Genève: Droz, 2003.

Humbert-Mougin, Sylvie, *Dionysos revisité: Les Tragiques grecs en France de Leconte de Lisle à Claudel,* Paris: Belin, 2003.

Hussher, Cécile, *L'Ange et la bête: Caïn et Abel dans la littérature,* Paris: Éditions du Cerf, 2005.

Iser, Wolfgang, *The Act of Reading: A Theory of Aesthetic Response,* Baltimore: The John Hopkins University Press, 1978.

Jauss, Hans Robert, *Toward an Aesthetic of Reception,* tr. Timothy Bahti, Minneapolis: University of Minnesota Press, 1982.

Klimis, Sophie, *Le Statut du mythe dans la poétique d'Aristote: Les fondements philosophiques de la tragédie,* Bruxelles: Ousia, 1997.

Labarthe-Postel, Judith, *Littérature et peinture dans le roman moderne,* Paris: L'Harmattan, 2002.

Leiva, Antonio Dominguez, Sébastien Hubier, Philippe Chardin and Didier Souiller, eds., *Études culturelles, anthropologie culturelle et comparatisme,* Neuilly-les-Dijon: Murmure, 2010.

Le Rider, Jacques, *Nietzsche en France, de la fin du XIXe siècle au temps présent,* Paris: PU de France, 1999.

Léonard-Roques, Véronique, *Caïn, figure de la modernité,* Paris: Honoré Champion, 2003.

Locatelli, Aude, *Littérature et musique au XXe siècle,* Paris: PU de France, 2001.

———, *Musique et littérature: Rencontres Sainte Cécile,* Aix-en-Provence: PU de Provence, 2011.

Lombez, Christine, *La Traduction de la poésie allemande en français dans la première moitié du XIXe siècle,* Tübingen: Niemeyer, 2009.

———, *Transactions secrètes: Philippe Jaccottet, poète et traducteur de Rilke et Hölderlin,* Arras: Artois PU, 2003.

———, ed., *Retraductions: De la Renaissance au XXIe siècle,* Nantes: Cécile Defaut, 2011.

Marty, Philippe, ed., *Eros traducteur,* special issue of *Loxias,* vol. 29, 2010, <http://revel.unice.fr/loxias/index.html?id=6073>.

Mellier, Denis, *L'Écriture de l'excès: Fiction fantastique et poétique de la terreur,* Paris: Honoré Champion, 1999.

———, *Les Écrans meurtriers: Essais sur les scènes spéculaires du thriller,* Liège: Céfal, 2001.

———, *La Littérature fantastique,* Paris: Seuil, 2000.

———, *Textes fantômes: Fantastique et autoréférence,* Paris: Kimé, 2001.

Montandon, Alain, ed., *L'Europe des politesses et le caractère des nations*, Clermont-Ferrand: PU Blaise Pascal, 1997.

———, ed., *Mœurs des uns, coutumes des autres: Les Français au regard de l'Europe: Une anthologie*, Clermont-Ferrand: PU Blaise Pascal, 1995.

———, ed., *Mœurs et images: Études d'imagologie européenne*, Clermont-Ferrand: PU Blaise Pascal, 1997.

Montandon, Alain, ed., *Écrire la danse*, Clermont-Ferrand: PU Blaise Pascal, 1999.

———, ed., *Le Livre de l'hospitalité: Accueil de l'étranger dans l'histoire et les cultures*, Paris: Bayard, 2004.

———, ed., *Littérature et anthropologie*, Nîmes: Lucie Éditions pour SFLGC, 2006.

———, ed., *Sociopoétique de la danse*, Paris: Anthropos, 1998.

Morel, Jean-Pierre, *Le Roman insupportable: L'Internationale littéraire et la France, 1920–1932*, Paris: Gallimard, 1986.

Moura, Jean-Marc, *Exotisme et lettres francophones*, Paris: PU de France, 2003.

———, *L'Europe littéraire et l'ailleurs*, Paris: PU de France, 1998.

———, *La Littérature des lointains: Histoire de l'exotisme européen au XXème siècle*, Paris: Honoré Champion, 1998.

———, *Littératures francophones et théories postcoloniales*, Paris: PU de France, 1999.

Murcia, Claude, *Nouveau roman, nouveau cinéma*, Bruxelles: Nathan, 1998.

Murdoch, Adlai and Anne Donadey, eds., *Postcolonial Theory and Francophone Literary Studies*, Gainesville: University Press Florida, 2005.

Nières-Chevrel, Isabelle, ed., *Littérature de jeunesse, incertaines frontiers*, Paris: Gallimard, 2005.

Noël, François, *Cours de littérature comparée,* 7 vols., Paris: Le Normant, 1816–28.

Oséki-Dépré, Inès, *Théories et pratiques de la traduction littéraire*, Paris: Armand Colin, 1999.

———, *Poésie et traduction*, Paris: Maisonneuve et Larose, 2004.

Pageaux, Daniel-Henri, ed., *La Recherche en littérature générale et comparée en France: Aspects et problèmes*, Paris: SFLGC, 1983.

———, *La Littérature générale et comparée*, Paris: Armand Colin, 1994.

———, *Littératures et cultures en dialogue*, Paris: L'Harmattan, 2007.

———, *Trente essais de littérature générale et comparée*, Paris: L'Harmattan, 2004.

Parizet, Sylvie, *Babel: Ordre ou chaos?*, Grenoble: ELLUG, 2010.

———, ed., *Mythe et littérature*, Nîmes: Lucie Éditions pour SFLGC, 2008.

Perrot, Jean, *Jeux et enjeux du livre d'enfance et de jeunesse*, Paris: Cercle de la Librairie, 1999.

———, *Le Secret de Pinocchio: George Sand & Carlo Collodi,* Paris: In-Press, 2003.

———, *Pinocchio: Entre texte et image*, Bern: Presses Interuniversitaires Européennes, 2003.

Picard, Timothée, *Wagner, une question européenne*, Rennes: PU de Rennes, 2006.

———, ed., *Dictionnaire encyclopédique Wagner*, Arles: Actes Sud, 2010.

———, *La Civilisation de l'Opéra: sur les traces d'un fantôme*, Paris: Fayard, 2016.

Plazenet, Laurence, *L'Ébahissement et la délectation: Réception comparée et poétiques du roman grec en France et en Angleterre aux XVIe et XVIIe siècles*, Paris: Honoré Champion, 1997.

Poulin, Isabelle, ed., *Critique et plurilinguisme*, Nîmes: Lucie Éditions pour SFLGC, 2013.

Prigent, Gael, *Huysmans et la Bible: Intertexte et iconographie scriptuaires dans l'œuvre*, Paris: Honoré Champion, 2008.

Prungnaud, Joëlle, ed., *Architecture et discours*, Lille: Presses de l'Université Charles-de-Gaulle Lille 3, 2006.

———, *Figures littéraires de la cathédrale 1880–1918*, Lille: PU du Septentrion, 2008.

———, ed., *La Cathédrale*, Lille: Presses de l'Université Charles-de-Gaulle Lille 3, 2001.

———, ed., *Les Monuments du passé*, Lille: Presses de l'Université Charles-de-Gaulle Lille 3, 2008.

Rallo-Ditche, Elisabeth, *Opéras, passions*, Paris: PU de France, 2007.

Saussy, Haun, ed., *Comparative Literature in an Age of Globalization,* Baltimore: The John Hopkins University Press, 2006.

Souiller, Didier, *La Littérature baroque en Europe,* Paris: PU de France, 1988.

———, *Calderon de la Barca et le grand théâtre du monde*, Paris: PU de France, 1992.

Souiller, Didier and Wladimir Troubetzkoy, eds., *Littérature comparée*, Paris: PU de France, 1997.

———, eds., *Manuel de littérature comparée*, Paris: PU de France, 1997.

Stead, Evanghélia, *L'Odyssée d'Homère,* Paris: Gallimard, 2007.

Steiner, Georges, *Antigones*, London: Clarendon Press, 1984.

Tomiche, Anne, 'Littérature européenne? Littérature occidentale? Littérature mondiale?', in *Europa zwischen Fiktion und Realpolitik/L'Europe: Fictions et réalités politiques*, ed. Roland Marti and Henri Vogt, Saarbrücken: Frankreichzentrum, 2010, pp. 19–34.

Tomiche, Anne and Philippe Zard, eds., *Littérature et philosophie*, Arras: Artois PU, 2002.

———, ed. with the help of Karl Zieger, *La Recherche en littérature générale et comparée en France en 2007: Bilans et perspectives*, Valenciennes: PU de Valenciennes, 2007.

Tomiche, Anne and Pierre Zoberman, eds., *Littérature et identités sexuelles*, Nîmes: Lucie Éditions pour SFLGC, 2007.

Troubetzkoy, Wladimir, *L'Ombre et la différance: Le Double en Europe,* Paris: PU de France, 1996.

Trousson, Raymond, *Thèmes et mythes: Questions de méthode*, Bruxelles: Éditions de l'Université de Bruxelles, 1981.

———, *Un Problème de littérature comparée: Les Études de thèmes: Essai de méthodologie*, Paris: Lettres Modernes, 1965.

Wajeman, Lise, *La Parole d'Adam, le corps d'Ève*, Genève: Droz, 2007.

Weber, Anne-Gaëlle, *A beau mentir qui vient de loin*, Paris: Honoré Champion, 2004.

———, *Les Perroquets de Cook: De la fabrique littéraire d'un lieu commun savant*, Paris: Classiques Garnier, 2013.

Westphal, Bertrand, *La Géocritique: Mode d'emploi*, Limoges: PU de Limoges, 2001.

———, *La Géocritique: Réel, fiction, espace*, Paris: Minuit, 2007.

9

Comparative Literature in India

Sayantan Dasgupta

MANY YEARS AGO, an essay entitled 'Comparative Literature in India' appeared in the *Yearbook of Comparative and General Literature*. It was one of the early attempts of our discipline to try and systematically define the contours of its Indian avatar and to historicize its development in this part of the world. The present essay takes as its point of departure this early essay, which predates it by more than half a century and which was instrumental in rationalizing in the context of its times Comparative Literature in India and making a strong case for locating it as a conjunctural practice. The initial essay remains a most useful account of the early history of our discipline in India and is testimony to the pedagogy that informed the first two decades of Comparative Literature here. Unfortunately, the essay does not seem to have got the recognition it deserved—neither for the approach it espoused, nor its limitations. It does not seem to have spurred on any substantial body of similar work on the history of Comparative Literature in India; publications and research on the topic have been at best sporadic, and at worst, almost non-existent.

The essay in question was penned in 1959 by Buddhadeva Bose, poet, scholar, writer and founder of the first university department of Comparative Literature in India at Jadavpur University.[1] It sought to outline first the political history that led to the emergence of the National Council of Education, whose avowed objective was to offer an alternative to the British-controlled colonial education system. It was from this council that Jadavpur University emerged. The essay then went on to discuss the aims and objectives with which Comparative Literature was introduced at Jadavpur. Finally, it proceeded to critique contemporary

* The present essay uses the title of the original Buddhadeva Bose essay and between submission for this volume and its publication has been published in Hindi translation in H.P. Shukla, ed., *Tulnatmak Sahitya: Saiddhantic Pranpreksh*, New Delhi: Rajkamal, 2015.

Single Literature pedagogic practices, discuss the salient features of the Jadavpur *school* (though nowhere in the essay does Bose mention the term) of Comparative Literature, and posit it in contradistinction to other existing approaches to the discipline. This essay betrays many of the anxieties of Comparative Literature as it existed in India at the time and many of which still characterize our discipline today. The pertinent issues raised by Bose make his essay an interesting starting point for our endeavor to locate Comparative Literature in India today.

At first glance, Bose seems to begin with a somewhat universalist notion of Comparative Literature, one that was part and parcel of the intellectual climate informing the field in its formative phase in the West. He writes: 'Wherever Comparative Literature is taught, there is the assumption that the literatures of the world form one comprehensive whole, with numerous historical and spiritual inter-relations' (Bose 1979: 88).[2] As a careful reading of the essay soon reveals, Bose is far from echoing an opinion that strives to privilege identity over difference. In fact, as he goes on to explain and justify the thrust of Comparative Literature at Jadavpur in its initial years, it becomes clear that he is pleading for a rationalization of Comparative Literature pedagogy in accordance with the imperatives of the pedagogical space in question. Thus, his 'Comparative Literature in India' is largely an essay on Comparative Literature at Jadavpur for the obvious reason that there was then no other Comparative Literature programme in India. It suggests that given the absence of resources available in American universities, Jadavpur should concentrate on a few well-defined areas of concentration—areas where expertise was available and which were of immediate relevance to the Indian context. Even the most cursory study of the first Comparative Literature syllabus at Jadavpur thus reveals that there were three distinct areas of focus. The first consisted of the classical Sanskrit tradition and the second was Bangla literature, the living literary tradition of Bengal, where Jadavpur University was located. Finally, there was 'Western literature', which formed a substantial part of the M.A. syllabus. There seems also to have been an attempt to try and locate Bangla literature in the context of the Sanskrit tradition, embodying therein perhaps something of the French School while adapting it to the more complex, multilingual Indian context. Bose justifies the importance of Western literature in the syllabus by pointing to the transactions that helped shaped the contours of Indian literature over the centuries.

This, then, was how Comparative Literature defined itself in India in the initial phase of its history. It seems to have already anticipated a 'quest for relevance' (Ngugi 87–110) long before this terminology came into currency. We also note that stress was clearly placed on the 'what' rather than the 'how' of Comparative Literature; questions of methodology were to become more important only much later. Even when Bose critiques the state of literary studies in India and highlights the advantages of doing Comparative Literature, he focuses largely on objects of study rather than on methodology.[3] Also to be noted is the way he tries to steer clear of gross nationalism and blind imitation of existing paradigms. When he cautions against the all-pervasive power of English departments in post-colonial India, he qualifies—'it is not *English* that these queries are directed against, but the *exclusive* hold of any single literature of the Occident .... We ... have felt that without forgetting our debt to English literature, our exclusive devotion to it has resulted in a considerable weakening of our culture' (Bose 1979, 90).[4]

This complicated relationship between Comparative Literature, universalism and nationalism has, of course, constituted a site of contest; it has, again, been at the basis of Comparative Literature's vision of itself as a conjunctural practice. The notion that Comparative Literature is not one but many, that it is by virtue of its quest for relevance and claims of inclusivity open to being reconstituted and refigured in a kind of *simulacrum* whereby the composition of centres and margins remains engaged in a state of flux, was subsequently reiterated by Swapan Majumdar. In 'Comparative Literature: Indian Dimensions', a paper presented at the First INCLA Convention in 1983, Majumdar noted that the engagement of Comparative Literature with the discourse of nationalism may not have been as inimical in India as it was in the West precisely because of India's colonial history (Majumdar 1987a: 13–22). He further goes on to state: 'it is precisely because of this predilection for National Literature—much too deplored by the Anglo-American critics as a methodology—that CL has struck roots in the Third World nations and in India in particular' (Majumdar 1987b: 53).

Indeed, the growth of Comparative Literature in India has historically shared a symbiotic relationship with the foregrounding of the concept of an Indian literature.[5] This relationship manifests itself in the systematic state-sponsored development of a corpus of works related to Indian literature, as well as in the various directions Comparative Literature would take in our country, viz., in the changes the Jadavpur syllabus would undergo over the years as well as in the different approaches to Comparative Literature that would emerge from other institutions.

II

The Sahitya Akademi, the Indian national academy of letters, was founded in 1954 with the objective of promoting the study of Indian literature and facilitating translation of Indian literary texts from the different *bhashas*. One of the first projects it undertook was the compilation of the *National Bibliography of Indian Literature 1901–1953*. This volume included Sindhi and English in addition to the languages then recognized in the Eighth Schedule of the Indian Constitution (Kesavan 1970: vii). The *Bibliography* turned out to be a very useful catalogue of Indian literature publications. It is important to mention this series and allied later attempts, such as the multi-volume *Encyclopedia of Indian Literature*, *Comparative Indian Literature*, edited by K.M. George, and Sisir Kumar Das's *A History of Indian Literature*. The specific study of modern Indian literature within the practice of Comparative Literature was almost non-existent before their appearance.

It was only in the late 1970s, when a major syllabus restructuring brought modern Indian literature in translation within the ambit of Comparative Literature in a significant way. This effort was further supplemented in a revamped M.A. syllabus at Jadavpur University in 1994. The point I am trying to make is that there was perhaps a symbiotic relationship at work here. As resources became increasingly available and seemed to develop Indian *bhasha* literatures became more visible, Indian Comparative Literature seemed to develop. They sustained the discipline at least partially, and may also perhaps be credited with having, in turn, been informed by it; they were surely part of a similar *Zeitgeist*. It is no coincidence then that the scope of Comparative Literature at Jadavpur expanded further in this phase to move beyond Sanskrit and Bangla to incorporate a larger Indian literature in a more meaningful way.

This trajectory can be amply demonstrated by an analysis of relevant Comparative Literature syllabi. The Jadavpur B.A. (Hons) syllabus in Comparative Literature was radically restructured in the late 1970s to incorporate a whole paper on 'Indian Literature other than Bengali in Translation'. To be doing Premchand's Hindi *Godan* in conjunction with masterpieces from other Indian *bhashas*, such as Thakazhi Shivsankara Pillai's *Chemmeen* and U.R. Ananthamurthy's *Samskara*, was a very significant move in an age when translations of such works were only just beginning to circulate, thanks to the efforts of bodies such as the Sahitya Akademi. The increased use of such translations indicates one of the trajectories our discipline would take across India over the next several decades.

While this move on the part of Jadavpur was part of the discipline's quest for relevance, the new syllabus was perhaps also a response to and worked in conjunction with developments in other parts of India. In 1974, the UGC had accepted R.K. Dasgupta's proposal to start an M. Lit. programme in Comparative *Indian* Literature in the Department of Modern

Indian Languages of the University of Delhi. ('Some Important Events in the History of Comparative Literature in India' 4). Again, in 1976, the University of Delhi hosted a seminar on Comparative Indian Literature, thanks to the efforts of Professor Nagendra. Within the next few years, a Comparative Indian Literature Association (CILA) would be formed. The intellectual climate demanded that Comparative Literature reformulate itself so as to negotiate the demands of Comparative Indian Literature and enhance the priority accorded to 'national literature', admittedly a paradoxical concept to use here. That this predilection would remain integral to the notion of Comparative Literature in India for some time was evident from the titles of books written by Comparative Literature scholars of the time. In 1987, Swapan Majumdar's book *Comparative Literature: Indian Dimensions* was published, once again reiterating the notion of Comparative Literature as conjunctural practice. Similarly, Amiya Dev's collection of essays, *The Idea of Comparative Literature in India* was published in 1984. Incorporating papers dating from 1977, Nabaneeta Dev Sen's *Counterpoints*, published in 1985, begins with 'The Concept of an Indian Literature Today: Another Name for Comparative Literature?' (Dev Sen 1985: 1–13), a paper she presented at the 8th Congress of the International Comparative Literature Association in Budapest in 1976. The emerging trend could not be clearer. It is also evident in Chandra Mohan's *Aspects of Comparative Literature: Current Approaches* (1989), one of the most influential anthologies of critical essays on Comparative Literature. Mohan's volume brought together some of the most important comparatists of the time from both India and abroad. His own essay examines Comparative Indian Literature, as do the contributions of Amiya Dev and K. Chellappan. In fact, Mohan writes in his 'Introduction': '[T]he confident tone of these essays on Indian themes is itself a demonstration that "Comparative Indian Literature" is a reality' (Mohan 1989: xiv).[8]

There were, of course, other 'new' areas that were secured by Indian Comparative Literature. 'Third World Literature', for example, which enjoyed substantial currency at least from the late-1970s onwards. New areas of interest also manifested themselves in the formulation of Jadavpur's M.A.-level Area Studies papers on the literatures of Africa, Latin America, and Bangladesh. Then there was literary theory, which, conspicuous by its absence in the first phase of Comparative Literature in India, entered the Comparative Literature syllabus in a big way in the 1990s; one instance of this development can be found in the M.A. syllabus that was made operational from 1994 at Jadavpur University—four out of the eight papers were constituted around literary theory. Still, the most significant and enduring change to be found throughout the entire country was the enhanced visibility and prominence of the study of Indian literature. And this trend was evident even in the syllabus we have just referred to—the 1994 Jadavpur M.A. syllabus, which had three optional papers where students could opt for either Western or Indian literature, meaning that one could get a degree in Comparative Literature with a specialization in Indian literature.

What is very important to note is that this opening up to 'other Indian literatures' was accompanied by a renewed stress on Bangla, the local language. Comparatists like Manabendra Bandyopadhyay engaged in translator activism by rendering scholarly work in Comparative Literature into the Bangla language.[9] He introduced to Bangla readers a vast corpus of modern Indian literatures, African literatures, and Latin American literatures through his various translation projects. Notable among these publications were his *Bhed Bibhed*, a thematically organized anthology of Indian short stories, the first volume of which was published in 1992, and the pathbreaking five-volume *Adhunik Bharatiya Galpa*, which introduced to readers of Bangla some of the most powerful works by modern Indian fiction writers such as Ismat Chugtai, Pendse, Phaniswar Nath Renu, Rajinder Singh Bedi, Ajeet Cour, Wajeeda Tabassum, Vaikom Muhammad Basheer, and Vijayadan Detha. Bandyopadhyay's project also included some of the more important scholars of the time, comparatists and non-comparatists, such as Sibaji Bandyopadhyay, Sourin Bhattacharya, Rusati Sen, Subha Chakraborty Dasgupta, and Ipshita Chanda.

III

For decades, Jadavpur had the dubious distinction of being the only department of Comparative Literature in the country. At one level, this distinction was symptomatic of a larger failure on the part of comparatists despite considerable effort to convince the rest of Indian academe about the efficacy, viability, and relevance of our discipline. Until quite recently, the number of institutions offering Comparative Literature as a *named* programme could be counted on one hand. Yet there is another side to this failure. Sisir Kumar Das pointed out that the success and impact of Comparative Literature in India could not be estimated in arithmetical terms. Writing in 1988, he opined,

> today, thirty-one years after the institution of that department, although the number of universities in India has almost doubled, the number of departments of comparative literature has not increased. However, this arithmetic does not tell the whole truth about the changes in attitudes in our literature faculties.

During the last fifteen years or so several associations have come up, and several departments have introduced courses that are known as Comparative Literature. These are indications of a new urge for the reorganization of the existing literature faculties. (Das 1989: 4–5)

Indeed, while the number of named Comparative Literature departments in India may not have increased during this period, there was a certain change that Comparative Literature managed to effect in these decades, as evidenced by the introduction of new courses or papers in Comparative Literature within other departments as well as by the revamping of the objects of study found in traditional Single Literature departments in India. 'English', for instance, has undergone considerable change. The syllabi of many English Literature departments in India today include the study of texts that seem to fit in more easily within the framework of a Comparative Literature curriculum. Thus, US American literature, Canadian literature, Latin American and Caribbean literature, and Translation Studies today cohabit with 'English' literature in English Literature syllabi at several Indian universities. Even Indian *bhasha* literature is now studied in English translation, a practice that Comparative Literature in India pioneered several decades ago and faced considerable resistance at that time for doing so. These developments mark the success of Comparative Literature, but they also point to the manner in which certain objects of study and methodologies propagated by and organic to Comparative Literature in India have been appropriated by other disciplines in their own quest to remain relevant in post-colonial India.

One also needs to take cognizance of the significant changes that have taken place in the decades after Sisir Kumar Das wrote his essay in the 1980s. Jadavpur is no longer alone in the institutionalized study of Comparative Literature in India. Veer Narmad South Gujarat University (Surat), founded in 1992, has a Comparative Literature programme and was the venue for the 7th Biennial International Conference of the Comparative Literature Association of India (CLAI) in 2005. It offers M.A., M.Phil., and Ph.D. courses in Comparative Literature with an emphasis on Gujarati literature. Telugu University in Hyderabad started its Centre for Comparative Studies in 1989 and renamed it as the Department of Comparative Studies in 1993. 'It aimed at developing inter-cultural and inter-disciplinary studies at the research level' ('Department of Comparative Studies, Telugu University' 5). In 1994, the University of Kerala at Trivandrum (now Thiruvananthapuram) launched a Centre for Comparative Literature ('Some Important Events in the History of Comparative Literature in India' 4), which organized the 5th CLAI Biennial International Conference in 2001. In 1994, the Department of Modern Indian Languages and Literary Studies of the University of Delhi added an M.A. in Comparative Indian Literature to its already existing M.Phil. programme ('News from Centres/Departments of Comparative Literature' 14). All these new programmes compete with institutions like Madurai Kamraj University, which had a Department of English *and Comparative Literature* since the late 1960s. Another institution where Comparative Literature exists (in a slightly different form in conjunction with English Literature) is Saurashtra University, Rajkot; the relevant department here is called the Department of English and Comparative Literary Studies.

Indeed, Comparative Literature has become more and more visible in India as an institutional entity since Sisir Kumar Das wrote his aforementioned essay. The rather haphazard manner in which it has grown highlights the need for an effective pedagogy of Comparative Literature as a conjunctural practice to be developed. Indeed, Comparative Literature has often taken on new dimensions and refashioned its contours quite radically as it has moved from Jadavpur University to other institutions. This development is perhaps desirable and reflects a trend that points to the dynamism of Comparative Literature as it is and can be practiced in India.

The last few years have been particularly productive for Comparative Literature in India; we have seen the fruition of many decades of struggle on the part of individuals, universities and associations to put Comparative Literature pedagogy on the map. The number of Indian universities offering Comparative Literature courses has grown substantially. Comparative Literature now occupies an important position in the curriculum at several of the central universities that have been recently established.

For example, the efforts to introduce Comparative Literature at the M.A. and M.Phil. levels at the Central University of Kerala, Kasaragod, bore fruit in 2009. That same year, the Central University of Gujarat (Gandhinagar) was established and already has an M.Phil.-Ph.D. programme in Comparative Literature. In 2010, the Centre for Comparative Literature at the Central University of Punjab (Bathinda) launched an integrated M.Phil.-Ph.D. in Comparative Literature (Mohan, Dasgupta, and Sharma 1). In 2009–2010, Rabindra-Bharati University started offering an M.Phil. in Comparative Literature and the first group of students have just graduated from the university (Dasgupta and Chattopadhyay, unpublished ms). One of the most important developments has been the launch of six subsidiary courses in Comparative Literature at Visva-Bharati University

(Santiniketan). The university has also recruited three faculty members in Comparative Literature and one expects a fully-fledged department to evolve there soon. It has also started M.Phil–Ph.D. programmes, and at the time of this essay to press, has just launched on M.A. programme in Comparative Literature.

These may all be recent developments, but they have their genesis in the past. What we are witnessing today—this 'sudden' efflorescence of Comparative Literature in its institutionalized form—is actually the result of academic activism carried out over the years, nay, over the decades by various actors among whom spearheaded initiatives in the various associations that have been in existence at different points of time—the Comparative Indian Literature Association (CILA), the Indian National Comparative Literature Association (INCLA) and CLAI.

IV

It is not without reason that Comparative Literature has been called an anxiogenic discipline (Bernheimer 1). The anxieties related to Comparative Literature are manifold—they resonate in the status of Comparative Literature as a reformist discipline and in its complicated questioning of 'equivalence' in a country where the visibility and number of teaching positions in Comparative Literature are miniscule in comparison to Single Literatures posts. Questions of academic content in our multilingual country, where the concept of a national literature is far more ambiguous than in most parts of the world makes the definition of Comparative Literature all the more essential. However, no history of Comparative Literature in India can be complete without mentioning something that has seldom been recorded in such narratives. I am speaking here of the contribution of the various Comparative Literature associations that have been in existence at various points of time in India.

There have been quite a few, some still-born, some quickly condemned to irrelevance or premature extinction, and some that went on for some time, but all of them in their own way offer insights into the development of our discipline in India. Some most useful work in this area was done many years ago by Swapan Majumdar, who compiled a list of 'Comparative Literature Associations in India' for the *ICLA Bulletin* (Majumdar 1986: 10–12). Unfortunately, this institutional trajectory is not an area that seems to have drawn much attention. Researchers of Comparative Literature have not followed up on this work with a history of those associations. My contention is that a careful study of documents relating to the agenda and work of these associations can provide a more holistic understanding of the narrative of Indian Comparative Literature itself. But this topic falls beyond the purview of this paper and will have to be taken up in the form of a separate venture. We can, however, at least attempt to record the paths on which our discipline may have traveled due to academic and administrative activities of these associations.

Majumdar lists four different associations that had been or were in existence at the time of his writing. Of these, the Delhi-based Comparative Indian Literature Association (CILA) and the Jadavpur-based Indian National Comparative Literature Association (INCLA) merged to form the Comparative Literature Association of India (CLAI) over the course of their joint conventions held at Jamia Millia Islamia in Delhi (1987) and at the Telugu University in Hyderabad (1989). From their inception, these organizations were involved in transforming the academic landscape of India and tried over the years to correct the asymmetries existing vis-à-vis Comparative Literature and other related disciplines. They also tried to propagate the cause of a more extensive presence of Comparative Literature in the Indian academic landscape.[10]

Thus, the 'Minutes of the First General Assembly of INCLA' dated 9 January 1983, records among other things, 'It is resolved that INCLA should take an active interest in the spreading of CL ... an immediate resolution was passed which is to be sent to all the Indian universities (to the UGC and to the Ministry of Education as well) asking them to include CL in their literature programmes, either by starting a separate department, or by including special papers in the single literature departments' ('Minutes of the First General Assembly of INCLA' 19). One notes here how INCLA strove to straddle the differential and the integrationist models of CL in its attempts to usher in a more holistic study of literature and culture.

Again, the minutes of the General Body meeting of the 3rd Biennial CLAI Congress (dated 21 April 1996) held at Telugu University in Hyderabad records that CLAI would strive to 'introduce Comparative Literature as an elective subject at the B.A. level in some colleges' (General Body Minutes, unpublished document). More significantly Resolution 5 ii) cites 'Another proposal of Dr. (Ashwin) Desai to the UGC to consider persons with Hons. degrees in a given Indian Language but M.A. in Comparative Literature, to be considered eligible for the teaching posts in respective Indian languages in schools/colleges was also considered'. This resolution points to how these associations of Comparative Literature tried to negotiate between the notion of Comparative Literature as an autonomous discipline with an integrationist model that strove to engage the administrative-bureaucratic machinery in devising possible routes or trajectories between CL and other disciplines.

This point is again in evidence in the papers of the Second Congress of the Comparative Literature Association of India hosted by the Department of Modern Indian Languages, University of Delhi, between 17 and 19 February 1993. The Congress, in its 'Resolution No. 2':

> resolved that the University Grants Commission and the universities as well as the State Education Departments be urged to (i) introduce Comparative Literature as a subject of study at all levels of college and university education—that is, at the levels of BA Subsidiary/Pass/Elective, BA Honours, MA, MPhil and PhD (and) (ii) recognize Comparative Literature as an equivalent subject for the posts of Lecturers, Readers and Professors in Literature Departments in colleges and universities. (General Body Minutes, unpublished documents)

These documents provide important pointers not just to the direction our discipline has taken in India but also to paths Comparative Literature has sought to follow, sometimes without as much success as we would have liked to have seen. The question of recognition still hangs fire in the Indian context and excites heated debate; the balance of payments vis-à-vis the recruitment of faculty between Comparative Literature and Single Literature departments is still as one-sided as it has always been in India; the number of Comparative Literature departments, too, is still modest, though rapidly on the rise. Yet Comparative Literature in India has perhaps never been as visible or as pregnant with possibilities as it is today. We cannot deny that we are living in interesting times with respect to CL in India today, despite all our angst and anxieties. Or, is it perhaps because of them?

NOTES

1. I stress this point because as Sisir Kumar Das has quite perspicaciously pointed out, while the history of Comparative Literature may have started *formally* in India with the establishment of the Jadavpur department in 1956, there was a long and sustained 'pre-history' of Comparative Literature in India. This prehistory included Rabindranath's lecture on Comparative Literature/*visvasahitya* at the NCE in 1906 as well as Bankimchandra Chattopadhyay's essay on 'Shakuntala, Miranda O Desdemona' (1873), the activities of the Fort William College which was established in 1800, and even the literary contact situations that existed in medieval India. For details, please see Sisir Kumar Das's 'Comparative Literature in India: A Historical Perspective' (Das 1989: 1–16). Swapan Majumdar also seems to hint in the same direction when he writes: 'Comparison as an attitude is age-old, but its uses on the pedagogical plane is a recent development in India' (Majumdar 1987: 7).

2. We may also note in this context Sisir Kumar Das's comments—'An assumption of the basic unity of the human race was certainly one of the main factors in the growth of comparative studies of religion and mythology and at the time [*sic*] scholars in their anxiousness to vindicate the universality of spirit overlooked the importance of diversities of human institutions and cultures' (Sisir Kumar Das, 'Comparative Literature in India: A Historical Perspective' in Mohan 1989: 7 and reprinted in this volume).
3. This point of view seems to have had sufficient currency among Indian comparatists. As late as 1989, we find this perspective echoed by Sisir Kumar Das in his essay, 'Muses in Isolation': 'I think comparative literature . . . is not different from the study of single literatures so far as the critical methodology is concerned, but differs only in matter and attitude' (Das 1989: 8–9).
4. In his essay, 'Muses in Isolation', Das enunciated this concern again a full 30 years after Buddhadeva Bose first expressed it so cogently. 'The only European literature—to be precise, the only foreign literature—that has taken a firm root in India is English. There is not a single university in the country without a department of English literature, nor is there a department of English literature which fails to attract a reasonable number of students' (Das 1989: 9). Again, he writes, 'I am not advocating for a ban on the study of English literature on the plea that it is a foreign literature or that it is the literature of the people who once ruled us. What I am asking for is the rationale of English literary studies in India' (Das 1989: 11).
5. Many would today disagree with the term and argue for its pluralistic incarnation, such as 'Indian literatures'. This may perhaps be read as being indicative of a moving away from a colonial anxiety which impelled one to highlight the unity in Indian diversity (as in the motto of the Sahitya Akademi—'Indian literature is one though written in many languages') in the decades immediately after independence when *diversity* within the unity tended to be emphasized. Nevertheless, I use the singular here because it relates to a phase of our narrative where the unitary nature of the concept was being established and propagated as part of a larger struggle for national integration.
6. Amiya Dev thus writes: '*Comparative Indian Literature* . . . has only assembled the diachronies—and that too in primarily generic rationale—with the more difficult task of synchronization left to future scholars. Still it is good spade work' (Dev, 'Towards Comparative Indian Literature', in Mohan 1989: 41).
7. A third volume was published posthumously. This volume dealt with the years 500–1399 and was subtitled 'From the Courtly to the Popular'.
8. Further evidence regarding the intellectual climate of the time can be seen in the two UGC circulars, one embodying V.K. Gokak's proposal that Indian literature be included in existing syllabi of Single Literature departments, and the other based on Motilal Jotwani's suggestion that M.A. studies in Single Literatures be replaced by M.A. in Indian Literature. See UGC Circular

Letter No. F5–5–85 (HR I) dated 25 March 1986, cited in Dev, 'Towards Comparative Indian Literature', p. 45.

9. I am indebted to Sibaji Bandyopadhyay for highlighting this particular aspect of the issue. Personal conversation.
10. I have argued elsewhere that the history of Comparative Literature in India has vacillated between two different ontological models that have contextualized the status of CL differently in terms of the hegemony of Single Literature departments. I call these two models the 'differential' and the 'integrationist'—the first envisages CL as a unique and autonomous discipline while the latter presents it as a space that shares contiguities with other literature departments. 'It could either posit Comparative Literature as an already formed entity that was *essentially* different from other already established normative literary studies and therefore one that could demand and would also have to fight on its own for a space of its own, a space in terms of university affiliation, studentship, and perhaps most importantly, of professional entrenchment, both academic and non-academic, or it could position it as a discipline that defined itself in terms of its dialogue with other disciplinary spaces, the danger in this case being of course that of being subsumed within the folds of more mainstream, more "powerful" disciplines'.

REFERENCES

Bandyopadhyay, Manabendra, ed., *Adhunik Bharatiya Galpa*, vols. 1–5, Calcutta: Bhurjapatra and Papyrus, 1985–93.

———, ed., *Bhed Bibhed 1: Danga, Deshbhag O Sampradayikatar Sarbabharatiya Galpa-sankalan*, Calcutta: Dey's, 1992.

Bernheimer, Charles, 'Introduction: The Anxieties of Comparison', in *Comparative Literature in the Age of Multiculturalism*, ed. Charles Bernheimer, Baltimore and London: The Johns Hopkins University Press, 1995, pp. 1–17.

Bose, Buddhadeva, 'Comparative Literature in India', *Yearbook of Comparative and General Literature 8* (1959). Rpt. in *Contribution to Comparative Literature: Germany and India*, ed. Naresh Guha, Kolkata: Jadavpur University, 1979, pp. 85–99.

Das, Sisir Kumar, *A History of Comparative Literature*, vol. 8, New Delhi: Sahitya Akademi, 1991.

———, *A History of Comparative Literature*, vol. 9, New Delhi: Sahitya Akademi, 1995.

———, 'Muses in Isolation', in *Comparative Literature: Theory and Practice*, ed. Amiya Dev and Sisir Kumar Das, Shimla: IIAS and Allied Publishers, 1989, pp. 3–18.

Datta, Amaresh, ed., *Encyclopedia of Indian Literature*, vol. 1, New Delhi: Sahitya Akademi, 1987.

'Department of Comparative Studies, Telugu University', *Souvenir of Third Biennial Congress of the Comparative Literature Association of India, April 20–22, 1996*, Department of Comparative Studies, Telugu University, Hyderabad, 1996, p. 5.

Dev, Amiya, *The Idea of Comparative Literature in India*, Calcutta: Papyrus, 1984.

Dev Sen, Nabaneeta, 'The Concept of an Indian Literature Today: Another Name for Comparative Literature?', in *Counterpoints: Essays in Comparative Literature*, Calcutta: Prajna, 1985, pp. 1–13.

George, K.M., ed., *Comparative Indian Literature*, vols. 1–2, Trichur: Kerala Sahitya Akademi and Macmillan India, 1984.

———, ed., *Modern Indian Literature: An Anthology*, vols. 1–2, New Delhi: Sahitya Akademi, 1992–93.

Indian National Comparative Literature Association News Bulletin, vol. 1, June 1983.

Kesavan, B.S., 'Introduction', in *The National Bibliography of Indian Literature*, vol. 3, ed. B.S. Kesavan, New Delhi: Sahitya Akademi, 1970, pp. vii–x.

———, B.S., ed., *The National Bibliography of Indian Literature*, vol. 3, New Delhi: Sahitya Akademi, 1970.

———, ed., *The National Bibliography of Indian Literature*, vol. 4, New Delhi: Sahitya Akademi, 1974.

Kesavan, B.S. and V.Y. Kulkarni, eds., *The National Bibliography of Indian Literature*, vol. 1, New Delhi: Sahitya Akademi, 1962.

Kesavan, B.S. and Y.M. Mulay, eds., *The National Bibliography of Indian Literature*, vol. 2, New Delhi: Sahitya Akademi, 1966.

Majumdar, Swapan, 'Comparative Literature Associations in India', *ICLA Bulletin*, vol. 7, no. 1, 1986, pp. 10–12.

———, 'Comparative Literature: Indian Dimensions', *Comparative Literature: Indian Dimensions*, Calcutta: Papyrus, 1987a, pp. 13–22.

———, 'Indian-Western Literary Relations: Problems of Acculturation and Appreciation', *Comparative Literature: Indian Dimensions*, ed. Majumdar, Calcutta: Papyrus, 1987b, pp. 50–61.

'Some Important Events in the History of Comparative Literature in India', *Souvenir of Third Biennial Congress of the Comparative Literature Association of India, April 20–22, 1996*, Department of Comparative Studies, Telugu University, Hyderabad, 1996, p. 4.

Mohan, Chandra, 'Comparative Literature in India: Recent Trends', in *Aspects of Comparative Literature: Contemporary Approaches*, ed. C. Mohan, New Delhi: India Publishers and Distributors, 1989.

Mohan, Chandra and Subha Chakraborty Dasgupta, eds., *CLAI Newsletter*, Delhi and Kolkata: Comparative Literature Association of India, August 2006.

Mohan, Chandra, Sayantan Dasgupta and Vasant Sharma, 'From the Editors', *CLAI Newsletter*, Kolkata: Comparative Literature Association of India, January 2013.

wa Thiong'o, Ngugi, *Decolonising the Mind: The Politics of Language of African Literature*, Oxford: James Currey, 1986, pp. 87–109.

10

Comparative Literature in India: The State of the Play

Ipshita Chanda

DO WE TEACH literature in Comparative Literature? Yes.
Do we teach literature in translation? Yes.
Do we teach the state-of-the-art European theory? Yes.

How then are Comparative Literature departments any different from all English literature departments in India that have waged battles against the establishment to teach a limitless variety of subjects we claim to be 'ours' (and have succeeded in no small measure)?

These are some of the questions that Comparative Literature has encountered in India in its sixty years of existence as an academic discipline. These questions also frame the issues that will be raised in this essay. In connecting these questions to events and responses, I am depending upon the concept of 'play' in my title to indicate the 'drama' inherent in the process. On a more mundane level, I use the metaphor of performance to illustrate the method of studying literature advocated by Comparative Literature as a discipline and its effectiveness in a multimedia-enabled interdisciplinary academic environment. I present the view of a practitioner of Comparative Literature who works in a context where such views are shaped and modified to address these issues from within that context. It is from this location that we raise the curtain on the state of play of Comparative Literature as a discipline in India.

Any intellectual practice, if it is to be institutionalized at a disciplinary level through syllabi and curricula, requires a method. But in the case of Comparative Literature, and perhaps in the case of literature as a subject of study, and a discipline, the nature of what is to be studied prevents the use of a rigidly framed unified method. Also, due to the diversity of the Indian languages, the practice of Comparative Literature in India, out of necessity, is grounded in a philosophy of pluralism. A society is plural in the way in which difference is perceived and negotiated by its members. Though these members belong to different cultural communities, shared systems operate in some specific areas of life, even though all major areas of life are not informed by similar systems of belief and practice. Coexisting with difference can be seen as the cornerstone of a plural society, such as India's. In such a society, quotidian existence itself necessitates what comparative practice demands: the willingness to open oneself to a world different from one's own. However, a single overarching grand narrative, which pedagogy and academia seem to demand presents a challenge on two counts; first, because the object of study is a work of art and second because it comes to being in such a society. It is with this caveat that we proceed.

Given its dependence on both temporal and spatial location, the method of Comparative Literature may be theoretically conceived of as a situated interpretive practice. The idea of a 'literary system' (Mohan[1], Majumdar[2]) may be utilized for understanding the inter-relationships between Indian languages, literatures, oratures and their nesting cultures. The interplay of these relations constitutes the literary field[3]. The study of literature as an expressive activity must be located in this field. On the Asian sub-continent, of which India is a part, contact at various levels and of different kinds has resulted in a plural society. A plural literary field is thus formed through reception and contact as shaping influences on cultural production as well as aesthetics. Besides, each literature is written in a language formed in a historically plural world.[4] In many cases, the boundaries between languages spoken in contiguous areas are porous; vocabulary, semantics and conceptual repertoires are shared. The practice of Comparative Literature in India has attempted to grasp this plurality through a diverse pedagogical agenda. For example, since multilinguality is the condition of Indian reality, the knowledge of languages can easily become the rationale for comparative literature practice in India, where the average student's exposure to more than one language can be taken as a base upon which to build.

If we accept the idea of Indian literature as a dynamic system composed of sub-systems with overlaps and divergences that operate across time and space, we may discern different kinds of resemblance among the languages spoken across neighbouring communities, thus giving rise to the idea of linguistic clusters. For the purposes of pedagogy, we think of literature as a particular use of language. In its literary and other uses, language mediates the layers of difference and identity at various levels of society. This usage is manifested and concretised in literature through location in a chronotope. In the Indian situation, a given time-space unit is inhabited by more than one language culture. The cluster theory of the comparative study of Indian[5] literatures advocates treating each cluster as a unit of study. But the cluster cannot be a closed unit: the inter-linguistic relations that exist across regional clusters are shaped by contemporary politics and continuously impact the language of literature and of daily use. The formation of modern Indian languages is the story of borrowing, lending, adaptation and transformation of linguistic and literary resources occasioned by contact between diverse language cultures, sometimes neighbouring and sometimes distant from one another. An understanding of the literary and lexical borrowing and lending, across language clusters that are geographically proximate as well as those which have been in contact with each other across space and time, is the basis of comparative literature pedagogy.

It is difficult to translate 'literature' meaning that which is written, into an Indian language while keeping this meaning intact. Various ideas of place, time, mode of transmission, form, content, purpose, addresser and addressee inform definitions of verbal art in different languages. Verbal art often appears as a supplement when words written and/or spoken extend themselves to music and painting. An example of a poetics based upon intermediality can be found in Bharata's dramatic theory,[6] which refers to three different types of experience originating in experience stemming from: the space of the stage, the body of the actor, and the 'content' of the play for the *Natyashastra*. The method of eliciting aesthetic response outlined by Bharata resonates across as an Indian language literatures, indicating that though there is variety in languages and language registers spatially and temporally differentiated, an existing its poetics informs the literary art or *kawya* and can throw light upon each of these experiences is integrated into the experience of 'rasa' by construction tradition of aesthetic object. The poetics proposed by Bharata is shared but rearticulated in the many Indian languages, whether it is through application or revision of his theory. Only a comparative study of this use will reveal the common bases of poetics in the individual Indian languages, and the singular difference of each from the other, a characteristic of the plural Indian literary system.

This brings us to the relation between Comparative Literature and Indian literature as subjects of study, which has been stated in the following manner:

Another provocative question to raise ... is with regard to the constituency of Indian literature within the form in which Comparative Literature is practiced in India today. One of the enduring ironies from the narrative of the development of Comparative Literature has lain in the fact that while Comparative Literature in the West was predicated initially on universalist notions of human identity and harmony—and this was, of course, catalysed by the contemporary socio-political context—the rise of the discipline in India was intimately tied up with the specific and the national—once again, thanks to the corresponding socio-political imperatives, very different in this case. This has made it important to look carefully at how a focus on the study of Indian literatures seems to have developed (if it has) within the hospitable terrain of Comparative Literature in India; this may manifest itself in different forms, of course, ranging from the establishment of courses specifically on 'Comparative Indian Literature' to effecting an inclusion of Indian literary texts as a thrust area within the label of 'Comparative Literature' itself.[7]

Some of the issues raised here have been extensively discussed for at least two decades. Many aspects may be highlighted in the larger context of the relationship between Comparative Literature and Indian Literature. So, the relations between the local language literature and the literature of the rest of India and, as a corollary, the relations between them, both individually and together, and different literatures of the world, come within the purview of Comparative Literature practice in India. The history of the practice of our discipline shows that writers and thinkers based in Indian languages, as well as those based in English but with an affinity for Indian languages, have been drawn towards the discipline[8]. Hence, the shape of Comparative Literature in India has been influenced by its relationship to the various Indian language-literatures, the literatures of the world in translation and English literature. Some schools[9] are of the opinion that it is best to let disciplinary definitions remain vague. Others, among whom I count myself, who teach the subject on a daily basis and have to answer questions regarding both the present and the future from students and parents alike, find it necessary to outline some tangible form which will define, if not our practice, then at least the location from which our practice can emerge, since located practice is the first lesson that Comparative Literature teaches us. Comparative Literature's ethics of engaging with the Other entails a special set of tools and procedures to read texts produced and received across cultures through locating recipient and 'guest' cultures in relation to each other. We can adapt these tools to read texts produced in any medium, provided we know the grammar of the medium itself, and how its materiality structures the work of art which is the object of both study and enjoyment.

The histories of modern Indian languages are testimony to their social and cultural plurality. If the local literature of any part of India is to be included in the Comparative Literature curriculum, then it must be located within the larger system of Indian literature, rather than taught in isolation. The struggle to institutionalize Comparative Literature in India has taught us that the relationship between the proportion of local, 'world' and English literatures can be addressed in imaginative ways. The context of production of any literary work is formed by the relationship between these three and the Indian literary system referred to at the outset though there is no place here to consider this relationship at length, it must be noted that the emergence of English as a language of literature written in India by Indians has effected a change in the Indian literary system which can be studied only though a comparative method. Similarly, the effect that the language its canons, literary and critical have had on the shaping of the literary systems in Indian languages becomes clear when studied through a comparative method. By the logic of the discipline, the study of these relationships is an irreducible part of any Comparative Literature syllabus taught in a particular linguistic region in India. But in our current pedagogy, the relational approach helps us to capture both the indeterminacy of literary art and the dynamics of the literary process is superseded by 'great texts written in language x' approach or by studies of thematic divergence/convergence with literatures in other languages, Indian and/or non-Indian. This dislocate the literary work from its place in the literary system of the language, deflecting the focus from literature as a special form of language use. Thus language, the very 'being' of literature, becomes an instrument rather than a form of creation, imaginative consciousness, merely a collection of signs in a socio-cultural document. This has resulted in an uneasy estrangement between Indian language literatures and Comparative Literature in India, Comparative Literature to the list of 'emerging' disciplines despite sixty years of existence. Consequently, we abandon language, through which literature comes to being, and reduce literary study to socio-cultural documentation. This summary brings us up to the present situation of Comparative Literature as practised in India, the relevance of its methods, and the paths of its intellectual and institutional development since the establishment of the first Indian Comparative Literature department in 1956.

Perhaps, in anticipation of the current state of play, practitioners of Comparative Literature in India had, no less than twenty years ago, mapped out a special trajectory for teaching Indian Comparative Literature.[10] The argument for the synchronic study and location in a diachronic comparative history, gained credence, resulting in Sisir Kumar Das's encyclopaedic work, *A History of Indian Literature*.[11] Here, the singularity, literal and metaphorical, of Indian literature as a category of analysis, formed the basis of the proposed model of historiography and led to some criticism that is favoured compartmentalization rather than 'integration'.[12] But, there is no disputing that Comparative Literature practice in India has paid scant and fragmented attention to the nurturing of this relationship between comparative method and the study of Indian language literatures. Hence, today, Comparative Literature as a discipline in India finds itself ill equipped to handle, and more importantly for the academic future of the discipline, to institutionalize, the comparative method required for the study of Indian literary cultures.

A deeper engagement of Comparative Literature as a discipline with Indian language literature departments through the development of a method for teaching the multiple Indian literary traditions is required. The basis for this is either proficiency in or instruction in more languages than simply one's mother tongue and English. This could well become the focus of future Comparative Literature syllabi in India. But this situation may not convince anyone that Comparative Literature should academically merge with one or many or any of the existing literature disciplines, new and old. Earlier, Comparative Literature departments in India often emerged from within English departments and sometimes, this is still the case.[13] In recent memory, a number of single literature departments, mainly European language literatures, have proved hospitable to Comparative Literature as a method, allowing their national literature syllabi to be framed from a comparative perspective,[14] even though they were not always clear regarding, which method to follow in executing this orientation. A few departments of literature like Bangla and Hindi[15] have begun to consider Comparative Literature as offering a viable method, but they are still few and far between. Such departments, in my opinion, are propitious destinations for Comparative Literature in India. The specification 'in India' involves creating a dialogue between Indian literatures, and linking the situation within which these literatures were created and are practised. Only then, gradually, Comparative Literature in India can begin to include the world outside the 'west' and its classical antecedents.

For a practitioner, the most productive way forward is an interrogation of our practice that examines the gaps identified within Comparative Literature in practice and theory, in general and particularly those that become evidence in a pluricultural multilingual country such as India. Colleagues in some parts of the country have emphasized that Comparative Literature's destination for the future will be found in Culture Studies. Doubtless many more such 'solutions' will emerge or are already in circulation. The questions come from colleagues, who are not convinced that Comparative Literature is not radical English or nascent

Cultural Studies or at the very least the unapologetic application of first-world or first-world-routed theory to local literatures. Such questions are also raised by students who come to find out what they are setting out to do. In response, this essay purports to recount the context of the discipline's institutionalization across the country. Much speculation on the place, use, logic, ideology and redundancy of Comparative Literature has been voiced from various theoretical and polemical perspectives. The purpose here is to engage with these questions from the point of view of a teacher of Comparative Literature in India.

Should the practice of Comparative Literature be different in India? Let us consider the single literature advocates who keep telling us, you do not read any literature 'completely'. By this statement they mean that you do not know the canon of any one language or literature completely. Does this criticism not alert us to the fact that the practice of Comparative Literature should be different here, where most of us grow up in a plurilingual environment and know at least two languages? For us, the canon includes what Sisir Kumar Das called the 'inherited'[16] texts such as the *Ramayana* and the *Mahabharata*. These epics are rarely read by Indians in the original. But an overwhelming number of modern Indian languages in the histories of their formation shows striking similarity. In most Indian languages there exists, therefore, at least one translation or retelling (more likely the latter) of the entire inherited text as well as various versions of select episodes. This is just one example of how the similarity among Indian-language literatures can only be fully grasped with a comparative method. If someone is really interested in answers to the list of questions at the head of this chapter, then this one instance should put to rest any reservation one might begin to have regarding the difference between Comparative Literature and English Literature as academic disciplines. But it still does not elucidate the specificity of comparative literary practice in India.

In what follows, I shall substantiate the view that the comparative method is effective for studying literatures located in the multilingual and plural literary cultures characteristic of the Indian situation. For example, almost twenty years ago[17] before the 'emerging' disciplines of Orality Studies, Media and Culture Studies and Performance Studies were ever conceptualized, the intermediality of the poetics proposed by Bharata and its influence on Indian language literatures, visual and performative arts were identified as areas to be studied by comparatists. This insight remained an observation and did not translate into practice until the emergent or new disciplines were established, and Indian practitioners of Comparative Literature found in these areas fertile ground for using existing resources from 'classical' and 'local' Indian languages. This appropriation was not done systematically to expand a Comparative Literature curriculum: rather, it is exemplified in work done by Comparative Literature scholars in these emergent disciplines, following the methods of Comparative Literature.[18] It remains a reality that we failed to orient our syllabi in keeping with our theoretical insights gleaned from researching the Indian situation and this is, again, only explicable by understanding the history of the discipline. The fruitfulness of this initial insight and its efficacy in the teaching of literatures Indian literatures can be illustrated with a couple of examples from comparative methods of teaching Indian literatures.[19]

On the hundred and fiftieth anniversary of Rabindranath Tagore's birth, students of Comparative Literature at Jadavpur University did a radioplay irreverently titled *McTagore 150*. The play follows an events team which hounds Rabindranath Tagore to refurbish his image and reinvent himself as a contemporary icon. Preparatory to the birthday celebrations, Rabindranath's exposure to varieties of music both Indian and non-Indian, classical and popular, become the object of investigation. The songs used in the play had tunes that Rabindranath had borrowed from different music systems, ranging from the Western to the Carnatic. Two of Rabindranath's most well-known songs were remixed, one as a rock version and the other as a jazz version retaining the original words. Both 'remixes' were tunes of popular Hindi film songs, while the original words were retained. Thus words and tunes were equally familier to the intended audience, though each belonged to a different language and nesting culture. So a number of cases of intermedial borrowing were actually constructed through the words in Bangla, the tunes from Hindi films songs, the script and its performance, illustrating the many interlinked processes that constitute acts of reception. Just as the entire repertoire of situation, symbols and formulae identified with Sufi poetry have become part of the vocabulary of modern Hindi film lyrics, creating a horizon of expectation for the modern reader and listener, similarly, varying thresholds of reception underlie the conceptualization and execution of character, say Valmiki's Rama,[20] and the Rama of the devotees, such as Tulsidas,[21] Kamban,[22] Krittibas,[23] to name a few authors of the local language renderings of the *Ramayana*. In 2008, the vast variety of *Ramayanas* was the focus of a students' seminar that included the Nepali, South Asian and women's *Ramayanas* as well as the study of the character of Hanuman in the Sanskrit version. These examples of the practice of comparative method, through capturing the play of difference both synchronically and diachronically reflect the dynamics of a literary culture derived from the inter-relationhips between various Indian languages and their literatures, which may be seen as individual entities formed from a plural base and part of a plural system.

As Amiya Dev states, Indian literature is an inter-literary condition.[24] Each language and literature has its own nesting culture, commensurate to a degree with other language literatures and their cultural fields. These overlaps become characteristic of a plural literary field, formed of shared repertoires of signification, common literary codes and common cultural processes by which the 'inter-literary condition' is changed or maintained. The examples cited here show how the plural culture of our location and our own specific position in that plurality can be made visible to our students both academically and practically as a part of our experience literary art and daily life. The aim, as that of Comparative Literature anywhere, is to locate oneself in time, place, and history, and to understand the dynamics of one's own culture as an interaction between the local and the specific on the one hand and the universal and the general on the other. In our case, Indian literature may be a viable category of literary study to the extent that it is possible to discern the degree to which individual language literary systems are commensurable with one another across time and space. This commensurability covers crucial areas that impact upon the inter-literary condition, and makes for plurality in terms of language and nesting culture. This allows us to imagine a category named India literature. It provides us with the basis of comparison. Beyond this lies the area of 'play'. Here, in the heterogeneity of individual languages and their plural life worlds, the literary text takes shape. And this brings us to the relationship of Comparative Literature to translation as activity and as literary text.

Comparative Literature is taught through translation. The criticism leveled at our practice is that since language itself is not available for study in a translated text, can Comparative Literature claim to be studying literature at all? I would address this criticism with the experience of teaching an astutely designed course on First Novels in Indian languages,[25] in a multi-lingual class as an optional course in the English department, not designed by a teacher of Comparative Literature. Among the students were readers of at least six languages. The novels were chosen from those languages, the translations were read by all, and the original language readers presented the text to the class. Here, the object of study, the literary text, comes to us not in the original language but in translation. As a scholar of Comparative Literature, my contribution was to provide a method to approach this diverse body of literature written in different languages. Language constitutes the literariness of the text and is the primary focus for the study of literature. But we did not as a class have access to the many languages of the many text. So we began with the location of the source language in its literary culture. Here the basis for understanding and the basis for comparison are similar—the 'Indian literary system' gives any Indian student of Indian language literatures, a reference point in her own language. In approaching a text written in a different language from a different geographical location is not a standard but a starting point from which the differences between Indian language literary systems arising can be shown against the background of a shared plural tradition.[26] I stated at the outset that the location of Comparative Literature practice shapes its direction and orientation: studying an Indian language text translated into English is different from studying a translation of the same text from one Indian language to another. Yet another situation is teaching that text in English to a class of non-Indian students. In all cases, the procedure is the same: by locating the text in the milieu of its production, the teacher attempts to instill a sense of the otherness of the text, indicating what is untranslatable through linguistic and extra-literary fact. For instance, the loss of the local register, the class and gender registers, even the special rites of passage and ways of life embedded in the source language are all issues that a comparative method addresses in the study of a translated text. It is imperative as part of this method itself to consider the structure of feeling as well as the specific literary system in the source language. In the case of a translated text, the frame of reference for literary study is created by establishing these parameters from the source language, so that the text is located in the source language milieu: the text itself is set off against this background. Hence, although there is no substitute for learning a language, the ambitious scope of Comparative Literature in a multilingual country like India is made possible through translation. A systematic study of translation practice connecting the source and target language milieux, will provide the linguistic and literary bases for teaching literature in translation, which forms a large part of Comparative Literature syllabi.

So if English Literature departments are teaching Indian language translations, and Cultural Studies departments are dealing with the other arts, and Translation Studies is an emerging discipline, what is the use of Comparative Literature? This question is not very new to Indian academe. I have attempted to answer this question by locating and outlining specific methods for specific kinds of pedagogical practice with objects of study that the emerging disciplines call their own, but which have been studied by the comparative method before those disciplines emerged.

Still—why does Comparative Literature need a method? Does English have a method? All literature disciplines have methods for reading literature from the literary system in that particular language. Also, a notion of literature and a method of literary reading deriving from that notion may well be shared by literatures in many languages and would form the material for a comparative study of poetics, as in the case of the poetics formulated by Bharata or that of Sangam poetry both of which were used by writers in different languages. But the tools of Comparative Literature extend by definition beyond single language literatures and in the Indian situation, this includes literatures written and oral, carried across time and place through travel and tradition. Though English has been cited as the ideal language for the practice of Comparative Literature in India,[27] it seems to be an obstacle in the study of Indian language literatures. This is because English studies do not (and do not need to, by virtue of their nomenclature) conceptualize Indian language literatures as systemically interrelated and commensurate to a particular degree. To return to the example of teaching through translation, the translated text for the student of English is a text in English, bearing certain literary codes and devices to which a hermeneutic like 'postcolonial' or 'feminist' may be applied. What other reason could there be for its inclusion as part of an English literature syllabus? But in a Comparative Literature classroom, the translated work and the act of translation are objects of study: the work is seen against the ground of an individual literary system which is a part of the plural Indian literary system. The codes and devices that bring the literary work into being therefore are not grounded in the 'English' literary system (itself a category for comparative study especially in a postcolonial situation). Rather, the ground for the translated text is formed through the interaction between the literary systems of the source and host languages. Thus, reading a translated text in any literary studies course of necessity must follow the method of Comparative Literature: this intails establishing a horizon for the meeting of the host and source languages in the text. Often this uncovers an irreducible difference between the life worlds of both—and that is the point at which the ethics of the method of comparative study enters the narrative.

Another question frequently asked of Comparative Literature students is: What do you do in Comparative Literature? What do you compare? Which implies that there is a 'doing' to this discipline that does not extend to any other Literary Studies discipline. No one asks what is 'done' in English or Bangla, other than reading the literature. We have tried to outline how a 'reading' is framed through a comparative method. But what happens beyond that? Literature is meant to elicit feeling:

it is our experience of 'worlds' that exist in the imagination how can the understanding of feeling follow a method? Does Comparative Literature as a discipline, then take an objective distance from the power of literature, or to put it less dramatically, from its very literariness?

Theodor Adorno describes a situation of engagement between thought and thing: 'If the thought truly realized itself [*entaeussern*] in the thing, if this counted for something and not its category, then the object itself would begin to speak under the thought's leisurely glance'[28]. The uniqueness of the literary sign will not allow it either to be subsumed within a systematic reading or be fully grasped by the 'sense-positing autonomy of the subject' (Adorno 2001: 36–9). Adorno's demolition of the Enlightenment view of the world was premised on the interrogation of the very notion of classificatory frameworks that mask what cannot be classified. Instead he proposes the reconceptualization of system in keeping with the critical impulse of philosophy that he wants to recuperate. This system is a 'constellation' of concepts, 'not constant, (which) congregate around historical factuality and allow interaction between them'[29]. As a functioning system, it is 'secularized into ... a latent force which ties disparate insights into one another (replacing any architectonic organization)'.[30] A literary work may be seen as such a system, internally ordered in relation to the larger systems of which it forms a part. Adorno then outlines the mode of thought that may replace closed-systemic thinking, and thereby, enable us to encounter the outside world. 'The structure of a mode of thought is no longer imposed on it by the authority and sovereignty by which it creates and generates its object from within itself but by the shape of whatever confronts it'(ibid., p. 39). An intersubjective space is, thus, created for literary understanding. But the 'understanding' that Comparative Literature aims for as the goal of its method, stems from an ethics that insists that the self is not a fully formed whole approaching an object. Rather, it becomes what it is when it reaches beyond what appear as its confines. Only when it enters the alien world of the other can it experience its difference as self. Hence it is not hospitality, interrelationships or the possibility of exchange between fully formed given entities, but openness that characterizes the practice of Comparative Literature.

If Comparative Literature as a mode of thought begins by opening itself to the world, can it be accused of enforced political correctness? I record here academic exercise, epistemological critique and pedagogic response based on learning the discipline through teaching it in the last twenty years. During this time, questions from the past that arose within the Humanities in general and Literary Studies in particular were directed towards the influence of continental theory, from where foundational mantras were gleaned to fashion a variety of disciplinary deities in various academic shrines. This process was coupled with the mandate of the national regulatory body for higher education, the University Grants Commission, insisting upon a change to the semester system, and defining goals in a way that encouraged the adoption of buzz words derived from the aforesaid disciplinary deities. The ideological orientation of particular strands of social and literary theory that arose from this contact with European thought at this particular juncture led to the institutionalization of thematic, or if a more sophisticated term is sought, discursive positions as the basis for disciplinary formations. The relationship between discourse and lived materiality began to be studied through the 'approaches' gleaned from ideological positions like feminism, Marxism, etc. applied through categories like 'writing from the margins', 'Postcolonial writing', 'minority writing', 'women's writing', 'Dalit writing', 'diaspora writing', and so on.

Comparative literature appeares to be caught in these extra-literary institutional cost currents and debates about its future and relevance never cease. While acknowledging Adorno's demolition of system and method in the strong and schematic sense, we must also clarify our view of literature. Is it tied to concept-ridden knowledge? We may consider Adorno's insight: 'Cognition holds none of its objects completely. It is not supposed to prepare the phantasm of a whole. It cannot be the task of a philosophical interpretation of works of art to establish their identity with the concept, to gobble them up in this'.[31] The work of art produced in another culture holds in itself the tension between the silence of linguistic and cultural untranslatability, and the eloquence of expression in a language not one's own. Comparative Literature methodically highlights this tension through the framing and location of the text in the space of contact between cultures.

But is Comparative Literature, because of this, in danger of contributing ethical justification for the near-fetishisation of 'otherness' and 'difference'? This translates into a peculiarly local problem: how to construct the other in a plural society? 'Contemporary approaches' to Comparative Literature taught in India include the gamut of European theory and Modern Indian Literary Theory. What is the intention behind this inclusion? How many systematic collections of literary essays in Indian languages, not to mention their English translations, have we made available for teaching? What would be the position of aesthetics in such a scheme? One could even go further in this stream of thought and ask how many classical traditions does Indian culture admit? These are all relevant questions to ask regarding the practice of Comparative Literature in India and may be answered by foregrounding the plurality of Indian languages and cultures, leading to a systemic understanding of their individual formations.

For the comparatist these reasons suffice to justify the classification 'Indian literature', not as a programmatic ideal but purely for the purposes of dealing with the material with which one is presented. The formation of Indian languages, the corpus of what Sisir Kumar Das called inherited texts and the phenomena of 'earlier seen' (pro-phane) and 'later seen' (meta-phane)[32] allow us to construct systemic narratives of Indian language literatures. Almost all Indian language literatures share many elements of this narrative. This did not occur because all of them participated in one uniform process in their formation. Rather, it was because they share local neighbourhoods inherited texts providing repertoires of themes, forms and symbols, and common histories, differentiated by degree and nature of contact with one another and with 'outside' influences. This results in interconnected but distinct linguistic formations in the plural literary field. Inasmuch as language and literature are linked, local politics and social organization as well as policies and events on the national or 'global' scale (like the linguistic reorganization of states), linguistic nationalism and the emergence of marginalized languages and literatures provide examples of pan-Indian phenomena, which have influenced the actual shaping of language. Hence, the study of literariness in an Indian language literature demands attention to these factors shaping the constituent literary systems. The alluring but challenging topic of poetics and/or aesthetics may well be a direction for future comparative work, if we can summon the will and expertise to introduce today's students to poetics and aesthetics from different philosophies of literature across the world. The understanding of our own literary systems, whether they are in our own language or in another Indian language is a task that Comparative Literature is yet to address comprehensively and systematically in India.

Finally, is Comparative Literature a study of literature, is it a study of theory using literature as source material or does it propose a theory of culture? Is it Cultural Studies that sometimes uses a literary text as source material? Venturing beyond the known world by opening the self to meet the other, is the foundational impulse of Comparative Literature. But if we fully appropriate what we meet beyond the known, can we still claim to respect the difference expressed in its singularity? Adorno cautions: 'Disaster threatens intellectual experience the more strenuously it ossifies into theory and acts as if it held the philosopher's stone in its hand.'[33]

Literary understanding cannot be dictated by theory or fixed by a fiat. At best, one can identify an aim and offer a method based on location and language-literary system, structured by a particular ethics of engaging the other. This entails reaching out with humility towards the other rather than appropriating it through explanatory frames or critical theories, allowing the play of difference to affectively engage the self: thus validating Comparative Literature as adequate for the study of the plural literary culture of India.

NOTES

1. Chandra Mohan, *Aspects of Comparative Literature: Contemporary Approaches*, Delhi: India Publishers & Distributors, 1989, p. 105.
2. Swapan Majumdar, *Comparative Literature Indian Dimensions*, Calcutta: Papyrus 1987; see also Majumdar, 'National Literature vis-à-vis Comparative Literature: The Indian Perspective and Point of View', in *Jadavpur Journal of Comparative Literature*, ed. Amiya Dev, no. 29, 1990, pp. 11–15.
3. Steven Totosy de Zepetnek, *Comparative Literature: Theory Method, Application*, Amsterdam, Atlanta: Rodopi, 1998, pp. 38–9; Sheldon Pollock calls it 'literary culture', *Language of the Gods in the World of Men: Sanskrit, Culture and Power in Pre-Modern India*, Berkeley, Los Angeles, London: University of California Press, 2006, p. 2.
4. Lachman M. Kubchandani, *Plural Language Plural Cultures: Communication, Identity, Sociopolitical Change in Contemporary India*, Honolulu: University of Hawaii Press, 1983, p. 6.
5. Aijaz Ahmad, 'Indian Literature: Notes Towards the Definition of a Category', in *In Theory: Classes, Nations, Literatures*, London: Verso, 1992, pp. 243–86.
6. Bharata, *Natya Shastra*, tr. Manomohan Ghosh <http://www.archive.org/details/NatyaShastraOfBharataMuniVolume1>.
7. See Sayantan Dasgupta, 'Locating Indian Comparative Literature Today', in *Comparative Literature: Mapping Milestones, Tracing Trajectories*, vol. 1 (forthcoming), Kolkata, UGC CAS in Comparative Literature Phase II, Jadavpur University.
8. Amiya Dev, 'Comparative Literature in India', in *Comparative Literature and Comparative Cultural Studies*, ed. Steven Totosy de Zepetenek, West Lafayette: Purdue UP, 2002, pp. 23–33.
9. See for example the exchange between Sisir Kumar Das and Sibaji Bandyopadhyay in *Granthacharcha 1778*, ed. Ashok Upadhyay, vol. 1, no. 1, Kolkata: Charbak, January 2014, pp. 247–58, with Bandyopadhyay taking this view.
10. Ayyappa Paniker, *Spotlight on Comparative Indian Literature*, Calcutta: Papyrus 1992, pp. 16–23.

11. Sisir Kumar Das, *A History of Indian Literature 1800–1910; Western Impact: Indian Response*, New Delhi: Sahitya Akademi, 1991, pp. 8–10.
12. Sisir Kumar Das, 'Integrated History of Indian Literature', Draft Working Paper, New Delhi: Sahitya Akademi, 2006; see also Amiya Dev, 'A History of Indian Literature', in *Indian Literature*, Sahitya Akademi, 2006; Harish Trivedi, 'The World as India: Some Models of Literary History,' in *Studying Transcultural Literary History*, ed. G. Lindberg-Wada, Berlin: Walter de Gruyter, 2006, pp. 23–31.
13. Witness the departments at the Central University of Kerala at Kasargod and of Gujarat at Gandhinagar and the Department of English and Other Modern European Languages at Visva-Bharati, Shantiniketan. In the first case, the degree is dual; at Visva-Bharati, Comparative Literature formed part of the English and Modern European Languages curriculum until it separated itself in 2013 as a Centre.
14. The syllabus for the English Department at the Central University at Kishengarh, Rajasthan, is a case in point.
15. The Hindi departments of Presidency University, Kolkata, or that of the Antarrashtriya Hindi Viswavidyalay, Wardha, are examples. At the University of Calucut, Comparative Literature is joined to the Russian department. At West Bengal State University, Comparative Literature is attached to the Bangla Department, though this is currently an administrative rather than an academic situation.
16. Sisir Kumar Das, 'The Idea of Literary History', in *Literary Historiography*, ed. I. Chanda, Literary Studies in India, vol. 1, Kolkata: Jadavpur University pp. 42–8.
17. Nabaneeta Dev Sen, 'The Concept of Indian Literature Today', *Jadavpur Journal of Comparative Literature*, vols. 16–17, 1978–79, pp. 97–106.
18. See for instance the introduction to Basu and Chanda, eds., *Locating Cultural Change: Theory Method Process*, Delhi: Sage; 2011, pp 1–18; I. Chanda, 'Women Writing Gender', in *Shaping the Discourse: Translations of Women's Writings in Periodicals between 1864–1947*, ed. Chanda and Bagchi, Kolkata: Stree, 2013.
19. See I. Chanda, 'The Comparatist as Teacher: Teaching Indian Literatures Through a Comparative Methodology', in *Quest of a Discipline: New Academic Directions for Comparative Literature*, ed. R.R.Yohanan, Delhi: Foundation Books, 2012, pp. 13–28.
20. Valmiki *Rāmāyaṇa* archive.org › [Texts collection] › [Opensource collection].
21. Tulsidas, *Sri Ramcaritmanas*, <http://gitapress.org/BOOKS/1318/1318_Sri%20Ramchritmanas_Roman.pdf>.
22. Kamban, *The Kamba Ramayan*, tr. P.S. Sundaram, ed. N.S. Jagannathan, Penguin, 2002.
23. Krittibas Ojha, *Krittibasi Ramayan*, Calcutta: Basumati Sahitya Mandir, 1926.
24. Aamiya Dev, 'Between the One and the Many: Rethinking Indian Literature', in *Jadavpur Journal of Comparative Literature*, no. 41, pp. 7–16; See

also Amiya Dev, 'Writing Indian Literary History', in *Historiography Literary Studies in India*, vol. 1, ed. I. Chanda, Kolkata: Jadavpur University, 2004, pp. 113–18.

25. M. Sridhar, 'Modernities in Indian Literature', Department of English, University of Hyderabad, July–november 2012.
26. See I. Chanda, 'Translating by the Ear', Introduction to Satinath Bhaduri, *Dhorai Chairt Manas*, tr. Ipshita Chanda, Delhi: Sahitya Akademi, 2013, pp. vii–xiv.
27. K. Satchidanandan, 'Mother Tongue, the Other Tongue: Indianising English', in *Quest of a Discipline: New Academic Directions for Comparative Literature*, ed. R.R.Yohanan, Delhi: Foundation Books, 2012, pp. 257–79.
28. Theodor Adorno, *Negative Dialectics*, tr. D. Redmond, Frankfurt: Surkhamp 2001 [1970], Introduction, pp. 36–9.
29. Theodor Adorno, 'Introduction', GS Volume 1, *Lectures on Negative Dialectics*, London: Polity 2008, p. 359.
30. Theodor Adorno, *Lectures on Negative Dialectics*, London: Polity, 2008, p. 38.
31. Theodor Adorno, 'Introduction', *Lectures on Negative Dialectics*, London: Polity, 2008, pp. 24–7.
32. Sisir Kumar Das, 'The Idea of Literary History', in *Historiography, Indian Literatary Studies*, vol. 1, ed. I. Chanda, Kolkata, 2004, pp. 42–48.
33. Theodor Adorno, 'The Essay as Form', in *Notes to Literature,* vol. 1, New York: Columbia, pp. 3–23.

REFERENCES

Adorno, T., *Negative Dialectics*, tr. D. Redmond, Frankfurt: Surkhamp, 1970.

———, *Lectures on Negative Dialectics*, London: Polity, 2008.

———, 'The Essay as Form', in *Notes to Literature,* vol. 1, tr. S.W. Nicholson, New York: Columbia University Press, 1991, pp. 3–23.

Ahmad, A., 'Indian Literature: Notes Towards the Definition of a Category', in *In Theory: Classes, Nations, Literatures*, ed. A. Ahmad, London: Verso, 1994, pp. 243–86.

Basu, P. and Chanda, I., eds., *Locating Cultural Change: Theory Method Process*, Delhi: Sage, 2011.

Bharata, *Natya Shastra*, tr. Manomohan Ghosh, <http://www.archive.org/details/NatyaShastraOfBharataMuniVolumel>.

Chanda, I., ed., *Historiography in the series Literary Studies in India*, Kolkata: Jadavpur University, 2004.

———, 'The Comparatist as Teacher: Teaching Indian Literatures Through a Comparative Methodology', in *Quest of a Discipline: New Academic Directions for Comparative Literature*, ed. R.R. Yohanan, Delhi: Combridge University Press, 2012.

Chanda, I., 'Women Writing Gender', in *Shaping the Discourse: Translations of Women's Writings in Periodicals between 1864–1947*, ed. Bagchi and Chanda, Kolkata: Stree, 2013a.

———, 'Translating by the Ear', introduction to Satinath Bhaduri, *Dhorai Chairt Manas*, tr. Ipshita Chanda, Delhi: Sahitya Akademi, 2013b.

Das, S.K., *A History of Indian Literature 1800–1910: Western Impact: Indian Response,* New Delhi: Sahitya Akademi, 1991a.

———, *A History of Indian Literature 1800–1910; Western Impact: Indian Response,* New Delhi: Sahitya Akademi, 1991, 1991b, pp. 8–10.

———, 'Integrated History of Indian Literature', Draft Vorking Paper, New Delhi: Sahitya Akademi, 1991c.

———, 'The Idea of Literary History', in *Historiography, Indian Literatary Studies, vol. 1,* ed. Ipshita Chanda, Kolkata, 2004.

Dasgupta, S., 'Locating Indian Comparative Literature Today', in *Comparative Literature: Mapping Milestones, Tracing Trajectories,* vol. 1, Kolkata: UGC CAS in Comparative Literature Phase II, Jadavpur University (forthcoming).

Dev, A., 'Between the One and the Many: Rethinking Indian Literature', in *Jadavpur Journal of Comparative Literature,* no. 41, Kolkata: Jadavpur University, 2006, pp. 7–16.

———, 'A History of Indian Literature', in *Indian Literature,* Delhi: Sahitya Akademi, 2006b.

Dev Sen, N., 'The Concept of Indian Literature Today', *Jadavpur Journal of Comparative Literature,* nos. 16–17, Calcutta: Jadavpur University, 1978–79, pp. 97–106.

Panniker, K.A., *Spotlight on Comparative Indian Literature,* Calcutta: Papyrus, 1992, pp. 16–23.

Satchidanandan, K., 'Mother Tongue, the Other Tongue: Indianising English', in *Quest of a Discipline: New Academic Directions for Comparative Literature,* ed. R.R. Yohanan, Delhi: CUP, 2012, pp. 257–79.

Kamban, *The Kamba Ramayan,* tr. P.S. Sundaram, ed. N.S. Jagannathan, Penguin, 2002.

Kubchandani, Lachman M., *Plural Language Plural Cultures: Communication, Identity, Sociopolitical Change in Contemporary India,* Honolnln: University of Hawaii Press, 1983.

Majumdar, S., *Comparative Literature Indian Dimensions,* Calcutta: Papyrus, 1987.

———, 'National Literature vis-à-vis Comparative Literature: The Indian Perspective and Point of View', *Jadavpur Journal of Comparative Literature,* no. 29, 1990, pp. 11–15.

Mohan, C., *Aspects of Comparative Literature: Contemporary Approaches,* Delhi: India Publishers & Distributors, 1989.

Ojha, Krittibas, *Krittibasi Ramayan,* Calcutta: Basumati Sahitya Mandir, 1921.

Pollock, S., *Language of the Gods in the World of Men: Sanskrit, Culture and Power in Pre-Modern India,* Berkeley, Los Angeles, London: University of California Press, 2006.

Totosy de Zepetnek, Steven, *Comparative Literature: Theory Method, Application*, Amsterdam: Rodopi, 1998.

Trivedi, H., 'The World as India: Some Models of Literary History', in *Studying Transcultural Literary History*, ed. G. Lindberg–Wada, Berlin: Walter de Gruyter, 2006.

Tulsidas, *Sri Ramcaritmanas*, <http://gitapress.org/BOOKS/1318/1318_Sri%20 Ramchritmanas_Roman.pdf>.

Valmiki, *Ramayana* archive.org › [Texts collection]› Opensource collection.

11

The Concept of the Margins in Comparative Literature in India

Subha Chakraborty Dasgupta

THE SUBJECT OF this chapter arises out of a concern articulated in a number of Comparative Literature conferences and seminars organized in India in the last few years—the non-inclusion or marginalization of particular groups, languages and voices. On a few occasions, the seminar topics focused on the themes of hegemony and the hierarchization of languages and literatures related to such languages, while on other occasions there were a number of papers on related topics, which dealt with substantial cases for inclusion of the marginalized within the hierarchical structure in question. A seminar that would gather the relevant strands of thought related to these concerns was eventually organized in 2005 by the Comparative Literature Association of India in Surat at the Department of Comparative Literature, South-Gujarat University. The seminar was entitled 'Poetics of the Margins: Reinventing Comparative Literature'. Needless to say, there was in the title an expression of dissatisfaction with Comparative Literature, as it was practised then—a plea that Comparative Literature be reorganized from a different perspective (with the foregrounding of the margins) or even that Comparative Literature studies be organized around principles dealing with the poetics of the margins. Incidentally, it may be noted that the state where this conference was organized, Gujarat, has a living tradition of oratures. It sponsors events where participation can run into the thousands. It is also the land of Jhaverchand Meghani, the reputed modern collector of folktales and the site of the Tribal Academy established by Ganesh Devy. The seminar produced a souvenir volume including an article by a social scientist on the state of tribal communities in Gujarat. The tribal population of Gujarat according to the 1991 census, constitutes 14.92 per cent of the total population, that is, about 6,161,775 of the more than 61 million inhabitants.

It is true that Comparative Literature in many parts of the world has often been organized around different key concepts[1]—early aesthetics, folk literature, influence studies, alternative canons of literature, questions of identity, and so forth. Static principles, while popular, always had a short shelf life in this discipline that flourishes due to its commitment to action, constant movement and change, and a pluridimensional approach to literature. Yet historical exigencies have to be acknowleged as well as literature's place in a given history. Both express and formulate certain demands to which Comparative Literature seeks answers. One such perspective, currently in vogue, is the formulation that posits Comparative Literature as a propitious site to examine marginality, and here I am speaking primarily of the Indian context, although it may not be wise to demarcate specificities so strongly in the realm of Comparative Literature. The moment of intense particularization is also the moment heralding a certain movement away from intercultural relations. It is also true that what elicits intense debate in one locale has repercussions in a wider context and, therefore, demands critical attention. If we need to recognize historical particularities, it is necessary to have single perspectives, which need to be built into the discipline not in any hierarchical form but through dialogic principles, retaining radical differences, bringing two disparate cultures face to face, failing perhaps to establish any viable relationship, and then starting all over again. If I speak of disparate cultures, it is because the gap between what is at the centre and what is far from the centre has widened enormously over the centuries. To borrow Edward Said's words in *Orientalism 25 Years Later*, 'we do need to concentrate on the slow working together of cultures . . . . But for that kind of wider perception, we need time, patient and sceptical inquiry, supported by faith in communities of interpretation that are difficult to sustain in a world demanding action and reaction' (2003).

Before going further, it is necessary to engage with the term 'margin' in the context of literature and literary studies. It is a contested term in literature and one of the questions repeatedly asked today is whether we are justified in bringing a term from political economy and its related hierarchies to the consideration of literature. The answer can simply be that literature is not outside the purview of the economic or the social in the general terminologies of Althusserian overdetermination. This justification, however, would only be partial, since the question also pertains to the ontological aspect of artistic activity, its singular way of being that necessitates other kinds of sounding boards and other organizational frameworks. Just as the notion of margins has been questioned, so too has the concept of the centre. I am reminded of a statement by Mahasweta Devi who was once asked whether she thought the tribal should be brought into the mainstream. She retorted, why should the ocean come to the river? What is designated the margin from one point of view could be designated the centre from another. But then again the ground reality is that in terms of privilege (and contrarily of non-privilege or exploitation), centres and margins do exist or are brought into existence, and an important area of work consists in studying the operating forces that bring such centres and margins into being in all spheres, including that of literature. It is in this context that pedagogical structures need to be investigated and reorganized. Along this line of centres and margins again, it is important to note that there may be many centres and many margins. Often marginality is viewed in terms of alterity, and in the context of literature, this would imply the existence of an alternative poetics and the assumption that the poetics of marginalized literatures is different from the poetics of literatures that are at the centre.

It we take up the case of oratures, marginalized in the context of print cultures, we find varying sets of poetic principles at work. Similarly, within oral contexts one discovers hierarchies of genres, centres and margins. In rural communities surrounding the metropolis in Bengal, for example, there are large community events such as the singing of *Banbibir pala*, where thousands gather to listen to the sorrowful plight of Banbibi and the eventual end to her sorrows with the intervention of Dakshin Roy, the protector of lives in the forests of the Sunderbans. There are also small community events where just the members of a family or an extended family may be involved in the enactment of a women's *vrata* held on a particular day of the year for the fulfilment of a particular wish beneficial to oneself, the larger family, community or the environment. Certain value codes are of necessity associated with oratures. Inter-relatedness, for instance, is a primary code as an oral text comes into being with relation to people in actual contact with one another, intervening implicitly or explicitly in the construction of the text. The principle of interrelatedness then takes on an added dimension within a given text giving expression to a world view, wherein everything that exists does so in an interlinked manner. In the past, particular attention has been paid to this interlinking, sometimes from the perspective of a non-anthropomorphic world, where man is not at the centre but where everything that exists has an intrinsic worth. However, inter-relatedness seems to be at odds with modern day principles of faster, forward and more. While it is also found in written literature as well, with certain differences perhaps, it does not appear as insistently, nor with the weight and wisdom of an entire tradition.

From the point of view of form, there is a tendency in oratures to compose a work from details that are semantically more or less independent. The technique is that of additive composition where unforeseen semantic breaks lead to surprises. A rhyme from one of the *vratas* is as follows: 'Fourteen flowers are my brothers/Brother, dear brother! I will make you wheat cakes, and what else? The world under one and twenty lamps'. It continues, 'Round Lotus, lotus round, hive of bee I make layers of lotus on lotus'.[2] The ordering of details is different—it does not proceed from an image of the whole but from an assemblage of images or units provided by tradition or the surroundings/events. Unexpected units arise from the perpetually new ordering of details, creating a greater space for meaning and new forms of creativity. A free combination of rhymed images serves to link the small and the fragile with the large and the cosmic, and create a constant passage between the two worlds, as it were. It would also be worth exploring the idea of additive composition in the context of the written. The organic text takes command from the centre even if in an oppositional mode. In the very formation of the additive text, history gets incorporated into its semantic core, that is, history in its lived contexts.

As a comparatist from the metropolis, I can enter the context of oratures as a visitor,[3] exchanging stories, anticipating, meeting, returning and then revisiting. Seeing oneself as a visitor in search of stories is quite different from being a researcher equipped with theories. There is neither the voyeuristic distance, nor the immediacy of an excess of preconditioned feelings. The comparatist's mode of being together will also include being apart, despite her engagement with what has been called the ethics of rapprochement. Stories have to be exchanged and meetings and visits have to continue.

II

Moving out from self-contained vernacular societies, one finds that when a story from the so-called margins is forced to enter into a dialectic relationship with all the forces acting on a particular social space, its very nature becomes transformed. There is the story of Rani Reshma and Chuharmal, performed as a folk-ballad and extensively commented upon by Badri Narayan in his book *Documenting Dissent* (2001). The lower caste people of Magahi and Bhojpuri regions of Bihar perform it now at a fair held every year at Chiradih (near Mokama) in remembrance of the low-caste Dusadh hero of the story. For the Dusadhs, it is a re-enactment of their glorious past. There are many variations of the story, but the basic core relates to the love of Chuharmal, a Dusadh chivalrous hero and Rani Reshma, the beautiful daughter of the local Raja of Bhumihar. The story is now a point of contention, an issue of conflict and violence between the Bhumihars and the lower castes of the region. It provoked four caste riots in Central Bihar, between 1970 and 1990. The story and its accompanying fair also figured prominently as a pre-election event. The story incidentally is often banned. In such instances, the Dusadhs perform a similar story with a similar rhythm and say that they feel good enacting it. In its many forms and its continuous renewal with reference to the series of enacted events it brings forth, this particular story in the *Veergatha* tradition distinguishes itself with respect to literature. It is also significant in its ability to mobilize dissent. One may argue at this point that the destiny of the meta-story has very little to do with the core story—but then, in orature specifically, and this ought to be so in literature as well, the story of the story is an integral part of the story-text. The borders become seamless as the story moves into context and another story begins, opening up an entirely new approach to narrativity and performance.

The trope of the visitor that I used in the context of the earlier story can only be used in a restricted sense here. It is no longer only a question of deep communication and its accompanying gestures. The realm of the symbolic spills over into the concrete and necessitates an equivalent move on the part of the comparatist who, one assumes in this case is also a performer, as well as those present. Literary responsibilities in this context would have to be redefined in accordance with the needs of the moment.

The question that we need to examine here is as follows: when are we dealing with literature in the context of a real situation and not in symbolic but in concrete terms? Are we compelled to deal with literature and its effects, and when are the effects immediate and of great magnitude? Are we still working with literature as it is known and studied within a literature classroom? Is there a pedagogical shift? The situation does open up certain perspectives within literature and makes the metropolitan student aware of its foundational dimensions, even though he/she may not be able to come to terms with the explosive excess contained in the story. At this stage, it may be worthwhile to remind ourselves that Comparative Literature is a disposition and a willingness to engage with the concept of literature from different terrains in a significant manner. The base line would always be closest to one's own area of contact, whatever form that contact may take, whether it be space, language, history or experience. It is then important to work out relations, discover them where they do not seem to exist, and if possible, move into terrains of radical alterity, if only to recover from falling into complacency and passivity.

Coming closer to the reality of the metropolis, concepts of the margins multiply manifold—narratives in local trains, poems or stories accompanying the sale of consumer items, wall graffiti and then a whole range of printed material, from lives of saints to praise songs and various kinds of manuals in verse form. It is often within this ephemera, so-called by the centre, that the 'word' springs into rhythm with a life of its own, as a part of the living processes of everyday life. It can be full of rare turns and surprises. The ludic impulse is also evident in this phenomenon, despite the fact that sometimes the creator may be living on the edge of survival. It can also be conceived without sentimentality, and most often, with a humour that has a certain subversive edge, destabilizing the ordered world of meanings in a subtle fashion. I am not sure that I can even speak of another margin, of *clochards* and madmen imagining themselves in various roles, talking to others, to themselves, where one encounters the raw cutting edge of words often from a region unknown to a gentlewoman—surrealistic, delirious literary experiences without a centre. One may also read in most of the above expressions, desperate attempts to build bridges, to communicate or simply to sell in order to survive. The world of 'ephemera' is also a space where one can experience the full implications of the contingent or the real. Meanings emerge and disappear—they are brought into being as one enters a certain space, and they disappear as one moves away from another space where a new set of meanings may emerge. This particular space will be quite radical to the comparatist. If she remains open to new forms of understandings and appreciations, there might not only be a radical democratization of literature and literary studies, but also an extension of the very concept of literature in the recognition of the agency of those who are not labelled 'poets' or 'authors'.

Within the metropolis, institutions of learning chart out another space with specific notions of centres and margins. In my language, I have in mind certain texts that may be seen as a complete rupture with a certain tradition of writing that is class-based and humanist despite explorations of the darker areas of society.[4] It must be remembered that Bengal did not have a strong Dalit movement in literature as in some other parts of India, where as a result mainstream literature had to acknowledge, and to a certain extent, enter into a dialectical relation with Dalit literature. The other tradition in Bengal represents texts based on a logic of subversion—they are fragmented and dispersed. They delineate those spaces in society that one would rather ignore. Some of them carry definite signposts and attempting to bring them into institutions would be tantamount to an erasure of their very spirit. But then again, as in the case of regions with a strong presence of Dalit literature, paying attention to such texts could bring into being a rich body of literature, and in this instance, richness would incorporate certain perspectives on life and society perceived to be right and just in the context of the crisis of justice in the present world. Such an aesthetics of subversion would necessarily be linked to a whole set of critical tools brought to bear on the existing faultlines in society.

In a restricted sense, we have been talking about the margins within a more or less local circuit, although some of the issues may be transcultural. Margins, of course, exist within a global system framed by the market economy. A CLAI Conference held in association with the Central Institute of Indian Languages, Mysore had 'Linguistic Hegemony and Identity' as the theme in 2003, and the Eleventh ICLA Congress held in Hong Kong in 2004 was titled 'At the Edge: Margins, Frontiers, Initiatives in Literature and Culture'. One may note that the term 'margins' in the context of the international body of the Comparative Literature Association linked up with frontiers and initiatives rather than with contexts of occlusion as in the national context. Also, when we speak locally we tend to limit conjectures and possibilities. The frameworks that we work with are less distanced, more immediate and necessitate both critical thought and action. Elsewhere, we work within broader frameworks, explore possibilities, work on nuances, engage with critical thought, but in a somewhat distanced manner. The comparatist poised within a network of broader frameworks, necessarily contingent in both cases, and also working in close connection with the local has to contend with tensions arising out of the different areas of need. One may reiterate at this point that Comparative Literature by consensus today, if one may use the word, is turned towards new understandings of literary phenomena by constant juxtapositions of different literary traditions and viewpoints. As a result, notions of margins and centres in the domain of Comparative Literature may, in fact, be conceptually non-existent. Our response to this position would be that, at the outset, we did bring in the notion of margins with reference to existing market structures that make certain kinds of literature invisible. This qualification does not allow space for certain domains of literary expression to flourish. It is a question of the Field of Forces that contributes to certain literary discourses flourishing at the expense of others. At one level, as others have argued before me and very effectively too, literary studies have to engage with these forces.

I would go further and say that comparatists should contribute to the creation of platforms that would allow such literatures and oratures to flourish. For their own sake, they should keep the discipline alive and not for the sake of the writer or *silpi* at the margins. In my first year undergraduate course on Comparative Literature, students inevitably tell me that Comparative Literature or *Tulanamulak Sahitya* is literature or *sahitya*, just as Bangla literature or English literature. Over the years, I have begun to see their point. Comparative Literature is worth its nomenclature in as much as it makes room for literatures, constantly unveils the invisible, creates opportunities for their visibility, uncovers creative energies, and as a consequence, fulfills its function as literature. Its entity as literature does not derive from a language and the history of its creative articulations, but from a comprehensive idea of literature as generated by different forms of creative expressions.

The ground reality is very different. Sisir Kumar Das would often talk about a discussion he once had with Henry Remak. He had agitatedly asked him, 'But why don't you take up the study of different Asian Literatures in your courses in Comparative Literature?' Remak smiled and answered, 'Each of us has to do what he or she can do best'. We do not have to be very ambitious—we can take up at least literatures within one other culture, one that seems to exist on a very different axis, that has remained invisible to a greater or lesser degree, and that in our context has had or can have important bearings and linkages. This literature needs to be taken up in all its density, involving a study of networks in operation within which it takes shape.

It is important at this point to enter directly into an area of discourse that has so far been peripheral to my engagement—the prevalent discourses on the margin within the first world, often articulated by third world intellectuals inhabiting the first world. There, the margin is a privileged space with necessary disciplinary support and often viewed in terms of a 'cosmopolitan alterity industry'. The non-aspiring elite within the Third World, and I mean the college teacher in suburbia who does not dream of going to northern metropolitan centres of study, often speaks of how pleasurable it is for her to engage with oratures. The appeal to the imaginary of the non-script sources, and the consequent enhancement of her understanding of literature, of certain aspects of life and living are underscored. It may on the surface be an engagement of the romantic kind, but not really so, as any journey into the context of oratures reveals layers of complexities calling for critical attention at every step. And again, a task pursued for its own sake, at its own pace, with little material gain, carves out its own little space of resistance to globalized market forces transforming lives and relationships. There is also the incidence of a Kuki girl from the North-East asking a teacher of Comparative Literature what she means by Comparative Literature in India when the syllabus reveals a complete absence of any of the living traditions of oratures from anywhere in India let alone the Kukis, whose numbers, she says, are diminishing everyday. As we enter the discursive domain of Comparative Literature, it is important to remember that issues are and will remain different in different parts of the world because they are felt and experienced in a different manner, expressed in a different texture and idiom, though in fact attention to such differences should also be a part of Comparative Literature studies. It is not a question of authentic marginality—the college teacher in suburbia is not marginal in the local context, on the other hand, what is termed marginal is very much a part of her history and from a larger perspective also a part of the planet's history—how one begins to acknowledge this fact and how it might lead to a rethinking of various civilizational structures is a different question.

NOTES

1. A version of this chapter was presented at the Congress of the Comparative Literature Association of India held in Surat in 2005.
2. Quotation from 'Tribhuvan Brata' in Dakshinaranjan Mitra Majumdar's *Thandidir Thole* (1909).
3. See Stephen Muecke, *Ancient and Modern: Time Culture and Indigenous Philosophy*, Sydney: UNSW Press, 2004.
4. An example here may be that of Nabarun Bhattacharya's *Herbert* (1994).

REFERENCES

Bhattacharya, Nabarun, *Herbert*, Kolkata: Dey's Publishing, 1994.

Narayan, Badri, *Documenting Dissent*, Shimla: IIAS, 2001.

Said, Edward W., 'Orientalism 25 Years Later: Wordly Humanism v. the Empire-builders', *Counterpunch*, 4 August 2003, (Retrieved from <http://www.counterpunch.org/2003/08/05/orientalism/>).

PART III

General Translation Theory

12

Towards an Indian Theory of Translation

Indra Nath Choudhuri

WHAT IS THE reason that a multilingual country with a 5,000-year-old civilization did not care to develop a well-founded translation theory or even discuss, if not elaborately, at least concisely, the nature, function and principles of translation. Bhadriraju Krishnamurti (1998: 38) by quoting M.B. Emeneau (1956: 3–16) points out that India is a linguistic area and, based on the same analogy, I might say that India is also a translation area. Being polyglots, we use more than one language while speaking or even thinking. However, the big question is why there is no single critical text specifying the art or science of translation parallel to the Sanskrit grammarian Panini's fourth-century BC *Ashtadhyayi* (literally, 'eight chapters') (Katre 1989) or Tholkappiyar's third-century BC Tamil grammar entitled *Tolkappiyam* (Rajam 1981) or Bharata's *Natyashastra*, an ancient Indian treatise on the performing arts, encompassing theatre, dance and music written between 200 BC and AD 200 (Ghosh 1951). One can presume that in the Indian context an exclusive attitude with regard to the Sanskrit language and privilege of the speakers, and their master narrative was responsible for this lacuna. To a greater extent, one would be correct in this assumption, as Suniti Kumar Chatterji has explained (Chatterji 1960: 94).

Polyglottism in ancient India, as Chatterji says, was responsible for the development of a 'translating consciousness' (1933: 172–190). Vatsyayana's term *lokopichanuvada*, or 'translatibility', suggests how far back we can trace India's theorizing on translation. Chatterji, in his book *Indo-Aryan and Hindi* (Chatterji 1960), has proved that a good deal of Sanskrit literature, particularly the *Mahabharata* and the Puranas, are based on a translation substratum from the literatures of Indo-Aryan languages which include the languages of Aryans, miscegenated Aryans, non-Aryans, and foreign speakers, in particular, settled groups who spoke Greek and old Persian. When Sanskrit attained a pan-Indian prestige status, its speakers became reluctant to disclose the translated character of this literary substratum.

We may be able to explain this oversight or occlusion theoretically by turning to the Russian formalists, who were of the opinion that in every literary tradition there is not one but several literary schools and that they exist in literature simultaneously (Crawford 2008: 209–19). Only one of them, however, represents the canonized crest. Sanskrit, in due course, achieved this status while the others existed obscurely. The superior position played down any role of translation from these languages into Sanskrit. With the passage of time, Sanskrit speakers came to hold the artistic creation in the Indian *bhashas* (regional languages) in contempt.

A prime example of this process can be seen in a legend that is usually associated with Gunadhya's *Brihatkatha*. Gunadhya, a poet of high merit and deep perception, wrote this book of stories in Paishachi language, a dialect once spoken in north-western India in Kashmir. When Gunadhya's *Brihatkatha* was composed during the seventh to the eighth centuries AD, Sanskrit was still the language of power, scholarship and arrogance. When Gunadhya presented the manuscript to scholars, they rejected it outright since it was not written in Sanskrit. In response to this humiliating insult, Gunadhya took the extreme step of burning the manuscript.

The legend goes on to relate that Somadeva, a distinguished scholar of Sanskrit, was able to rescue one-seventh of the manuscript by persuading Gunadhya not to burn the complete work. This portion (2400 slokas) of the recovered manuscript was translated into Sanskrit by Somadeva as the *Kathasaritsagara*. Later on, Kshemendra, another very distinguished scholar of Sanskrit, also translated the extant manuscript in 7500 Sanskrit verses, as the *Brihatkathamanjari*. In fact, Somadeva's work was the first book translated into Sanskrit from any other Indian language. There exist other translations available in Sanskrit from Pali Buddhist texts, but in general Sanskrit held an elitist approach to literature. Other languages were simply not translated into Sanskrit.

Although Sanskrit scholars and writers did not care to translate from *bhasha* literature into Sanskrit, they were quite concerned about the issue of translation in the multilingual society in which they lived. Faced with linguistic divergence, they were forced to investigate different aspects of language, learning and teaching. They wished to distinguish universals from common notions in the various languages and chart the distances between them. They also had to deal with the complex relationship between words and meaning, language representation, and logic. All these issues still have relevance for our understanding of ancient Indian linguistics and help in creating a viable theory for translations today.

There are scattered insights and oblique hints given in different texts, as well as the actual principles observed by the practitioners of literary translation in almost all the Indian languages stretching over several centuries, that can be pieced together to develop an Indian theory of translation. Some examples of these texts are the *Aitereya* or *Gopatha Brahmana*—a large number of Brahmana texts were written between 1000–600 BC to explain the Vedic texts, rites and customs (Malaviya 1986; see also Mitra and Bhushana 1872); the Sanskrit grammarian Panini's *Ashtadhyayi*; Yaska, another Sanskrit grammarian who succeeded Panini during the sixth or seventh century BC, wrote his book on the etymology of Vedic terms, the *Nirukta* (Sarup 2002; Krishna 1990);[1] Kayyata's eleven-century *tika* (commentary) named *Pradipa*, Mahabhasyakar's eleven-century commentary on Panini's grammar attributed to Patanjali (Raja 1990); Kulluka Bhatta's *tika*, the *Manavartha Muktavali* (AD 260) on Bhartrihari and the *Manusmriti* (between thirteen and fifteen centuries) and Vatsyayana's first-century BC commentary, along with the *Varttika* by Uddyotakar on Gautama's *Nyayadarshana*, the book of logic (Tarkatirtha 1985; Vidyabhusana 1971). The actual principles observed by the practitioners of literary translation in almost all the Indian languages stretching over several centuries can be pieced together to develop an Indian theory of translation.

Here I must admit that I have little knowledge of 700 to 800 years of the common era's *bhasha* tradition and also the explicative discussion in the Prakrit and Apabhramsa of Jam aesthetics about which D.R. Nagaraj, A.K. Ramanujan's successor at Chicago, gave a brilliant exposition in a Sahitya Akademi seminar many years back on 5 October 1996 in Bangalore. While piecing together what has been said about translation in a variety of texts, one can realize that in the Indian context the term for translation is *anuwad*, and it signifies the repetition of what is enjoined by a Vedic text with a different wording. But repetition is not understood as a literal word by word rendering of the original from source to target language. In the Indian context, the reader is never a passive receiver of a text in which its truth is enshrined. The theories of *rasa* and *dhvani* suggest that a text is recoded by the individual consciousness of its receiver so that he/she may have multiple aesthetic experiences and hence a text is not perceived as an object that should produce a single invariant reading. Unlike the Western approach to tradition, any deviation on the part of the reader-translator is not a transgression in Indian translation. The Indian translator always has the freedom to interpret the text if he or she does not disturb the core of the piece and it always remains constant, what André Lefevere refers to as the 'invariant core' of a translated text (1976, 1981: 52–8).

One of the greatest advances in twentieth century Western literary study is that theoreticians like Roland Barthes saw the role of the literary work as that of making the reader not so much a 'consumer' as a 'producer' of the text (1970: 4). Julia Kristeva's notion of 'intertextuality' was also profoundly significant because the very acceptance of all the texts that precede and surround a work allows the reader—translator to interpret, clarify, and translate (1980: 69). The ancient Indian view that translation is nothing but repetition also suggests that translation is primarily a clarification or interpretation that is obtained by repetitive utterances. To an Indian society, steeped in an oral literary tradition of *smriti* and *shruti*, differing versions become the norm rather than an exception. The method of producing an authentic and 'pure' text, as practised in Europe, particularly during the colonial period, was an alien notion for Indians. To the Indian mind, translation is rebirth where the *atman*, the text's soul or invariant core, remains constant, while other aspects take on a new form.

Moreover, in addition to analysing the notion of repetition (*vidhivihitatasyanuvachanuvadah*: to repeat in words according to rules in translation), the *Gopatha Brahmana* reflects on the doctrine of the purpose-fulness of translation (*saprayojanamanuvadah*: translation is always with a purpose) in Sanskrit poetics and the fact that it cannot be simply explained by the utility theory of supply and demand. Translation problems are more aesthetic than purely linguistic and functional. Therefore, *prayojana* should be understood as aesthetic delight (*sakalaprayojanamaulibhutaanandam*: the ultimate objective of literature is a state of blissfulness) according to Mammata (2005: 2), an eleventh-century AD Sanskrit rhetorician. He was of the opinion that literary translation is not just a replication of a text in another verbal space and period. Instead, a translated text raises the question of how translation functions as an aesthetic activity.

The essence of translation lies in the preservation of meaning across two different languages. This notion leads us to the central issue of equivalence in translation. In Madhavacharya's *Jaiminiya Nyaya Mala-Vistara* (1865), it is said that the revelation of meaning is translation: *jatasyakathanamanuvadah* (1.4.6), and therefore equivalence here does not mean a search for sameness but something which is revealed. Even Shakespeare in 'A Midsummer Nights' Dream' did not accept the theory of sameness for translation. The play is of common men, kings, queens and fairies with magical power. One of the characters named Puck turned the head of Bottom, a weaver, into that of a donkey to satisfy Oberon's desire to play a joke on his wife Titania. Bottom's friends were very scared and felt as if they were haunted by some evil spirit. One of his friends, Snout, called out, 'O Bottom, thou art changed!' His friend Quince went a step further and retorted, 'Bless thee, Bless thee! Thou art translated' (Act III, Scene 1). In other words, for Shakespeare, translation denotes a complete transformation of the original.

An adequate translation is semantically, pragmatically and dynamically equivalent because a translator is confronted with a range of interpretabilities and his task is to analyse consciously the superstructure of content based on a complex fabric of language. Revelation of meaning depends upon etymology (*yoga*) and interpretation is based on conventionally established usage (*rudhi*), which is always stronger than *yoga*. Translation, therefore, is not verbatim reproduction but an imaginative recreation and retelling in the target language.

Indian theoreticians understood that the literal meaning of an utterance is only a part of its total meaning and that those who try to analyse literal meaning may completely lose sight of its real or inner significance. More than literal meaning, however, the ancients looked for a text's inner significance which is rooted in the context of the verbal art. It determines the 'literariness' of the artifact and, without this knowledge, a translation is never successful. Both the verbal and cultural contexts, therefore, facilitate the recoding of the text by the reader-translator for the purpose of emancipating *artha* (meaning) from material reality (Jonardon 2006: 23). Kayyat, and even Tholkappiyar (third century BC) refer to *pramanaantar* or the contextual meaning that occurs when transferred translation becomes a reality.

In contrast, the Buddhist logicians talked about mental or conceptual images, which do not have their counterpart in the objective world, as conceived by Mimamsa and Nyaya philosophers. They refused to believe there are any real connections between words and external objects. *Netti-Prakranam*, a Buddhist guidebook for commentators, emphasizes the context theory of language and investigates the structure and play of a text's word fabric (Nanamoli 1962).

In the famous Tamil grammar, the *Tholkappiyam*, context plays an important role in resolving problems of meaning. Bhartrihari (fifth century AD) identifies four types of context factors that are significant for understanding verbal art (Iyer 1977: 136; 1983: 273):

(a) *sansarga* (two things known to be related, e.g. *savatsadhenu*: cow with her calf).

(b) *viprayoga* (relation between two things disappears, e.g. *avatsadhenu:* cow without a calf).
(c) *sahacharya* (e.g. Rama-Laxmana, here Rama is not Parashurama or Balarama. The compound here identifies Rama as the brother of Laxmana).
(d) *Virodhita* (*ahinakula*: opposition or a hostile relation, e.g. snake and mongoose).

Besides *anubachanam* (the notion of repetition), *saprayojanam* (purposefulness of a text/aesthetic delight), *jatasyakathanam* (revelation of meaning is not a search for sameness) and *pramanantaram* (contextual meaning) as explained earlier, Ayyappa Panikar introduces other useful concepts prevalent in medieval Indian translations of Sanskrit classics that, in fact, reveal everything worth knowing regarding Sanskrit theories on translation. These concepts include *anukriti, arthakriya, vyaktivivekam* and *ullurai* (Paniker 1996: 36–45; 1998: 39–48).

1. *Anukriti* is an imitation of the original. One can imitate only what one is not. The product of imitation is not the same text but a similar one.
2. *Arthakriya* involves placing emphasis on the manifold ways in which meanings are enacted in different texts. It focuses on the creation of meaning, addition, omission, displacement and expansion.
3. *Vyaktivivekam* denotes the rendering of meaning as it is inferred by the reader or its interpretation as based on *anumana* or the inference potential of a given passage.
4. *Ullurai* is a Dravidian term that primarily means inner speech, which is not the heard melody but the one unheard or the speech within. In a literary text, *ullurai* plays a crucial role.

These concepts confirm the existence of a distinctive Indian theory of translation that underlines the creative freedom enjoyed by medieval Indian reader—translators to produce viable, fully localized translations with a visible absence of anxiety on their part regarding authenticity.

These initial translators attended to their jobs with few inhibitions. They rarely maintained a word-for-word or line-for-line discipline. Their categories were nothing akin to the TL (target language) and the SL (source language) or the mother tongue and the other tongue. The poet/writers executing *bhasha* renderings of Sanskrit texts treated both languages as their own. They had a sense of possession with respect to the Sanskrit heritage. In fact, the whole medieval *bhakti* movement of poetry in India sought to translate the language of spirituality from Sanskrit to the language of the people and liberate the scriptures from the monopoly of a restricted class of people. They saw to it that their translations became a means of reorganizing society.

In the case of Jnaneswara or Jnanadeva, a distinguished poet of medieval Marathi devotional poetry (thirteen century AD and his book *Bhavartha Dipika* (popularly known as the '*Jnaneswari*') was free translation of the *Bhagavad Gita* (Bahirat 1956). Within the scope of this work, this great philosopher and *poet* subsumes the knowledge of the *Nath* tradition in order to wed it to the *bhakti* movement. The original text, the *Gita*, is a set of dialogues, between Saunaka and rishis in the Nimisha forest, between Sanjaya and Dhritarasthra, and between Krishna and Arjuna. In translating it, Jnanadeva adds two more levels of dialogic tension: the first involves the oral level of the conversation between the poet and his guru Nivrittinath and the second, the lexical level of dictation given by the poet to his scholiast Satchidananda. In adding these levels, the poet endows the oral component with legitimacy as a form of literature as valid as the written word. He thereby underlines that the *Jnaneswari Gita* is more a *suta* (to be sung in another language) text than a *mantra* (Sanskrit verse) text. We find contained in these subversions and shifts the seeds of an emerging and very complex Indian theory of translation. Devy is of opinion that Indian consciousness is 'translating consciousness' and it exploits the 'potential openness of language systems'. He believes `if we take lead from Phenomenology and conceptualize a whole community of 'translating consciousness', it should be possible to develop a theory of inter-lingual synonymy' (Devy 1993, 139–141). W.B. Quine could apply, in this case, the thesis of indeterminacy of translation and cast his aspersions on this kind of a theoretical formulation (Quine 1960), but the Indian theoreticians would say that there is no reason to be skeptical and fastidious about exactness and accuracy.

It is obvious that medieval India did not believe in literal translation even though Indian writers were familiar with the concept of a verbatim translation known as the *chhaya* (shadow) of the Prakrit text into Sanskrit, which is frequently found in Sanskrit drama. Indians preferred adaptation to *verbatim* translation. The *Tolkappiyam* mentions that a vali (an adapted work) can be of four kinds: abridged, expanded, abridged and expanded, or translated in accordance with the Tamil traditions. Kamban (eleven-century AD Tamil poet and author of *Ramaavataram*, popularly known as *Kambanramayanam*, the Tamil version of Valmiki's *Ramayana*) belongs to this school of translation. He did not aim for literal paraphrasing, but sought to create a living translation.

It reminds us of FitzGerald, the English translator of the *Rubaiyat of Omar Khayyam*, who once said, 'I shall anytime prefer a living sparrow than a stuffed eagle' (quoted from a letter by FitzGereld to E.B. Cowell, 27 April 1859: 4). Translated texts are both word-bound and world-bound. The tradition of translation in medieval India was world-bound but not word-bound.

But where should one set the limits for creative freedom? When does a version become subversion? When does a deviation lead to distortion? One can cite counter-texts like *Ravanayana* or *Meghnadbadhkavya* (epic in Bengali language of the nineteen century related the story of the *Ramayana* by Michael Madhusudan Dutt) or feminist versions of the *Ramayana* in Bengali (Padmavati's *Ramayana*) and other languages or parodies of the *Mahabharata* like *The Great Indian Novel* by Shashi Tharoor. They are certainly not translations in the orthodox or ordinary sense of the term. But they exhibit inter textuality—each work provokes us to think of the other texts.

The West, in contrast, has always been obsessed with the anxiety of authenticity. Perhaps it began with the attempts to translate the Bible into the different languages of the world that this issue of authenticity became so significant. According to G.N. Devy, the European literary tradition that was reared on Christian metaphysics has always alluded to translation as a 'perpetual exile', a move away from the origins and an effort to resituate one's own origin. In the West, translation is feared as an intrusion of the 'other'. Sometimes this intrusion is desirable because it helps define one's identity. The King James Bible and Martin Luther's Bible translation proved excellent examples of how quests for identity often 'translate into acts of literary defiance' (Devy 2009: 182).

European literary historiography is, in fact, steeped in a tradition that has always been suspicious of the 'other'—the Europeans feared foreign culture entering in their lives through translation. Inversely, India possesses a high capacity to assimilate alien cultures. Its acceptance of Vedantic oneness has always paved the way for obliterating difference between *swa* and *para* (the self and the other) (Devy 1998; pp. 143–7). In the modern period, translation in the West has been studied from a variety of perspectives: the discourse analysis by Paul Valery (referred by Whiting 1978), the Cultural Studies approach by George Steiner (1975), theoretical linguistics by J.C. Catford (1965), psychoanalysis by Andrew Benjamin (1992), structuralism by Roman Jakobson (2006: 21), the deconstruction by Derrida (1978, 1980: 218–27), gender studies by Lori Chamberlain (1992) and, of course, postcolonial discourse analysis by Lawrence Venuti (1986: 179–212). The influence Venuti has exerted on translation studies, by his advocacy of *foreignizing* as against *domesticating* translation forms as a part of postcolonial discourse analysis. All these approaches consider translation as a complicated linguistic and literary act, whereas in India it tends to be viewed as an inevitable way of life and the focus has been more on the pragmatic aspects of translation.

Among post-structuralist thinkers, Jacques Derrida, in particular, questioned the absolute position that a literary text occupied in traditional critical discourse and argued that each new instance of reading the text is a different occasion to experience the absence of meaning. Derrida, thus, granted translation the status of literature since the translator, like a creative writer, signifies meaning as an independent presence and develops a more dynamic theory between the relationship of meaning and language (1999: 423–46).

Bhartrihari's exposition of the *sphota* theory almost anticipates Derrida. The Indian poet maintained that the relation between *nada* (phonetic manifestation) and *sphota* (semantic realization) resembles the reflection of the sun in the flowing water. The reflection of a steady object can acquire the movements of a water current (Vakyapadiya, *Brahmakandam* (kanda/chapter 1), 1965: 48–50). No reflection is possible unless there is a substance to contain it. Yet the reflection in itself and by itself is nothing. Meaning exists in language not as a positive presence but as an absence that reflects its independent presence (Bhattacharya 2002).

I suspect that this view was very much prevalent in India and contributed unconsciously to the construction of a theory of translation. In modern times, such an understanding was endorsed by Sri Aurobindo who held that a translator is not necessarily bound to the original; he can make his own poem out of it, if he likes, and that is the general practice.[2]

However, the Indian view is reader-oriented; it does not neglect the basic desire of a reader to approach translation in order to understand and enjoy the original and not to make a new creation out of it. One reads translation primarily in order to come out from one's own cultural prison and create a vantage point from which one can observe, understand, and enjoy the happenings of another culture (Varney 2008: 113–31).

In contemporary India, plurilingual authors, writing in the language of the ex-colonizer or in the various Indian *bhashas*, are challenging and redefining many accepted notions in translation theory. We can no longer merely limit ourselves to the conventional notion of linguistic equivalence or ideas of loss and gain which have long been a staple of translation theory because of the extensive use of different *upabhashas* by Indian writers such as Kambar, Debesh Roy, Krishna Sobti and others;

the creation of a new language by Dalit writers; and the use of tribal languages in multilingual contexts. These are the languages of the 'in between', occupying an intermediary space and challenging conventional notions of translation by seeking to create new models for translation theory. Once these developments are seen and accepted as a part of a historic process, only then can we be able to analyse and explain the Dalit and *grammin* (rural) literary heterodoxy and translate it (Choudhuri 1997: 31–32). In the process, we should be able to create an Indian translation theory and add new insights to it and affirm the importance of a moral and radical deconstructive path.

I started my essay with a story of Gunadhya's *Brihatkatha* and I now end it with another story narrated by Alexander Dow, who translated Farishta's *Tareekh e Farishta* (1606) as *History of Hindostan* (1768 to 72 in 3 vols) from Persian into English and also commented on the difficulties of translating from Sanskrit into English or Persian both for himself and the Mughal emperors. Dow tells the legendary tale of the great scholar Faizi, one of the nine jewels of the Mughal Emperor Akbar, who had changed his name and travelled to Varanasi to study the Vedas under a learned Brahmin with the ultimate intention of translating them into Persian (Dow 1768: xxvi-vii) Faizi acquired the necessary knowledge of Sanskrit after ten years of study but he also fell passionately in love with the daughter of his guru. The Brahmin was delighted to have his daughter married to his disciple but when the repentant young man revealed the deception to his guru that he was not a Brahmin but originally a Muslim, the Brahmin Guru ordered him to stop his learning in the Vedas immediately. He also forewarned him not to translate the knowledge he had acquired. As the legend goes, Faizi returned hone with a wife but no translation. In comparison to Faizi in the sixteenth century and Dow in the eighteenth century, our situation in the twenty-first century of translating Sanskrit or *bhasha* texts into English or another Indian *bhasha* is far less problematic and considerably more propitious. With the increase in translation activities, the development of an Indian theory of translation now becomes plausible.

Such a theory would not reject the pragmatic approach of sameness in translation but would go a step further towards emotionally reconstructing a verbal art into a different language. In the process, metaphorically, if the text looked like a golden chain with a pendant but in its recreation in another language, if it lost its chain but not the pendant, and if the pendant looked attractive, then one should not hesitate to say to the translator, 'Congratulations, you have nailed it.' In this context, I will conclude with a couplet from Iqbal (1935–2003), one of the most distinguished Urdu poets, which is apt for our understanding of Indian translation consciousness: 'Transcend your reason although it is a glow, it is not your destination; It can only the path to the destination show' (Iqbal 2003: 65).

NOTES

1. See Krishna, 1990, Chapter 3 for a detailed account on Yaska.
2. In the matter of translations, Sri Aurobindo seems to have held the not unreasonable, if perhaps unorthodox, view that mere literalness or word for word equation was not the ideal towards which one should aim and, in fact, he once wrote to Dilip Kumar Roy, an Aurobindonian and a great singer: 'a translator is not necessarily bound to the original he chooses; he can make his own poem out of it, if he likes, and that is what is very often done' (Sri Aurobindo: The future poetry, p. 431). But it should be equally clear that, if 'literalness' should not mean dullness, flatness or deadness ('turning life into death and poetic power into poverty and flatness'), 'freedom' should not mean a sheer tangential escape into regions altogether new. A literary (not literal) translation is no students' crib but neither should it involve a transmogrification. Good translations like Dryden's *Virgil* and Fitzgerald's *Omar Khayyam* are equally great poems, by virtue of their finish and their essential fidelity to their originals' (Sri Aurobindo 1949: 208); cf. George Sampson, 'Dryden's Virgil is literally Dryden's Virgil ... Its readers were already familiar with Virgil's Virgil, and wanted to know how a great English poet would treat that familiar story, (George Sampson and R.C. Churchil,1970: 341).

REFERENCES

Bahirat, B.P., *The Philosophy of Jnanadeva: As Gleaned from the Amrtanubhava*, Delhi: Motilal Banarsidass, 1956.

Barthes, Roland, *S/Z (1970)*, translated by Richard Miller, London, Jonathan Cape, 1974

Benjamin, Andrew, 'Translating Origins: Psychoanalysis and Philosophy', *Rethinking Translation*, London: Routledge, 1992.

Bhattacharya, Sibajiban, *Bhartrihari and Wittgenstein*, New Delhi: Sahitya Akademi, 2002.

Bhatt, Kulluka, *Mauusmriti: with the Sanskrit Commentary Manavarthamuktavali*, Delhi: J.L. Shastri and S.C. Banerji, 1996.

Catford, J.C., *A Linguistic Theory of Translation: An Essay in Applied Linguistis*, London: CUP, 1965.

Chamberlain, Lori, 'Gender and the Metaphorics of Translation', in *Rethinking Translation: Discourse, Subjectivity, Ideology*, ed. Lawrence Venuti, London and New York: Routledge, 1992.

Chatterji, Suniti Kumar, *Indo-Aryan and Hindi*, Calcutta: Firma K.L. Mukhopadhyaya, 1960.

———, "Polyglottism in Indo-Aryan", pp. 177–190, Proceedings of 7th Oriental Conference, Baroda, 1933, Poona.

Choudhuri, Indra Nath, 'The Plurality of Languages and Literature in Translation: The Post Colonial Context', pp. 439–43, *Meta Journal des traducteurs Meta/Translations*, Montreal, vol. 42, n. 2, 1997 and Translation and Multilingualism: Post-Colonial Context, (ed.) Shantha Ramakrishna, pp. 31–32, Delhi, Pencraft International 1997.

Crawford, Lawrence, 'Viktor Shklovskij: Difference in Demamiliarization, Comparative Literature', *JSTOR*, vol. 36, 1984; article reprinted, 2008, pp. 209–19.

Derrida, J., *Writing and Difference*, London and New York: Routledge, 1978.

———, 'Des Tours de Babel', in *Theories of Translation*, pp. 218–27, (ed.) R. Schulte and J. Biguenet, Chicago: University of Chicago Press, 1980, pp. 218–27.

———, 'What is a Relevant Translation?', pp. 423–46 in *The Translation Studies Reader*, ed. L. Venuti, London & New York: Routledge, 1999.

Devy, G.N., 'Language, Culture, Translation', presented at the Workshop on Language, Culture and Translation at IIC, p. 182, New Delhi, from 31 October to 1 November 1990

———, *On Many Heroes: An Indian Essay in Literary Historiography*, pp. 143–47, Sangam Books Ltd,, London, 1998

———, *Postcolonial Translation: Translation and Literary History–An Indian View*, p. 182 London: Routledge, 1999.

——— *In Another Tongue: Essays on Indian English Literature*, pp. 139–141 Madras: Macmillan India, 1993.

Dow, Alexander, *History of Hindostan, English translation of Vol. 1 of the Persian book by Muhammad Qasim Hindu Shah Astaravadi Firishtah*, pp. xxvi–vii, London: T.Becket and P.A. De Hondt, 1768,

Emeneau, M.B., Language, Vol. 32, No. 1 (January–March, 1956), pp. 3–16, Linguistic Society of America, Washington, 1956.

Fitz Gerald, Edward, Letters of Edward Fitz Gerald in 2 vols, p. 4, London, MacMillan, Vol. 2, 1901.

George Sampson and R.C. Churchil, *The Concise Cambridge History of English Literature*, Chapter VIII, p. 34 Cambridge, 1970.

Ghosh, Manomohan, *Bharata's Natya Sastra, English Translation*, Calcutta: Asiatic Society of Bengal, 1951.

lqbal, Allama Baal-e-Jibreel, *The Best of Iqhal*, 1935; tr. Kuldeep Salil, p. 65, repr., Delhi: Rajpal, 2003.

Iyer, K.A. Subramania, *The Vakyapadiya of Bhartrihari with the Vritti*, original text, Kanda 2, verse 315, p. 273, Motilal Banarasidas, 1983, Poona: Deccan College, Poona, 1963.

———, *Vakyapadiya of Bhartrihari with the Vritti, Kanda 1*, translation, pp. 48–50, Poona Decan College, Poona, 1965.

———, *The Vakyapadiya of Bhartrihari with the Vritti, English Translation of Chap. 2*, p. 136, Delhi: Motilal Banarsidass, 1977.

Jakobson, R., *On Linguistic Aspects of Translation, an essay*, 1959; repr. in Translation *Studies Reader*, p. 126, ed. Lawrence Venuti, London, 2000.

Jonardon, Ganeri, *Artha: Meaning*, p. 23, London: OUP, 2006.

Katre, Sumitra M., *Astadhyayi of Panini, English Translation*, Austin: University of Texas Press, 1987, repr., Delhi: Motilal Banarsidass, 1989.

Krishna, Matilal Bimal, *The Word and the World: Judia's Contribution to the Study of Language*, London: OUP, 1990.

Krishnamurti, Bhadriraju, *Language, Education and Society (Language Development)*, New Delhi: Sage, 1998.

Kristeva, Julia, *Desire in Language: A Semiotic Approach to Literature and Art*, tr. Thomas Gora, Alice Jardine and Leon. S. Roudiez, Columbia University Press, 1980.

Lefevere, Andre, *Leuven Colloquium on Literature and Translation*, p. 192, Rodopi, B.V. Amsterdam–Atlanta GA 1988.

———, 'Beyond the Process': Literary Translation in Literature and Literary Theory' pp. 52–59, in *Rose Marilya Gaddis*, ed. 'Translation Spectrum': Essays in Theory and Practice, State University Press, Albany, 1981.

Madhavacharya, *The Jaiminiya-Nyaya-Mala-Vistara*, London: Trubner & Co., 1865 (available in digitized form from the holdings of Harvard University).

Malaviya, Sudhakar, ed., *Aitereya Brahmana*, pt. 1, Varanasi: Tata Printing Press, 1986.

Mammata, *Kavya Prakash*, with English Translation by Dr. Ganganath Jha, p. 2, Varanasi: Bharatiya Vidya Prakashan, 2005.

Mitra, Rajendralal and Harachandra Vidya Bhushana, eds., *The Gopatha Brahmana of the Atharva Veda Bibliotheca Indica*, Asiatic Society of Bengal, Calcutta, 1872.

Nagaraj, D.R., *Listening to the Loom: Essays on Literature, Politics, and Violence*, New Delhi: Orient BlackSwan, 2012.

Nanamoli, Bhikkhu, *Netti-Prakaranam* (The Guide, a Buddhist text), tr. Nanamoli, Bristol,: The Pali Text Society, 1962.

Paniker, Ayyappa K., 'The Anxiety of Authenticity: Reflections on Literary Translations', in *Translation: Its Theory and Practice*, pp. 36–45, ed. A.K. Singh, 1996, New Delhi; Creative Books,

———, 'Towards an Indian Theory of Literary Translation', pp. 39–48 in *Translation: From Periphery to Centrestage*, ed. Tutun Mukherjee, New Delhi: Prestige Books, 1998.

Quine, W.B., *Word and Object*, Cambridge, Mass: MIT Press, 1960.

Raja, K. Kunjunni, 'Philosophical Elements in Patanjali's Mahabhasya', in *Encyclopedia of Indian Philosophies*, vol. 5, ed. Harold G. Coward and K. Kunjunni Raja, Princeton: Princeton University Press, 1990.

Rajam, V.S., *A Comparative Study of Two Ancient Grammatical Traditions: The Tamil Tholkappiyam compared with the Sanskrit Rgveda-Pratisakhya, Taittiriya-Pratisakhya, Apisali Siksha, and the Astadhyayi*, Ph.D. Thesis, University of Pennsylvania, 1981.

Sarup, Laksman, *The Nighantu and the Nirukta of Sri Yaskacharya: The Oldest Indian Treatise on Etymology, Philology and Semantics*, London: H. Milford 1920–1, repr., Motilal Banarsidass, 2002.

Sherry, Simon, *Gender in Translation: Cultural Identity and the Politics of Transmission*, London and New York: Routledge, 1996.

Steiner, George, *After Babel: Aspects of Language and Translation*, London: OUP, 1975.

Sri Aurobindo, *Letters of Sri Aurobindo*, third series (*On Poetry and Literature*), Bombay, Sri Aurobindo Circle, 1949.

———, The Future Poetry, p. 431, Sri Aurobindo Birth Centenary Library, Pondichary, 1997.

Tarkatirtha, Amarendramohan, *Nyayadarsanam with* Vatsyayana's *Bhasya and* Udyotkara's *Vartikka*, Delhi: Motilal Banarasidass, 1985.

Venuti, Lawrence, 'A Translator's Invisibility', *Criticism: A Quarterly for Literature and Arts*, vol. 28, no. 2, 1986, pp. 179–212.

———, *The Translator's Invisibility: A History of Translation*, London and New York: Routledge, 1995.

Varney, Jennifer, 'Deconstruction and Translation: Positions, Pertinence and the Empowerment of the Translator', pp. 113–31, *Journal of Language & Translation*, vol. 9, no. 1, March 2008.

Vidyabhusana, Satis Chandra, 'Nyaya-bhasya by Vatsyayana', *A History of Indian Logic: Ancient, Medieval and Modern Schools*, Calcutta: Calcutta University Publication, 1920; repr., Delhi: Motilal Banarsidass, 1971.

Whiting, C.G., *Paul Valéry*, Paris: Athlone Press, 1978.

13

The Epiphany of Difference: From Linearity to Simultaneity

Jasbir Jain

WHY IS IT that some of us prefer to read comparatively? What, in fact, is Comparative Literature? In recent years there has been a growing fascination for it in academe and several university departments have now added the word 'comparative', partly through compulsion, on account of the growing recognition of India's plurality, partly in order to extend literary studies to Asian and African writing, and partly also because of the increased interest in translation studies. This expansion of the discipline put to rest the fears expressed in the Bernheimer report (at least, as far as India is concerned) and introduced a host of other fields that can be considered as competitors to Comparative Literature—intertextuality, cultural studies, film studies and other related disciplines, such as music and painting, thus conferring a certain cohesive wholeness on the discipline. Actually, this expansion brings us closer to Gayatri Spivak's view that Comparative Literature should be all encompassing. In the *Death of a Discipline*, Spivak also heralded a new beginning in the Global South. The shift has been one of location, concerns and perspectives.

Despite this expansion and upsurge of interest, all is not well. For me personally, it has been a season of discontent and concern. A great deal that is now passing as Comparative Literature, is not comparative. Often, surface linkages miss out on the rich texture of the text, the culture and the context. It becomes difficult to distinguish between the comparative approach and other critical approaches fostered by modernism, post-modernism and new historicism. It is equally difficult to say what the gains or the losses of a given approach might be. The discipline is yielding to the pressures of popularity and losing its rigour. Its methodologies remain undefined and hazy. If we are seriously concerned with the future of the discipline, there is need to debate its methodologies and practice more exacting standards. A brief look at the history of India's relationship with Comparative Literature reveals certain trends. It has gone through a phase of influence studies, then moved on to cultural relativism and has also negotiated with modernism/postmodernism. The first two trends, though shared with western cultures, locate themselves in an unequal relationship, which for us in India, was one subordinated to political realities.

The significant questions that tend to resurface every generation and need to be addressed frontally are very basic. What is Comparative Literature and what does it mean for us in India? What is the main objective of reaching across to the other? Is it the search for difference or for similarity, or is it the need to be assured of one's own identity? Or do we work with comparisons mainly to work out a chronology and a history? The very location of comparative studies in a multiplicity of temporal and theoretical dimensions needs to be developed more emphatically if it is to be meaningful and worthwhile. Its essence is located as much in language as in culture and therefore both thematological studies and comparisons within monolingual literatures need to be placed in perspective. Perhaps the value of any comparative study lies in the way it sets meaning free from both textual as well as historical confines. Strangely enough, though we begin with specifics, the traces of the universal embedded in our discipline keep surfacing, allowing us to forget difference. Comparative literary studies are placed under an obligation to work simultaneously in more than one culture and it is only natural for ideological and historical situations to be shaped differently. Edward Said, in the essay 'Traveling Theory', traces both the significant ways in which ideas travel and undergo change as they relocate into new settings, which can be selective in their acceptance or mold them according to their own cultural and political requirements.

The present paper deals with four categories, which even as they overlap, merit individual consideration. The first of these involves the nature of the self along with its overlappings into identity and subjectivity; the second moves to the relationship with the 'Other/s', while the third focuses on the reciprocal embeddedness of culture and language as it challenges the limits of translation (and the risks of interpretation *only* through translation); and the final category traces the pleasure of reading comparatively as specificity transcends its confines to result in an epiphanic experience which decentres the text, places the reader simultaneously in several different worlds, expands his/her imagination and understanding, and brings to it what Heidegger refers to as the 'element of adventure' (Heidegger 180).

Self, subjectivity, and identity are words that are interrelated, yet quite different from each other. Cultures are always reluctant to dispense with their identities. They may acknowledge some slight shifts and internal evolution but hold fast to their external rootedness in their origins and identities. They create new political ones based on the constructs of language, religion, politics or even resistance. But the core basic identity of an individual is constituted by unconscious absorption through the process of growing up, through the tales our grandmothers have narrated, the customs our mothers practiced and the behavioral codes our fathers instilled in us. No matter how varied the sources of culture and no matter how conflictual they may or may not have been, cultures have a tendency to build themselves on an accumulative sense of identity which incorporates the religious and ethical forces prevalent in a given environment. Working through personal practices and experiences, cultural identities anchor themselves in race, religion and history. These markers of identity are more often than not also barriers hindering the manner in which we relate to the Other.

One has to move beyond this limited idea of identity, located in externals and in inherited and collective frameworks, in order to discover the Self, which is an individualized consciousness, responding to or resisting its environment. Various kinds of images crowd the mind like a shattered mirror, a diamond or stone, or light radiating from a centre, or the shoots of a plant claiming independence despite the commonality of roots. The Self is symbolized by all the above and as it sparks, it very often transforms inherited notions of identity. Histories of resistance, reform, conversion or migration have created new identities and new cultures which are marked by difference and, as such, are important to any effort at comparisons, whether literary or cultural. Their role in relationships in any study of significance and their explanation for the birth of subjectivity through the process of resistance are also significant. The Self is born out of the tension between the existing reality and the desire to change it; it implies agency, an ability to self-reflect and to think of oneself as a subject. Subjectivity becomes a much larger challenge, if one begins to explore different concepts of the Self in other cultures. Psychological or philosophical ideas, which grow out of successive reconsiderations also have semi-scriptural or religious origins. The opposition between the 'given' and personal will has shaped our histories. Hall in his work *Subjectivity* discusses Descartes's *Discourse on the Method* and the comments of later critics, specifically Garrett Thomson, who viewed the Enlightenment thinker's attempt 'to reconcile the conflict between the new science and the old religion' (qtd. by Hall 20). The fact that Descartes's works were banned is in itself a significant hint. Books that are banned mark the subversive shifts in culture that provoke reinterpretation. In his work, *From Socrates to Sartre: The Philosophical Quest* (1984). T.Z. Lavine observes that Descartes's thoughts on the concept of subjectivity introduce a chasm between the subjective consciousness and the external physical and social being (Hall 20).

The *Upanishads* also observe that the Self is the means of knowing, of understanding, of desire and its fulfilment. It is in relationship to the Other that one transcends the Self. Similarly other cultural texts and religious reform movements expressed in narratives such as Buddhist and Jain stories, *kathas* (tales) and myths, depict existing relationships, and, in the process, alter them according to their own needs, whether moral or political. Myths and their various retellings mark a questioning dialogicity, they form a significant part of both history and the present. All these interactions and shifts within encompassing religious or national cultures and their various offshoots and breakaways contribute to the construction of identity through the encounter with the Other (Currie 92–94). Otherness denotes the presence of the absent, as we see in Toni Morrison's *Playing in the Dark* where she writes about the way the marginal (absent) presence of the blacks in society was instrumental in constructing white culture. Again in her Tanner Lecture 'Unspeakable Things Unspoken: The Afro-American Presence in American Literature', Morrison writes about her own writing and the way it has intervened and disturbed the single-culture narratology. But every piece of writing is not necessarily backed by authorial elaborations; it is for the reader to enlarge the scope of these and similar insights.

The Other has been imagined in various ways and relationships with it have a history of imitation, cloning, simulation, withdrawal, hatred and rebellion. Is the Other the repressed or the desired Self, alter ego or something mysterious? Kate McGowan views alterity as a relationship both of difference and deferral. The process of relating it to cultural studies and analysis helps define the concerns of the comparatist as an important method of observing the Other as moving outside and beyond the text. One of the symbols McGowan uses are the twin towers of the World Trade Centre in New York, which Jean Baudrillard had singled out as an example of duplication becoming monolithic and no longer, 'opening out to the outside world' (qtd. by McGowan 80). Thus imitation and simulation can detract from otherness and dialogue. The originality of the referent is lost. While commonalities connect, differences mark identities. Differences act like a powerful flow of life-saving water from the sluices of a dam that bars understanding. In the semiotic system, language is the first sign, but symbols and artefacts provide other signs that even as they represent and reinforce meaning, proceed to sow the seeds of difference. The multiplicity of signs and the additive multiplicity of their meanings are the ways of going across, of opening up a text from a different time, history or culture. Going beyond embedded symbols, emotional responses reflect anxieties of annihilation, separation, or exile.

For a long time, civilisations have been viewed through binary divisions such as good and evil, illusion and reality, centre and margins, haves and have-nots. This tendency has surfaced in history and philosophy master and slave binary) and has found its way into structural analysis, playing a dominant role in colonial histories and infiltrating literary studies. Binary divisions or comparisons tend to be stark and unequal. True, post-structuralism and plurality have broken the syndrome in some measure but a residue lingers tenaciously in mental and emotional structures. Love and hate is one such example. Does nothing exist in-between? The histories of peace initiatives as well as of terrorist activities also can be viewed in this context. McGowan considers difference to be a major issue in the world. Difference matters. But 'are there some differences more real or more important than others? For anyone engaged in cultural struggles over meaning, there will of course always be instances within which the priority of one particular manifestation of difference will seem more urgent than the other. But the particularities of differences are, potentially at least, endless' (McGowan 89). McGowan proceeds to observe that if one has to go beyond mere relative terms, it is important not to essentialize difference. In fact, plural societies have continuously thrown up varying models for adjusting difference: tolerance, side-lining, subordinating and marginalizing, and at times war. There has also been a search for reconciliatory measures and more compassionate or empathetic accommodations. In Indian culture, the *bhakti* movement combined resistance with openness. The Indian situation, when located within the political history of the last sixty years, marks a period of fluctuations from secularism and liberalism towards an essentialization of identities. At this point of history, the ethnic affiliations geographically outside the country are playing a disruptive role as are certain internal divisions. From the issue of temple entry for Dalits, society has shifted to segregated churches, gurudwaras and temples. The contrary movement can be seen in the tendency to assimilate tribals into dominant groups. Writing and interpretation reflect these issues and hence they locate themselves in a simultaneity of local and archaeological histories. Working out the meaning of the Self and the Other necessitates not only knowledge and reflection, but also what I refer to as a 'memory-dig', a peeling away of the many layers of personal and historical consciousness and unconsciousness in order to unravel the camouflaged meaning of a symbol. The challenge here lies in the way one can find to open a symbol and liberate it from its fixity in tradition.

What is present is visible and gives the appearance of a stability that is reinforced by the written word. But the task of interpretation is multifold when the origins and attachments which hold its stability are examined closely. Retelling is one way of destabilizing the word and freeing its centre from its fixity. This subversion is marked by the Sanskrit term *vakroti*, a poetic term describing when images deviate from an expected echo and introduce something new. It is not only a differentiation of ideas, but very often one of sound and intonation. Writers in every literature experiment by playing with existing meanings, ideas and structures: anti-hero (Hardy), anti-narrative/dis-narrative (Kafka), silence (Beckett) or language (James Joyce). Vijayavardhana in his *Outlines of Sanskrit Poetics* writes, 'those aspects of *vakrokti* known as *prakaranavakrata* and *prabandtia-vakrata* deal with the changes effected by the poet in the original story to suit his requirements when the plot in the original story is selected from existing tradition' (129). These shifts may be of substitution or omission or through the introduction of new elements. Is *vakroti* close to Derrida's concept of play that he discusses in 'Structure, Sign and Play in the Discourse of the Human Sciences'? Derrida speaks of a structure which provides a balance but even as it forms itself, it also closes off the play which it opens up and makes possible. As centre, the substitution of contents, elements, or terms is no longer possible (279). But Derrida goes on to note that the very thing which was instrumental in structuring the centre, escapes structuring. This last point is a difficult idea to grasp. How does it escape structurality and how does it remain outside the totality? If the existing centre is replaced by another centre, what kind of a relationship does it have with structure? Derrida proceeds by questioning both substitutions and centres. Perhaps the disruptive force is contained not only by another centre but by looking at structure as a function and not as a centre. Its dislocation is brought about by the sign-substitutions that come into play, which may often be the insertion of earlier absences or a combination of opposites. Derrida makes a further distinction between sign and signifier and points out that while we cannot do without sign, it is the word signifier which 'must be abandoned as a metaphysical concept' (281). This move destabilizes the reliability of the existing relationship between sign and signifier, opening out innumerable interpretative possibilities. The meaning of a word is elusive and even when heavily ensconced in its context, it has a habit of shifting relationships. Commenting upon the Derridean concept of *différance* and his rejection of a stable centre and affixed sign, Mark Currie writes that a sign also functions by positing a common denominator, a common essence and sameness, through the process of suppressing difference, by claiming dominance, it also acts as an exclusionary act and suppresses temporal differences (Currie 57). This focus on the unreliability of the sign raises several other questions related to the written word and in this connection, the very act of and dependence on translation.

But before I move to that very crucial question, I would like to turn to Gurbhagat Singh's views on logo-centrism. Singh examined the differential approach to linguistic structures, especially where a plurality of languages exists (1997). In the essay 'Comparative Literature: Towards a Non-Logocentric Paradigm', working through a discussion of Derridean thought in relation to texts from a variety of cultures, Singh observed that the literary text 'becomes a decentred monad or a schizophrenic unit radiating its special ironic, dualistic or better, *visista-atavistic*, qualified non-dualistic, energy—to use this notion from Ramanuja—by being centred in its own cultural problematic. And in this process as it stretches its semiosis and poesis to the last limit' (77). In order to render this process possible, a transcultural-non-logocentric critical theory has to be worked out (Ibid.). Hence, Singh points out, difference is of utmost importance. It is ironic that while Derrida talks of *différence* and *différance* and values a certain decentring, his consciousness of his Jewishness is repeatedly voiced as a redeeming aspect in Singh's assertion that he also prioritizes the 'spiritual' since Derrida in his essays, *On Forgiveness* and *Cosmopolitanism*, works within the Abrahamaic tradition. These realities demonstrate the need as well as the possibility of inhabiting two worlds simultaneously and not in a linear fashion.

Sanskrit poetics is neither as static nor as pure as it is often presumed to be. Its history and development provide evidence of an openness to other languages, and traditions such as Prakrit and Persian. An openness in its narrative forms contributed to its development. It is a mistake to focus all attention on the *Natyashastra* and more specifically the *rasa* theory. Sanskrit poetics also has a tradition of questioning, shifts and changes—at least right up to the twelfth century as Mirajkar traces in his essay, 'The Relevance of Indian Literary Theory'. One would add that the aesthetics of orality both in poetry and narrative, classic theatre, folk literature and modern prose narrative share this trait.

Comparative Literature today increasingly depends on translated texts and, in many cases, without even the minimal access to the original language, or its nuances or with only a nodding acquaintance with its culture. Indian writing in English presents an altogether different set of problems. While the original writing in English, as several writers have acknowledged, is in itself a translation, the translations from other Indian languages pose even more serious issues for the non-culture reader. It needs to be granted that language and culture are not synonyms. We find in the English writing by Indians a form of diasporic writing that is seen and believed to be the face of India in the Western world. This diasporic literature overshadows the writing located in India as well as the writing in other Indian languages. This situation occurs primarily for two reasons: the sheer volume of readership in English far exceeds the readership in many other languages and the cultural representation (and hence interpretation) is less dense (for the non-cultural reader), having already been mediated by the writer. In Rushdie 'Imaginary Homelands', refers to the diasporic writing as 'translated', in the sense of going across. Similarly, the India-based writer Shashi Deshpande in the essay, 'Where Do We Belong?' discusses how writing in English in India limits the author by isolating him/her from the language of the people. Deprived of the vitality that comes from writing in the language of the people (34) there is also a blurring of *différence* and a corresponding loss in the act of representation. One has to find ways to get around this dilemma. Speaking of her own experience as a writer, Deshpande notes 'when we write in English, we are, in effect translating' (37). There is also a third reason for diasporic writing's greater visibility. These writers, in most cases, stay away from specificities, what Nayantara Sahgal once refered to as engaging with the raw reality. Thus, there is a cultural dilution with the narrative ordinarily taking place in urban, metropolitan locations. Similar to the India-based Indian writing in English, translated texts also face problems, despite being more authentically rooted in culture. They often run counter to the metropolitan novel. Hence, my serious objection to Susan Bassnett's liberal approach that foreign readers accept Third-World translated texts as an adequate substitution for the original. A comparatist must be bilingual, if not trilingual or multilingual. A monolingual comparison misses the essentials. In support of my argument regarding the inadequacies of translation, I turn to Alan Bass's Introduction to his translation of Derrida's *Writing and Difference* (1977). Bass writes 'the translator, constantly aware of what he is sacrificing, is often tempted to use a language that is a compromise between English as we know it and English as he would like it to be in order to capture as much of the original text as possible'. Bass further adds, 'This compromise English, however, is usually comprehensible only to those who read the translation along with the original' (Bass xiv). Bass points to the eternal problem faced by translators when translating from the source language into the target language. Whatever goes into the nature of this compromise becomes the element missing from both the translated text and the diasporic text. Bass then asks whether any translation can be made to signify the same thing as the original text? How critical is the play of signifiers—etymological play, stylistic play—to what is signified by the text (xv)? A partial answer is provided by Derrida in the fact that the history of metaphysics has never ceased to impose upon semiology (the science of signs) the search for a 'transcendental signified', that is a concept independent of language (cited by Bass xv). Derrida refers here to the concept of transformation, while P. Lal used the terminology 'transcreation'. Does this process really solve the problem of unravelling the meaning and accommodating the degree of shift in translated texts? How does one recapture or recreate the element lost in the compromise that Bass evokes? The practice which several translators in contemporary India have begun to follow is to depend heavily on the language and culture of the original for transferring the essence of meaning by carrying over defining terms, syntax, and, at times, even the source language, in an attempt to capture the lilt, rhythm as well as the anguish articulated in the writerly struggle to express the inexpressible that is present in the original. Two recent translations that I have read from languages I do not know that adhere to this practice are Kalyana Rao's Telugu novel, *Untouchable Spring* translated by Alladi Uma and M.Sridhar and Sarah Joseph's *Gift in Green*, translated by Valson Thampu. They transport the reader into another world where the difference is not merely of experience, but of a host of other things ranging from survival to faith, Alladi and Sridhar use fractional sentences and different rhythms as they weave the narrative through historical and emotional time. The same-culture reader, of whose historical subconscious this history is a part, can with some patience fall into this rhythm of broken, half-complete sentences but a reader from another culture may or may not have the necessary patience or devotion to attempt this movement. Does this mean unfamiliarity with a culture or a language is an impenetrable barrier? Not necessarily. But there are differences between readings where the reader seeks engagement in order to gain familiarity or know about a culture and readings which initially locate themselves in a familiar culture. A glance at academic syllabi demonstrates how texts can be either culturally neutral, deal with abstractions like identity, or reflect known histories. Very rarely is the effort made to go to the specifics of these texts as they are woven into the texture of a culture. (It is true that epics often find a ready acceptance across cultures. Is it because their narration is surrounded by commentaries and annotations?)

A translation's close relationship with the interpretative act suggests that comparative reading necessitates a similar 'going across'—not in curiosity, not merely in search of sameness or difference but in search of knowledge, the epistemological differences and processes of knowing and moving beyond the text. At some point the connection with ideas, thoughts and philosophies results in a widening of the mind, it frees writing from fixity and opens up other worlds. In the last few months, I have been reading three different kinds of works: the classics of Russian and European fiction—from Gogol to Kundera: a host of translated novels from Indian languages (Malayalam, Tamil, Telugu) and Hindi and Punjabi writing in the original. The result was that my mind was flooded with insights into morality, continuations of tradition, narrative experiments, differences in meaning, the constant shadow of the political, not merely as a matter of history but as influencing the formation and control of ideas and the freedom of policy and development. These writings revealed hidden emotional dimensions and the difficulties of living amidst uncertainty, fear, and insecurity. Strangely this conglomeration of experiences across time, space, histories and language left me with a feeling of being liberated, able to relate to the Other and move out from my own positions. Reading comparatively is an act of growth, it bridges gaps and takes one out of a linear flow to experience the simultaneity of life. But this experience happens only when the approach is free from structural frames, works simultaneously with multiple cultures and histories, is empathetically conscious of alterities and differences, aware of the indigenous and is prepared to work outside the text.

REFERENCES

Bass, Alan, Translator's Introduction, *Writing and Difference*, ed. Jacques Derrida, London: Routledge and Kegan Paul, 1978, pp. ix–xx.

Currie, Mark, *Difference*, The New Critical Idiom Series, London: Routledge, 2004.

Derrida, Jacques, *Writing and Difference*, tr. Alan Bass, London and Henley: Routledge and Kegan Paul, 1978.

———, 'Structure, Sign and Play in the Discourse of Human Sciences', in *Writing and Difference*, tr. Alan Bass, London and Henley: Routledge and Kegan Paul, 1978, pp. 278–93.

Deshpande, Shashi, 'Where Do We Belong: Regional, National, or International?', *Writing From the Margin and Other Essays*, New Delhi: Viking, 2003, pp. 30–60.

Hall, Donald E., *Subjectivity*, New York and London: Routledge, 2004.

Heidegger, Martin, 'Letter on Humanism (1947)', ed. David Farrell Krell in *Heidegger*: *Basic Writings*, London: Routledge, Special Indian Edition, 2012 [1978], pp. 147–81.

Joseph, Sarah, *Gift in Green* (Malayalam), tr. Valson Thampu, New Delhi: Harper Perennial, 2011.

McGowan, Kate, 'Alterity', *Key Issues in Critical and Cultural Theory* [2007], Jaipur: Rawat Publication, 2009, pp. 79–101.

Mirajkar, Nishikant D., 'The Relevance of Indian Literary Theory', in *Comparative Literature: Theory and Practice*, ed. Amiya Dev and Sisir Kumar Das, New Delhi: IIAS and Allied Publishers, 1979, pp. 263–84.

Morrison, Toni, 'Unspeakable Things Unspoken: The Afro-American Presence in American Literature', The Tanner Lectures on Human Values, University of Michigan 1988, <http://www.tannerlectures.utah.edu/lectures/morrison.toni.pad>, pp. 123–63.

Rao, Kalayana G., *Untouchable Spring (2000)*, tr. Alladi Uma and M. Sridhar, Hyderabad: Orient BlackSwan, 2010.

Rushdie, Salman, 'Imaginary Homelands', in *Creating Theory: Writers on Writing*, ed. Jasbir Jain, Delhi: Pencraft International, 2000, pp. 213–24.

Singh, Gurbhagat, 'The Betrayal of Polyphony: Blocked Possibilities of Criticism in India', in *Nativism; Essays in Criticism*, ed. Makarand Paranjape, New Delhi: Sahitya Akademi, 1997, pp. 84–94.

———, 'Comparative Literature: Towards a Non-logocentric Paradigm', in *Comparative Literature: Theory and Practice*, ed. Amiya Dev and Sisir Kumar Das, New Delhi: IIAS and Allied Publishers, 1989, pp. 71–8.

Spivak, Gayatri Chakrovorty, *Death of a Discipline*, New York: Columbia University Press, 2003.

Vijayavardhana, G., 'The Vakroti Theory', in *Outlines of Sanskrit Poetics*, Varanasi: The Chowkhamba Sanskrit Series, 1970, pp. 124–35.

14

Beyond Orientalist and Postcolonial Constructs: The *Telos* of Translation Studies from the Perspective of Comparative Indian Literature

E.V. Ramakrishnan

DURING THE last three decades there has been a perceptible change in the way translation has been viewed in India. As a student I hardly came across any reference to translation in the English literature classroom or in the literary criticism of Malayalam where translations were taken for granted. We all read Dostoevsky, Brecht, Chekhov, Kafka, Camus, Sartre, Ionesco, Pirandello and Neruda, not to mention Tagore, Premchand, Bankimchandra, Saratchandra and Tulsidas etc. without ever bothering to find out who translated them or how their texts worked as translations. Today, in India, translations of Indian literature are being produced and marketed by major publishers and translators have acquired greater visibility. They are invited to major literary festivals and they are counted among writers. The emergence of Translation Studies in the West has had its impact in India but, as an interdisciplinary field of study, Translation Studies is yet to make its presence felt in the Indian academy. Social scientists and culture theorists assume that translation need not be taken into account in the production of knowledge about any society. A similar cognitive block seems to operate in the case of media studies, film studies or performance studies. Translation is not receiving the attention it deserves in the constitution of the basic premises of the field. Comparatists have greater responsibility in engaging with Translation Studies. However, they have not paid attention to the fact that in a multilingual society, categories such as 'literature', 'literariness', 'text', and 'reader' need to be configured differently from what they are in a monolingual, monocultural society. In this paper, my primary objective is to indicate the vast potential of

Translation Studies in India as an area of interdisciplinary research from the perspective of Comparative Studies in Indian Literature. Since translation is still understood in terms of a transfer of texts between two languages, its relations to the literary system as a whole and its role in shaping the shifts in literary sensibility and bringing about radical changes in literary culture from a macro point of view are largely uncharted. In a multilingual society like India, translation has to be understood in all its manifestations, as traffic across cultures assumes many forms across textual, visual and performative traditions in contexts ranging from oral to digital, over a period beginning with the patronage of kings to the emergence of print capitalism. Attempting to map the field from the beginning of the last millennium is a colossal task but a large body of dedicated scholars have begun to work together to make it happen. Such an attempt will enable us to re-conceive Comparative Indian Literature as a field with its own protocols and pedagogy. Comparative Indian Literature and Translation Studies overlap repeatedly as we consider issues in literary history, reception aesthetics, thematology, genealogy or the coming of the book in Indian languages. Hence both disciplines have a bonding that is too intricate and symbiotic to ignore. In the course of this essay, we shall see how the foundational moments of modern Indian languages and their nodal moments of mutations into complex literary traditions with their own internal dynamics are deeply implicated in translation in all its forms.

We also need to remember that language is the site where, very often, social, cultural and political battles are fought in India. Alternatively one may say that socio-political conflicts invariably acquire cultural and linguistic overtones, necessitating negotiations with and through languages. Some of these fault-lines that cause fissures and ruptures run deep and will have to be factored into the discussion regarding the shifts of our cultural terrains. Here it would be instructive to recall how, in the first place, modern Indian languages came into being around the beginning of second millennium, overthrowing the hegemony of Sanskrit, a language which had reigned as the sole preserve of intellectual and literary expression for over a thousand years. Equally instructive is the way in which modern Indian languages shifted gear in the wake of the colonial encounter, assimilating and resisting elements in the 'superior' external literary traditions without losing their own ground. The fact that within a period of less than a century modern Indian languages brought into their creative expression forms such as the novel, the short story, the autobiography, the personal and reflective essay, modern drama and literary critical discourse is no mean achievement. That translation played a significant role in these engagements with the Other has not received the attention it merits. The foundational moment of modern Indian languages as well as their coming of age as major world literary languages in the context of colonial/imperial assault: these are two contexts that cannot be comprehended without exploring the role of translation as a creative mode of intellectual negotiation and social/political assertion.

I

One of the major cultural shifts that happened in India or throughout South Asia, as Sheldon Pollock argues, was the decline of Sanskrit and its replacement by regional languages as the medium of intellectual discourse and literary composition. From roughly 900 CE, Sanskrit lost its monopolistic status as the pan-Indian language of high culture. This event was accompanied by the assertion of regional forms of articulation both within court and outside. Pollock uses the term 'vernacularization' to describe this linguistic and cultural shift (Pollock 2011: 330–338). I would prefer to use the term 'regionalization' as the term 'vernacular' carries unpalatable cultural baggage. Pollock offers a working definition of 'vernacularization' in these words:

> Vernacularization is here understood—not a priori or stipulatively but from tendencies visible in the empirical record—as the historical process of choosing to create a written literature, along with its complement, a political discourse, in local languages according to models supplied by a superordinate, usually, cosmopolitan, literary culture. (Pollock 2011: 23)

This shift towards modern Indian languages takes place in Kannada in the ninth century, in Telugu around the tenth century, Marathi around the thirteenth century, Gujarati around the twelfth century, Malayalam around the fifteenth century, and in Assamese, Bangla and Oriya around the fifteenth/sixteenth century. In his discussion of the Kannada scene, Pollock identifies certain features of the process of 'regionalization', two of which may be relevant for our main subject. He finds a correlation between 'vernacular innovation and a reconfiguration of the culture-power order' (ibid.: 336). As the new political discourse rooted in the region gained ascendancy and consolidated its position, Sanskrit yielded its place as a cosmopolitan language. The identification of the region and its people with its language marks a moment of transition when the regional language begins to function 'as the primary code of political communication' (ibid.: 337). As Pollock puts it, this is the moment when 'aesthetics of vernacular power' began to produce 'a new power of vernacular aesthetics' (ibid.: 338).

Pollock's central argument regarding a transfer of power from Sanskrit to modern Indian languages assumes the unequal power relations between them as a cultural given, without going into their content. He never discusses problems of caste in the context of production of knowledge in India. He is eager to point out that Sanskrit was not monopolized by Brahmins in India. However, it remains a mystery how and why the language of gods remained out of bounds to large sections of lower caste people and women in India. In his eagerness to incorporate the cultural shifts in India into a universal model that is dictated by the paradigms of the European Reformation, Pollock erases the differences between the regions within India with reference to their modes of adopting and shaping new literary cultures centred around regional languages. The plurality of the Indian situation marked by deep heteroglossia is not reflected in his argument. For instance, the trajectories of Malayalam and Kannada are not the same as far as the response to the Sanskrit cosmopolis is concerned. It has been argued that after the rise of regional languages into separate, independent languages, Sanskrit occupied a cultural space within many of these regional discourses, largely through its pre-eminence as the language of knowledge and its rich traditions of poetics. In her study of the evolution of Marathi language and culture titled, *Language, Politics and the Public Sphere*, Veena Naregal cautions against the adoption of categories derived from the European Reformation, and says: 'The literarisation of the vernaculars here did not lead to a redefinition of aesthetic norms and ideas of cultivation or notions of collectivity, as happened through the Renaissance' (Naregal: 41). She further argues that in the case of Marathi, the rise of 'vernacular' textuality was mediated through the 'high' textual traditions of Sanskrit. But this is not borne out by facts. In his book, *Religion and Public Memory: A Cultural History of Saint Namdev in India*, Christian Lee Nvetzke shows how public memory plays a crucial role in the creation of Namdev's image as a saint-poet in Maharashtra. The oral performance of *kirtan* to which the common masses could relate emotionally laid the foundation for his subsequent fame and reception. Nvetzke observes:

> Namdeo is a key figure in Maharashtra as well as central, western, and northern India, and virtually ubiquitous in the Hindu and Sikh religious-literary traditions of these regions from the fifteenth century to the present, a period spanning Sultanate, Mughal, Maratha, and British rule as well as post-Independence India. (Nvetzke 2008:1)

This popular domain is absent in Pollock's discussion of 'vernacularisation' in India. He also fails to note that even the regions from which modern Indian languages emerged were multilingual to the core. The ninth century Kannada text *Kavirajamarga*, which Pollock discusses at length, shows that *desi* traditions are characterized by multiplicity; not even the thousand headed Vasuki can describe all the poetic styles that are available in Kannada (Ramakrishnan 2011: 27). That Sanskrit was never the language of the masses is an accepted fact. In the large number of translations of the epics, the *Ramayana* and the *Mahabharata*, the local literary traditions enter into the narrative, creating a dialogic relation between the *marga* and the *desi*. For instance, in the Oriya version of the *Mahabharata* translated by Sarala Das, the *Bhagavat Gıta* is omitted. The situation for rendering the *Gıta* was very much there, but Sarala chose to exclude the great statement the *Gıta* makes from his narrative (B.N. Patnaik 2012: 48). There are several episodes in Sarala's *Mahabharata*, where the regional version does not follow the original. This is how the native reader who lives his everyday life in the world of the region is incorporated into the text. That translations of the Sanskrit routinely deviated from the canonical text has to be seen from the perspective of assimilating the region into the narrative. This does not make it less of a translation. In fact, all the major renderings of the *Ramayana* and the *Mahabharata*, deviate from the canonical Sanskrit text in several ways largely because of the ethical burden these poets carried as translators. Their primary responsibility was to the living speech community of which they were a part. They spoke in the present tense even when the stories they told belonged to the past. Their language was the common heritage the people had created over centuries and they now sensed the great responsibility of investing it with a literary text that would give a core regional identity to the people. The complete identification of these poets with their regions and polulations is what gives their texts new poetic meaning. The first major literary text of Marathi, *Jnaneswarı* is a retelling of the *Bhagavat Gıta*. In his rendering Jnanadeva incorporates 'his own dialogue with his guru, Nivrittinath on the one hand, and on the other with his raptly attentive audience, Sacchittananda, the scholiast who committed the text to writing' (Ganesh Devy 1998: 47). By the time Jnanadeva comes to the sixth chapter of the *Gıta*, he confidently asserts the primacy of his mother tongue's power in these words: 'My language is Marathi, but I will compose this work with such beautiful words and style that it will easily surpass nectar' (ibid.: 48). This clearly shows that the writers of regional languages were not merely reproducing the *kavya* tradition from Sanskrit but addressing a living speech community through their writing, by deviating from the original wherever they were called upon to do it. They were producing new texts for a contemporary society because the creative impulse in that society had matured to a stage where Sanskrit would not satisfy their needs of creative expression. Orientalists wanted to freeze India into a timeless frame where everything durable in India came from its classical past. Sheldon Pollock subscribes to the same ideology though he gives it a package that is contemporary.

That each of the modern Indian languages produced translations of the great Indian epics during the period from the tenth to sixteenth century is a fact that should alert us to the churning that was happening across India during this creative upsurge of translation. The distribution of the *Ramayana* across modern Indian languages will help us understand this complex trajectory: Assamese (fourteenth century; Madhav Kandali); Bengali (fifteenth century; Krittivasa); Gujarati (seventeenth century; Premananda); Hindi (sixteenth century; Tulsidasa); Kannada (twelfth century; Nagacandra or Abhinava Pampa); Kashmiri (eighteenth century; Prakasha Bhatta); Malayalam (seventeenth century; Thunchat Ezuthachan), Marathi (sixteenth century; Ekanatha); Oriya (sixteenth century; Balrama Dasa); Tamil (tenth century; Kambar); Telugu (sixteenth century: Molla). The cognitive grid that produced these translations attests to the presence of a domain of social imagination deeply embedded in the cultural practices of the people dating back to the period around 500–800 CE when modern Indian languages began appearing in their rudimentary forms. What Sheldon Pollock fails to trace is this domain of social imagination that has shaped the modern Indian sensibility across its several languages, strongly resisting the hermetic aesthetic of a hegemonic language like Sanskrit. It is significant that Sheldon Pollock does not mention the word 'translation' not even once in his massive tome on Sanskrit language that runs to 684 pages of which the index is about 38 pages. This cognitive blockage is derived from Orientalist mindset where anything worthwhile in India has to be in Sanskrit and at least a thousand year old.

The gap between the 'high' culture of Sanskrit and the 'common' practices of the masses has always been apparent to the discerning scholars of regional languages. It is true that this gap has remained untheorized untill modern print cultures altered the power relations between the traditional 'kavya'-centred literary tradition and the modern print-centred prose tradition in the nineteenth century. The large number of prose-based literary forms such as the travelogue, short story, biography, autobiography, novel, personal essay etc., that emerged in the nineteenth century did not subscribe to paradigms of Sanskrit aesthetics. *Bhakti* poetry which constituted the initial impulse for the translations that inaugurated modern Indian literary traditions, marked a shift away from Sanskrit poetics as it used forms such as '*vachana*' and '*abhang*' for literary composition to address the elite as well as the masses.

The defiance of hierarchy as institutionalized in the caste system and the assertion of collective aspirations of the people towards a shared experiential world characterize much of *bhakti* poetry in the regional languages. The rise of Manipravalam in Malayalam points to the emergence of a participatory cultural space where the cosmopolitan and the local interpenetrate, enabling Sanskrit to retain its legitimacy within a regional cultural framework. Though Manipravalam existed in varying degrees in all South Indian languages, only in Malayalam did it become the standard medium of composing poetry. This is because Malayalam, in its development towards an independent language, had to confront the hegemonic structures of both Tamil and Sanskrit: translation becomes the mode of negotiation in these confrontations of culture and power between opposing experiential locations. Manipravalam in Malayalam enables the native speech community to retain a regional cosmopolis without being subservient to the dominating power of Sanskrit or Tamil.

U.R. Ananthamurthy has argued that modern Indian languages have successfully negotiated the hegemonic status of Sanskrit through translation. He comments:

> The philosophers say that there is a little fire somewhere in the *atma* (soul) which can digest anything; this is known in Sanskrit as the *Jeernagni*, the digestive fire. I consider the Indian *bhashas* the great *Jeernagnis* of India, because they digested Sanskrit at one time, as they digest Europe now. They have been transacting with different languages in this manner all through their history. (Ananthamurthy 2014: 87)

Ananthamurthy points to the direction in which translation studies should move in India. Modern Indian languages have internalised the epistemological structures of Sanskrit, along with other similarly placed languages of antiquity, to such an extent that they could confidently confront the challenges of colonial modernity embodied by English. The postcolonial theorists of Brazil have advanced a theory of translation as cannibalism in the context of their colonialist ruptures. One of its leading proponents, Else Vieira, in her paper, 'Liberating Calibans' remarks:

> Cannibalism is a metaphor actually drawn from the natives' ritual whereby feeding someone or drinking someone's blood, as they did to their totemic 'tapir,' was a means of absorbing the other's strength, a pointer to the very project of the Anthropophagy group: not to deny foreign influences or nourishment, but

to absorb and transform them by the addition of autochtonous input. Initially using the metaphor as an irreverent verbal weapon, the Manifesto Antropofago stresses the repressive nature of colonialism. (Vieira 1999: 98–99)

What is significant here as well as in Ananthamurthy's view is the perception of a deeper process at work in the field of translation in societies like India and Brazil, as well as a concern with ideology and epistemology. That translation is a way of producing knowledge has been recognized by Indian languages all throughout their histories. Translation Studies in India need to recover this teleology grounded in knowledge production. This is possible only if we view the two moments—the one that marks the beginning of modern Indian languages, during the first half of the second millennium, moving away from the hegemonic structures of Sanskrit and similar languages, and the other one during the nineteenth century, confronting the equally dominant colonial structures of epistemology—not as isolated and disconnected events but a part of the larger matrix of the history of knowledge production in the country through translations that happened within Indian languages.

No theory can emerge based on our experience of translating Indian texts into English. These English translations only fulfil a larger need of the globalised world. That is why the project of translating Indian classics into English undertaken by the Murthy Classical Library under the general editorship of Sheldon Pollock has to be seen as part of an 'Orientalist' project. In his note titled 'Why a Classical Library of India?', Pollock argues that books written before 1800 alone will be chosen for translation. He pays tribute to multilingualism in India but finds its great tradition 'ruptured' by colonialism. For him 'knowledge' means what is contained in ancient Indian classics. In a lecture titled 'What is Indian Knowledge Good for?' Pollock argued that, with the passing away of languages like Pali and Prakrit, everything valuable in Indian tradition will get erased and the decline of Sanskrit is the worst crisis India has experienced in its history (Pollock 2013). He fails to see that Indian languages as dynamic entities were required to negotiate political structures of power by producing new types of knowledge. If they developed new genres and took to print culture which enabled them to recover their past for a new literate audience, the question of 'rupture' needs to be reconsidered. A.R.Venkatachalapathy in his scholarly analysis of the coming of print in Tamil literary culture, *The Province of the Book*, shows how the process was deeply implicated in several other narratives such as that of patronage, emergence of the public sphere, production of textbooks, rise of the popular novel, birth of the woman reader, etc.

(Venkatachalapathy 2012: 13–19). If India had stayed with its ancient classics without moving onto these new phases of cultural history, it would have become the exotic museum that scholars like Pollock and the orientalists before them would like India to be.

II

The shift from Sanskrit to regional languages in North India happened at a time when Persian and Arabic emerged as languages of authority, with the consolidation of political power by the Mughal empire. The spheres of influence exerted by Sanskrit, on the one hand, and Persian and Arabic on the other, remained mutually exclusive as their power and authority were derived from different traditions and sources. The shift towards modern Indian languages assumes visibility in the textual traditions of *bhakti* and the enabling role played by Persian and Arabic in this process needs to be noted. Sufi poetry and the Islamic world-view have played a crucial role in shaping the poetic discourse of *bhakti*. Arabic and Persian were languages of intellectual discourse, and not merely those of civic authority. By the thirteenth century, South Asia had been constituted as a cultural domain of great intellectual rigour through Persian and Arabic. In her introduction to *Poetics and Politics of Sufism and Bhakti*, Kavita Punjabi comments: 'The influence of Sufism permeated the whole of the Islamic world from Persia right up to the borders in Bengal, combining Arabic and Persian influences with indigenous languages, literatures and folk cultures, and drawing the latter into the wide open Persio-Arabic network, even as it transformed Indian literatures and society in significant ways' (Punjabi 2011: 6). This evidently shows that the literary world of India during the period from the thirteenth to the eighteenth centuries was characterised by a deeply resonant multilingualism which writers like Pollock refuse to acknowledge. A poet like Amir Khusru (d. 1325) wrote in Persian, Hindwai and Brajbhasha, and was fluent in Turkish and Arabic. As mentioned above, Namdev's poetry cuts across many languages in western and northern India. This deep-rooted and widespread multilingualism transcended the political boundaries and opened up social spaces. The lexical influence of Persian and Arabic can be seen even in the works of Eknath (roughly 1270–1350) who composed poetry in Marathi in the fourteenth century (Naregal 2001: 16/23n). One of the key reformers of the nineteenth century, Raja Rammohun Roy was well-versed in Persian and Arabic, besides Sanskrit showing that this multilingual tradition continued well into the nineteenth century. Raja Rammohun Roy's first book was a treatise, *Tuhfat-ul-Muwahiddin*

(A Gift from the Monotheists) in Persian with an introduction in Arabic. In this book, Rammohun underlined the need for 'rational approach to religions and religious experience' and drew the attention to the 'achievement of monotheism throughout the world' (Saumyendranath Tagore 2009: 10–11). Obviously, rational approach could be derived from Persian and Arabic as well.

This multilingualism also led to an intellectual ferment in medieval India leading to dialogues between different ideologies and philosophies. Jonardon Ganeri, in the essay, 'Intellectual India: Reason, Identify, Dissent' comments:

> India in the 17th century, the century after Akbar, was a place of great intellectual excitement. Muslim, Hindu and Jaina intellectuals produced works of tremendous interest, ideas circulated around India, through the Persianate and Arabic worlds, and also between India and Europe. (Ganeri 2009: 258)

In 1656, the year in which Dara Shikoh's grand project of translating 52 Upanishads from Sanskrit into Persian was achieved, the French physician and philosopher, François Bernier, was in India and translated the works of Descartes and the empiricist Gassendi into Persian. Thus, much before the advent of colonial education, the ideas of the Enlightenment were available to Persian-knowing elites of India. It was through the translation of Bernier's *Travels in the Mughal Empire* into English that Dryden culled material for his play, *Aurangzeb* (1675). Ganeri asks:

> With Gassendi's work translated into Persian even before it was available in French, and the monotheistic pantheism of the Upanishads and Dara Shukoh already in France and England years before Spinoza's *Ethics* were published, what more dramatic evidence could there be of the rapid global circulation of ideas in the 1660s and 70s? (ibid.: 260)

Arabic and Persian were not merely languages of the court and administration, but the mediums of intellectual discourse that impacted the world-view of discerning Indians. Their liberating influences provided a powerful impetus for the *bhashas* to question and subvert the hegemony of the Sanskrit cosmopolis. This also means that before the arrival of English, India had already been in dialogue with the West and had contributed to the rise of modernity in the West through its own dialogic traditions. This intellectual history was effectively erased from public memory with the banishment of Persian and its traditions from the subcontinent. This also meant a shift from the multilingualism of medieval India to the bilingualism of the nineteenth century, where English became the intellectual language and Indian languages their inferior other.

In Kerala, the rise of Malayalam as a literary language occured at a time of political turmoil in the hundred years between 1650 and 1750, when the Portugese and the Dutch were engaged in a war for supremacy on the Western coast. The Portugese had made their presence felt in Cochin (today's 'Kochi') and the Arabs were entrenched in Calicut (today's 'Kozhikode') under the patronage of the Samorin. By the end of the seventeenth century (1660 to be precise), the Portugese commercial empire in Indian waters gave way to the Dutch who were subsequently displaced by the British in another wave of attacks and counter-attacks. The presence of Portugese missionaries in Kerala contributed to the development of prose through translations of the Bible and the publication of grammars and dictionary. Malayalam was deficient in prose though there was a certain tradition of writing in royal proclamations and courtly documentation. The new 'missionary Malayalam' obviously followed a trajectory that was different from the highly Sanskritised Malayalam or the earlier variety of Malayalam derived from Tamil. Many varieties of Malayalam, such as Arabi Malayalam and Jewish Malayalam, developed during the long periods of Kerala's contacts with the various communities from other parts of the world. Malayalam contains a large number of words from Persian, Arabic, Portugese, Dutch and many other European languages. It was through this hybridisation that Malayalam emerged into a 'modern' language, capable of dealing with the larger project of modernity. To say that its 'cosmopolitan' tradition was an imprint of the Sanskritic model is to falsify history.

Languages such as Malayalam used translation as a mode to negotiate the multiple life worlds they inhabited. It must be remembered that Sanskrit rarely translates other texts and its resources were not openly accessible to most of the people in India. One of the reasons why colonial administrators patronized Sanskrit was this 'purity' that made it the ideal medium to recover an Aryan antiquity. Max Müller says: 'But what is far more important than its merely chronological antiquity is the antique state of preservation in which that Aryan language has been handed down to us' (Max Müller 2000: xvii). Orientalists as well as Anglicists refuse to engage with the multi-lingual ethos of the regional languages and their cosmopolitan traditions. William Carey, one of the reputed Serampore missionaries, who translated the *Ramayana* into Bengali in 1802 (he was also a scholar of Marathi, Telugu and Hindustani), comments:

> If any language could be adopted as the universal medium of communication with all the different Indian nations it would be Sanskrita, which is indeed not only the key to all Indian literature, but also the parent of every language spoken throughout India. (Quoted from Balaji Ranaganathan 2009: 73–74)

While Orientalists translated classical India into modern European languages to construct a grand narrative of its Aryan past, Anglicists harped on the lack of rational discourses and scientific temper in modern Indian languages. Charles Grant who is one of the first Anglicists to spell out the white man's burden finds print as an effective vehicle for dominating the native consciousness. He writes:

> The art of printing would enable us to disseminate our writings in a way the Persians never could have done, though their compositions had been as numerous as ours. Hence the Hindoos would see the great use we make of reason on all subjects, and in all affairs, they also would learn to reason, they would become acquainted with their own species, the past and present state of the world; their affections would gradually become interested by varying engaging works, composed to recommend virtue, and to defer from vice; the general mass of their opinion would be rectified, and above all, they would use a better system of principals and morals. (emphasis added; Ibid.: 83)

Reason becomes an organizing principle for recovering one's past as well as knowing one's place in the world. Indian languages are now required to conform to this paradigm which is derived from the discourses of Enlightenment rationality. The 'othering' of Indian languages is achieved though the deployment of a moral economy where they are banished to the realm of the irrational. Indian languages are repeatedly referred to as dialects incapable of transmitting 'modern' knowledge. Macaulay's infamous minute states:

> All parties seem to be agreed on one point, that the dialects commonly spoken among the natives of this part of India contain neither literary nor scientific information, and are moreover so poor and rude that, until they are enriched from some other quarter, it will not be easy to translate any valuable work into them. (Ibid.: 85)

The intense multilingualism and the shared metaphoric universe sustained by Indian languages were disputed by the hegemonic structures of colonial power.

The fuzzy nature of pre-colonial society enabled communities to relate to the pan-Indian Sanskrit cosmopolis on their own terms but the colonial authority had a hegemonic hold on all their faculties including imagination, necessitating a reworking of all their resources and discourses. The conceptual grid of colonialism has at its disposal the elaborate cognitive apparatus of rationality as an organizing principle. This is why the introduction of English, along with the advent of print, set in motion an unprecedented process of standardization from which no Indian language could escape without risking extinction. English occupied the space marked by modernity, appropriating to itself the power of arbitration regarding the nature and content of modernity. Sanskrit fell from its pedestal to the status of an archaic language. The process of modernization that was now underway demanded that regional languages internalize the logic of rationality and empiricism that had already been initiated by print. The internal economy of regional languages became differentiated, acquiring an elitist high form that equipped it with features of English and Sanskrit. Many varieties of modern Indian languages now came to be relegated to the level of dialects, while those closer to the elite variety gained greater currency and value.

Modernity in the colonial context manifests itself in the political-cultural discourse of nation and nationalism. Orientalists and Anglicists, seemingly opponents in their authentication of Sanskrit and English respectively, both pan-Indian languages, effectively meet in the narrative of the nation that has to reconcile the requirement of an uninterrupted history of unitary discourses with a present where a univocal rationality could be embodied in a homogenized contemporary idiom. Regional linguistic traditions become the other in this scheme of a past that is imagined as future. Instead of designating nation as a work in progress, in all its imperfect visions and revisions and complex living heteroglossia, nation was given an imagined unity in its Sanskritic high tradition and this constructed homogeneity was consecrated and canonized through a pact with discourses of universality and objectivity under the façade of a false modernity. In this enactment of culture-power conjunction, region becomes a fragment, a lack that is forever suspect and incomplete. The earlier confidence which Indian languages had asserted against Sanskrit and developed their own independent literary styles could not be recovered in their encounter with English largely because of the political power of the hegemonic colonial apparatus.

In the nineteenth century, Persian was progressively replaced by English throughout India: in 1832 in the Bombay and Madras Presidencies and in 1837 in Bengal Presidency. This set in motion a process which gradually resulted in the Sanskritization of Indian languages under the patronage of the state. The fracturing of the shared composite culture of Hindi/Urdu as a case in point reflects the disastrous consequences of the cleavage that developed in North India. The founding moment of the linguistic divide that finally deepened into the communal divide and the two-nation theory can be seen in the order issued by Anthony Mac Donnell, Lt. Governor of NWP&O on 18th April, 1900 allowing permissive use of Devanagari in provincial courts (Alok Rai 2000: 17).

This subtle move, in effect, put the colonial stamp of approval on the legitimacy of Sanskritized Hindi as against Persianized Urdu which was perceived as a threat by the Hindu elite. In the 1870s and 1880s, the Hindustani in the Persian script gave way to Hindi in the Nagari script. The pedants of Fort William College and the missionaries of Serampore contributed in their separate ways to the institutionalization of Sanskritised Hindi. This is also the time when print media had begun a crucial role in the shaping of the subjectivities of various communities. To quote Alok Rai:

> The rough beast of cultural differentiation—of amputation and self-mutilation leading eventually to civil war and partition—was formed in new parallel nurseries of which were the innocent and certainly unintended consequence of colonial education policy. (Ibid.: 95)

The subjectivities legitimated by a centralized nation-state demand allegiance to the *langue* of elite discourse and not the *parole* of the popular multi-lingual heteroglossia. Here then is the fault-line that animates the conflictual terrain of the regional Indian languages. The contestations that have accompanied the formation of the public sphere in regional speech communities have repeatedly problematised the elitist positions embodied in nationalist narratives.

III

I will conclude this discussion with a brief note on the role of missionary Malayalam in the shaping of modern Malayalam prose. As was pointed out above, the mainstream literary tradition of Malayalam up until the eighteenth century was made up of poetry and had not developed a viable form of prose for articulating ideas, feelings and attitudes. With the coming of missionaries in the sixteenth centuries, things began to change. Here we need to remember that the missionaries had an impact on Indian languages as a whole. In a lecture titled 'Languages of India in their Relation to Missionary Work' on 28 April 1875 on the occasion of the annual meeting of the Society for the Propagation of the Gospel, Revd. Robert Caldwell outlines the nature of the contributions being made by missionaries to the major languages of India as well as to minor tribal languages. He begins by outlining the complexity of the linguistic situation in India where a large number of languages are spoken:

> Not including English, the language of government and of the higher education—not including Sanskrit, the literary language of the Brahmans

and other Indo-Aryans—not including Persian, the literary language of the Muhammadans—not including any of the languages spoken on the frontier side of Indian frontier, such as Beluchi, on the north-west, or the Burmese dialects spoken on the eastern side of the Bay of Bengal—reckoning only the languages spoken within the boundary line, but including the native states as well as the British provinces, and the aboriginal tribes of the hills and forests, as well as the more cultivated races—the number of languages spoken in India cannot fall short of a hundred. (Caldwell 2007: 577)

Towards the end of the lecture he says:

We have seen that Christianity is now being taught in about seven-and-twenty Indian languages, or including the literary languages—Sanskrit and Persian—in nine-and-twenty and that amongst twenty three of the peoples by whom these languages are spoken. Christian truth has assumed visible shape, through the formation of amongst them of congregations of Christians. I trust therefore the time is coming—it will soon come—it will come perhaps almost before we are aware—when every language and dialect in India will be consecrated to Christ. (ibid.: 587)

Missionaries did not turn to the traditional prose for their models of writing but to the ordinary speech of the common people and this revolutionized the manner in which Malayalam prose was written. Scholars of Malayalam have been reluctant to recognize the role of missionaries in the development of Malayalam prose. A veteran scholar of Malayalam like S. Guptan Nair in his introduction to the book on *Missionary Malayalam* by P.J. Francis, harps on the proselytizing role of the missionaries which, according to him, prompted them to opt for the common speech current in society (Francis 2006: 7). While this is true, the fact remains that they saw language from the outside and transformed it to suit the demands of writing discursive prose where ideas and feelings could be communicated. The first travelogue written in Malayalam in 1780, *Vartamanapustakam* by Paremmakkal Thoma Kathanar is remarkable for its detailed account of the social conditions of Kerala Christians in the eighteenth century, apart from the references to the problems faced by Christian sects in Kerala. P.K. Parameswaran Nair, the eminent literary historian, observes that 'many qualities rare in Malayalam prose of those times such as the systematic presentation of ideas, division into paragraphs, rational ordering of sentences could be traced here' (Parameswaran Nair Smaraka Trust 150). L.V. Ramaswami Iyer, a prominent linguist of the early twentieth century has noted the Latinate syntax of early missionary writings. He writes:

The journey man prose of these Missionaries, particularly of the more recent periods, is 'coloured' by what may be called the 'Latinistic' outlook. Ideas, comparisons and turns of expression are cast in the Latinistic mould; constuctions of Malaylam are imitated or adapted from those of the Latin speeches; new compounds and phrases are coined on the analogy of those existing in the speeches of south of Europe; and sometimes even the words and forms of Malayalam are so chosen as to correspond to the South European outlook. (ibid.: 142)

Historians of Malayalam prose like Prabhakara Varier tend to argue that, given the conditions of transformation in the eighteenth and nineteenth centuries, the Sanskritized prose of the seventeenth century would have developed into its modern form, even without the intervention of missionaries. He says: 'If we examine the development of prose from the seventeenth to nineteenth centuries, it can be seen that a new clear prose is gradually emerging. Missionary prose has not played any role in this process' (Varier 2004: 104). But this contradicts the facts. The intervention of print, translations of the Bible, the publication of dictionaries etc., constitute an important stage of colonial modernity that redefined the direction taken by the Malayalam language. Benjamin Bailey (1791–1871), a Protestant priest from Dewsbury, Yorkshire in England, not only translated the Bible into Malayalam and produced a monumental Malayalam-English dictionary that took 28 years of labour, but also created the types for printing of Malayalam, creating a standard form for the Malayalam alpahabet, and altering the manner in which we write Malayalam. As the first Principal of the Kottayam College established by the Church Mission Society, he was the first to introduce English into the curriculum of college education in Kerala. The round and shapely Malayalam type he introduced in the place of the square-type Malayalam letters went on to become the standard type for writing and printing Malayalam, making him the first typographer of Malayalam. In translating the Bible into Malayalam (first published in 1829) he used an idiom that incorporated colloquial words and common idioms, thus moving away from the high Sanskritic style. The first Malayalam book to be printed in Kerala, *Stories translated from English for the benefit of Small Children* was printed in the modern Malayalam type developed by him and published in 1824. What is central to the present argument is that the imprint of colonial modernity can be seen in all the projects initiated by Bailey: the translation of the Bible, production of Malayalam types, introduction of English and the establishment of the Malayalam printing press. He effectively laid the foundation for a new Malayalam prose that led to the rejuvenation of literature in the modern phase.

What displaces the Sanskrit-centred high tradition is the combination of the projects of modernity that brought about changes in the dissemination of literature, educational curriculum and modes of relating to the others in society. The new literary forms such as the novel, the short story, the autobiography etc. did not develop from the earlier prose forms but under the impact of the new prose which had internalized the logic of the new print. However, it has to be noted that the new hierarchy, with English occupying a superior status both as administrative intellectual medium, and Malayalam being seen as a medium of the masses, further created a schism in the world of culture that deepened into a major fault-line of our socio-cultural domain. Here we need to see the complex linguistic and cultural scene in a single language in India, namely, Malayalam, which defies easy generalizations. This is why we have to be wary of post-colonial constructs in the area of translation which tend to see India as a single unit. Postcolonial theory is concerned with only those issues that touch upon the Anglo-American academy. It fails to go deep into issues that originate in the multilingual contexts of India. One of the basic responsibilities of Indian comparatists is to be ethically responsive to the linguistic and cultural realities of India as embedded in texts produced in Indian languages. Indian comparatists cannot work with translations alone; they have to return to the original languages of the subcontinent. That there is hardly anything in postcolonial critical tradition which can enable them to explore the ground reality in India makes them lonely figures, but loneliness is the price you pay for the ethical commitment to the cause of your language and its people.

It is significant that at a crucial stage of its development of prose, Malayalam internalized the syntactical features of South European languages. By the time *Varthamanapustakam* came to be written in 1785, missionary Malayalam had developed a robust prose style capable of expressing a range of ideas about society, religion, art, architecture and moral values. Another book written during this period was *Jnanamuthmala* (A garland made of the pearls of wisdom) that appeared in 1784. C.L. Antony, an eminent linguist of the last century, in his analysis of this text demonstrates how it marks a significant advancement in the development of Malayalam prose by incorporating the colloquial language of central Kerala. It carries the stamp of its times in several of its syntactical and grammatical features, but there is no denying the fact that modern Malayalam prose developed from this kind of missionary prose. Antony says the foundation of modern prose in Malayalam was established in the works of missionary prose. The first Malayalam book to be published (in 1811) was the New Testament (with 504 pages) that was printed in the Courier Press of Bombay. Benjamin Bayley's Malayalam-English dictionary appeared in 1846 and continues to be a standard lexicon. It was titled 'A dictionary of high and colloquial Malayalam and English' and included large number of words of every day usage from all the communities in southern Kerala.

The impetus for the transformation of Malayalam into a modern language came not from Sanskrit but from its encounter with European languages and its incorporation of the local and everyday speech of the living community. This is where it parted company with the Sanskritic tradition which had fossilized Malayalam into a language with very little expressive power. This process, strangely enough, secularized Malayalam by giving it the capacity to address the common people through various periodicals that began to appear from 1847 onwards. The translations of Shakespeare that became available in the latter part of the nineteenth century and the early novels such as *The Slayer Slain* were all written in the language that developed from missionary Malayalam and leaned heavily on the spoken varieties of Malayalam in different parts of Kerala. In an editorial written in *Malayala Manorama* on 11 February 1893, the editor says that of the seventeen periodicals published in Kerala six were weeklies, one appeared thrice a month, four appeared twice a month, and the remaining six were monthlies (E.V. Ramakrishnan 2011: 25). The shift from orality to print happened through the medium of missionary Malayalam. Missionary prose, while being encapsulated within colonial modernity, was the product of a public sphere where 'inherently unstable identities in a stratified society could be visualized from new perspectives' (Ramakrishnan 2011: 161). The new public sphere was characterized by its resistance to elitist notions of culture and politics.

In conclusion it may be stated, keeping the example of Malayalam in mind, that modern Indian languages used the emancipatory potential of colonial modernity as embodied in English to turn away from the hegemonic hold of Sanskrit during the period between the eighteenth and twentieth centuries. Similarly, in their foundational moment they relied on the creative potential of the popular domain to confront the hegemony of Sanskrit. What is at work here is the dynamics of the multilingual culture that is deeply ingrained in its own structure enabling it to view with suspicion those categories that seek closure and finality. As in the case of Sanskrit, the presence of English created a new hierarchy where modern Indian languages were required to approximate themselves to the epistemological models set by English with its professed rationality. As a result of this false hierarchy, the symbiotic relations between Indian languages came to be viewed with suspicion and distrust, as languages became increasingly insecure in their competition with English. Modern Indian languages also distanced themselves from their oral resources that had been relegated to the irrational pre-modern domain. The Other of modern languages is now located within the languages themselves and this accounts for the embattled state of their present being. The task of the comparatist is to recover this Other and articulate its being in an attempt to negotiate an emergent dialogic relation.

REFERENCES

Antony, C.L., *Bhashapatanangal*, Thrissur: Kerala Sahitya Akademi, 1989.

Caldwell, Dr. Robert, 'The Languages of India in Their Relation to Missionary Work' (Republication from the Archives), *Tapasam*, vol. II, issues 3 and 4, 2007, pp. 574–88.

Devy, G.N., *Of Many Heroes: An Indian Essay in Literary Historiography*, Hyderabad: Orient Longman, 1998.

Francis, P.J. Advocate, *Pathiri Malayalam: Oru Vichitanam*, Kottayam: Current Books, 2006.

Ganeri, Jonardon, 'Intellectual India: Reason, Identity and Dissent', *New Literary History*, vol. 40, no. 2, Spring 2009, pp. 247–63.

Kartha, K.S.P., ed., *Oru Yatrayute Katha* by Paramekkal Thoma Kathanar, Thiruvananthapuram: Sony Books, 1989.

Kaviraj, Sudipta, 'Writing, Speaking, Being: Language and the Historical Formations of Identities in India', in *Language and Politics in India*, ed. Asha Sarangi, New Delhi: OUP, 2010.

King, Robert D., *Nehru and the Language Politics of India*, New Delhi: OUP, 1998.

Müller, Friedrich Max, *India: What it Can Teach Us?*, Delhi: Penguin, 2000.

Naregal, Veena, *Language Politics, Elites and the Public Sphere*, New Delhi: Permanent Black, 2001.

Novetzke, Christian Lee, *Religion and Public Memory: A Cultural History of Saint Namdev in India*, New York Chichester: Columbia University Press, 2008.

Panjabi, Kavita, *Poetics and Politics of Sufism and Bhakti in South Asia: Love, Loss and Liberation*, Hyderabad: Orient BlackSwan, 2011.

Parameswaran Nair Smaraka Trust, *Malayala Sahitya Charitram 17um and 18um Nootantukalil*, Kottayam: Current Books, 2001.

Patnaik, Bibudhendra N., *Introducing Saaralaa Mahaabhaarata*, Mysore: Central Institute of Indian Languages, 2012.

Pollock, Sheldon, *The Language of the Gods in the World of Men*, New Delhi: Permanent Black, 2011.

———, 'What is Indian knowledge good for?', First Balvant Parekh Memorial Lecture, Baroda: Balvant Parekh Centre for General Semantics and Other Human Sciences, 2013.

Rai, Alok, *Hindi Nationalism*, Hyderabad: Orient Longman, 2000.

Ramakrishnan, E.V., *Locating Indian Literature: Texts, Traditions, Translations*, Hyderabad: Orient BlackSwan, 2011.

———, *Anubhavangale Aarkkanu Peti?*, Kottayam: D.C. Books, 2012.

Ranganathan, Balaji, *Orientalism and India*, New Delhi: Creative Books, 2009.

Tagore, Saumyendranath, *Raja Rammohun Roy*, Makers of Indian Literature Series, New Delhi: Sahitya Akademi, 2009.

Varier, K.M. Prabhakara, *Malayalam: Mattavum Valarchayum*, Sukapuram, Thrissur: Vallathol Vidyapeetam and Current Books, 2004.

Venkatachalapathy, A.R., *The Province of the Book: Scholars, Scribes and Scribblers in Colonial Tamilnadu*, Ranikhet: Permanent Black, distributed by New Delhi: Orient BlackSwan, 2012.

Vieira, E., 'Liberating Calibans: Readings of Antropofagia and Haroldo de Campos' poetics of transcreation', in *Postcolonial Translation: Theory and Practice*, ed. S. Bassnett and H. Trivedi, London and New York: Routledge, 1999.

15

Revisiting Translation: Towards Fine Arts and Architecture

Anisur Rahman

CANONS: OLD AND NEW

As the most engaging and never-ending site of human activity, translation has collected a huge mass of material around itself in terms of theoretical discussions and personal narratives. In addition, there is a large variety of material lying around in unspecified categories. Re-visiting this site for all its massive capital of theory and practice in the second decade of the twenty-first century is like moving through seven continents and wondering at the exclusive exhibits one sees. One arrives ultimately, if one does, at one's own location where structures and forms of meaning reside in the marks and motifs of a site, as also the *langue* and *parole* of a people. The matter gets complex with the realization that all verbal expressions remain fluid and that all intents are arbitrary at best. So, how does a text in translation become a receptacle of meaning, when language remains fluid and the supposed meaning in a language only arbitrary? By using the metaphor of a long and arduous voyage through seven continents and considering the complex ways language and meaning operate in a translated text, I wish to posit that while all acts of translation and theorization are rooted in given cultural and linguistic spaces, there can be no possibility of developing a discourse on translation, unless it is contextualized in time, space, history, and culture.

Although lying buried in deep past, there are institutions that tell a different story. When I say this, I have in mind the Chang'an School in China, Plato's Academy in Greece, the great library of Alexandria in Egypt, the academy of Jund-e Shapur in Persia, Bait-ul Hikma in Iraq, and the School of Toledo in Spain. In constructing a great variety of knowledge systems, these institutions laid down the classical tradition of developing contiguities with various peoples, faiths, and languages. These seats of comprehensive learning emerged and survived as empires of knowledge construction, and as seminal sites of negotiation among people in diverse locations as such as Greece, Persia, Arabia, Europe, China, and Japan; that flourished within faiths as different as Islam, Christianity, and Buddhism; and languages as varied as Greek, Arabic, Latin, and English. While knowledge systems pertaining to philosophy, grammar, mathematics, and sciences saw their efflorescence in these sites, translation too started to develop as an art. In ancient India, we have the example of individuals, rather than institutions, in figures such as Kumarjiva who translated Sanskrit Sutras. Later, with the arrival Portuguese, Dutch, and British colonizers, followed by the Jesuit missionaries, travellers and political emissaries created conditions for the construction and dissemination of new knowledge. The establishment of the College of Fort William in Calcutta was instrumental in knowledge production and translation. Such efforts kept multiplying in subsequent years with the establishment of other institutions throughout the colonial period.

Given this history, I should like to propose that, like the Continental Drift, there is something we might call the Translational Drift operating today. In its engagement with postcolonial theory and practice, translation has moved towards, as well as drawn away, in a richly ambiguous way, from traditional norms of writing and reading. It has developed as a formidable site of intense debates on race and history. At the new sites of literary production, translation is subjected to contestations in the spheres of society, politics, identity, and the larger configuration of the nation state. Even though nation states pretend to cooperate with each other for the sake of political expediency, correctness, or necessity, they have, in fact, drawn apart in order to safeguard their hidden and proclaimed agendas. As such, literary production and translation are required so that these different sites might better chart a way of difference for themselves and deny their belonging to a universal order of mixed or blurred identities. Unlike earlier times, translation today has no empire; there are, instead, sites of divergent and convergent ideologies where dominant and subaltern constructions regarding language and textual formation, history, and cultural configurations are hotly debated. In the postcolonial and postmodern world, translation survives in contested spaces where it works through the politics of negotiating with various components of a text and the world represented in the text.

TOWARDS FINE ART AND ARCHITECTURE

By summarizing instances of translations from the classical and postclassical periods, I wish to build an argument that translation has essentially been a cultural engagement with acts of language and the structures of ideas. I will elaborate further by drawing parallels from the field of architecture. Just as every building follows certain structural principles, every translation follows a set of rules in its reconstruction of a text. Extending this logic further, I may add that just as every building speaks a language of its own; every translation discovers its own idiom. I might also propose that just as a translator brings language to a text, and text to a language; the architect also brings bricks to a building, and a building to bricks. Both the architect and the translator, in devising their modes of expression, create their own artefacts—their own configurations of language and ideas.

With this basic argument in hand, let me pursue my case further. A translator appropriates different strategies for different texts, just as an architect does for different building types. So every literary form whether it be fiction or poetry, drama or prose, epic or lyric, essay or memoir, calls for different strategies of translation. Similarly, every building type whether it functionas as a theatre or amphitheatre, tower or skyscraper, mall or motel, hut or hotel, gymnasium or stadium, needs a different set of principles for its constructions. Just as a good text has to stand out in order to become canonical, a good piece of architecture too has to prove sustainable in order to become a classic. Let me take this argument one step further and isolate the structural elements that distinguish a literary text from architecture. No literary text, or text in translation, can ever be structured without its base in figures of speech such as image, simile, or metaphor; myth, symbol, or allegory; allusion, antithesis, or irony; metonymy, personification, or hyperbole; oxymoron, paradox, or pun. In the same manner, no work of architecture, which can be viewed as a text of another kind, can ever be composed without making use, for example, of items such as beams, columns, or spans; aisles, arcades, or pathways; domes, arches, or towers; labyrinths, basements, or attics; porches, porticos, or balconies. Furthermore, both literary texts as configured in translation and structural designs as translated into buildings need a primary mind-mapping and concept-mapping as the bases for their structures. Once these two structures are complete in their external form, they need chiselling. So, a work in translation goes through an endless process of revisions in order to pass as a final product possessing a certain beauty and appeal. Similarly, a building achieves these ends with molding, festooning, or etching, as the facade may demand. As the translated text acquires its own voice and maintains its acoustics, the architectural text too reverberates with its own sounds and echoes. In the ultimate analysis, both of them approximate a condition of architectural mythology, which may be considered to be the height of artistic achievement.

Both works of art, the text in translation and the building in execution, acquire their ultimate expression when they are presented as pleasantly readable and comfortably habitable spaces. The interiors and the exteriors of both 'texts' breathe life once they are properly adorned with appropriate colors and figurative designs. The translator, like a painter, approaches the color wheel to make his choice of colors. He has a large variety of the primary, secondary, or tertiary; complimentary, neutral, or fugitive shades from which to choose. He also has to decide on color durability and scheme; color separation and space; color temperature and quality, in order to contextualise the text in translation, or architecture in its final execution. The exposure to light and management of silhouettes, in terms of single or double exposure, and two-dimensional or multi-dimensional visualizations must impart a sense of completion to the 'text'. It is here that the artist and architect join hands and, complimenting each other, make a work artistically successful. In the final analysis, the translated text and the completed building emerge as naturalist or impressionist, realist or surrealistic, abstract or concrete works of art. In this viable execution lies their appeal and the possibility of their eventual canonization.

A PATTERN LANGUAGE

With reference to the argument that translation is a cultural engagement with language, I would like to dwell upon the concept of 'Pattern Language' put forth by the innovative architectural theorists Christopher Alexander, Sara Ishikawa, and Murray Silverstein[1] who engage the basic idea of how certain tools and techniques create designs. They argue that even common people are capable of creating architectural patterns, which are akin to linguistic patterns. Drawing on basic linguistic composition, they suggest that pattern language in architecture is also composed of vocabulary, syntax, and grammar, and that these three elements are configured in complex ways to create designs. Pattern language, they believe, offers solutions to structural problems and facilitates good design. They envision the architect as someone who solves problems by creating designs, with the help of vocabulary, syntax, and grammar. Words embody meaning, and work through grammar. Meaning and grammar are, thus, inseparable. They play a necessary role in creating designs. As such, a collection of words once put together, creates a structure and all the components of this structure are logically combined to create a language that ultimately creates the architectural design. Since architecture based on pattern language is a thing of utility for the user, it serves as an object of empowerment.

Another significant part of the pattern language model is the context, which gives it meaning. Pattern language works through the principle of striking a balance between divergent elements. It acquires strength or character in relation to another design either within or outside the architecture itself. Its value is thus imparted through comparison. Pattern language establishes a hierarchy in the complex web of languages that ultimately writes the 'text' of the building and constitutes a philosophy of its construction.

It would appear that the key issues in pattern language are vocabulary, syntax, and grammar; problem, solution, and context; balance, empowerment, and design. The architect identifies a project, discovers its context in relation to its intended users, views potential problems in terms of balancing the work, and arrives at a solution in terms of how best to complete the project with the maximum utility and pleasure accruing to the user or reader. In relation to this thesis, I may propose that translators too are writers of pattern language who work with their own vocabulary, syntax, and grammar. They identify a text just as architects identify their projects. They know their context in terms of their readers as architects know their own works in relation to their users. Both the writer and the architect balance their acts of 'languaging' their problems. Both work towards achieving pleasure and empowering their users/readers. Developing a multidisciplinary approach and drawing upon the disciplines of literature, biology, and geometry, I may further suggest that translation is a symbolic, metabolic, and parabolic activity. As a symbolic act, translation provides a source of cultural empowerment, an indication of the comparative growth of a people. As a metabolic act, it is a process of acquiring energy and multiplying new cells for better survival. If not done properly, translation may devolve into a parabolic activity in which an object, thrown into the air, falls back on the ground like a parabola.

THE CONTEXT OF THE TEXT

Finally, I would like to examine the above propositions in relation to some translation practices. I have chosen examples from translators themselves who view their activity in a theoretical fashion. In translating Jalaluddin Rumi, Reynold A. Nicholson is deeply concerned with the problem of accuracy. 'My translation seeks to reconcile the claims of accuracy and art:' he says, 'it is therefore in prose' (ix).[2] In translating Kabir, Arvind Krishna Mehrotra finds a parallel between the Kabir text and its translation. 'As with Kabir text', he says, 'so with this Kabir translation; it is made keeping the text's inclusive genius in mind' (xxxi).[3] While translating Anantha Murthy's *Samskara*, A.K. Ramanujan was primarily concerned with textual formation. 'I have tried to make the translation self-contained, faithful yet readable'. He also maintained that the 'translator hopes not only to translate a text, but hopes (against all odds) to translate a non-native reader into a native one' (not paginated). In translating Mahasweta Devi, Gayatri Chakravorty Spivak reports an intimate dialogue with the author. 'To my great delight, among the first things Mahasweta Devi said to me . . . 'Gayatri, what I am really enjoying in your translation is how you've shown that dialect can be dignified''[4] (viii). Interestingly, my last example is not from a work of translation but from one written originally in the English language but creating a keen sense of the writer's mother tongue. In his Introduction to *Twilight in Delhi*, Ahmed Ali writes, 'Many who have read only the translation tell me they cannot believe it could have been written originally in English; and some have even said that I must have written it in Urdu and then translated it into English. On the other hand, some have refused to read the Urdu version because, they say, the English original is untranslatable' (vii).

An analysis of the translators' intentions and methodologies as mentioned above would show that all these translators are essentially concerned with the problem of language. The questions of accuracy, fidelity, cultural transference, tone and tenor, in short, all the clichés turn out to be attendant issues. We see this process exemplified by Ahmed Ali, who writes two languages and preserves two cultures simultaneously when he chooses to construct his story through verse in a particular sequence of his novel. He describes a scene where fakirs come begging:

> They stood before the doors and sang a verse or just shouted for bread or pice or, tinkling their bowls together, they waved their heads in frenzy, beating time with their feet, singing for all they were worth:
>
> Dhum! Qalandar, God will give,
> Dhum! Qalandar, God alone;
> Milk and sugar, God will give,
> Dhum! Qalandar, God alone . . . (17)

I am not familiar with the Urdu verse that the fakirs in Ali's days are singing, nor do I know how it could form a part of his memory. The important point is that he chooses to preserve a cultural condition and record that condition in another language. I may only guess that what the fakirs sang could have been something like this:

Dhum Qalandar, Allah dega
Dhum Qalandar, Allah hi Allah
Doodh aur shakkar, Allah dega
Dum Qalandar, Allah hi Allah

We may have one more example in a couplet he renders in English:

Betake your way, O breeze of the Spring,
Frolic not with me:
You are in a playful mood,
But I in one of ecstasy. (32)

Those with knowledge of the Urdu language and its literary culture, would immediately recognise the source of this couplet:

Na Chhed ai nikhat-e baad-e bahaari raah lag apni
Tujhe atkheliyan soojhi hain, hum bezar baithe hain

The fictional plot is thus illuminated by this intervention which I would consider linguistic in nature; it serves to distinguish the text. In translating Mir and Ghalib, Ali explains his concerns in yet another way when he notes that the 'retention of rhyme would have meant either sacrificing sense or faithfulness to the originals, or distortion of syntax, or both' (106).[5] The examples quoted above substantiate that all these translators develop their own versions of pattern language; they negotiate with vocabulary, syntax, and grammar; context, problem, and solution; design, balance, and empowerment. They perform their tasks in a cultural context since all texts (and all architectures) exist in a cultural time and a cultural space.

NOTES

1. C. Alexander, S. Ishikawa and M. Silverstein, *A Pattern Language: Towns, Buildings, Construction*, New York: OUP, 1977.
2. In his 'Preface' to this volume Nicholson continues: 'Obviously English verse cannot convey the full verbal sense of oriental poetry without lapsing into grotesque doggerel; the translator must either profess a general adherence to his author's meaning ... or arising above the letter, he must catch the elusive spirit of his original and reproduce it in a worthy form. Of this the highest and rarest kind of translation, Fitzgerald's Omar Khayyam is a classic example. I have done my best to avoid gratuitous banalities, when no misapprehension was possible' (ix).

3. In his 'Introduction', after engaging with various other methodologies employed earlier for translating Kabir, Malhotra sums up his methodology as follows: '*Songs of Kabir* is both a work of translation based on the best available critical editions and . . . a further elaboration of Kabir's corpus, taking its place alongside those that have already been in existence for hundreds of years' (xxxiv).
4. In her 'Translator's Foreword', Spivak begins by making a basic statement about her way of approaching the text at a primary level to produce a translation of great competence: 'It has been my practice to underline the words in English in the original. It makes the text awkward to view'.
5. In his 'Note on the Translations', Ali further notes: 'If I had allowed my interpretations to enter, the translated poems would not have remained Ghalib, as Fitzgerald's translations are not Omar Khayyam. So, I have left the translations, like the originals, unexplained, so that each reader can interpret the poet in accordance with his sensibility, as he does the poetry of T.S. Eliot' (107).

REFERENCES

Alexander, C., S. Ishikawa and M. Silverstein, *A Pattern Language: Towns, Buildings, Construction*, New York: OUP, 1977.

Ali, Ahmed, *Twilight in Delhi*, Bombay: OUP, 1966.

———, *The Golden Treasury: An Anthology of Urdu Poetry*, New York and London: Columbia University Press, 1973.

Mehrotra, Arvind Krishna, *Songs of Kabir*, India: Hachette, 2011.

Nicholson, Reynold A., *Selected Poems from the Divani Shamsi Tabriz*, Cambridge: University Press, 1898.

Ramanujan, A.K., *Samskara*, Delhi: OUP, 2009.

Spivak, Gayatri Chakravorty, *Chotti Munda and His Arrow*, Kolkata: Seagull Books, 2002.

16

Negotiating Difference: Minority Discourse and Translation

Assumpta Camps

THIS ESSAY looks at how difference is currently negotiated from the perspective of minority discourses and how such negotiation informs the task of translation, in a time when the dynamic of intersections and mediations shaping today's developments in contemporary literature falls under the rubric of cultural translation. Linguistic conflict is crucial to the creative trajectory of transcultural authors. Bilingual, they are torn between their mother tongue and the majority language that many of them choose for their writing. Caught between languages and cultures that are sometimes very distant from one another, transcultural authors need to discover in these interstices a literary voice that can express their cultural, linguistic and social reality. The challenge for them is to find a form that pays respect to their own minority cultural universe (often oral), a universe to which they wish to give visibility and literary substance. This search takes transcultural authors on a journey of exploration that not only arrives at no easy solutions, but also seeks genuinely intercultural communication from which minority discourse can emerge. In this effort, translation plays an absolutely critical role. Quite often, these authors negotiate with the dominant culture through translation: they perceive themselves through translation; they write and are written about through translation; and through translation they aspire to attain their own voice within the dominant discourse.

From this perspective, it is necessary to bear in mind that transcultural literatures involve a process of translation in and of themselves. As the Indian critic G.N. Devy (1998) reminds us, many literary traditions

* This essay has been written within the Research Project FFI2009-10896, directed by Assumpta Camps, and funded by the Spanish Government.

in postcolonial spaces have been born precisely in acts of translation. In Devy's view, communities exist possessing what he calls translating consciousness (Devy 1998: 154–5), that is, a consciousness that emerges in multilingual communities in which a language of colonial domination has attained a privileged status in terms of its communicative and creative possibilities without overriding the various autochthonous languages within such communities. Similarly, Pérez Firmat speaks of the need for a translation sensibility in his study on the importance of translation in the development of Cuban literature (Pérez Firmat 1989: 1), and Bergvall refers to the translative awareness (Bergvall 2000: 252) of multilingual authors who continually develop their fictions around the complex concept of (un)translatability between two or more languages and cultures. As we shall see, these various approaches are similar to the transcultural experience. Their negotiation of difference in order to make room for minority discourse, draws on the idea of writing from the standpoint of translation.

TRANSCULTURAL LITERATURES

Located between frontiers, in the problematic cultural and linguistic interstices created by the clash and interaction of various cultures, the narrative work of transcultural authors, present to a great extent in the postcolonial sphere, encompasses an emerging area where the forms of these encounters have taken on their own distinct voice. Their literary efforts possess a critical dimension in that they aim to rewrite and move away from the representation that others, within the dominant discourse, have made of them, marginalizing, censoring, hiding or stereotyping their cultural identities first in a colonial and subsequently in a postcolonial setting.

This essay makes use of the concept of 'transculturation', borrowed from Latin American cultural criticism. In broad strokes, transculturation refers to the process by which cultures meet. This encounter produces changes in the contact societies and a creative response arises in the transitivity between cultures, particularly when the cultures come from dissimilar positions of power. Transculturation is an avenue by which minority discourses make their way in this intercultural relationship; it is not predicated on the idea that individual cultural traditions disappear, but rather that they undergo continuous development, in dialogic interaction. In this process, some features of both cultures are lost, while others are gained, giving rise to new communicative forms and possibilities (Sales 2001).

We start from the premise that minority discourse makes room for itself through the narratives of transculturation produced by bilingual and bicultural authors, who fictionalize a communicative issue that is resolved by an operation of translation. Bicultural (not merely bilingual) authors are also, and above all else, translators; they are mediators between the languages and cultures that make up who they are, yet do not exist on the same plane. Their work leads to a unequal intercultural dialogue that involves taking a stance with respect to the dominant, hegemonic discourse. Doubtlessly, writing in this context means translating. At the same time, however, it involves negotiating the difference between the autochthonous culture (relegated to the periphery) and the hegemonic culture, which is typically Western and sets itself up as central and canonical.

As we know, translation and power are inextricably linked. From the postcolonial sphere, retranslation or the use of translation is postulated as a means of resisting hegemonic structures. Indeed, translation studies in recent decades, particularly from the nineties onwards, have assumed that translation goes beyond the strictly linguistic area, functioning as an activity of intercultural, creative and social mediation, a communicative process that always unfolds within a social, cultural and political context. It is not necessary to insist here that one of the main avenues of imperial oppression is precisely the exercise of control over language, which is not only a social phenomenon, but can also become an instrument of institutional power. Seen from this perspective, the postcolonial use of non-dominant and minoritized languages poses a real challenge in the social and political sphere, because many transcultural authors adopt what has come to be called the Caliban strategy, formulating their response in the 'language of empire' in which they have been educated.[1]

For better or worse, the global expansion of languages such as Spanish or English cannot be denied in today's world. As we know, such languages do not belong to a single nation in particular. A multitude of communicative varieties have sprung up in places where they have been introduced as official idioms and they have, over time, taken on a life of their own. In the confrontation between so-called global languages and minoritized languages, transcultural narrators see a possibility of transforming and promoting the hybridisation of hegemonic languages from within and through the lens of minority cultures.

Today, choosing the dominant language, i.e. a global language, for literary creation, is an increasingly common path. In some sense, the choice can be viewed as an act of submission to the dominant discourse and the suppression of minoritized languages and cultures. However, it also marks a privileged space 'from which' to undertake resistance and promote transcultural interaction: a space where the discourse of power can be made plural from within the system. This process involves using language to communicate what would otherwise remain unvoiced, concealed and marginalized. Preserving a minority language and culture from annihilation is also possible through an artist's choice to create in a global language, as a valid communicative intermediary, and insert into that language cultural features of the minority tradition, language, and culture, thus turning the global language into a hybrid vehicle of this other language and culture. With this translinguistic option, the transcultural author steps into the transnational repertoire and market. As Steven Kellman (2000) has pointed out, the 'translingual writer' is 'a writer who resides between languages' (Kellman 2000: 9), 'inhabiting' this interstitial space and fighting to establish authority and a voice in a foreign language that may, at the same time, prove problematic for the writer because of earlier social or colonial imposition. For bilingual narrators, writing in a language other than their mother tongue is sometimes a choice and sometimes a necessity, arising from the social imbalance between languages. Whatever the case, the choice is never naïve; it has a political dimension. Such authors aspire to convey their culture and their vision to the world. The challenge lies in finding expression in a strange language that they must learn to make their own. Therefore, literary creation that brings out the minority discourse of languages and minoritized cultures originates in an operation of cultural translation that is not only creative, but critical. Indeed, such authors invent narratives in which the language of writing, just as a palimpsest, does not succeed in fully occluding the linguistic and cultural diversity that nurtures their works.

Contemporary transcultural literature features a wide panorama of bilingual subjects writing in a global language. Examples abound: Indians writing in English (e.g. Salman Rushdie, Vikram Chandra, and V. S. Naipaul), Maghrebi authors writing in French (e.g. Tahar Ben Jelloun, Assia Djebar), Egyptians writing in English (e.g. Ahdaf Soueif), Turks writing in German (e.g. Emine Sevgi Özdamar, Jakob Arjouni), Iranians writing in Dutch (e.g. Kader Abdolah), Africans writing in Spanish (e.g. Donato Ndongo, Mohamed El Gheryb), Tunisians writing in Italian (e.g. Salah Methnani), Quechua-speakers writing in Spanish (e.g. José María Arguedas), and many more. In the same vein, some multicultural literary experiences in the United States are of great interest. For example, Rosario Ferré and Esmeralda Santiago are Puerto Rican authors who are bilingual in Spanish and English and self-translate their novels from Spanish to English (Ferré) or vice versa (Santiago), noting the painful recreation of the narrative subject in the process of cultural translation in which they are consciously inscribed. By contrast, the Dominican-American Julia Álvarez and the Cuban Cristina García have Spanish as their mother tongue, but they write in English, the language that they have learned and mastered and in which they have (re)created themselves.

THE CHICANO LITERATURE: A CASE STUDY

A particularly interesting case centres on Chicano writers, such as Sandra Cisneros, Carmen Tafolla, Lorna Dee Cervantes, Ana Castillo and Gloria Anzaldúa, who negotiate difference with the hegemonic discourse based on their bilingual and bicultural stance in a unique space, the borderlands of the US and Mexico where they live. Their works shift back and forth between Spanish and English, adopting extremely interesting code-switching in their narratives, and allowing for a bilingual reading of their texts.

The border is a territory full of contradictions and conflicts, of contacts and transgressions, where the frontier is an 'open wound' that delimits a space in which safety and risk coexist, and which defines what we are and what we are not: belonging and exclusion. The borderland is also a space of uncertainty, a contradictory place of double inscription—neither the one nor the other, but both at the same time. In the parlance of Homi K. Bhabha, we could say that it represents the uncanny space of imposture.[2]

Living on the border means living on the margins and, at the same time, preserving intact the ability to move from one space to another, from one identity to the next, from one language to another: not only from English to Spanish (or vice versa) but also from standard English to slang, to standard Spanish, to Mexican Spanish, to the dialect of northern Mexico, to Chicano language and its varieties, to Tex-Mex Spanglish, to Pachuco, etc. At the point where cultures meet, languages contaminate one another and take on new life in the form of Chicano Spanish, a language born out of the reality of the new borderland identity, almost like a secret language, like one's own homeland.

Those who live on the border tend to be alienated from both their own mother culture and the dominant English culture: they live on a cultural border, at the limits, in a reality where translation and cultural transfer are common, and where hybridization is not only a natural feature but a defining one, observable at the level both of ethnicity and language. As Samuel Weber has pointed out, subjects under those conditions experience the anxiety of that double inscription, since anxiety is the affective address of a 'world [that] reveals itself as caught up in the space between frames: a double frame or one that is split'.[3]

The borderland exists beyond the purely geographical, for it is a metaphor not only for the clash or contamination between cultures, but also of a certain state of mind. As Bhabha has brilliantly stated it:

> [the] borderland culture of hybridity . . . articulates its problems of identification and its diasporic aesthetic in an uncanny, disjunctive temporality that is, at once, the *time* of cultural displacement, and the *space* of the 'untranslatable.' (Bhabha 1994: 322)

The borderland is a metaphor of this 'in-between space' that celebrates cultural mixing and where hybridism can be projected towards other realities not necessarily identified with a political frontier. In fact, it appears in any context of cultural hybridization, be it a postcolonial context or the settling of minority cultures in First-World countries. What is interesting here is to analyse this cultural hyphenation and the effect of this mixing on the textual experience of these authors from the point of view of their negotiation of difference within the minority discourse. It is also significant to study the implications for translation beyond this liminal space for erratic cultural identities. In the work of Sandra Cisneros, for example, we are facing not just one frontier—the Mexican-American border—but several: as a woman, as a member of the Chicano collectivity, and as a writer.

The border, therefore, is a privileged place in which to consider issues of cultural transmission and the relationship with the Other, as well as to redefine ourselves in light of how the Other sees us. It is an ideal viewpoint for observing the cultural centre from the periphery, and the cultural periphery from the centre that allows the emergence of silenced minority discourses.

Cisneros' work, originating in this plural reality, is almost inevitably bilingual, and we often find words in Spanish (in its different varieties) in it. Her writing, however, is more than straightforward bilingualism: Cisneros writes in English, but she often uses Mexican syntax, introduces numerous set phrases, Mexican idioms and proverbs, which are sometimes translated literally into English and Texan Spanish. Her writing is thus not only bilingual, but bicultural; it supports itself through translation, where language, identity and culture become concepts subject to continuous negotiation. Through this peculiar form of writing, the author is constantly seeking to create an effect of strangeness that surprises the reader.

A brief extract from her novel *The House on Mango Street* offers a good example:

My Name

In English my name means hope. In Spanish it means too many letters. It means sadness, it means waiting. It is like the number nine. A muddy colour. It is the Mexican records my father plays on Sunday mornings when he is shaving, songs like sobbing. . . . At school they say my name funny as if the syllables were made out of tin and hurt the roof of your mouth. But in Spanish my name is made out of a softer something, like silver, not quite as thick as sister's name—Magdalena—which is uglier than mine. Magdalena who at least can come home and become Nenny. But I am always Esperanza. (Cisneros 1989: 10–11)

Demonstrating an astonishing degree of metalinguistic reflection, the girl narrator, who is Chicana and bilingual, centres the enormous experiential weight of her bicultural dichotomy on the meaning of her name, which she is able to translate into English, transforming it into a bridge between the languages and cultures that make up who she is. In this way, the author reflects in her work on how such an experience can also be difficult and even harrowing, particularly in childhood.

TRANSLATION AND POSTCOLONIAL STUDIES: LOOKING FOR NEW TRANSLATION STRATEGIES

In the field of translation studies, the proximity between the translation process and creative writing has been described differently by Maria Tymoczko (Tymockzo 1999; 2000), who presents translation and postcolonial literature as instances of intercultural writing that emerge from the intersection between different literary systems. In Tymoczko's view, the translator and the postcolonial writer are mediators who can only be differentiated by the extent to which each one transposes and translates both a text and its cultural universe:

The primary difference is that, unlike translators, post-colonial writers are not transposing a text. As background to their literary works, they are transposing a culture—to be understood as a language, a cognitive system, a literature (comprised of a system of texts, genres, tale types, and so on), a material culture, a social system and legal framework, a history, and so forth. (Tymoczko 1999: 20)

However, Tymoczko notes that a more significant disparity between these two literary activities concerns the demands that they make (Tymockzo 1999: 21). While the translator faces the dilemma of fidelity to the text that must be translated, the writer has greater freedom to select cultural elements that will be translated into an original text. In her conclusions, Tymoczko (2000) stops short of claiming that postcolonial fictions 'are' translations, she suggests that they share formal and functional elements. Without lapsing into generalizations, I would say that transcultural cases, in fact, do exist in which a fiction 'is and functions as' a translation: of itself and of an entire cultural world. They offer unique examples of self-translation arising from the bilingualism of their authors. However, the situation becomes more complex when we examine the translation of transcultural narratives, which involve a secondary operation of translation.

Translating Chicano literature, as with any borderland reality, is undoubtedly a complex procedure because the original texts are already loaded with textual and contextual nuances that are difficult to transfer. This multiplicity involves, on the one hand, a special relationship between the original text (hybrid) and the translation (which, it could be argued, is of necessity also hybrid). It also obliges us to adopt a different positioning with respect to the subject/object of the translation. In approaching the original (and its meaning) the reader is ultimately forced to make certain shifts in emphasis (Joysmith 1996).

For many people, the translation of borderland textualities is a 'talking back', that is, a procedure of reversed (re)writing (which, as for Sandra Cisnero's work, would only be strictly true in the case of a translation into Spanish). What emerges is thus a hybrid translation, neither Mexican nor American, of a hybrid original text that likewise is neither American nor Mexican.

However, the translation of this type of transcultural writing calls for special translation strategies as well as commitment from the translator. Gayatri Spivak, from a postcolonial point of view, poses an interesting case of a visible translator committed to cultural subalternity. She has noted that 'You cannot translate from a position of monolinguist superiority' (Spivak 1993: 195). In addition to other aspects of this indisputable truth, Spivak offers interesting reflections on the ethics and politics of translation, particularly in her well-known text *The Politics of Translation* (Spivak 1993), which takes a feminist and post-structuralist approach to postcolonial translation and critiques Western strategies of translation as 'Westernizing'. She points to their tendency to homogenize, approaching so-called 'Third-World literatures' without mediation of any sort, as though they were immediately accessible. In common with A. Berman (Berman 1984; 1985), Spivak takes a stance in favour of a specific degree of literalness. She supports an intermediate discourse that breaks the effect of immediacy that the reader can have of the text, offering a sense of the original's differential specificity. Spivak also holds the view that the most appropriate approach to take when introducing texts of minority cultures, particularly from the so-called Third World, to Western culture is for the translator to have a sound familiarity with the literary production of the language being translated in order to know how to discriminate some texts from others. Beyond these reflections, Spivak's contributions in this area are also of great interest when she puts her approach into practice, for example, when translating into English from Bengali—a language that is already a hybrid—the works of a postcolonial author like the Bengali activist Mahasweta Devi, who has a strong commitment to the tribal communities of India.[4]

In conclusion, in the context of transcultural literatures, when narrating constitutes translating in and of itself, the act of translation challenges us to assume an ethical commitment born out of respect not only for cultural and linguistic diversity, which nourishes the text from the start, but also for the minority discourse that sustains it. Today, more than ever, translation as a constant negotiation leads us into dialogue with difference and it may even open the way for the emergence of a minority discourse that has until now been silent.

NOTES

2. In the famous words of Caliban to Prospero: 'You taught me language; and my profit on't is, I know how to curse. The red plague rid you for learning me your language!' (Shakespeare 1610: 976).
3. See Bhabha, Homi K., *The Location of Culture*, London and New York: Routledge, 1994, Chapter 8).
4. S. Weber, *Return to Freud: Jacques Lacan's Dislocation of Psychoanalysis*, Cambridge: CUP, 1991, p. 161.
5. As we know, Mahasweta Devi writes in English (the language in which she studied) as well as in Bengali, but she has written most of her literary works in Bengali, employing it as a dominant code that hybridizes English and other languages used in India.

REFERENCES

Albertazzi, Silvia, *Lo Sguardo dell'Altro: Le letterature postcoloniali*, Roma: Carocci, 2000.

Bhabha, Homi K., *The Location of Culture*, London and New York: Routledge, 1994.

Berman, Antoine, *The Experience of the Foreign*, tr. S. Heyvaert, New York: State University of New York Press, 1992.

———, 'Translation and the trials of the foreign', tr. Lawrence Venuti, in *The Translation Studies Reader*, ed. Lawrence Venuti, 2000, London and New York: Routledge, 1985, pp. 284–97.

Cisneros, Sandra, *The House on Mango Street*, London: Bloomsbury, 1989.

———, *Caramelo o Puro cuento*, tr. Liliana Valenzuela, 2003, Barcelona: Seix Barral, 2002.

De Courtivron, Isabelle, ed., *Lives in Translation: Bilingual Writers on Identity and Creativity*, New York: Palgrave MacMillan, 2003.

Devi, Mahasweta, *Chotti Munda and His Arrow*, tr. Gayatri Chakravorty Spivak, 2003, Oxford: Blackwell, 1980.

———, *Imaginary Maps*, tr. Gayatri Chakravorty Spivak, London and New York: Routledge, 1995.

Devy, G.N., *Of Many Heroes: An Indian Essay in Literary Historiography*, New Delhi: Sangam Books/Prestige, 1998.

Kellman, Steven G., *The Translingual Imagination*, Lincoln/London: University of Nebraska Press, 2000.

Pérez Firmat, Gustavo, *The Cuban Condition: Translation and Identity in Modern Cuban Literature*, Cambridge: CUP, 1989.

Sales, Dora, 'Transculturación narrativa: Posibilidades de un concepto latinoamericano para la teoría y la literatura comparada intercultural', *Exemplaria: Revista de Literatura Comparada/Journal of Comparative Literature*, vol. 5, 2001, pp. 21–37.

Shakespeare, William, 'The Tempest' in *The Complete Works of William Shakespeare*, ed. W.G. Clark and W. Aldis Wright, 2 vols., New York: Nelson Doubleday, vol. 2, 1610, pp. 971–92.

Spivak, Gayatri Chakravorty, 'The Politics of Translation', in *Outside in the Teaching Machine*, London and New York: Routledge, 1993, pp. 179–200.

———, *Death of a Discipline*, New York: Columbia University Press, 2003.

St-Pierre, Paul, 'Translating Cultural Difference: Fakir Mohan Senapati's *Chha Mana Atha Guntha*', in *Translation and Postcolonialism: India*, ed. Paul St-Pierre, Numéro spécial, *Meta*: *Translator's Journal*, vol. 42, no. 2, 1997, pp. 423–38.

Tymoczko, Maria, 'Post-colonial Writing and Literary Translation', in *Post-colonial Translation: Theory and Practice*, ed. Susan Bassnett and Harish Trivedi, London and New York: Routledge, 1999, pp. 19–40.

———, 'Translations of Themselves: The Contours of Postcolonial Fiction', in *Changing the Terms: Translating in the Postcolonial Era*, ed. Sherry Simon and Paul St-Pierre, Ottawa: University of Ottawa Press, 2000, pp. 147–63.

Weber, S., *Return to Freud: Jacques Lacan's Dislocation of Psychoanalysis*, Cambridge: CUP, 1991.

17

Translating India as the Other: Partition and After

Sukrita Paul Kumar

TO TRANSLATE is to carry across. In 1947, with the actual transfer of power to two sovereign nations on the Indian subcontinent, the euphoria of Independence could hardly be savoured amidst the barbarity of the ensuing communal frenzy. With daggers drawn in an atmosphere of suspicion and fear, people went berserk and became captives to violent urges: killing, raping and assaulting each other. They fled to the other side of the border for life and security with a hope of coming back home sometime later. In the words of Mushirul Hasan, it was as if '[t]he civilizational rhythm of the subcontinent was being irreparably destroyed'.[1] That was Partition. India was cracking up. On the surface, it was the end of an era and the beginning of another. But Radcliff's pen could in no way have clipped human consciousness with the mere drawing of borders between India and Pakistan.

People carried their old *basti(s)* or community dwelling(s) to their new ones and their past to their present. They gradually went through a process of translation, assimilation and change, to eventually evolve new stabilities and identities. By the early twentieth century, with the process of colonization by the British, and thanks to the struggle for independence, different states and regions were consolidated and India began to be clearly perceived as a single country: the country that sought freedom from the British. But then along with this freedom came the bloodshed of Partition and the dislocation of several million people. Carrying within themselves shadowy borders, the brick and mortar of their homes, the gullies and lanes of their cities, the migrants on both sides of the borders also transported their memories of sorrows and happiness, their sociology and culture.

The protagonist of Intezar Husain's Urdu novel, *Basti*,[2] Zakir, constantly mediates and modifies his past in accordance with the significance and nature of his present. Zakir teaches history and is professionally dealing and actually grappling with the linearity of time flowing uninterruptedly. He psychologically confronts the discontinuities and ruptures juxtaposed with the images and experiences of the past flashing before his eyes. His sense of personal history calls for a fundamental rethinking of historiography. Problematizing his experience of history, he thinks, 'How boring it is teaching history to boys. Other people's history can be read comfortably, the way a novel can be read. But my own history? I'm on the run from my own history—and catching my breath in the present. Escapist. But the merciless present pushes us back again toward our history. The mind keeps talking'.[3] His stream of consciousness oscillates between the so-called past and his present blurring all divisions of time.

The inevitable question then is, how is he going to come out of the hypnotic nostalgia of the past that presents itself to him repeatedly in the form of Roopnagar, (literally, the city of beauty). The author could have named the setting after a real city in India. But, he instead makes up a city in order to emphasize the social and natural harmony of that pre-Partition town. Partition has disrupted the harmony of Roopnagar and ironically, it is the memory of this disruption that brings the protagonist back to the now and connects him with the present, twenty five years later.

As evidenced in Rahi Masoom Raza's powerful Hindi novel *Adha Gaon*,[4] many Muslims could not quite work out and understand the logic behind Muslim nationalism. Nor did the majority of Hindus and Sikhs have any grasp of the two-nation theory. Trapped in the crossfire of hatred between the two communities in 1947, thousands fled their homes with no destination in mind. 'India' and 'Pakistan' were mere territorial abstractions[5] for people who had no sense of the newly demarcated frontiers. They had little knowledge of how Mountbatten's Plan or the Radcliffe Award would change the destinies of millions and tear them apart from the familial, social, and cultural moorings.

In the Urdu novella, *Khwabro (Sleepwalkers)*[6] by Joginder Paul, Deewane Maulavi Saheb suffers from no sense of loss only because he has taken refuge in insanity. In Karachi he is thoroughly convinced that he is still living in Lucknow. Although set in Karachi, the novella opens with the assertion 'This is Lucknow . . .'. As soon as the *mohajirs* 'recovered their breath after reaching Karachi, the entire city emerged from their hearts, brick by brick'.[7] In the waking hours, they come to terms with the new location, in their sleep, however, they throng to the Ameenabad Chowk of Lucknow. In *Basti*, reality appears to Zakir swathed in an eerie half-light, at times making the past more real than the present. Both *Basti* and *Khwabro* examine how the process of assimilating the past to the present passes through, as it were, a twilight zone. It is a liminal space in which there are occasional flashes of revelation. When Roopnagar empties, Zakir reflects 'Yar, how strange it is that the same town becomes more meaningful for those who had to leave it'.[8] It had become for him all the more meaningful because he had moved to Pakistan. In *Khwabro*, Ishaq Mirza writes to Hashim describing a similar perception: 'Subhan Allah! Lucknow is actually here .... Over there, we could never figure out where Lucknow had vanished from Lucknow ... Bhai, the reality of Lucknow after all lies in the elegance of Lucknow .... Actually you are the genuine Lukhnavis ... settled here in your Lucknow'.[9]

In both these novels, it is the second generation, Zakir in *Basti* and Ishaq Mirza in *Khwabro,* who perceive the true status of the cities from which they fled with their fathers. In his mind, Deewane Maulavi Saheb never migrated. He has forever remained in Lucknow. Nor have Zakir's father and mother left either. Their consciousness remains with their family heirlooms lying locked in the storeroom of their mansion in Roopnagar. They have to go and get these heirlooms before termites destroy them. Zakir muses; 'Is time a termite, or is a termite time?'[10] Abbajan of *Basti* and Deewane Malauvi Sahib of *Khwabro*, both remain rooted, attached, and inert despite their migration while their sons Zakir and Ishaq Mirza are wanderers forever, despite their settlement in their homes in Pakistan. Ishaq marries a Sindhi girl, as if announcing himself to be different. He then creates a third reality, born out of a past given to him by Deewane Maulavi Saheb and a present which is distinctly post-Partition. *Basti* was written in 1979 and *Khwabro* in 1990, many years after the actual experience of Partition, yet these novels record the movement into time, across time and even beyond time. In *Basti*, Ammi says: 'Oh, what does time have to do with it.... Time always goes on passing'.[11]

Though the novel *Basti* seems to cover a span of only a few months in the life of Zakir, in effect it evokes through flashback the entire cultural backdrop of centuries of Muslim history. The main connection with modern history is to be found in 1857, moves to 1947, then to 1965, and finally to the 1971 disintegration of Pakistan. Gradually Roopnagar becomes a vague and distant reality with the new slogan 'Crush India' coming in 'like a whirlwind'. India emerged as the Other, it is defined through hatred, going beyond translation. Zakir identifies Roopnagar also with his beloved, Sabirah—who did not migrate to Pakistan. The political entity called 'India' thus becomes distant yet something with whom to be reckoned. Regarding Roopnagar,

Zakir acknowledges: 'If something happened to this city how could I bear it?'[12]

In *Khwabro*, Deewane Maulavi Saheb actually comes out of *his* Lucknow of the mind when a bomb explodes in his *haveli*. He is driven to his senses only to slip into another false belief articulated quite delicately in the novel. He is in Karachi temporarily, merely on a visit, waiting to go back to his Lucknow. His grandson Salim quickly disabuses him of this delusion: 'But this is Lucknow, Bade Abbu!' says the lad, running after the ball at the end of the novel. This is the Lucknow that is only a part of Karachi, a Lucknow recreated with a difference. It includes the presence of the Sindhi cook who brings another dimension to its culture. The process of absorption, of exclusion within the politics of Pakistan and, inevitably, the ongoing love-hate relationship with India are the new local dynamics of Karachi.

The seeds of communalism sown and nourished by vested political interests are not very visible on the ordinary level of existence prior to Partition. They surface, however, after Partition with an unbounded fury, capturing cities, *qasbas*, and various other locations. In his novel *Laute Hue Musafir* (*The Migrants Who Came Back*), Kamleshwar, the well-known Hindi writer, told his tale of a *qasba* in U.P., which came into the grip of chaos and the clutches of communal suspicion. This novel introduces the reader to a cobbler, a cycle-repairer, small craftsmen and struggling youths. It narrates their everyday, simple conversations demonstrating the faith and love that existed between Hindus and Muslims in that small town. Then a mental division begins to develop between these two groups. The novel opens with the memory of dream-like scenes depicting what is called Ganga-Jamuna culture, when, for example, on the occasion of *Muharrum*, *taziya* (replica of the tomb of Husain carried in processions during Muharram) would pass through a Hindu locality and Hindus would sprinkle rose-water on it with utmost reverence. Muslim women would come and peek out of the *chics* (curtains) hanging on their doors for a *darshan* or viewing of the Ramleela.

But after 1945, latent communal feelings in this *basti* began to simmer and gradually the bonds of love and faith in people's hearts began to collapse. With Partition, there was a mass exodus. Naseeban abandoned her mud house. The *jhopadi* (hut) remained amidst the debris and ruins of old houses and hutments as mere signs of former life in that *qasba*. A large group of Muslim migrants left this *basti* with the faith that they would eventually reach Pakistan. They never did. Somehow they were dispersed along the way here and there in that *zilha* (locality) and did not come back lest the Hindus take offence. Strangely, the Hindus too had fled because of the heavy Muslim presence in the region. Iftikar, a character in the novel, perceives his fate clearly: 'Even if Pakistan comes to exist, of what use will it be to us. In Pakistan, too, we will after all be *ikkawallahs*, pulling carts and horses'.[13]

The real struggle, as the novel subtly establishes, is between the rich and the poor. Though there no conflagrations in the area, many hearts were consumed by the flames of hatred. All those poor migrants had no means of realizing their Pakistan. Naseeban is the lonesome witness of the desolation of the *basti*. More importantly, she also bears witness to the scene years later, of the return of the grown-up children of those lost migrants come to the *basti* in search of labour. Partition had dispersed the older generation and the *basti* had disintegrated. However, with the emergence of industry and the establishment of tube wells, new prospects for employment and survival came into being. There were signs of development and progress. The India of this *basti* causes Naseeban to smile with hope and good cheer. Naseeban's eyes twinkle and she cries with happiness: there is an instant recognition. The descendents had returned, as the narrative emphasizes, to be housed in their homes, on this side of the border within the geo-political entity that is India. Their fate is not that of the protagonists in Intezar Husain's novella, where 'the city has already burned, but our tails are still burning'.[14]

Just as in *Laute Hue Musafir*, where the children of the migrants find old homes and have new prospects, so too do Zakir and Afsal come 'home' in *Basti*, if only to visit the graves of the older generation. Upon his return, Zakir decides to write a letter to Sabirah 'before the parting of her hair fills with silver, and before the keys rust'.[15] This act represents his liberation, his moving on, connecting and rebuilding rather than remaining in the framework of the existential psychosis engendered by Partition. Obviously, this move is not easy since the politics of the country have constantly fueled the flames of conflict with sporadic riots and curfews. In Karachi as in Bhiwandi, in India as in Pakistan, the legacy of Partition manifests itself in ethnic and communal tension.

In Ali Imam Naqvi's touching Urdu short story 'Dongarivari ke Gidhh' ('The Vultures of the Parsi Cemetary'), Hormoz and Pharoz, the cemetery attendants, panic one day when they discover that there are no vultures attending to the corpses. The police commissioner explains the situation to the board:

> All of them are flocking to the Kharki, Raviwar Peth and Somwar Peth, the areas where riots have broken out . . . . Oh those Hindus and Muslims are at each other's throats again. There's been a riot. The bastards they've torched everything,

houses, shops, even ambulances and hearses, the whole lot. The street is littered with corpses. One right on top of the other. Piled high. Our vultures ... well, they're having a field day there. And that police commissioner ... he said after the street's been cleaned up, the vultures will come back on their own accord'. 'Even if the street's cleaned up—so what? What makes you think the vultures will return? This fucking India ... there's a riot everyday here, everyday a fire, everyday people die. The vultures will come back?? The hell they will!'[16]

When life is thus disturbed, whether through Hindu Muslim violence or through riots in Karachi from tensions between the *mohajirs* (Pakistanis whose parents migrated to north India during or after Partition) and 'natives', it is as if Partition has never ended; it is being carried across time. This situation continues to be expressed in poetry, short stories, and longer fiction. If translation is dissemination and a metaphor for travel, then one certainly finds pertinent examples in Khushwant Singh's *A Train to Pakistan*, Krishan Chander's 'Peshawar Express', Bhisham Sahni's 'Amritsar Aa Gaya' or Gulzar's 'Khauf'. In such narratives, the train's travel across borders, they fear, hatred, vengefulness, sadness, and bewilderment back and forth between the two nations.

Writers describe different forms of ethnic and racial violence in these multifaceted and multilingual texts. To what extent are the geographical spaces politically defined? How are these identities determined and perceived? What conceptual formulations may be at work that perhaps contradict reality? These questions suggest some of the complexities casting a shadow over any simplistic readings of the nation. Histories exist within histories and nations within nations. As Muhammad Umar Memon remarks in the 'Introduction' to his novel, the writer explores in the character of Zakir his cultural identity as it extends back through Muslim history. This professor of history, as a citizen of the new nation seeks to reconcile the consciousness of being a Pakistani with the past he carries from India on both a personal and a collective level. In fact, there has to be a juxtaposition of the personal with the collective histories of migrancy and exile. Different ideologies and politics formulate and construct the idea of the nation.

Migrancy, it is evident, also means the migrancy of ideas and histories. The new location, therefore, becomes a site for internal and external conflict between the Self and the Other, the Other as the Self, and the Other face to face with the Self. When Ghani the Mussalman in Mohan Rakesh's story 'Malbe Ka Malik' (His Heap of Rubble)[17] comes to India seven years after Partition and views the rubble of his house, the experience destroys the walls he has psychologically preserved. He has to come to terms with new realities. The professed ideology of the nation-state, which earlier may not have had any meaning for him, becomes real and we are led to imagine that he goes back to a Pakistan that is now freshly defined. India translates itself as the Other. These texts suggest how obvious territorial imperatives work to protect the self.

The story of Partition and India will remain only half-told if we do not pay attention to the plight of the innumerable women who were mauled, raped, and abused in the mayhem following Partition. In Rajinder Singh Bedi's Urdu story 'Lajwanti', the girl who is, to her husband, known as Lajjo before Partition, becomes deified for him as Lajwanti (touch-me-not) after she was gruesomely assaulted at the hands of men during Partition. While the husband can have reverence for her, he can no longer feel any love or passion for her. He can respect her and deify her, but cannot bring himself to have a normal relationship with a 'dishonored' wife. The loss of a woman's honor transforms everything. Lines from Amrita Pritam's Punjabi poem 'Aj Akhan Waris Sah Nun' describe the crucial and touching difference between the pre- and the post-Partition scenario with regard to women's fate: the female Self gets translated as the Other to herself as well as others:

Today I implore Waris Shah
to speak up from his grave
and turn over a page of
the Book of Love
When a daughter of the fabled Punjab wept
He gave tongue to her silent grief
Today a million daughters weep
But where is Waris Shah
To give voice to their woes?'[18]

It is difficult to forget the poignant scene from Bhisham Sahni's Hindi novel *Tamas* in which during a riot a large group of Sikh women jump into a well in order to save their honor. The women pile up in the well until it becomes so full that the last few of them cannot jump into it! Women were totally removed from both the political decisions that created the chaos as well as the violent horror that followed. Yet, they were the prime targets of brutality from both communities. The Pakistani Urdu writer Farkhanda Lodi's story 'Parbati', written soon after the 1965 Indo-Pak War, depicts a culturally composite portrait of female identity in the character of Parbati/Parveen. The author suggests that women know no frontiers: 'she had forgotten that there are countries on this earth, and countries have borders and borders are guarded'.[19] In contrast, as the Pakistani-centric Samina Rahman has observed, when there is that mirror effect between the two hostile worlds, where each reflects and imitates the other (and in fact creates the Other), humanity is abandoned.[20]

From within the existential angst of homelessness, Indian and Pakistani writers influenced by Partition have continually deconstructed the past when India signified home. This India has now become the Other. Their narratives of the present react, counter, and readjust the memories of the past. The concept of the nation, recently developed as a major theme of academic discussion, is no longer confined to a simple geo-political space, but constructed by a series of concepts, ideologies, and histories. Partition destabilized the unquestioned legitimacy of earlier ideals, further problematizing the very idea of nation and identity.

India is now to be seen as distinct from Pakistan which, in turn, has to determine its own identity. India was initially translated as the Other by all those who carried their own India across borders and across time. Indeed, the relationship between the original Self and the translated Other is in harmony, only when primal connections are realized. But, the conflict between the two is exacerbated when the perception of what was done does not match one's memory of the original.

NOTES

1. Mushirul Hasan, ed., *India Partitioned: The Other Side of Freedom*, New Delhi: Roli Books, 1995, p. 10.
2. Intezar Husain, *Basti*, tr. Frances W. Pritchett, New Delhi: Harper-Collins Publishers India, 1995.
3. Ibid., p. 83.
4. Rahi Masoom Raza, *Adha Gaon*, translated into English as *The Feuding Families of Village Gangauli* by Gillian Wright, Penguin Books, 1994.
5. This expression is used by Mushirul Hasan in the Introduction to *India Partitioned: The Other Side of Freedom*, New Delhi: Roli Books, 1995.
6. Joginder Paul, *Khwabro*, translated into English by Sunil Trivedi and Sukrita Paul Kumar as *Sleepwalkers*, New Delhi: Katha, 1998.
7. *Sleepwalkers*, p. 12.
8. Husain, *Basti*, p. 142.
9. Paul, *Sleepwalkers*, p. 46.
10. Husain, *Basti*, p. 149.
11. Ibid., p. 148.
12. Ibid., p. 167.

13. Kamleshwar, *Laute Hue Musafir*, Allahabad: Lokbharti Prakashan, 1961, p. 61.
14. Ibid., p. 254.
15. Husain, *Basti*, p. 263.
16. Ali Iman Naqvi, 'The Vultures of the Parsi Cemetery', in *India Partitioned: The Other Side of Freedom*, ed. Mushirul Hasan, New Delhii: Roli Books, 1995, p. 295.
17. Mohan Rakesh, 'Malbe ka Malik', translated into English as 'His Heap of Rubble' by Harish Trivedi, in *Breakthrough*, ed. Sukrita Paul Kumar, Shimla: IIAS, 1993.
18. Amrita Pritam, 'Aj Akhan Waris Sah Nun', tr. N.S. Tasneem, ed. K.M. George, *Modern Indian Literature,* New Delhi: Sahitya Akademi.
19. Farkhandha Lodi, 'Parbati', *In Her Own Time*, tr. and ed. Samina Rehman, Lahore: ASR Publications, 1994, p. 71.
20. Samina Rehman, *In Her Own Time*, Introduction, Lahore: ASR Publications, 1994.

REFERENCES

Hasan, M., ed., *India Partitioned: The Other Side of Freedom*, New Delhi: Roli Books, 1995.

Husain, I., F.W. Pritchett, tr., New Delhi: Harper-Collins Publishers India, 1995.

Kamleshwar, *Laute Hue Musafir*, Allahabad: Lokbharti Prakashan, 1961.

Lodi, F., 'Parbati', tr. and ed. S. Rehman, *In Her Own Time*, Lahore: ASR Publications, 1994.

Naqvi, A.I., 'Dongarivari ke Gidhh' ('The Vultures of the Parsi Cemetery'). ed. M. Hasan, *India Partitioned: The Other Side of Freedom.*

Paul, J., *Khwabro*, tr. S. Trivedi and S.P. Kumar, *Sleepwalkers*. New Delhi: Katha, 1998.

Rakesh, M., 'Malbe ka Malik'. ('His Heap of Rubble'), tr. H. Trivedi, in *Breakthrough*, ed. S.P. Kumar, Shimla: IIAS, 1993.

Raza, R.M., G. Wright, tr., *The Feuding Families of Village Gangauli*, New Delhi: Penguin Books, 1994.

Pritam, A. 'Aj Akhan Waris Sah Nun', tr. N.S. Tasneem, in *Modern Indian Literature*, ed. K.M. George, New Delhi: Sahitya Akademi.

Rehman, S., 'Introduction', S. Rahman, *In Her Own Time.*

PART IV

Case Studies

18

The Urdu Premchand: The Hindi Premchand

Harish Trivedi

Besides being acclaimed for his literary genius, Premchand (1880–1936) is accorded the unique distinction in Indian literary history of having founded and consolidated the modern novel into not one but two of our major languages, Urdu and Hindi. Yet, curiously, those who know the Urdu Premchand hardly acknowledge that he also moved on to write in Hindi, while those who know the Hindi Premchand like to pretend that Premchand did not even exist before he ventured into Hindi. Thus, in his pioneering and immensely influential history of Hindi literature (1929; rev. 1940), Ramachandra Shukla begins his discussion of Premchand with the Hindi short stories he published in 1916, while Premchand in fact had been publishing novels and short stories in Urdu since 1903. Shyam Sundar Das in his equally important work on Hindi language and literature (1930) describes the Hindi *Sevasadan* (1919) as Premchand's 'first original novel' while in fact he had published five novels in Urdu before then, and as late as in 1977, in the comprehensive 16-volume history of Hindi literature, we find the plain and forthright announcement that 'The Age of Premchand' begins in 1918, again more or less with the Hindi *Sevasadan* (Shukla 1940: 505; Das 1930: 505). Conversely, through some unconscious misappropriation, Syed Ehtesham Hussain writing in 1963 claims the Hindi *Godan* (1936) to be the Urdu *Gaudan*, which was in fact published three years after Premchand's death in someone else's translation in 1939. In sharp contrast, Masood Hussain Khan, for this very reason, wants to throw *Gaudan* out of Urdu literature altogether. He wrote that '*Gaudan* has no place in the history of Urdu fiction.'

* This essay first appeared in *Aspects of Comparative Literature: Current Approaches*, 1989.

Similarly, Jafar Raza in a book published in 1983 insists throughout, against the force of much of the evidence he himself cites, that Premchand went on writing equally in Urdu and Hindi to the end of his days, while Muhammad Sadiq, swinging to the other extreme in his magisterial *History of Urdu Literature* (1964; rev. 1984) cautions his readers: 'It is not generally known that Premchand's novels have all been translated from books originally published in Hindi' (1984, 439).

Such partisan or purblind misrepresentations of the other Premchand are due probably to that secular piety or benign bigotry, which has regulated most utterances in our century about the Hindi-Urdu or indeed the Hindu-Muslim question. It is the purpose of this paper to confront and critically appraise the indisputable facts that after having published five novels and approximately sixty short stories almost exclusively in Urdu over the first twelve years of his writing career, from 1903 to 1915, Premchand moved steadily but surely towards Hindi. He at first published in Hindi journals some of his stories that were originally published in Urdu and then during 1918–19, he rewrote and published, first in Hindi, his sixth novel under the title *Sevasadan* while its original Urdu version *Bazar-e-Husn* lay unpublished for another four years due to the lack of a publisher. Finally, starting with *Kayakalpa* in 1924, he settled down to write all his subsequent novels originally in Hindi, which were then first published in Hindi as well. Though Premchand would occasionally, and only occasionally, write some of his shorter pieces, both fiction and non-fiction, in Urdu even beyond 1924, Hindi became overwhelmingly the vehicle of his major fiction after that date right up to his death, months after the publication of *Godan* in 1936.

This linguistic transition effected over the middle decade of his writing career was of crucial significance for Premchand as a writer, both for the reasons that caused it and for the consequences that flowed from it. In what follows, an attempt is made to elaborate and analyse these causes and consequences in a not only strictly literary but also a wider linguistic, cultural, political and 'communal' perspective, in order to appreciate their full import.

II

Premchand himself explained time and again that the reason why he moved from Urdu to Hindi was that in Urdu there was a dearth of publishers, and that by switching to Hindi he would not only ensure 'prompt and profitable publication but also gain many more readers.

TABLE 18.1: Number of books published in UP in Urdu and Hindi, 1881–1910

	1881–90	*1891–1900*	*1901–10*
Urdu	4380	4218	3547
Hindi	2793	3186	5063

SOURCE: Francis Robinson, 'Table VII', *Separatism Among Indian Muslims*, Cambridge, 1974, p. 77.

That he was only too right about this fact is borne out by the history of his publications throughout his career, as amply documented by himself in letters to his friends and editors' (Rai 1982: 103–4, 110, 125–6, 191, 205, 206).

The point of interest here is that even ten or fifteen years before Premchand actually said so, i.e. around the turn of the century, it would have been preposterous to imagine that there could be a dearth of Urdu publishers for a writer of his abilities, especially in comparison with Hindi publishers. In the meantime, however, a lot had changed, as is borne out by the figures in Tables 18.1 and 18.2.

The reasons for such a dramatic reversal can be traced back to the year 1837, when, together with the introduction of English as the official language at the higher levels, Urdu had been officially adopted as the leading North Indian vernacular so that all individuals, whether Muslim or Hindu, simply had to learn it if they wanted to get on in the world. However, towards the end of the nineteenth century, Urdu found itself increasingly besieged by a persistent and populous demand for its optional substitution or even complete supercession by Hindi, and a fateful blow was dealt in the year 1900 when the government conceded the optional use of Hindi in the Nagari script for official and judicial purposes in Uttar Pradesh (UP). The curt response of Lord Curzon, then Viceroy, to the

TABLE 18.2: Number and circulation of newspapers in UP in Urdu and Hindi, 1891–1911

	1891		*1901*		*1911**	
	No.	*Circ.*	*No.*	*Circ.*	*No.*	*Circ.*
Urdu	68	16,256	69	23,757	116	76,608
Hindi	24	8,002	34	17,419	68	77,731

SOURCE: Francis Robinson, 'Table VII', *Separatism Among Indian Muslims*, Cambridge, 1974, p. 78.

protests against this decision indicates his perception of the wider sectarian implications of this apparently innocuous issue: 'The howls of Mussulmans merely represent the spleen of a minority from whose hands are slipping away the reins of power, and who clutch at any method of arbitrarily retaining them (Curzon to Anthony MacDonnell 1965: 259).

This crucial breakthrough for Hindi had been achieved by the sustained efforts of many individuals and organizations spearheaded by the Nagari Pracharini Sabha (established 1893)[2] which has been justly described as 'a political promoter for the cause of Hindi' (Gumperz and Das Gupta, 1971, 138) during this period. Shortly afterwards, in 1910, the Hindi Sahitya Sammelan was founded, which developed and sustained very close links with the Indian National Congress at least until 1935, during which period Hindustani or Hindi gradually came to be adopted by the Congress as the *rashtrabhasha*, and not only as a vehicle of nationalism but indeed as one of its major planks, so that if one could not go to jail in the cause of *swaraj*, one could learn Hindi or wield the spinning wheel as the next best contribution to the great struggle. Finally, at a controversial meeting of the Bharatiya Sahitya Parishad at Nagpur in 1936, which Premchand attended and over which Gandhi presided, the Mahatma laid down the ruling that the language of the Parishad, and by implication the language of the country, was going to be not 'Hindustani' in which the now much reduced Urdu could still have claimed a half-share, but 'Hindi or Hindustani' in the Nagari script (Rai 1982: 354–7).

That this struggle for supremacy between Urdu and Hindi had a strong economic dimension as well, again running broadly along communal lines, is reflected in a statement made by Bharatendu Harishchandra to the Education Commission for the North-West Provinces and Oudh. He wrote that 'If Urdu ceases to be the court language, the Mussulmans will not easily secure the numerous offices of Government, such as peshkarships, sarishtadarships, muharrirships, etc., of which at present they have a sort of monopoly' (Qtd. In Robinson 1974: 75–6). This point proved prophetically true, as indicated by the statistics that the proportion of subordinate official jobs held by the Muslims in UP, where they constantly constituted around 14 per cent of the total population, went down from 63.9 per cent in 1857 to 45.8 per cent in 1886–87 to 34.7 per cent in 1913 (Brass 1974: 143; Robinson 1974: 46).

In the larger context of these inextricably interrelated linguistic, political and economic developments, it can be clearly seen that Premchand's switch from Urdu to Hindi was less an individual, personal choice and more a historical compulsion.

III

Even at the specifically aesthetic and literary level, Urdu did not have, by way of a congenial literary tradition, much with which to hold Premchand back. It has been determined that of the fourteen major Indian languages, Urdu was distinctly the last to emerge out of its 'medieval' period into the 'modern' (Majumdar 1987: 46). In fiction, there had been only two novelists of any note before Premchand, Ratan Nath Dar 'Sarshar' (1846–1902) and Abdul Halim 'Sharar' (1860–1926),[2] who again represented between them, as it happened, some of the fissures which were forming from within the reputedly 'composite' identity of Urdu language and literature. Sarshar, a Hindu, had in his *magnum opus*, *Fasana-e-Azad*, celebrated with great relish the common life of an incredible variety of people found among the Lucknow of the Nawabs, while Sharar, in novel after novel set in the Spain of the *jehads* or the Arabia of the early centuries of the Muslim era, had attempted to revive the pristine glory of Islam in a mode of fiction which, in imitation of Hamlet's list of hyphenated hybrid literary forms, may well be called 'the historical-fantastical-political'.

So palpably different were these two contemporaries that sporadic skirmishes would break out between their respective admirers in the Urdu literary journals of the day, in which each party would argue for the superiority of its idol with an almost theological fervour and resourcefulness. Premchand himself intervened in one such running battle in 1906 (in which Chakbast, incidentally a Hindu, according to Premchand, had written a critically just account of Sarshar, in reply to which one Hakim Barham Sahab Gorakhpuri had not only run Sarshar down but also 'extolled Hazrat Sharar to the high heavens'); he came down comprehensively in favour of Sarshar, and in the process once referred to his favourite writer not by name or pen-name but as 'Panditji', as Sarshar was by birth a Kashmiri Brahmin (Premchand in Rai 1962: 59–72).

The all-too-brief tradition of the Urdu novel, which Premchand inherited had, thus, already developed communal overtones. Premchand's perception of the situation would have been especially acute, for in the early part of his career he had been, even as he wrote in Urdu, something of a Hindu revivalist-patriot, as his early stories of Rajput or Bundelkhand valour bear out. In any case, the existence of a Hindu writer in Urdu had always been a rarity and something of an anomaly, and Premchand seems to have been conscious of it. In an astoundingly frank appraisal of his situation in 1915, he wrote:

I am now practising to write in Hindi as well. Urdu will no longer do . . . Has any Hindu ever made a success of writing in Urdu that I will? (Rai 1962: 104).

To Premchand's anguished rhetorical question, Grahame Bailey provides a statistical answer in the concluding chapter of his history of Urdu literature, which contains the following passage:

About 250 authors have been mentioned in this work. Apart from Prem Cand, . . . only eight are Hindus, the rest are Muhammedans. The only famous writers among them are Daya Shankar Nasim, Ratn Nath Sarshar, and Durga Sahae Suroor. Hindu authors of real ability prefer to write in Hindi. (Bailey 1979: 102)

Another more extensive history of Urdu literature further corroborates Premchand's sense of being an unwanted alien in the domain of Urdu literature, and it does so from the other side of the fence, as it were: '. . . this much will have to be admitted that Muslims continued to treat him more or less as an outsider (Sadiq 1984: 439).

On the other hand, when Premchand did cross the gulf of this 'cultural-communal divergence' (Brass 1974: 134) to begin publishing in Hindi, he was welcomed on the other side with a warmth that was distinctly more than literary. In his 'Preface' to Premchand's first book in Hindi, a collection of seven short stories under the metaphoric title *Sapta Saroj* (Seven Lotuses), Pandit Mannan Dwivedi Gajapuri wrote in terms highly redolent of Hindu culture:

Premchandji occupies a very high place among the Hindu virtuosos of Urdu literature. . . . It is a matter of joy that mother-tongue Hindi has of late attracted his heart. Premchandji has entered the Temple of Nagari to offer worship and the Mother has adopted this glorious loving son Prem by embracing him to her bosom (1917).

IV

Moving beyond the apparently personal and straightforward, but in fact, highly symptomatic and complex historical reasons for Premchand's switch from Urdu to Hindi, we can now examine the consequences of this switch, its significance, and how and where they are manifested in his works.

It may be argued that the consequence of Premchand's literary 'code-switching' was to effect a sea-change in the original connotation of that word, 'a sea-change/Into something rich and strange' (Shakespeare 400–01). By moving to Hindi, Premchand appears to have obtained a metamorphic release from an inappropriate and constraining literary situation, in which his own perceptions of life and his literary inclinations had run in one direction, while the grain of the language he had been trained to use by early education and social expectations, as well as the grain of the literary tradition inhering in that language, had run in quite another direction. The tradition of Urdu language and literature had throughout been urban and urbane, while Hindi, clearly more the language of the common folk at least at this stage of its evolution, related Premchand back to the only life he knew and which alone could form his proper subject-matter, his true quarry. Significantly, at the height of the Urdu-Hindi controversy at the end of the nineteenth century, Urdu had been described by its own partisans as 'the language of refinement and of upper and civilized classes of people', and it had been urged to be 'the duty of Government . . . not to consult the whim of the peasantry' who were identified as the champions of Hindi (Anon 1900: 69).

In a broader perspective, Premchand's entry into Hindi, already emerging as the adopted national language, put him squarely in the mainstream of national life and nationalist politics. It is no coincidence that Premchand's active and practical conversion to Gandhian nationalism should have occurred almost right in the middle of the final phase of his other conversion from Urdu to Hindi, which can be dated from 1918 (when he completed the Urdu *Bazar-e-Husn*) to 1924 (when he started *Kayakalpa* in Hindi). On 15 February 1921, a week after he had heard Gandhi address a public meeting to promote Non-Cooperation in Gorakhpur, Premchand resigned the comfortable government job, which he had held for twenty-two years. These two departures may be regarded as major turning points in his life and writing career. The sense of liberation that Premchand felt on resigning government service is caught in all its thrill and exhilaration in two short stories he wrote within the next few weeks, 'Lal Fita' (Red Tape) and 'Vichitra Holi' (A Special Holi). The liberation that Hindi afforded him is captured not in one or two works that immediately followed, but writ large over the rest of his career.

V

The significance of Premchand's switch from Urdu to Hindi can be best appreciated in the evolving context of his career seen as a whole. Some indication of the direction of this evolution may be understood by looking briefly at his first novel and his first short story, both of course in Urdu—the transitional novel *Bazar-e-Husn/Sevasadan* and a short story from the same period, and finally by outlining a pattern of thematic progression as reflected in the final phase of his career following *Sevasadan*, to which all his major novels belong.

Premchand's first novel, published serially in 1903–04, was *Asrar-e-Ma'abid* whose title was later translated by its Hindi editor as *Devasthana Rahasya* or, literally, *The Secrets of the Sanctum Sanctorum*. It is written in the sprightly, pert and even internally rhyming Urdu prose style, which was generally current at the time and which Premchand had derived basically from his favourite Sarshar. It has for its subject the moral degeneration of brahmin temple-priests and young Hindu widows, both of whom find religious worship a convenient pretext for the pleasures of the flesh. However, such is the dichotomy here between the received form and the intended content that an acute social evil never rises above being a lovers' ruse, and the tone that could have been expected to be scathingly reformist turns out to be merrily salacious.

Another remarkable feature of this work is an abruptly erupting purple patch in the middle of Chapter Two, which is heavily loaded with Arabic and Persian. Here is a brief sample:

> *Is do angusht ki zaban men vo qoowat-e-goyai au zor-e-bayan kuja ki us qudarat-e-kamila ka ek shimma bhi mariz-e-bayan men la sake jisake mahaz adna ishare par yah gulzar sarapabahar wajoodpizir hua. Is deeda-e-kor men wah teziy-e-bisarat kuja ki us sana'at-e-ezadi ka mushahira kar sake jisaki jat se yah gunagoon khilaqut zahoor men ai.* (Anon, 1900, 69)

This passage goes on for nine pages and is meant to depict a self-contained episode involving the Hindu holy trinity of Brahma, Vishnu and Mahesh! The Hindi editor, obviously nonplussed by this passage, suggests that it is a parody of such a style, but there is not the slightest trace of any such ironical intention in the text. A more probable explanation for this oddity may be to regard it as a virtuoso piece performed by an unknown new writer in his maiden work in order to establish his credentials. And if it turns out to be a trifle overdone, it is because all such show-off performances are liable to be so if undertaken out of a sense of insecurity. Interestingly, in the very last year of his career as now in his first, Premchand once again produced a remarkably Persianized piece, this time meant to be delivered as a speech, because he had mistakenly assumed that his audience was going to be composed exclusively of highly literate Muslims. When one member of the prospective audience quaked before such heavy literary artillery at a pre-view, Premchand laughed one of his famous loud laughs and said: 'Well, I said to myself—let me write a language that will show them . . .'. After a pause he added, 'After all, I am the son of a kayastha, am I not!' (Rai 1982: 347).[3]

Premchand's first short story, 'Duniya ka Sabse Anmol Ratan' (1907; The Rarest Gem in the World) begins, as per Urdu tradition, in a remote 'pan-Islamic' setting, with a languishing-lover hero and a cruel-mistress heroine stereotypically called Dilfigar and Dilfareb—the kind of stuff that would have warmed the cockles of Sharar's own revivalist heart. But the denouement, curiously, is as heavily revivalist Hindu as the beginning was Muslim. In conclusion, it is the last drop of a dying Rajput warrior's blood, which is acclaimed as the rarest gem in the world by both Dilfigar and Dilfareb, while the point is deftly skirted that this particularly precious drop of Rajput blood might very likely have been shed in battle with a Muslim army!

Of *Bazar-e-Husn* or *Sevasadan*, the transitional novel, the titles themselves are symptomatic of the shift in Premchand's sensibility. Amorous beauty and the marketplace are highlighted in the Urdu title while in contrast, more austere concepts of home and social service constitute the Hindi title, for a novel which is substantially the same in both versions. The Urdu title promises one more variation on the popular theme of the life of a prostitute, treated sometimes naughtily and nearly always amorally in Urdu, as in Mirza Muhammad Hadi Ruswa's classic *Umrao Jan Ada* (1899), while *Sevasadan* connotes idealistic reformism as it also recalls by half-allusion such contemporary social reform organizations as the Bharat Sevak Samaj and the various Seva Samitis.

The radical transformation of the title is fully matched by innumerable minor and local, but culturally consistent changes, through which Premchand rendered this novel from Urdu into Hindi. Thus, in the opening paragraph of the novel, a reference to the '*pak daman*' of a character is replaced by plain '*satcharitrata*' in Hindi for the lack of a comparable metaphor, while a female character is described as '*satisaddhvi*' in Hindi when she was understandably no such thing in Urdu. Elsewhere in the novel, '*Bankebihari*' in Urdu (referring to Lord Krishna) is devoutly turned into '*Shribankebihariji*' in Hindi, '*begar-zana andaz*' becomes in an overkill of translation '*nishkama bhava*', while '*majlis khatm hui*' becomes '*sabha visarjit hui*'. '*Usne intezam-e-khanadari ki nahin, khat-nafs ki talim pai thi*' is altered completely to become '*Usne grihini banane ki nahin, indriyon ke anandabhog ki shiksha pai thi.*[4] The accumulative effect of numerous such changes is not only a 'Hindification' of the Urdu version but, through subtle cultural connotations, also a 'Hinduisation', which may seem artistically apt enough in a novel where all the major characters are Hindu, whose social ambience is comprehensively Hindu, and whose protagonist Suman is not only a Hindu but indeed a brahmin with a mother piously named Gangajali! Conversely, the emotive significance of even the name Suman (which means 'flower' in Hindi) is liable to be lost in Urdu where it is so spelt that it can be read as the meaningless 'Samau'—which is indeed how one Urdu critic consistently refers to her. (Sadiq 1984: 440–41, 444).

In the same year that *Sevasadan* was published, Premchand sat down to write a short story for the Urdu magazine *Kahakashan* of Lahore but found, when he had finished it, that he could not really send it there. As he explained to the editor Imtiaz Ali Taj: 'I have recently written another story, "Atma Ram" . . . . It has turned out to be so utterly Hindu that it is not suitable for *Kahakashan*. I may take *you* to be a Hindu but your readers certainly are not Hindu' (Rai 1962: 107). This story is about an aged, devout village goldsmith, Mahadeva, who is attached above everything else in the world to a parrot eponymously and symbolically named Atmaram, literally embodying the popular Hindu belief that the soul, the *atman*, is like a bird which flies out of the body upon death, as in the common Hindi phrase '*prana pakheru ur jana*'. Mahadeva is best known in his village for chanting at all hours of the day and night two lines from his favourite *bhajan:* '*Satta Gurudatta Shivadatta Data/Rama ke charan men chitta laga*.' The climax of the story occurs when Atmaram, the parrot, escapes from his cage, and Mahadeva follows it high and low to try and tempt it back. As Premchand describes it in Hindi:

> [The parrot] would now come and settle on the top of the cage, and now sit at the door of the cage and look at its bowls for food and water, and then fly off. If the Old Man was *moha* incarnate, the parrot was incarnate *maya*. This went on till it was evening. The struggle between *maya* and *moha* was lost in the darkness (Premchand, n.d., 122–9).

As is evident, Premchand significantly plays on essentially Hindu concepts like *maya* and *moha*, which can hardly be translated into any other language, and on submerged metaphysical metaphors of the bird and the soul. No wonder the story proved to be a little too much for the Urdu-Muslim readers of *Kahakashan*. If Premchand was to go on writing more such stories when the spirit moved him to write them, he could hardly have gone on writing them in Urdu.

VI

In conclusion, we may survey briefly the distinct thematic development of Premchand after his transition to Hindi. His five Urdu novels before *Bazar-e-Husn* had been slight, formally derivative or undistinguished, and altogether less than successful, as Premchand himself later acknowledged. However, immediately after completing *Bazar-e-Husn* in May 1918, he began *Gosha-e-Afiyat* (first published as *Premashram* in Hindi in 1921), his first novel extensively concerned with peasant life, while his first short story dealing with a peasant hero, 'Balidan', also appeared in 1918. In his authoritative biography of Premchand, Amrit Rai has described with great vividness the process of sudden illumination through which Premchand now came to see that his true and proper theme, his forte, had not been the kind of urban-social issues he had written about before, so much as it was the life of the villages and villagers which he himself knew best through his upbringing and observation.

Next, and directly following his resignation from government service, he produced his grand epic of the Gandhian nationalist movement, *Rangabhumi* (1924), which remained till the publication of *Godan* his own favourite among his novels. His next novel, *Kayakalpa* (1926), though it contains some twaddle about rebirth, also has his most forthright and up-to-date depictions of the Hindu-Muslim communal riots. This book was followed by *Nirmala* (1925–26), a poignant tale of the suffering of a young wife mismatched to a man old enough to be her father, with stepsons old enough to be her lovers. The novel is far more authentic in its attack on some aspects of Hindu society than any of his previous efforts in Urdu had been, such as *Hamkhurma-o-Hamsawab* (1906), *Kishana* (1907?), and *Jalva-e-Isar* (1912). Next came *Ghaban* (1931) a novel, which is abruptly jerked away from excoriating another social evil, the greed for jewellery, into a sub-plot involving patriotic terrorists. *Karmabhumi* (1932) with its predominantly nationalist concerns, formed a companion piece to the similarly titled *Rangabhumi*, and finally came *Godan* (1936), the classic account of subhuman misery, fatalistic resilience and the crippling subjugation of the Indian peasantry. It is in these novels and the short stories of the later phase that Premchand found the fulfilment of his true sensibility and genius—it is in these works that the essence as well as the substance of his achievement lies.

In his *History of Urdu Literature*, published in the middle of Premchand's career in 1928, T.G. Bailey had prophesied of Premchand: 'He will never attain the heights which are within his reach unless he goes back to his tales of the village life which he has lived, and the Hindu villagers whom he understands. Those tales alone ring true, and only they enable him to express his soul'.

Thus, according to Bailey, the path to creative truth for Premchand lay through the lives of Hindu villagers. It needs to be added that Premchand's path to these Hindu villagers, as well as to the mainstream of national and nationalist life, lay through Hindi, and that it was only after his metempsychosis, the transmigration of his creative soul from one linguistic body to a more naturally appropriate one that he fulfilled himself as a writer.

VII

The case of Premchand's transition from one language to another raises some further questions, which may have implications of a wider, theoretical nature of some relevance to a comparative study of Indian literatures. First, it prompts us to ask to what extent a writer's world-view is determined by the language he writes in, and whether such determination is more sharply highlighted rather than less so if the writer happens to be bilingual. Second, does a writer switching from, say, Oriya to Bengali, or from Gujarati to Marathi, require such pervasive cultural adjustments as were necessary for Premchand? If not, is Urdu then something of a special case among Indian languages, comparable in its non-Sanskritic non-Dravidic provenance and composition not to other Indian languages but, say, to Indian English?

Third, since Premchand is not the only Indian author to have moved from a smaller and declining language into a more widely spoken and vigorous one in order to gain a little more money and many more readers, and since we have some Indian writers today who are probably making more money and winning more admirers in a more widely spoken language into which they are translated than in the smaller one in which they originally write, are we here studying in fact not one isolated case but a social and economic force of centripetal tendency, which may eventually prove to be of tremendous consequence in the development of Indian literature? And, lastly, is Premchand's case at all comparable to the cases of some foreign writers who have moved not only from one language to another but also from one country to another (or several others), and who may or may not have found the language of their later adoption creatively as congenial as their first language? Among the more notable of such writers are, of course, Vladimir Nabokov and Samuel Beckett.

NOTES

1. For two illuminating accounts of the campaign for Hindi, written from distinct points of view, see Robinson (1974: 69–78) and Brass (1974: 127–38).

2. A possible third could have been Nazir Ahmad (1836-1912), 'if he could have been persuaded to write novels rather than improving tales' (Russell 1970: 122).
3. The speech was Premchand's presidential address to the first conference of the Indian Progressive Writers' Association held at Lucknow on 9 and 10 April 1936.
4. The quotations here are taken from the Hindi *Sevasadan* (1919, pp. 1, 19–20, 21 and 25), and from the corresponding passages from the Urdu *Bazar-e-Husn* (1923; repr. 1954).

REFERENCES

Anon, *A Defence of the Urdu Language and Character*, Allahabad, 1900.

Bailey, T.G., *A History of Urdu Literature* (repr.). [1928], Delhi: OUP, 2008 or available at: <http://www.columbia.edu/itc/mealac/pritchett/00urduhindilinks/bailey/bailey.html>.

Brass, Paul R., *Language, Religion and Politics in North India*, Cambridge, 1974.

Char Laghu Upanyas, New Delhi, n.d.

Curzon to Anthony MacDon'nell [1 June 1900], in S. Gopal, *British Policy in India, 1858–1905*, Cambridge: CUP, 1965.

Das, S.S., *Hindi Bhasha aur Sahitya*, Allahabad, 1930.

Gumperz, John J. and J. Das Gupta, 'Language, Communication and Control in North India', in *Language in Social Groups: Essays by John J. Gumperz*, ed. Anwar S. Dil, Stanford: Stanford University Press, 1971.

Majumdar, S., *Comparative Literature: Indian Dimensions*, Calcutta: Papyrus, 1987.

'Pahale Samskaran ki Bhumika' [1917], in *Sapta Saroj.*, Calcutta, 1954.

Premchand, 'Sharar aur Sarshar', in *Vividh Prasang*, ed. Amrit Rai, Allahabad, 1962, pp. 59–72.

———. *Manasarovar*, VII, pp. 122–9, Allahabad.

Rai, A., *Premchand: A Life*, tr., Harish Trivedi, New Delhi: People's Publishing House, 1982.

Raza, J., *Premchand: Urdu-Hindi Kathakar*, Allahabad, 1983.

Robinson, F., *Separatism Among Indian Muslims*, Cambridge: CUP, 1974.

Russell, R., 'The Development of the Modern Novel in Urdu', in *The Novel in India: Its Birth and Development*, ed. T.W. Clark, London, 1970.

Sadiq, M., *A History of Urdu Literature*. Delhi: OUP, 1995.

Shakespeare, *The Tempest*, I.ii. 400–1.

Shukla, R., *Hindi Sahitya ka Itihas*. Kashi: Lokbharati Prakashan, 1940.

———, *Hindi Sahitya ka Brihat Itihasi*, vol. IX, Varanasi, 1977, p. 129.

The Urdu Premchand: The Hindi Premchand

Afterword

THE ESSAY reprinted here was presented at the first conference of the Comparative Indian Literature Association (CILA) held at the University of Delhi from 5 to 7 January 1984. In this Afterword, it may be useful to take stock of how Comparative Literature has played out and developed in India over the last three decades, by surveying its institutional history as well as its thematological evolution.

CILA had then only recently been founded by Professor Sisir Kumar Das, Tagore Professor of Bengali in the Department of Modern Indian Languages, University of Delhi, and that Conference was its first notable activity, its coming-out party. The session (or 'panel') on the last day in which I presented my paper was chaired by another luminary of the field, Professor Amiya Dev of the Comparative Literature Department, Jadavpur University, Calcutta, who was then the President of the Calcutta-based Indian National Comparative Literature Association (INCLA). He was also the editor of the *Jadavpur Journal of Comparative Literature* for which he promptly appropriated my paper as soon as I had finished reading it.

These details are worth recounting because they represent a formative phase in the development of Comparative Literature in India. Das had set up CILA in 1981 mainly to signal and consolidate a groundswell for the sub-discipline of Comparative Literature in Delhi that had been visible since 1977. Until then, the one and only home of Comparative Literature in India had been the Comparative Literature Department founded at the Jadavpur University in Calcutta in 1956. There was between CILA and INCLA (established 1982) the utmost cordiality and collegiality. Sisir Das and Amiya Dev had for long been the best of friends, and anyhow, the forest of Comparative Literature in India was far too small for two lions to stake out distinct and separate turfs within it. So, at a joint conference co-convened by the two associations in 1988 in Hyderabad, CILA and

INCLA merged to form an association under a new name and banner, the Comparative Literature Association of India (CLAI).

The present nomenclature is a definite improvement on both the old ones. INCLA suffered from the paradox that it called itself both 'National' and 'Comparative', thus, flouting a basic tenet of Comparative Literature that it must go beyond a single language and a single nation. And though less flagrantly, CILA too seemed guilty of the same fault, for it was dedicated not to 'Indian Comparative Literature' but rather to 'Comparative Indian Literature', the latter formulation signifying that it was within the domain of Indian Literature that all the comparative study was to be undertaken.

The present name, 'Comparative Literature Association of India', seems more liberal or at least non-committal in this regard. But it may be acknowledged that in practice, Comparative Literature in India continues to be perhaps no wider in scope now than ever before, and what we do is in effect Comparative Literature within and among the Indian languages and literatures. This may seem narrow and ghetto-like but when one looks closely, it is perhaps hardly more so than what goes on in the name of Comparative Literature elsewhere in the world.

An episode that Sisir Das often recounted is illuminating in this regard. When Das (who had a Ph.D. from London, had been a post-doctoral fellow at Cornell, and knew Greek) first met one of the doyens of Comparative Literature in the West, René Wellek, he asked Wellek why Western comparatists like him paid so little attention in their work to 'Japanese Literature, or Chinese, or Persian'—and Wellek here interrupted to complete Das's question, 'or Sanskrit?' He then put a hand on Das's shoulder and said, 'One should do what one can' (qtd. in Trivedi 1997a, 5).

I think that cured Das and all the rest of us of any supposed obligation to try and do the kind of Comparative Literature that would also involve the West. If they don't, can't, and won't do us, why should we slavishly hanker to try and do them? India has as many major languages, both classical and modern, as Europe, each with a rich literary history, and that should suffice for us, as their languages and literatures suffice for the West. (There are, of course, some honourable exceptions on both sides but they only prove the rule.) This may explain why I never did get round to comparing Premchand's bilingualism with that of Nabokov or Beckett, a follow-up project, which I mention towards the end of my essay above. Nor, to the best of my knowledge, has anyone else, from either the East or the West. One does what one can.

So, I too have gone on doing what I can, and this has meant in part that I have, since 1984, returned more than once to the rich quarry

I identified here, Premchand and bilingualism, in order to dig more deeply and open up other seams. This was my second comparative paper, while my first too, in 1978, had concerned Premchand, being an analysis of his wholesale adaptation into Hindi of George Eliot's minor classic *Silas Marner.* Later, I examined another adaptation by Premchand of a Western work, Anatole France's *Thais,* from an explicitly postcolonial point of view (Trivedi 1997b). On another occasion, with new evidence and arguments, I revisited the explosive question of Premchand and Urdu and Hindi, placing it in a longer chronological perspective as part of a broader narrative of the evolution of Hindi language and literature in the twentieth century (Trivedi 2003).

The question of Urdu, Hindi, and Premchand, which I had more or less wandered into, was indeed highly combustible and as had become abundantly clear to me as soon as I had finished reading my paper out at that conference in 1984. A long discussion then ensued, which it would be an understatement to call heated. A lady academic from the Aligarh Muslim University Dr Zahida Zaidi (who taught English and was a well-known poet and playwright in Urdu, as I came to know later) stood up at the back of the auditorium and castigated me at length for even daring to suggest that Premchand had ever moved on from Urdu to Hindi.

Then, Dr Kamal Kishore Goyanka, a Hindi scholar from my own university, Delhi, got up from his seat, strode up to the stage, occupied the lectern, and began denouncing me for sullying Premchand's status as an iconic Hindi writer. He went on and on, getting more and more agitated and angry, until the chairperson Amiya Dev (who is short and slim as Goyanka is tall and sturdy) left his chair, went up to Goyanka, put an arm round his waist, and physically escorted him off the stage, down the steps, and back to his seat. Dr Goyanka and I have since come to know each other better. He has also proved to be over these decades one of the most assiduous and prolific Premchand scholars of our generation. He has published among other works a pioneering dual-language Hindi-Urdu edition of a selection of twenty-five of Premchand's short stories, thirteen of which were first published in Urdu and twelve first published in Hindi (Goyanka 1990). This selection is, of course, only a sample of Premchand's oeuvre, but it is significant that of the thirteen stories included here, which were first published in Urdu, ten had appeared by 1920, while of the twelve stories first published in Hindi, ten appeared after that date. This chronology cogently substantiates the case I had already argued in my paper above that Premchand wrote and published in Urdu up to a certain point in his career, and thereafter, moved to Hindi for writing most of his short stories and all his novels.

In any case, this paper delivered in 1984 was my baptism by fire into Comparative Literature. Actually, what proved controversial and provocative was not so much any issue concerning Comparative Literature itself as the question of Urdu and Hindi, and by obvious implication (as indicated by my two major interrogators) of Muslims and Hindus, and the great and separatist gulf between them that already existed in Premchand's time and that ultimately led to Partition, the division of India on the basis of religion into two nations, India and Pakistan. The relationship of one language and literature to another was apparently no mere academic matter, but could have been, at least in some particular historical contexts, momentous and even have had cataclysmic consequences.

In fact, so deeply ingrained were the issues I dared to discuss in this essay that they found subliminal manifestations in the unlikeliest of places. In late December 1983, Sisir Das asked me to go over the draft programme of the forthcoming conference, written out in his own bold and fair hand, before it was sent to be typed on those stencil sheets from which one made cyclostyled copies in those antediluvian pre-computer pre-photocopy days. Das was as meticulous as he was erudite, and I could detect only one error: he had put down the title of my paper as 'The Urdu Premchand; the *Hindu* Premchand'. The word 'Hindi' as misspelt here forms a beguiling rhyme with 'Urdu', and that may have been part of the explanation for the error. But there was also possibly a subconscious reason for this 'Freudian slip', which related to the vexed and deep-rooted Hindu-Muslim history of the sub-continent, subtly internalized and hardly distinguishable in many accounts from the Hindi-Urdu divide. Hindi and Urdu are commonly taken to be the languages of Hindus and Muslims, respectively—especially by the speakers of the other language—and it is a pertinent part of a wider comparative agenda to investigate the sources and the cultural history of these beliefs, perceptions and (mis) apprehensions (Trivedi 2012).

To go back to the present state of Comparative Literature in India (as indeed worldwide), it now exists under two kinds of threats of encroachment: one, from Postcolonial discourse, which has been around for at least a couple of decades and has won many converts, and two, from the trending conceptualization of a new field of study called World Literature, which is just now heaving into view. Postcolonial discourse has in part stolen the thematological thunder from Comparative Literature, by providing a common platform for exploring connections and comparisons, both cultural and political, between the various literatures of the vast and far-flung parts of the world that were once under colonial rule. But it is World Literature, which appears to pose a greater challenge to

Comparative Literature as it has essentially a similar agenda as Comparative Literature and claims to be even broader in scope. World Literature is, thus, in direct contestation with Comparative Literature for the same (inter)disciplinary space.

In India, unlike in the West, World Literature is yet to make waves, but for one substantial exception. In a new collection of nineteen essays on Comparative Literature, five essays are grouped together in a section titled 'World Literature and Comparative Literature: A Dialogue', both the essays in the opening section, 'Introduction', also participate substantially in this dialogue, and two more essays later in the volume in another section also feature the term 'World Literature' in their respective titles (Ramakrishnan et. al. 2013: 3–103, 107–16, 125–33)—and that adds up to nearly half the book.

Judging by past indications, these disciplinary contestations (or turf wars) will first be staged and resolved in the West, and will then be followed by a largely cloned but partially modified resolution in India. Indications of this localizing process are already to be discerned in the volume mentioned above. It would appear that World Literature is an attractive proposition for some eminent Indian comparatists partly because it may offer an opportunity to reconceptualize and appropriate 'the World' to India's advantage! Thus, T.S. Satyanath posits against the Western English-language canon of World Literature a very different canon as visualized by an Indian poet, Kuvempu, in his own language Kannada in 1947, in which he evoked right at the beginning (as a pious cosmopolitan gesture?) Homer, Virgil, Dante and Milton, and then proceeded to name three classical Kannada poets, four Sanskrit poets, and one poet each from Hindi, Bengali, Persian, Tamil, and Indian English, all within a space of five lines (cited in Satyanath 2013: 71–2). This roll call of great epic poets comprising mostly Indian writers may seem hardly more lop-sided than some Western anthologies of World Literature of the past.

But the last word here belongs perhaps to Amiya Dev, who ostensibly is content to fill his basket of World Literature with just one egg, really, in an essay titled 'Tagore as World Literature' (Dev 2013: 107–16). He evokes in it a whole range of the greatest writers of the world—Dante and Goethe, Maupassant and Chekhov, Schiller and Mann, Tolstoy and Gorky, Sa'di and Hafez—with regard to some aspect or the other of the multifarious achievements of the '*vishva-kavi*' (world-poet) Tagore. The bottom-line appeal of the new conglomerate called World Literature, thus, would seem to be that we in India can now aspire to claim a bigger slice of the world cake. And Premchand too may prosper for, unlike most great authors of the world, he wrote in not one but two languages and may possibly be entitled to two bites of the cherry!

REFERENCES

Dev, A., 'Tagore as World Literature', in *Interdisciplinary Alter-natives*, ed. E.V. Ramakrishnan, H. Trivedi and C. Mohan, New Delhi: Sage, 2013, pp. 107–16.

Goyanka, K.K., ed., *Premchand ki Hindi-Urdu Kahaniyan*, New Delhi: Bharatiya Jnanpith Prakashan, 1990.

Ramakrishnan, E.V., H. Trivedi and C. Mohan, eds., *Interdisciplinary Alter-natives in Comparative Literature*, New Delhi: Sage, 2013.

Satyanath, T.S., 'World Literature in the Context of Indian Literatures', in *Interdisciplinary Alter-natives*, ed. E.V. Ramakrishnan, H. Trivedi and C. Mohan, New Delhi: Sage, 2013, pp. 63–74.

Trivedi, H., 'Comparative Literature in India: Formation and Formulation', *New Comparison: A Journal of Comparative and General Literary Studies*, Special Issue on 'Comparative Literature in India', vol. 23, Spring 1997a, pp. 3–12.

———, 'India, England, France: A (Post-)Colonial Translational Triangle', *Meta: Journal des traducteurs*, vol. 42, no. 2, 1997b, pp. 407–15.

———, 'Hindi and the Nation', in *Literary Cultures in History: Reconstructions from South Asia*, ed. Sheldon Pollock, Berkeley: University of California Press, 2003, pp. 958–1022.

———, 'Muslims and Hindus: Urdu and Hindi', in *Islamicate Traditions in South Asia: Themes from Culture & History*, ed. Agnieszka Kuczkiewicz-Fras, New Delhi: Manohar, 2012, pp. 213–45.

19

The Oral, the Written and Memory: A History of Indian Aphasia

Ganesh Devy

LITERARY HISTORIOGRAPHY in India is a task that might defeat practically anyone owing to several reasons. The multiplicity of languages and a long literary past of three millennia make literary historiography in India a daunting task. The span of literary pasts of varied length for different languages poses yet another difficulty. The Eighth Schedule of the Constitution presently lists only twenty-two languages. But I am thinking of all the languages in India including those that have become extinct and have or have had literature produced in one form or the other. How does one approach in this regard the question of constructing a truthful, authentic, viable, pragmatic, functional, proper, descriptive history or a focused history? How does one construct any type of history or histories at all? Writing the history of English Literature in England is like maintaining a garden where you know the names of all the species, the age of the plants, their blossoming seasons and the fruits to be expected. This is not to say that England's literary historiography has no challenges, yet attempting to chart it is humanly possible. But Indian historiography is like entering the mythical 'Naimisaranya', where there is no beginning or end in sight. No single description will be entirely 'reasonable' in Indian literary historiography.

What is India? Is India a nation, a political reality or a philosophical category? Once Gandhi was asked about what he thought of western civilization. He promptly responded saying, 'It's a good *idea*'. For most of us, India cannot be thought of in terms of a singularity. The idea of India for Kashmiris who have migrated to Delhi, the idea of India for people in the north-eastern states, the idea for the terrified tribal in Chattisgarh, Jharkhand, and Orissa or even their outraged 'protectors', all seem to be differently constructed. India may mean one thing to the non-resident diaspora. It can mean something very different for you and me. In such a context of diverse perceptions historiography becomes a challenge.

When analysing literary history, one can find a terrible mix-up between the oral and the written that is guided, conditioned or distorted by what I have called 'amnesia'. All our important literature in the past was produced, received, circulated and remembered orally. Writing became an established practice after the arrival of printing technology during the colonial period. I am not talking about Vedic literature, liturgical literature or texts as such. Imagine fourth- and fifth-century dramas that were produced orally. These dramas were never read by people since there was no paper available. Texts as such were circulated through oral means. The same can be said for the perpetuation of '*sangeetha*' (music) tradition.

In the case of oral texts, there was no possibility of a second edition. There was no oral circulation of drama in a fixed language. At the most memorizing with the help of a text could involve the use of script. Depending on the audience, the language of the text varied. Let us think of the earliest mention of the *Mahabharata*: initially it was called *Ithihaas* (*Jaya-itihaas*). Many of us believe that history as a discipline has come from the West. But we must remember that the *Mahabharata* was called some kind of *history*. Certainly, it is not history in the Hegelian sense of the term. Let's not be chauvinistic or exaggerate the nature of history that existed prior to the colonial period in this country. The *Mahabharata* was history of a certain kind. In fact, a thousand years later, when Rajsekhar was thinking of history, he said it was of two kinds—one of many heroes and another of a single hero. He said that the *Ramayana* is a historical text with a single hero. But we know that the *Ramayana* is not an accurate historical text. I am not personally categorizing the *Ramayana* as history, but I am just calling attention to Rajsekhar's assessment. Rajsekhar said that the *Mahabharata* is history because the *Mahabharata* says so itself. That indeed was the earliest form of the *Mahabharata*. But the first reported version, in the Bhandarkar Institute version, tells of the time when the *Mahabharata* was being recited. At that time Ugrashravas comes to an *ashram* (think of it as some kind of college or University) and recites the verses to the students. They like the poetry and ask him to repeat it. Ugrashravas says that he has already recited the verses once and that he can easily repeat them. He says he knows 8800 verses but there are other sages who are equally proficient whose individual versions are not necessarily in the same language. They became assimilated into a single language text at some late date, when the first corpus of the *Mahabharata* was compiled.

The *Mahabharata* is a good example of a typical linguistic composition of traditional Indian literary texts. Like Homer's epic, it is one great epic i.e. passed down orally from one generation to another generation. The Indian epic is accommodative of many languages and very much part of the literary tradition. Think of the playwright: what is the difference between Shudraka, Kalidasa, or even those later day and more 'sophisticated' playwrights, since they invariably knew several languages? One of the theoreticians (in Sanskrit poetics) while looking at various literatures noted that there were so many *Ritis* and proposed the *Riti Sidhanta.* Thus literature could be composed at once in any number of ways in any number of languages.

There is a little story about the mother of all stories in this country—*Kathasaritsagara* (*Bṛhat Katha*). Śiva and Parvati often indulge in the business of storytelling. Parvati always likes new stories to be created for her. She therefore complains to her divine consort who was busy in responding to his devotees that he risked neglecting her. Śiva takes up the challenge of creating a new story exclusively for her. Parvati insists that the story should be only for her and no one else. She demands an exclusive story-telling session. So they create a special bower for her to listen to the story in privacy. But two of the *Ganas* try to eavesdrop. They are curious to know what Śiva is telling to Parvati. She notices the two intruders and curses them with complete amnesia: 'You'll be born in another form and you will forget all these wonderful stories'. They appeal to Śiva and out of his generosity; he softens the curse. There will be a possibility of recollecting what they forget, but that will be a sad thing in their lives. The two *Ganas* are then born as human beings: Vararuchi and Gunadhya. Vararuchi starts remembering these stories as Śiva said, but in a Paisachik language and not in Sanskrit. The moment he remembers he wants to write down the stories. He catches hold of an animal, and since he has no ink and pen he cuts the animal and with a sharp instrument dipped in the animal's blood, he starts writing on its skin. Gunadhya, his companion, recites the stories. One is formulated in the written tradition and the other in the oral tradition. They take the stories to the King asking him for patronage. The King sends them back because the stories they have brought are in the Paisachik language and not in Sanskrit. Heartbroken, they return to the forest and start burning the stories one after the other. But Gunadhya wants to read them out before they are destroyed, and is heard by all the animals and birds. They come listening keenly to his charming stories. The animals and birds forget to drink and eat. They become thin and one such lean bird gets served for lunch at the King's court. The King turned angry and asked, 'how come there is no food in my kingdom?' Somebody tells him about the recital of the stories in the forest and that all the animals and birds had forgotten to eat food. The King rushes to the forest and saves the remaining part of the manuscript from the fire. The story in the Paisachik language also becomes a great story in the Sanskrit language. Several texts come together. The oral and the written stay together in our tradition. This phenomenon happened everywhere in India—equally so in Kerala, in Assam, and elsewhere.

Because we had our own ways of remembering the past, our own styles of historiography, we decided that certain texts could be reinterpreted and rendered differently from time to time. An original text could be brought back to life in the form of translation. In India, translation was never looked down upon when compared with the original. Translation and the original were accorded the same importance. Translation was not treated as something that had fallen from paradise into hell. Jnaneshwar (Jnana deva) rewrote the *Gita* from Sanskrit into Marathi. *Jnaneshwari* (Jnaneshwar's commentary on the *Gita*) was also worshipped by the people. Prakrit was not seen as inferior to Sanskrit. Oral was not deemed inferior to the written word. Writing was not understood as sacred, but the oral was however treated as sacred. Vacha/speech was a goddess, as was Sanskrit at times. A particular form of writing was therefore thought to be not so important. If we look at the issue of writing from a sociological point of view, we find that it emerges when agrarian societies started moving towards an early capitalistic aspiration, when there is some accumulation of surplus. Imagine yourself in the pastoral age slowly moving towards becoming an agrarian society, then to semi-industrial, industrial, capitalistic, and then to a global capitalistic age. When the shift from the pastoral to the agrarian takes place, human beings started thinking of saving themselves from hard labour. There are limits for the human body that we cannot escape: we move perpendicular to the earth, whereas all other animals and birds move parallel to the earth. The spine is both our great boon and our curse; bending the spine is a bother. All our choices in life have evolved in such a way that the body can avoid bending down. Pastoral work or hunting rarely required frequent bending. Agriculture required bending down, touching the ground repeatedly. Therefore, in the process of sociological evolution, humans felt the need to employ others, animal or human, to do their agricultural labour. In order to employ a person for labour, one needs to have a surplus. I grow something this year and save a little bit of it, give it you and in the future you do my work. When these transactions became complex, carefully remembering them became necessary. In order to record these memories, marks were made on rock surfaces, on trees or on any such material so that those memories could be communicated from one generation to the next generation, providing a record of the surplus one's ancestors produced and invested in the labour of other people. This need to record marks the birth of scripts all over the world. Remember that the geometrical forms used for 'writing' numerals are often accepted as the first graphical signs for vowels used by that speech community. Most vowel sounds have graphical similarities with graphical features of the numbers used by that society. This process is scientifically established, it's not my fancy, and historical linguistics has accepted the origin of scripts in this fashion.

Scripts have no 'logical' relation with the languages they represent. A given language is never dependent for its growth or decline on the script in which it is written. Having a well developed script does not ensure the superiority of a given language over other languages. A language can never be considered lacking in valuable aspects, if it has not developed a script for itself. For example, the English language still does not have a script of its own. English uses the Roman script. Yet, it is a mighty language. We cannot dismiss it as a dialect of Latin.

No script is a perfect representation of vocal symbols, graphic symbols, and orthographic symbols. That's why when you write in your own language or in English there are so many sounds that are difficult to represent and you make many compromises. Each written script establishes a convention. When I say 'Rama is the King of Travancore', the way I write the word Rama in the regional script establishes a convention. One learns to associate the sounds with the graphical symbols. They are not quantitatively equivalent to verbal signals. Hence any script can represent any language. Many languages have fared well without having scripts for themselves.

When the British arrived in this country, we decided that the written was more important than the oral. India had started using paper in the thirteenth century. The Turkish paper merchants in Delhi had become extremely prosperous; they were equivalent to the Narayana Murthis (IT Barons) of today. Delhi's state structure was rooted in the paper industry. Prior to that time, India communicated through oral traditions that were basically committed to written form. For example, in the days of the Marathi poet Tukaram, the practice was for a poet to write something and the writing was copied into different versions since printing was not possible. In those days, copies were pretty expensive. Writings on paper/ manuscripts/copies, according to certain reports, were sold and purchased for thousands of rupees. That's the time when excellent orthography also was cultivated. Good handwriting became a value in education that has now disappeared with the onset of the computers. A poet would write his poems and also sing them. The dramatist wrote a version of a play but its actual presentation would be quite different. People heard poems in the oral form, while written forms were also available. It is said that Tukaram's enemies found it difficult to tolerate his rising stature and popularity, and so they decided to collect all his works and sink them in the Indrayani River. After some days those bundles of papers surfaced. Although the water blotted the ink, the poems had nevertheless circulated orally resulting in Tukaram's poems being remembered. There is a similar story of the latter-day poet Ghalib. In the last years of his life, Ghalib used to *write* verse but he did not know where his verses were. Once he was walking along the Ganga and heard a beggar singing one of his poems. Ghalib had tears in his eyes. 'Where did you find this?' the deeply moved poet asked, and the beggar said 'I've got this' and showed him a paper. Ghalib did not have a record of the song himself. So the oral and the written existed together. Once the British came to this country, the written became sacred.

The sacredness of the written originated not in the attitude of the British toward writing or orality. It originated in the British system of land records. Land ownership had to be written and all those land laws from 1763 to 1924 strengthened the idea that in order to establish one's identity and legal existence, one had to have something in writing as testimony. At the end of the eighteenth century, we accepted the new colonial legal system. So many Indian languages were put into script (print media) at this time. The colonial government appointed one Lalluji Lal at Fort William in Calcutta to create scripts for Indian languages or use already available scripts. Most Indian scripts were based on Brahmi. Lalluji Lal put only some languages into print. He did not go round the country to find out which language was spoken by more people, which language had a better future, which one was old, eminent and so on. It was not a rational study; he decided to put Indian languages into script in an entirely subjective way. Literature only started getting printed in those languages.

When we became independent, the Government of India prepared a list of languages, the Eighth Schedule of the Constitution, in which only those languages put to script by the British were enumerated. States were given only to those languages that had a print culture. As a result of this ruling, we have linguistic states in the country. But on the borders of these states, language groups are distributed and people with different languages are scattered on both sides. Look at the 'adivasis'—the Bhils, the Gonds, the Santhals, the Mundas—who inhabit four states. The Bhils are scattered in Maharashtra, Madhya Pradesh, Rajasthan, and Gujarat; the Gonds in Maharashtra, Madhya Pradesh, and Chhatthisgarh; the Santals in Bengal, Jharkhand, Bihar, and Orissa. Since they had languages which were not in print, these groups could be scattered to different states of the country. It was not the fault of these people and not because they did not have a literary past. This action occurred because of colonial intervention.

In 1961 when the census was carried out, India reported the existence of 1652 mother tongues. In 1971, the census (decadal census) reported only 109 mother tongues. How did the census statistics decrease from 1652 to 109? Is it because the government failed in its record taking? The census reports usually come out five or six years after the census is recorded. So the 1971 census came out in 1976 or 1977. In 1971, a war had taken place outside India that resulted in the splitting up of East Pakistan and West Pakistan. East Pakistan became a separate nation on the question of language. Bangla was not included in the educational system of East Pakistan and, as a result, East Bengal became Bangladesh. Since this event happened next-door, the Government of India became very nervous about language diversity. So when the 1971 census data appeared, it disclosed statistics for only those languages spoken by more than ten thousand individuals. Thus the census reported 108 languages; the 109th was described as 'all others', which included the remaining thousands. Children, who are born in these other language will, therefore, never get schooling in their mother tongues. It is obligatory on the part of the Government of India to provide money only for education in languages listed in the Eighth Schedule of the Constitution. So there are no schools, colleges and universities for other languages though occasionally there are radio programmes in these other languages. Children do not learn their own mother tongue but learn other languages. They feel shy of mentioning other languages as their mother tongues. Languages are dying in this fashion. We have as of today about 700 languages in this country. As per the forecast of 'Ethnologue' (a famous website) and of UNESCO, India will by the end of this century have possibly not more than one-tenth of these languages left. Approximately 800 languages will become obsolete.

What do these languages hold in them? They hold knowledge about ecology. I was compiling a list of Himalayan languages in three states—Jammu and Kashmir, Himachal Pradesh and Uthrakhand—and found that there are over one hundred terms for snow. They have a word for snow which falls on muddy waters, snow which falls in the latter part of the afternoon, the first and last phase of snow and so on. All these terms indicate great knowledge of the environment in these days when we are all worried about climate change and global warming. We are losing or we are bound to lose such information.

In the Parliament of India, only 4 per cent of Indian languages are heard; 96 per cent are never heard. Each language presents a worldview. It combines a community's imagination as well as its memory. Each language portrays a unique world. I will mention how imagination and memory combine together in a language. Consciousness—supported by the sensory capabilities of the human body in time and space—makes sense of the world only through constant encounter with time and space. It is imagination that helps us organize space through a series of images. Images of external objects bombard our mind through the eye and the mind then organizes them as a created replica of space. This is why the imagination is so important. What about memory? Humans have conceptualized time unlike other animals. Only human animals speak in a complex language. Other animals can refer only to the present—a dog or a dolphin may have limited memory. Humans however, have conceptualized time in a complex manner. Some Indian languages have six varieties of the past tense, others have four. If a language has six forms of the past tense, there can be at least six different approaches to looking at the past, six measurements of the past time. It has taken a very long time for human beings to arrive at the formulation of the past tense. The present tense was easy. The present tense refers to 'fact or truth' and the past tense tells a 'lie' or fiction. Telling a 'lie' demands a much more complicated process in the brain. In the evolutionary history of language, it took nearly two lakh years or so for the humans to formulate something in the past tense. We first conceptualized time and, in order to come to terms with it, we devised the past tense in language. If we had no memory, we would not have been able to manage the past. I remember today that I am the same person that I was yesterday. It is through memory that I am able to put together the past and the present, and create a sense of continuity in existence. Every language organizes the world on its own terms, in terms of its own unique interpretation of space and time. In this country, when we lose 96 per cent of our languages we lose so much of our stock of world-views. In other words, we lose almost our entire intellectual capital on which a historiography of India is created. I think it is time for us to look at these issues with an alertness of mind and rearrange the conceptual categories that we have inherited and have accepted unquestioningly.

We were told sometime back, two hundred years ago, that Indians had no sense of history, that India had only a *cyclical* sense of history, and that Indian time ran in cycles. None of these dicta are true. Think of Bhartrihari, the fourth century grammarian, he added another book to his *Vakyapadiya* (a grammar text). This book or section of the book was called the *Kaalasamuddesh*—i.e. how to understand tenses or time. In the *Kaalasamuddesh*, Bhartrihari maintain that time has various possibilities. One kind of time is like a fixed road. We are the wayfarers while time does not move, but we walk through time. The second description is that time is like a water-well from which we keep on drawing, trying to deplete it, but time returns to its own source. For the third description, he gives the example of a person who trains birds. The trainer ties a very thin string to the claws of the pigeon and pulls it in order to train and control the bird. These strings are invisible. Bhartrihari teaches that time is like the trainer of birds. All of us are like birds and time controls us—time tells us how far we will fly. This is not a cyclical sense of time. Clearly, then, we have a linear sense of time, multiple time, and dynamic time. This is only one example. The Chinese, Arabs and Russians have also produced histories and historiographies with different conceptions of time.

Two hundred years ago, during the colonial period, if Indians were told that we had no sense of history, it was because of the analogy that the English made between us and animals. We had to be convinced that we were closer to animals that had no sense of history than to an advanced race such as the British. We somehow accepted this narrative. Until today, many of us believe that history has come to us only through Hegel in Germany or Hobbes and Locke in England. I think, time has come for us to look at the question of what is literature, what are the oral and the written, what is this amnesia that we have accepted.

Worst of all is the fact that we are 'sentencing' (I am using that word quite advisedly) so many languages in this country, silencing them, and imposing certain debilitating conditions on them. The Greek language bequeathed us the term 'aphasia'—loss of speech that happens because the brain cannot communicate with the speech organs, or the speech organs themselves are deficient. But there is a different kind of 'aphasia' where, in a country like ours, speaking a language is treated as a kind of backwardness. Rather than taking pride in a a large number of Indian languages, we are imposing severe 'aphasia'on them. I think the time has come for us to look at the question. The time has come to asks how we define the oral and the written. We need to question this amnesia that we have accepted.

This story was written by Mahasweta Devi. In Maharashtra in the Amaravati district, there is a tribe called the Korkus. In the early 1990s, the

Korkus started dying in large numbers from sickle cell anemia (a genetic ailment), a typically tribal disease in the country. The Government of Maharashtra appointed a committee. The doctors went there and came back saying that it was a genetic disease and nothing could be done. At that time, I was working with Mahasweta Devi on nomadic communities. I invited her to visit the Korku community in Amaravati. We went together and saw a devastated landscape. She came back and wrote the following story.

When the Korkus realize that they will all die, they decide to die in a dignified fashion rather than mourn over their predicament. They build a cottage and wait there to die when their time comes. The last of the Korkus, Mahadu (Mahadev), a young boy, waits in the cottage to die. A doctor who has done a lot of research on the effects of malnutrition visits Mahadu and injects a fluid into his body. This fluid is known to have improved the conditions of people battered by sickle cell anemia. The doctor sees that after he has injected Mahadu with the fluid, the boy's health improves. The doctor immediately leaves for Geneva to present a paper in a science conference on the success of his invention. But Mahadu is waiting in the cottage, hungry and alone.

The Korku forest was given to the British for the construction of wooden logs to put under the railway tracks. The railway line from Howrah to Surat is made from the Korku trees. Mahadu, while waiting in the cottage, hears the whistle of a train and suddenly feels the smell that comes as the fragrance from the past pervades his senses; it comes from the timber snatched away from his ancestors. He rushes to the train and jumps into it. The train takes him to Bombay and there, lo and behold, he sees a strange thing. For the first time in his life, he sees food. He feels hungry; he feels the hunger of generations. He starts eating and eats everything. Because there is not enough food for him in Bombay he starts eating the Victoria Terminal building, the Bombay University and many other tall structures of the city. His stature grows tall and his head touches the sky. Then he bends down and drinks the Arabian Sea, rises again, raises his hands and plucks the stars from the sky, and starts rewriting the history of the Korkus. If we do not do it for their benefit, then they will do it. For themselves, they will create a new Historiography and a new Literature.

20

Indigenous Playwriting and Globalization

Marc Maufort

Over the past few decades, the phenomenon referred to as 'globalization' has become a staple feature of our world. This process was already announced in the Enlightenment by Immanuel Kant, whose related concept of cosmopolitanism nonetheless betrayed a Eurocentric emphasis on the universal (Knowles 56).[1] Nowadays, globalization usually designates, as Dan Rebellato points out, the complex web of political, cultural, and economic relationships between nations on a truly intercontinental scale (Rebellato 4–12). This new world vision has not failed to generate its specific criticism. In the field of Comparative Literature, let it suffice to mention David Damrosch's reinvention of the Goethean concept of World Literature as a 'mode of circulation and of reading', revealing a literary network between different nations (5). In the realm of postcolonial studies, Gayatri Spivak's idea of 'planetarity' emphasizes meaningful interaction with forms of otherness (73). If globalization fosters positive exchanges between different world cultures, it simultaneously favours cultural sameness. Accordingly, theater and postcolonial critics Helen Gilbert and Jacqueline Lo endorse an extended form of cosmopolitanism devoid of 'traditional associations with privilege and with impartiality to the demands of the local' (Gilbert and Lo 4). Such reinvigorated cosmopolitanism emphasizes the possiblities of local resistance against the homogenizing tendencies of globalization. Despite Gilbert and Lo's pioneering efforts in the field of postcolonial and multi-ethnic theater, much still needs to be explored in the relationship between Indigenous playwriting and globalization, particularly as Gilbert and Lo limit their study to the Oceanic stage. Further, comparative literary studies have mainly focused on globalization in the field of fiction or poetry, as Damrosch's and Spivak's works quoted above indicate. This essay therefore seeks to show how Comparative Literature's methodology can enhance our understanding of the ways in which Aboriginal playwrights negotiate globalization.

As I have shown elsewhere, Aboriginal playwriting is a literary phenomenon that has gained increasing importance since the 1980s (Maufort 2003: 147–231; 2010: 139–73). One could argue that this growth has been favoured by the pervasive focus on minority discourses typical of the late twentieth century. During this period, more and more Aboriginal work was published throughout the world. Globalized publishing markets allowed for a wide distribution of previously unavailable material. Aboriginal drama from countries such as Australia, New Zealand, and Canada was performed internationally, during such events as the Edinburgh Festival, to cite but one example. Further, in some cases, Aboriginal companies from various countries joined forces. The collaborative work of Māori/Pacific Islands artist Miria George and the Toronto-based Native Earth Performing Arts provides a case in point (George 121). However, as I shall suggest below, globalization, while it increases the visibility of Aboriginal playwriting, can also constitute an obstacle to the articulation of an intensely localized aesthetic, as international readers or audiences do not always wish to engage with the specificities of the foreign cultures they encounter. They ghettoize, indeed exoticize, material from diverse cultures as similar facets of the broad category of Aboriginal writing.[2]

In this respect, comparative literatary studies, I would contend, are particularly useful. Most Aboriginal literary works are too often examined within the framework of national literatures, albeit through the lens of postcolonial theory. In addition, analysing Aboriginal literature from a non-Native perspective is fraught with the problematic issues of voice appropriation, a tendency often understood as adopting a Eurocentric, if not dismissive, approach to Indigenous material. The increasingly non-Eurocentric focus of comparative literary studies can help remedy this pitfall. A mere cursory look at the work performed by ICLA research committeees in recent years would suffice to demonstrate the discipline's cosmopolitan perspective. Comparative Literature's methodology forces non-Native researchers to engage with a plurality of Indigenous cultures from different regions of the world. Focusing on an array of culturally distinct works limits the danger of cultural appropriation precisely because this method enables an appreciation of the diversity of non-Western aesthetics. This essay offers glimpses of how Comparative Literature's methodology can fruitfully help understand Indigenous playwriting, particularly with regard to its reconfiguration of traditional realism.

Contemporary Indigenous theater in North America and Australasia offers an ideal comparative vantage point from which to examine the ways in which Native playwrights have reinvented traditional Euro-American dramatic realism so as to assert the uniqueness of their culture in today's 'global village'. Through such a repositioned stage realism, they seek to avoid the homogenizing gaze of Western audiences and readers, who tend to rely exclusively on hegemonic positioning systems in order to navigate the worlds of Native literature and drama. The ways in which Native playwrights use other artistic genres in an attempt to hybridize stage realism constitutes a hitherto understudied aspect of this resistance against globalization. As this essay will attempt to show, borrowings from extra-literary forms of art play a paramount role in forging local Indigenous idioms. The three case studies examined here explore this aesthetic device in some detail by comparing Indigenous playwrights from North America and New Zealand. Canadian *Métis* playwright Marie Clements blends dramatic art and photography in her recent *The Edward Curtis Project: A Modern Picture Story*. The works of the US-based Spiderwoman collective explicitly refer to the art of Hopi weaving and quilting. In *Winnetou's Snake Oil Show from Wigwam City*, the actors articulate a new genre called 'storyweaving'. In Aotearoa/New Zealand, Briar Grace-Smith's magic realist play *Purapurawhetū* is structured on the process of weaving a sacred Māori *tukutuku* panel. These plays thus evade the Eurocentric conventions of Aristotelian linearity. The analytical tools of Comparative Literature enable scholars to foreground the wide range of transgeneric devices used by these Aboriginal dramatists.

I

In her remarkable body of experimental plays, Canadian *Métis* dramatist Marie Clements offers striking instances of this innovative blurring between theater and other art forms. *Burning Vision* (2002) focuses on historical events that took place in the North West Territories in the late nineteenth century and throughout the twentieth century. The play focuses, in particular, on the economic exploitation of radium ore at the expense of the health of the Dene Indians. While this substance was primarily meant to cure cancer, it ironically served to destroy Hiroshima and Nagasaki. This play links events which took place in nineteenth-century Dene communities in North America with what occurred in Japan. The first pages of the published version of the play provide a map of the Great North, on which various events are chronologically listed in small inserts. This distortion and expansion of conventional time-space coordinates indicates Clements's desire to redefine the very boundaries of what constitutes drama. In a subsequent work, *Copper Thunderbird* (2007), Clements literally equates her play with the paintings of Aboriginal artist Norval Morrisseau. This painter's final epiphany is enacted as a communion with the creatures he depicted throughout his career. The entire stage literally transforms into a Morrisseau canvas, in a transgeneric fusion of theater and painting. As creatures represented in the canvas appear on the stage, they exclaim in a chorus-like fashion: 'We are Norval Morrisseau' (81).[3]

In *The Edward Curtis Project: A Modern Picture Story*, a joint project with photographer Rita Leistner (2010), Clements blends dramatic text and photographic art in order to debunk Western stereotypes of Native Americans. Clements's and Leistner's undertaking is a response to the anthropological work of photographer Edward Sheriff Curtis (1858–1952) who photographed and documented the life of Native Americans extensively in the twenty volumes of his influential book, *The North American Indian* (1907–1930). While his work still retains considerable historical value, it is nonetheless frequently criticized for its romanticized depictions of Native Americans. Like many of his contemporaries, Curtis regarded these Natives as examples of a 'vanishing race'. In their collaborative works, Clements and Leistner sought to avert Curtis's gaze of appropriation. Leistner devised an exhibit of photographs counterpointing Curtis's sentimentalizing stance. The pictures were on display at the same time that Clements's play was performed. The public was invited to view both the exhibit and the play. Moreover, the pictures were published in the printed version of the project, thus integrating the two art forms. Unlike Curtis's photographs, Leistner's pictures are often conceived as dyptichs offering striking contrasts between Natives depicted alternatively in their contemporary, Westernized, garments and in their traditional regalia. Thus, Leistner's photographs prompt us to question the reliability of photographic perception. Do they actually convey the whole complexity of Native American identities?

A similar question is addressed in Clements's companion script, which is highly experimental. In her desire to challenge Curtis's photographic 'framing' of Native subjects, Clements resorts to a variety of media extending beyond the literary mode, such as 'photography, archival film, video, archival writing, Euro-Aboriginal and Aboriginal-Euro orchestral scores, wax cylinders, and magic lanterns' (9). Unlike Curtis, she tries to offer non-stereotypical portraits of her characters. Further, the recurrence throughout the script of words referring to sight indicates Clements's wish to undermine photographic truthfulness. Characteristically, Curtis carried a small glass in his pocket, described as 'a stereoscopic lens from a camera ... brought back from the Civil War' (35). This act readily emphasizes Curtis's reductionist perspective.

The play could be seen as a long stream-of-consciousness in which a depressed Native, Angeline, undertakes an arduous journey towards regeneration. Angeline successfully confronts ghost-like apparitions, including Curtis himself and his photographed subjects. As a mixed race individual of Dene and Russian Canadian extraction, Angeline feels her real identity has been stolen by Western culture. On the advice of her psychiatrist, she reads Curtis's photographic book about the Natives. Thus, she metaphorically embarks upon a therapeutic 'vision' quest that ultimately leads her to a firmer sense of her Aboriginal identity. In this process, she manages to evade Curtis's sentimental framing. From the very start, the play's concern with contemporary photographic art stands in marked contrast to Curtis's techniques. Says Angeline: 'My mother's walls were filled with pictures . . . evidence of our success as a family . . . . Mixed race marriage. Contemporary' (11). Further, the script is interspersed with metatheatrical excerpts from Curtis's public lectures about Native Indians. In the midst of one of these lectures, Yiska, Angeline's boyfriend, aggressively confronts Curtis in an attempt to resist his gaze of appropriation. As the stage directions indicate, Yiska's speech is delivered in the Peigan language, although the script readily transcribes it in English: 'I am not for your eyes. . . . lower your need to see what is not for you. . . . I am not for your eyes. Stay where I cannot see you and you cannot see me' (27). Yiska openly criticizes Curtis's photographic practice: 'YISKA: You were taking pictures of your idea of them. Big difference' (53). Further, Curtis feels pursued by the gaze of a Native he once photographed, Alexander Upshaw: 'He's looking at me. His eyes are following me' (39). Opposition to Curtis intensifies as the photographer himself becomes aware of his negative influence on Native culture: 'A baby was trying to be born, stuck, they said because of me. Stuck between flesh and spirit, between surviving and vanishing. Because of me they said . . . Was it real? It was real' (56). In his final confrontation with the Hunger Chief, a timeless creature, who is a 'bear-like leader of all peoples and all nations. A shaper of storms and clear skies' (8), Curtis meets with his death. In these last moments, he becomes one with the Natives he once photographed: 'CURTIS: . . . I've nothing left. HUNGER CHIEF: Then you are finally one of us. The only way a white man can become an Indian is to starve . . . You want to live with the Indians, then you must die with us. . . . *parts of Edward Curtis's Indians begin to develop as negative images . . . Shots of spirits emerge and move forward*' (59–60). This reunion proves to be fatal. The Native spirits strip Curtis of his clothes, calling him a thief. Ironically, Curtis's own creatures kill him: '*EDWARD CURTIS sinks down into the lake. The INDIANS begin to disappear as they submerge in the water*' (61).

In contrast, Angeline simultaneously undergoes a spiritual rebirth. She now clearly identifies what Curtis failed to reflect in his photographic art, the suffering of the Indians. She experiences a vision of three Native children who died in the snow. Apparently, they accidentally froze to death as they accompanied their father, who had been trying to bring one of them to a doctor. Angeline feels compassionate: 'I began to take my coat off . . . the layers I had put on . . . I took off and I put them on their little bodies . . . It was so cold . . . and they were so alone. . . . I laid down with them, covering them with a blanket the best I could . . . I rocked them into their sleep, tucking them in' (65). As the ghost of Curtis suddenly appears, Angeline asks him to take the picture of this unromantic, indeed tragic, event. To which Curtis responds: 'I can't take the picture . . . because I'm not alive. You are' (66). Thus, the concluding moments of the play emphasize Angeline's newly-found agency as a potential photographer chronicling a different aspect of the Native predicament. As she embraces her boyfriend, she asserts her ability to see and understand who she is: 'Take me back . . . I am ready to see everything. . . . We have survived despite what you can, or cannot see. . . . We have survived across time, across place, to love each other towards a new day' (66–67). Thus, Angeline has successfully overcome the crippling impact of Curtis's photographic art. All in all, Clements's references to the Western art form of photography paradoxically enable her to develop an innovative Native idiom that literally explodes Western concepts of dramatic linearity.

II

Similar examples of transgeneric cross-fertilization can be found in Aboriginal playwriting originating in the United States. For instance, the works of the Spiderwoman collective explicitly refer to the art of Hopi weaving and quilting. The Spiderman group consists of Lisa Mayo, Muriel Miguel, and Gloria Miguel, all women of Kuna/Rappahannock descent. In *Winnetou's Snake Oil Show from Wigwam City* (1988), the collective is joined by the Chichimec/Otomi actress Hortensia Colorado, whose Aztec background draws a link between First Nations and Chicano people. In *Winnetou*, the actors develop a new genre they refer to as 'storyweaving':

They take their name from the Hopi goddess Spiderwoman, who taught the people to weave and said, 'You must make a mistake in every tapestry so that my spirit may come and go at will'. Spiderwoman has prophetic insight into the future, speaks all languages, and by nature of being a spider is ever present to give and to guide. The women call their technique of working 'storyweaving', in which they create designs and weave stories with words and movement, creating an overlay of interlocking stories, where fantasy and power are comically intertwined.[4] (230)

The setting encodes the collective's use of First Nations material. Indeed, it foregrounds 'Spiderwoman's signature backdrop made of different pieces of cloth to form a hodgepodge patchwork quilt' (234). Further, *Winnetou* relies on a hybrid blend of Native elements and Western metatheatrical devices, in an echo of Clements's techniques. The entire play can be seen as a challenge to realist representation: it constitutes a parody of Wild West Shows, which enacted outrageously racist and simplistic characterizations of First Nations people. An embedded metatheatrical performance appropriates Hopi quilting in order to create a highly personal stage language, thus offering Spiderwoman a particularly appropriate weapon to challenge Western mimesis. Winnetou, the central character/stereotype, provides the best instance of the White violation of First Nations authenticity and thus recalls to some extent Curtis's sentimentalizing gaze. Indeed, he is depicted as an extremely naïve 'Noble savage' betrayed by his German friend Gunther. Through a series of character transformations and loosely linked vignettes, the script dramatizes the negative aspects of White appropriations of First Nations spirituality. However, this performance piece concludes with a reaffirmation of cultural independence and an ultimate rejection of American materialism.

As a typical example of *mise en abyme*, the play's embedded Wild West Show bears the same title as that of the overarching work: 'Winnetou's Snake Oil Show from Wigwam City'. It is introduced by Princess Pissy Willow—herself a stereotype drawn to the point of absurdity. After ingesting the Snake Oil, various characters feel relieved of their afflictions. First Nations magic is thus reduced to a marketable product. Metatheatrical parody further heightens when, having selected a fair-skinned member of the audience, the collective invites him to become a First Nations person. This ironic 'transformation ceremony' is meant to literally alter a White member from the public into a photocopied Native (255).

In the play's final moments, the sisters' epiphanic awareness contradicts Gunther's claim that the Indians comprise a 'sick and dying race', an oppositional stance reminiscent of *The Edward Curtis Project* (260). The last scenic image suggests spiritual regeneration, as the sisters now repossess their Aboriginal culture: 'LISA: Our homes are not in museums. We are not defeated. We are still here' (262). This rebirth suggests a return to the Native values encoded in the Hopi quilt backdrop that serves as an essential feature of the setting throughout the play.

III

Spiderwoman's practice of weaving invites comparison with Māori playwriting from Aotearoa/New Zealand. The theatrical exploitation of other art forms is particularly noticeable in *Purapurawhetū* (1997), a play by the highly regarded Māori dramatist Briar Grace-Smith.[5] In this play, Grace-Smith develops a form of magic realism that is clearly linked with Māori legends and the art of weaving, specifically as the weaving of a sacred *Tukutuku* (ornamental) panel. Magic realism, as Jeanne Delbaere reminds us, presupposes the absence of boundaries between the world of the living and the supernatural, an Indigenous feature pervading Grace-Smith's play. Magic realism, Delbaere argues, is often used by postcolonial or minority writers to express a reaction against the centre, against hegemonic society, thus constituting a sign of resistance against globalization. It serves to designate a fracture in the real resulting in a transitory conflation of phenomena that Western spectators would consider incompatible. Thus foregrounding the contiguity between ordinary reality and the world of ancestors, magic realism articulates an Indigenous worldview differing markedly from Western modes of perception. What Delbaere describes as 'mythic realism', a variant of magic realism, emanates from the supernatural features of the environment itself. This concept, to which I shall refer as mythic magic realism for the sake of consistency, can be expanded to incorporate texts engaging the mythical cosmologies of Indigenous people (Delbaere 252–53).

Purapurawhetū tells the story of a *tukutuku* weaver, Tyler, who effects through his craft the reconciliation of a whole Māori community, Te Kupenga (signifying 'net'). Their name obliquely refers to the connectedness that is yet to be achieved. In the type of *tukutuku* panel called *Purapurawhetū* (literally meaning 'weaving panel of stars'), each stitch represents a star, which is itself linked to an ancestor spirit. As the weaving progresses, the story represented by the panel unfolds in the presence of the audience. The set of the play comprises two areas, the beach and the weaving workshop. In Māori mythology, the beach represents a liminal space of in-betweenness connecting the real world with the supernatural. In this specific instance, it constitutes a kind of purgatory, in which Hohepa searches in vain for his lost inheritance, symbolized by his dead son, Bubba. In contrast, the weaving area is associated with Tyler's sacred *tukutuku* panel, which he seeks to complete before the opening of the new community *marae* (place of gathering; the spiritual centre of a Māori village). The play dramatizes a quest for roots, for Māori identity, the attempt to repossess the land confiscated by the Pākehā (New Zealanders of Anglo-Celtic descent) people (23). The genuine reunion will be achieved, the play suggests, when the Māori community finally gets rid of all Pākehā materialistic values and rediscovers the spirituality of Māori myths, as encoded in the *tukutuku* panel. The play's action thus moves towards forgiveness. The family ancestor, Awatea, eventually lifts the curse that has transformed the community into a wasteland.

The first scenes introduce the main characters, Hohepa, Tyler, and Hohepa's greedy second son Matawera who wears Hohepa's *taonga* (treasure), a sign that Tyler takes to mean that he has usurped power and legitimacy. Tyler does not think he possesses the *mana* (honour) necessary to heal the community. The sense of uprootedness that fractured the community after Bubba's death is powerfully expressed by Hohepa: 'Such a confusing day, every memory lost. . . . The clouds have covered the sea with their own image, and I can find nothing. . . . So cold, so cold and all alone' (37). The action of the play further relies on a ghost-like character, Kui, a near-blind old woman. She is the reincarnation of the deceased Aggie, Hohepa's former wife and Bubba's mother. She represents the spiritual legacy of Māori tradition, whose presence brings about the lifting of the community curse. She feels deeply in touch with the sacred significance of Tyler's woven panel, which she describes as a *tukutuku* suggesting the harmonious reunion of the fractured family in the netherword (38-41).

In Act III, Aggie reveals that Bubba was meant to become the leader of the *whānau* (family). As such, he was to be given the same name as the community ancestor, Awatea. However, he was cruelly drowned by his jealous half-brother, Matawera, before he could be properly named. Hohepa's hope for peace and regeneration finds its realization at the end of the play. Eventually, the old man feels persuaded he has found his Bubba again, in a kind of epiphanic moment: '*Hohepa leaps back, amazed. He has seen his baby*' (100). Hohepa further suggests that Bubba has now inherited the name of his ancestor Awatea. This repossession of spiritual identity really occurs through the art of *tukutuku* weaving, as the voice of Bubba indicates: 'They are weaving my story. Daddy' (105). Further, Matawera eventually accepts Bubba being given his true name, thus exorcising his own evil nature in a final gesture of spiritual reconciliation.

The last scene, entitled 'Purapurawhetū', marks the completion of both the drama and the *tukutuku* weaving. In the last moments of the play, the name of Bubba/Awatea is metaphorically woven into the *Purapurawhetū* panel, which encodes the spiritual reunification of the *whānau*. The curse is lifted, as the spirit of Bubba/Awatea affirms the healing power of naming, a typical Māori belief: 'AWATEA: The place where I dance is an over place./An above place./From here we can see everything./We touch and circle and laugh./Mostly we sparkle./My name is Awatea' (111). Thus, Grace-Smith's fusion of the Māori art of weaving and theater enables her to lend a sacred dimension to her work, in the form of a local theatrical idiom that clearly differs from the stage language developed by Clements and the Spiderwoman collective, a further sign of the multiple ways in which globalization can be negotiated. Indeed, her use of magic realism combines with Māori weaving to create a unique stage aesthetic.

* * *

Summing up, my three case studies demonstrate that Aboriginal playwrights, in different regions of the globe, freely borrow from various artistic genres in an attempt to escape the constrictions of Euro-American realism. The complex patterns of these writers' dramatic techniques and transgeneric devices reflect the specific characteristics of their Native cultures in an increasingly globalized age. This rapidly developing artistic phenomenon will require the careful scrutiny of Comparative Literature specialists in decades to come.

NOTES

1. I have provided a more comprehensive theoretical account of globalization criticism in the introduction to a special issue of *Theatre Research in Canada*, co-edited with Reid Gilbert (Gilbert and Maufort).
2. Throughout this essay, I shall use the terms 'Indigenous' and 'Aboriginal' interchangeably, emphasizing their transnational connotations. By contrast, the terms 'Native' and 'First Nations' (a typically Canadian phrase) will primarily refer to North American Indigenous material.
3. I have offered a more thorough analysis of Clements's *Burning Vision* and its historical focus in an essay entitled 'Voices of Cultural Memory: Enacting History in Recent Native Canadian Drama' (170–75). Likewise, additional background information on *Copper Thunderbird* can be found in my essay entitled 'Celebrating Indigeneity: Contemporary Aboriginal Playwriting

in Canada and Australasia' (102–107). Marie Clements's dramaturgies have attracted so much critical attention in recent years that a special issue of *Theatre Research in Canada,* guest edited by Reid Gilbert, was devoted to her entire work (*TRiC* 31.2, 2010).

4. In my book *Labyrinth of Hybridities, Avatars of O'Neillian Realism in Multi-ethnic American Drama (1972–2003),* I have provided a detailed analysis of Spiderwoman's hybridization of O'Neillian realism in this particular play (156–59).
5. For more details about Briar Grace-Smith's reinvention of Western codes of stage realism in this particular play, the reader should turn to my book, *Transgressive Itineraries. Postcolonial Hybridizations of Dramatic Realism* (224–31).

   Also of importance in this context is Chandra Mohan's team work on Indian and Pacific literature in the framework of his ICLA-sponsored research committee: 'Research Committee on Literary and Inter-Relationships between India, its Neighboring Countries, and the World'.

REFERENCES

Clements, Marie and Rita Leistner, *Burning Vision*, Vancouver: Talonbooks, 2003.

———, *Copper Thunderbird*, Vancouver: Talonbooks, 2007.

———, *The Edward Curtis Project: A Modern Picture Story*, Vancouver: Talonbooks, 2010.

Curtis, Edward Sheriff, *The North American Indian*, 25th anniversary edn., Cologne: Taschen, 2005.

Damrosch, David, *What Is World Literature?*, Princeton and Oxford: Princeton University Press, 2003.

Darby, Jaye T. and Stephanie Fitzgerald, eds., *Keepers of the Morning Star: An Anthology of Native Women's Theater*, Los Angeles: UCLA American Indian Studies Centre, 2003.

Däwes, Birgit, ed., *Indigenous North American Drama: A Multivocal History*, Albany: SUNY Press, 2013.

Delbaere, Jeanne, 'Psychic Realism, Mythic Realism, Grotesque Realism: Variations on Magic Realism in Contemporary Literature in English', in *Magical Realism: Theory, History, Community*, ed. Lois Parkinson Zamora and Wendy B. Faris, Duke University Press, 1995, pp. 249–63.

George, Miria, *Urban Hymns*, in *Three Plays: Young and Hungry*, Wellington: Playmarket, 2010, pp. 119–77.

Gilbert, Helen and Jacqueline Lo, *Performance and Cosmopolitics: Cross-cultural Transactions in Australasia*, Houndsmill: Palgrave Macmillan, 2007.

Gilbert, Reid, ed., Special Issue on Marie Clements, *Theatre Research in Canada*, vol. 31, no. 2, 2010.

Grace-Smith, Briar, *Purapurawhetū*, Wellington: Huia Publishers, 1999.

Figueira, Dorothy and Marc Maufort, eds., *Theatres in the Round: Multi-ethnic, Indigenous, and Intertextual Dialogues in Drama*, Brussels: P.I.E. Peter Lang, 2011.

Knowles, Ric, *Theatre and Interculturalism*, Houndsmill: Palgrave Macmillan, 2010.

Maufort, Marc, 'Celebrating Indigeneity: Contemporary Aboriginal Playwriting in Canada and Australasia', in *Theatres in the Round*, ed. Dorothy Figueira and Marc Maufort, 2011, pp. 91–108.

———, *Labyrinth of Hybridities: Avatars of O'Neillian Realism in Multi-ethnic American Drama (1972–2003)*, Brussels: P.I.E. Peter Lang, 2010.

———, *Transgressive Itineraries: Postcolonial Hybridizations of Dramatic Realism*, Brussels: P.I.E. Peter Lang, 2003.

———, 'Voices of Cultural Memory: Enacting History in Recent Native Canadian Drama', in *Indigenous North American Drama*, ed. Birgit Däwes, New York: SUNY Press, 2013, pp. 159–76.

Maufort, Marc and Reid Gilbert, 'Introduction: Canadian Performances/Global Redefinitions', *Theatre Research in Canada*, vol. 34, no. 1, 2013, pp. 1–5.

Rebellato, Dan, *Theatre and Globalization*, Houndsmill: Palgrave Macmillan, 2009.

Spiderwoman Theater, *Winnetou's Snake Oil Show from Wigwam City*, in *Keepers of the Morning Star*, ed. Jaye T. Darby and Stephanie Fitzgerald, pp. 229–62.

Spivak, Gayatri Chakravorty, *Death of a Discipline*, New York: Columbia University Press, 2003.

Zamora, Lois Parkinson and Wendy B. Faris, eds., *Magical Realism: Theory, History, Community*, Durham and London: Duke University Press, 1995.

21

In Quest of the Other: Literature, Methodology, and Ethics—Reflections on Calvino's *If on a winter's night a traveller*

Sieghild Bogumil-Notz

COMPARATIVE LITERATURE AND THE FIRST PERIOD OF CULTURAL STUDIES

AT THE VERY moment when Comparative Literature was conceived as a systematic field of study, i.e. in the second half of the nineteenth century, there was no doubt that literature had to be placed into a non-literary context. In this regard, Herder, a German Romantic poet and thinker of the eighteenth century, assumes a pioneering role by focusing on the prominent role climate, landscape, historical conditions, and the character that a given population plays in the creation of a literary work. In other words, Herder stressed the geographical and cultural context that shapes individual languages and literatures. The nineteenth-century French philosopher and historian, Hippolyte Taine, then conceived these contextual references in the language of his epoch, underscoring, as he put it, the 'race', the 'milieu', and the 'moment'. Thus, Comparative Literature, since its very inception as an academic discipline, took into account specific cultural contexts. The external components even became so predominant that the classical question of the inherent aesthetic quality of a literary work became less significant. Scrutinizing the intrinsic value of a literary work accepted by all 'men of good taste' beyond any geographic and temporal difference was rejected as the primary method of analysis. Instead, critics changed their orientation and began to base their aesthetic evaluation on the very differences themselves. The specific national, historical, and social contexts, as the foundation from which creation originates, became the basis for aesthetic value. The quality of a literary work was evaluated according to the density, intensity, and the extent of its representation. A literary work was judged by how it reflected the conditions under which it was produced. The relationship between work/ author and non-literary conditions was regarded from the perspective of cause and effect, firmly tied together by the idea of a logical, scientific mechanism of representation. Thus, positivism as a scientific method entered into the comparative literary criticism that, at its best, produced something akin to what we today call Cultural Studies.

We can pause here and examine what can be considered not only a methodological threshold, but more profoundly an epistemological clash in order to examine in greater depth this epoch-making moment and reflect on what actually occurred when classical aesthetics were replaced. It can be acknowledged that literary critics were aware of literature's 'other Self', that is, history as a literary category, or rather, history as a narrative that narrates literature or says what literature is meant to say. History *is* already literature. The old Aristotelian controversy between minor history only telling facts and philosophical literature dealing with probabilities and necessities[1] has after more than two millennia found a new formulation. History gives birth to literature. However, history as the constitutive Other of literature obliges critics to proceed with their endless quests for the Other. Calvino's novel, *If on a winter's night a traveller* offers a particularly striking example of this process. It is not our aim here to discuss all the methodological aspects of Calvino's work. A summarizing glance will suffice.

For more than a century, positivism has held sway, although various movements and schools have intervened. As a method, positivism constantly changed its shape under the influence of the diverse currents in literary studies, such as the sociological perspective fiercely defended in England by H.M. Posnett, *Geistesgeschichte*, psychological or formalist trends. Moreover, the meaning of literature itself has changed, just as the stories change in Calvino's novel—until the linguistic turn asserted itself in the sixties and seventies and relegated historical-literary narratives to the background.

COMPARATIVE LITERATURE AND THE CULTURAL TURN

Art undergoes transformations, as Celan pointed out in *The Meridian*. It is 'tenacious', a 'long living' problem, and 'eternal'. Since 'art continued living', literature as a historical narrative necessarily rebounded. It came back under the auspices of Cultural Studies. Having been practiced in the United States and Great Britain[2] for several decades, Cultural Studies became a topic of inquiry in Germany in the last decade of the twentieth century. Conceived as a 'cultural turn', Cultural Studies had a similar effect in literature as the above-mentioned focus on history in literature. Dismissing textual autoreflexivity, its construction, deconstruction, and the exclusivity of language as the literary medium, critics called for the inclusion of Cultural Studies in literary studies or even the replacement of literary studies with Cultural Studies.[3]

In response to such reformulations, the question to be asked is whether anything new has, in fact, surfaced since the nineteenth century. Of course, one difference is immediately striking. After a century of epistemological and methodological history, the notion of culture has completely changed. It now includes all areas beyond traditional literary fields, such as popular culture, the history of the everyday life, anthropology, gender studies, media and communications, the role of institutional influences, and problems of globalization. But, it also includes new methods such as New Historicism, discourse analysis, etc. All human products, material and immaterial, private and public, are now part of the concept of culture; they include theoretical, autocritical, and interdisciplinary perspectives as well as questions of interculturality.[4] Cultural Studies today are founded on a dynamic concept of culture in opposition to the restricted static cultural system of Herder and Taine. Dynamics are, in fact, emphasized since the notion of interculturality and its implicit presupposition of mutual encounter and exchange have shifted to encompass the unlimited concept of transculturality. Its starting point is the awareness of globalization. Cultural Studies are grounded on the assumption that, in a globalized world, cultures, languages, and literatures cannot be clearly defined. Their boundaries are fluid; areas inter-penetrate each other. Cultures, languages, and literatures are hybrid and need a new methodological and even a new linguistic approach.[5] However, here as before,[6] the 'baby is thrown out with the bath water' and Comparative Literature as a discipline is at stake.[7] The baby is the text and like a baby, it is an open, hybrid personality, but a personality nevertheless. One can see that literary studies in general and especially Comparative Literature are strong or weak depending on the attention they pay to the text.

This observation leads to another difference. Actually, literary studies do not blindly submit to Cultural Studies. Certain comparatists are particularly opposed to it, even though they generally accept that the all embracing point of view is inherent in Comparative Literature itself. Cultural Studies, thus, became a challenge to the discipline. Yet, the methodological position of most European comparatists was quickly articulated. It was and is still not a question of opposing Cultural Studies on principle and excluding its followers from the comparative approach to literature. But Cultural Studies must not, as it was the case during the positivist period, dictate how we analyse texts. On the contrary, literary texts continue to be the core of the discipline. They may be hybrid and open, but no less the unit of measure, even though they might exist in fragmentary form. Here again, Calvino's novel offers a striking example. One can say that the text is surrounded by a kind of perforated border. It is like a human being who is nothing on her own but who nevertheless has her own personality. Thus, instead of admitting that the text is submerged by the polyperspectivism of the mammoth discipline of Cultural Studies, one accepts the latter in order to support the expansion of the field of Comparative Literature, to contribute to enlarging the corpus of literatures under examination, and to develop heterogeneous fields of research.

Finally there is a third important difference between this current formulation and traditional Cultural Studies. The target of traditional Cultural Studies was different. In opposition to Goethe's claim for a *Weltliteratur* in lieu of national literatures, the Romantics successfully established the national literatures as well-defined entities. They were interested in Cultural Studies insofar as it offered the basis for comparison and contributed to the revaluation of the individual literary work's literality. This limitation had a long life. Only after one hundred and fifty years, since the so-called cultural turn and the idea of globalization (which can be considered the other side of the same coin) have the boundaries between the two formulations begun to break down. The consequence is a renewed interest in Goethe's concept of *Weltliteratur*.[8]

GOETHE'S CONCEPTION OF *WELTLITERATUR* AND THE OTHER

Our interest here is not to trace all the facets of the notion of *Weltliteratur* nor its history. Instead, we want to point out the features this concept has in common with the contemporary idea of literary globalization. The parallel between *Weltliteratur* and global literature at first may seem quite strange, yet both concepts call for comparison, since they have their source in a similar historical situation. Both notions emerged at a time of great technical and scientific innovation that produced a general acceleration and expansion of economic and communicative exchange. Also, in the eighteenth century, distances ceased to matter—new speed in modes of transport facilitated easy interconnectivity. The increase in daily, weekly, and monthly journals, the boom of translations, individual travel, and a flourishing culture of personal correspondence all contributed to bring nations and literatures together. Goethe clearly expressed the analogy between technical innovation and literature in a letter to Carlyle encouraging both himself and his friend to make more liberal use of new communication options.[9] Literature becomes an international phenomenon beyond European boundaries. Here again, the comparison does not at first glance seem evident. The invention of the steam engine and the acceleration of the postal service cannot be compared with the high speed and global connection of today's high-tech aviation and the internet. Yet, as Manfred Koch points out, in spite of all the differences in the degree and density of today's world-embracing communication, the process is structurally the same.[10] Goethe was aware of the transformations of his day, especially of the worldwide economic exchange that he took as a model for literary exchange. One projects onto the Other one's own qualities and, in turn, appropriates the qualities of the Other for oneself, as seen in Goethe's use of Shakespeare. In his conversation with Eckermann on 18 January 1825, Goethe refers to what we currently call an intertextual procedure: 'Thus my Mephistopheles sings a song of Shakespeare, and why should he not? Why should I take the trouble to invent one on my own, if the one of Shakespeare was just right and said just what it had to say?'[11] World Literature, for Goethe, is not a static token, but the product of a communicative process in which the author's rights do not exist. Rather, all texts can contribute to the larger text of *Weltliteratur.* This notion is not limited to knowledge of all other literatures accessible in a given epoch. Rather, *Weltliteratur* produces a new kind of globally intertextual text similar to a genuine hybrid text. Goethe defends this sort of hybridity: 'Let us be versatile! Little Brandenburg turnips are delicious, best when mixed with chestnuts, and both these noble fruits grow far off from each other.—Do not object to find in our diverse writings beside the Western and Northern forms also the Eastern and Southern ones'.[12] No doubt, Goethe refers to his 'hybrid' text par excellence, the *West-Östlicher Divan.*

At the same time, Goethe combines his vision of a new World Literature with the ethical claim for a new humanity. He stresses that by looking at other literatures, one becomes aware of convergent and divergent orientations that allow us to exceed the limited nationalist conception of literature the Romantics claimed at the time. Examining the Other actually helps to minimize one's own difference. As a consequence, particularities give way to an understanding of humanity as a whole. Awareness of the Other does not guarantee peace for Goethe. He did hope, however, that people would become less cruel and less arrogant.

Even if they do not start loving each other, they may become more tolerant: '[...] we repeat that it is out of the question that nations shall think in the same way, rather they just shall become aware of each other, understand each other, and, if they do not love each other, they should at least learn to tolerate each other'.[13] World Literature is a process of transnational interaction where national differences are ignored in order to educate people and contribute to a unique universally cultivated society of a perfect humanity. Especially in the eighteenth century, literature had not only a pedagogical but also an eminently political dimension.

When Goethe championed literary exchange in order to promote *Weltliteratur*, he had a clear understanding of the importance of the Other. However, the poet broaches as a matter of course an issue that has become today a complex and complicated theme. According to classical philosophy and ethics, the human being is the same at every place and at every time beyond any historical, geographical or social considerations. Kant defines the autonomy of the subject in the following manner: man acts according to a priori rules which, in principle, originate in him as an individual with responsibility to both humanity and himself, and from which universal rules can be derived. Man, by following these laws, finds the dignity of a moral and, therefore, free being.[14] Thus, differences are not relevant and the Other is a problem for Goethe since the Self and the Other are identical. In a conversation with Eckermann, the poet defines his position with all desirable clarity: 'The world always stays the same, [. . .] the conditions repeat themselves, one nation lives, loves and feels like the other one, so why should one poet not write poetry like the other one? The situations of life are alike, so why should the situations of the poems not be alike?'[15] Intellectual property does not exist; every poet can say the same thing under similar conditions. Consequently, everyone can make use of the utterances of the other. World Literature as an accumulation of 'hybrid' texts is self-evident.

However, the question is whether Goethe can really be considered to stand side by side with critics such as Homi K. Bhabha in his defense of hybrid texts as a viable approach to the Other. Does Goethe really anticipate the actual discussion of whether and how we can understand the Other? Having applied this notion to Goethe, we perhaps should put it in quotation marks or speak of 'a sort of' hybridity. Indeed, Goethe's intertextuality seems to produce a 'hybrid' text that, in spite of an apparent similarity on the surface, has nothing in common with it. Hybridity presupposes a consciousness of differences. In contrast,

Goethe excludes and even annihilates this consciousness. Therefore, we cannot properly speak of hybridity with regard to Goethe's conception of the world's literary texts. Rather, they are a kind of patchwork with smooth transitions. The individual's contributions are scarcely recognizable, as in the case of the *West-Östlicher Divan*, whose poems are in part based on the poetic correspondence between the aged Goethe and his young mistress, Marianne von Willemer. In this compendium, the poet included poems or parts of poems the young lady wrote in response to poems by Goethe.

THE ENCOUNTER WITH THE OTHER IN THE CURRENT ETHICAL DISCUSSION

In the present context, we do not pretend to offer a summary of the current discussions on Otherness[16]. The following reflections attempt instead to underscore the direction severe discussions have taken in recent years.

Cultural Studies today focuses mainly on difference. The perspective has generally been imposed by changes in the world's economic situation. In the case of our discipline, the concept of World Literature has become global literature. In the context of the global village, differences necessarily prevail, leading to new transformations which in turn, provoke identity shock. One had to realize that the Other is completely unknown to oneself. This experience engenders disorientation and insecurity. Emmanuel Levinas in particular, concentrated on scrutinizing Otherness. In his work *Totality and Infinity* (1961), he examined how the face-to-face relationship is always incongruent. There cannot be an assimilating dialogue or any kind of hermeneutic understanding. On the contrary, the incongruity of the face-to-face is, in fact, the real encounter. For Levinas, it is a question of one's responsibility for the Other and maintaining this incompatibility.

Gilles Deleuze proposed another answer to the problem of encounter. He introduced the perspective of the nomad and claims that nomadic life is the 'strongest exercise of depersonalization',[17] of throwing oneself 'into the mental position',[18] a method of those who think in a different manner. It is the only way, he argued, to find one's own identity.

Cultural critics like Homi K. Bhabha or Edward Said have questioned the domination of Western cultural politics and colonialism's repression of the Other. They have both ensured that one can no longer ignore the issue of difference, be it on the linguistic-literary, cultural, or political front. In *The Location of Culture* (1994), Bhabha suggested a solution to this problem. Even though his focus was on a concrete political engagement of minorities and minority cultures, he questioned how one encounters the Other. In this regard, his approach resembles that of Levinas. Indeed, Bhabha invites the readers to respect the Other insofar as the utterance of the one meets the utterance of the Other without any mediation. Opposites join each other without themselves intermingling. They form rather a hybrid whole, with meaning emerging out of the interstices produced by the shock of encounter. In a hybrid text, differences speak and create new meanings. There is no restrictive comparison,[19] no annihilating amputation or distortion. We encounter free manifestations of diversity, producing new and unknown meaning.

How can this work? Bhabha exemplifies this process in his commentary on installations by the Puerto Rican multi-media artist Pepón Osorio and the poem *Names* by the Caribbean poet Derek Walcott. These works of art offer striking examples for the unmediated encounter of different cultures. But can such a shock also be produced within the same culture? Following Levinas, any Other, even within the same culture, is unknown. Perhaps this is exactly the starting point of Calvino's novel *If on a winter's night a traveller*, which exemplifies the encounter with the unknown at the core of one's own intimate space.

In view of Bhabha's or Said's global political engagement, the shift into the private sphere of everyday life may seem a fanciful disregard for urgent global challenges. However, daily life is not pure emptiness; on the contrary, it is the stuff of which dreams are made. The more the course of events (or even non-events) is plain, the more a meaningful transformation of the discontinuity underlying any hybrid manifestation becomes obvious. In this regard, Calvino's novel can provide a framework for the passage from blank space to the sense-producing practice of hybridity.

If on a winter's night a traveller

Calvino's novel, *If on a winter's night a traveller* (*Se una notte d'inverno un viaggiatore*, 1979) is quite curious. It is composed of a series of beginnings to novels. Opening with the first novel that stops abruptly, the fictive Reader seeks in vain for a novel that actually comes to a conclusion. Only at the end of the novel does the Reader almost finish the first novel he wanted to read at the beginning. He then discovers that it is none other than 'If on a winter's night a traveller' written by the fictive author Calvino. In other words, the Italian author Italo Calvino (1923–85) takes up the topic of the complexity of otherness by including and beginning with his own identity and demonstrating how we can or cannot approach the

Other and what it means to approach the Other. The way the Reader looks for the Other leads us as readers to question the possibility of any practical encounter with the absolutely unknown Other.

The fictive reader called 'Reader' is without any personal qualification which could be seen as 'indiscreet' (33)[20] Throughout the entire novel, the omniscient narrator quite intimately addresses this Reader with the second-personal pronoun 'you'. The reader begins to read a newly published fiction entitled 'If on a winter's night a traveller' written by a fictive author called Calvino. After thirty pages, the story is interrupted and the second chapter begins with the following comment of the narrator: 'You have now read about thirty pages and you're becoming caught up in the story. At a certain point you remark' (29)—in short, the novel starts again nearly from its beginning, and so it does again and again until the end of the book. Angry about the defective production of the edition, the Reader returns to the bookshop in order to exchange the book. However he is told that the book he wanted to read is not the book he had begun to read. The bookbinder has been mistaken; he has confused the pages so that the Reader had actually read the beginning of a Polish novel entitled 'Outside the Town of Malbork' by Tazio Bazakbal. Since the Reader had liked the beginning of this book, he abandons his search for the novel of Calvino and takes the Polish novel in its place. Yet again, he is the victim of an error, since the new text had nothing to do with the novel by Bazakbal. Even before the end of the first chapter, the text is interrupted every two pages by two blank pages, 'blank, printed; blank, printed; and so on until the end' (43). The Reader loses the thread of the narration, asks himself whether there is any relationship with the Polish novel. His consultation of dictionaries and encyclopaedias regarding the quite strange personal names and toponyms does not help, and he remains very confused. He tries to phone the female reader Ludmilla whom he has come to know in the library. She has had the same problem with Calvino's novel and had also wanted to continue reading the Polish book. When the Reader first saw the female reader, he felt immediately attracted to her: 'And so the Other Reader makes her happy entrance into your field of vision, Reader, or, rather, into the field of your attention; or, rather, you have entered a magnetic field from whose attraction you cannot escape. Don't waste time, then, you have a good excuse to strike up a conversation, a common ground, . . . go ahead, what are you waiting for?' (29). The encouragement of the Reader by the narrator is the signal for the love story to develop during the novel, although it goes unnoticed by us as readers. Its vicissitudes are as confusing as the imbroglio of the novels. Indeed, for a long time, the Reader cannot make contact with Ludmilla and has to speak on the phone through an intermediary (her pushy sister). In short, both plots are intimately tied together in such a way that they reflect each other. The story of reading and the desire to read parallels the tale of the erotic desire. In other words, there is no difference between the love of reading and the love of a person. As the novel demonstrates, they have the same impact on the characters. Professor Uzzi-Tuzzi's and Ludmilla's discussions on the act of reading touch upon the theme of identity: 'Reading', the Professor says, 'is always this: There is a thing that is there, a thing made of writing, a solid, material object, which cannot be changed, and through this thing we measure ourselves against something else that is not present, something else that belongs to the immaterial, invisible world, because it can only be thought imagined, or because it was once and is no longer, past, lost unattainable, in the land of the dead'. Ludmilla continues: 'Or that is not present because it does not yet exist, something desired, feared, possible or impossible.... Reading is going toward something that is about to be, and no one yet knows what it will be' (65). This last remark makes a very valid point: to read is the encounter of the Other as the absolute unknown—it is akin to love.

We readers are, however, unaware of the situation. The suspense of the novel makes it resemble a detective story, focusing on the male and female readers' search for the novel they want to read, whether it is Calvino's novel or the Polish one which they learn is actually yet another book, entitled 'Leaning from the Steep Slope' by the Cimmerian writer Ukko Ahti. This book, in turn, reveals itself to be the beginning of still another novel, i.e. the Cambrian novel 'Without fear of vertigo and wind' written by an author whose pseudonym is Vorts Viljandi and who has written in Cimmerian and Cambrian, the convolutions continue on and on, until the end. The source book, so to speak, Calvino's novel, is long out of sight even as the Reader pursues endlessly his quest of the 'Other' which leads him from book to book and, at the same time, from the bookshop to the female reader, to Professor Uzzi-Tuzzi, to his Cambrian rival Galligani, and finally to the publishing house of all these novels. There, a new dimension of the imbroglio emerges with reference to the existence of a translator, Ermes Marana, who wrote the translation of the Cimmerian or Cambrian novel. The editor learns that Marana does not know a single word of Cimmerian or Cambrian. Later, Marana pretends to translate the book by the Polish author Bazakbal, which is actually the French work, *Looks down in the gathering shadow*, written by the Belgian author Bertrand Vandervelde. The publishing house then tries to follow the translator's attempts to trace all the novels and to replace those copies that are already in print. The Reader continues to make a number of errors until he finally comes into possession of a single copy of the last novel. The Reader is allowed to read it, and again, it has nothing to do with any of the previously mentioned novels. The original novels and their sources are fading away in the same way as the authors do. The translator Ermes Marana lives up to his namesake, the god Hermes. He is not only the messenger of Zeus and the God of thieves and impostors, but also the god of travellers, the inventor of numbers, weights, and the alphabet. He can tell the future and he is the author of esoteric writings. As Hermes Trismegistus, he is the god of arcane knowledge. Through his various impostures, everything disappears and, logically, he does so, too. He himself epitomizes imposture: 'All the papers in the Marana business have vanished. His typescripts, the original texts, Cambrian, Polish, French. He's vanished, everything's vanished, overnight' (100). One would say that nearly all the meanings of his name coalesce in his character as an impostor.

Meanwhile, the Reader is taken to a third fictional level: he does not read a novel or the translation of a novel, but the copy of the translation of a novel. The translator communicates exclusively by letter and explains the chaos he has caused in the following manner: As time passes by, the names on the book covers come to mean nothing. They can disappear, their works may not survive, they can be attributed to an anonymous author or different works can be ascribed to a single author (88). The editor confirms: 'The author was an invisible point from which books came, a void travelled by ghosts' (88). This assessment is immediately proved by the actions of Marana who now becomes ubiquitous, travelling the five continents. He mails letters whose stamps do not correspond to the country from which they are sent; their chronology is also incorrect, and they consist of a mass of tangled topics. One letter speaks about an old Indio called the 'Father of Stories' whom some consider 'the original source of narrative material, the primordial magma from which the individual manifestations of each writer develop' (101). Some consider him to be a visionary putting himself into contact with others of similar temperament through the use of hallucinogenic mushrooms. Others think he is a reincarnation of Homer or of other famous authors. In short, even the originary narrative source is obliterated. Meanwhile, the narrative form of the letters changes: from commercial information to fantastic mystifications, to detective stories, to Scheherazadian tales, to the plot of a hi-jacking, and so forth. At the same time, the female reader undergoes change. However, the Reader, who lives all these narratives as events of his own life, can see only one face behind the different female figures, the visage of Ludmilla. What remains is the imbroglio of the plot lines, or, as the title of one of the fragmentary narratives says, 'a network of lines that intersect'. What also remains are the two other constituents of the narrative, i.e. the Reader and the narrator. Even though they become multiple—the Reader at the end splits into eight types and the narrator, in chapter VIII, assumes the role of the Irish author Silas Flannery without giving up his function as the narrator—the Reader, Ludmilla, and the narrator are firm references throughout the endlessly deviating novel.

The more the narratives become confused and ultimately vanish in the mist of a non-ending fictionalisation, the more Ludmilla takes shape. She and the nameless male Reader slowly approach each other even though she is as elusive as the books they seek. Nevertheless, the love story progresses until both are lying in bed making love. It is the moment when Calvino directly identifies the act of reading with the erotic act: 'Ludmilla, now you are being read. Your body is being subjected to a systematic reading.... And you, too, O Reader, are meanwhile an object of reading: the Other Reader now is reviewing your body' (132). The love story continues to be mediated by the story of reading so when the Reader decides at the very end of the novel to marry Ludmilla, this turn of events seems sudden. The seventh reader asks the first one (i.e. the Reader) whether he really believes that a story should have a beginning and an end, the narrator responds: 'You stop for a moment to reflect on these words. Then, in a flash, you decide you want to marry Ludmilla' (215). But for those who have realized the intersection of the two stories, the conclusion is not surprising: it coincides with the Reader finishing the novel 'If on a winter's night a traveller'.

STRAIGHT THROUGH THE CHAOS—THE OTHER

Calvino's novel is an extremely intricate novel. Even the narrative thread highlighted above is confusing and entangled. It gets lost, appears again, changes, and then deviates. The chaos is absolute. The Reader, as well as readers are confronted with the pure otherness which is intangible because it is constantly changing. Neverthless the Reader finally does meet Ludmilla. She is ever-changing in so far that the Reader lends her features to all the fictive female figures he encounters in the different novelistic fragments. However, the narrator underscores that even in the most intimate union they are disunited: 'At the moment when you most appear to be a united *voi*, a second person plural, you are two *tu's* more separate and circumscribed than before. (This is already true now, when you are still occupied, each with the other's presence, in an exclusive fashion. Imagine how it will be in a little while, when ghosts that do not meet will frequent your minds accompanying the encounters of your bodies tested by habit)' (132). The Other remains unattainable. The same history does not unite the I and the Other. On the contrary, it provokes an endless quest for the Other. Each episode, no matter how meaningless, not only entails the whole past life of the Self but merges together with other events or other lives of the Self. All these kinds of lives finally find each other and compose a whole life, 'my life' (92).

In light of this reading of Calvino's novel, the initial question of this essay becomes pertinent: How does one communicate with the Other? The answer, while logical, may be surprising. The consequence of all the hybrid lives of the Self leads to the following conclusion: when one narrates one story, all the other stories inevitably burst forth. Narration opens 'a space full of stories', says the protagonist of one of the novelistic fragments, 'that perhaps is simply my lifetime, where you can move in all directions, as in a space, always finding stories that cannot be told until other stories are told first, and so, setting out from any moment or place, you encounter always the same density of material to be told' (92). Thus, even the most marginal, anecdotal episodes and the most meaningless details are worth narrating for two reasons. It is a generally known fact that the identity of a person is a hybrid whole constituted by other lives. Moreover, one not only lives necessarily all kinds of otherness, but the Self Is Located in otherness. Thus, the Other inevitably appears as a part of one's own life with all its unattainable distance, just as one's own life is unattainable in its whole amplitude. The Other is as intangible as we are ourselves immeasurable. In this regard, the I Is the Other, as Rimbaud and, before him, Nerval both noted. Finally, one cannot speak anymore of the Self; he/she is for ever the Other. The I constituted in narrative is a permanent source of challenge, desire, enrichment, and love. Following its challenge and appeal, one comes to interact with what is still Other. The love story of the Reader and Ludmilla shows how communication is not possible in an absolute sense. This lack of ultimate reason, termed by Derrida the absence of origin, its presence represents the point where our existence is rooted is ineffable and alien. It makes all our actions and gestures contingent. At the same time, it initiates and stimulates fragments of dialogues that make the novel or life move forword.

The question then arises: How does one live in this otherness? Calvino shows that it is by following the challenge and through desire. Even if one gets hopelessly lost, one cannot really be lost. There is nothing that would not be in one's own interest. Following Calvino, one could formulate a new motto: Dare to be a traveller. In the context of global literature, differences, i.e. the Other as opposed to the Self, prevails. We should begin to think of ourselves as the Other, we should undertake the quest for the Other, even the most distant and alien Other. We should search for part of ourselves in order to complete our lives through such continual transformation. 'The best way to learn to know oneself is to look for understanding the Other'.[21] It is the kind of nomadism that Deleuze calls for, yet with a major difference: the transgression is no transgression and it does not entail depersonalisation. On the contrary, the Self as the Other finds in what is still Other greater fulfilment and accomplishment. One does not abandon anything, rather one becomes enriched. I am not making a plea for any relativism, irresponsibility, or selfishness. Quite the contrary, seeking the Other on behalf of ourselves implies a reorientation in regard to ethics, identity, and difference.

The question then becomes: how does the relationship between the Self and the Other impact on the aims and methodology of Comparative Literature? It is clear that the concept of national literature has to be revised. It has become obsolete insofar as all the 'other' literatures belong to a single national one that is no longer national but global at its very origin. The literary material of the comparatist is one literature in its worldwide dimension. This concept of global literature is different from the notion of World Literature as well as from our current understanding of globality because both imply the idea of distinction and transgression of the Self and the Other. One might object that most of the 'other' literatures can only be known in translations. It is not really a problem, because translations are a part of the literature of the target language. Therefore, comparatists should henceforth focus on translation. Another objection can be refuted in the same easy way. To conceive a unique literary corpus that includes all literatures does not mean to assimilate the other literatures in the sense of Goethe's intertextual reading. There is a notable difference: continuity between texts is actually rare, whereas breaks are significant, as Calvino's novel shows. Constant discontinuity impedes assimilation or disfiguring reading. It becomes then the challenge for the comparatist to develop a new methodology, since the former mode of comparison is obsolete. General ethical, philosophical, and cultural topics become significant and lead to a new definition and understanding of the discipline, of the human being, of the concept of literature, and of its objectives.

A last question might be added: How does one negotiate such a mammoth task? A new tactic needs to be formulated: Dare to be a traveller and accept the challenge. Calvino again points us in the right direction: his Reader is tenacious and persists in pursuing his desire of reading even though—or rather just because—the object is always deferred. Thus, his desire remains desire, unfulfilled and always a challenge, as strong as erotic desire and, as we have noted, the two cannot be separated. The Other in its many forms continually stirs up desire. The Other is particularly challenging, since it consists of endless variations. Each Other involves his/her own network of narratives; the encounter with this Other results in other new narratives (133). Thus, an end of reading is not in sight. Calvino's text poses a stirring challenge for the comparatist, inviting him or her to engage in endless reading, contribute to 'other' approaches and to 'other' huge textual horizons that create 'other' histories.[22]

NOTES

1. Aristote, *Poetics*, in: Aristote, *Poétique*, Texte établi et traduit par J. Hardy, Paris: Société d'édition «Les Belles Lettres», 1965, chap. 9.
2. See Markus Fauser, *Kulturwissenschaft*, Darmstadt: Wissenschaftliche Buchgesellschaft, 2004, p. 32.
3. See Doris Bachmann-Medick, *Cultural Turns: Neuorientierungen in den Kulturwissenschaften*, Reinbek: Rowohlt, 2006, pp. 8–9.
4. See among others Johannes Anderegg and Edith Anna Kunz, eds., *Kulturwissenschaften: Positionen und Perspektiven*, Bielefeld: Aisthesis, 1999.
5. See the introduction to Dorothee Kimmich and Schamma Shahadat, eds., *Kulturen in Bewegung: Beiträge zur Theorie und Praxis der Transkulturalität*, Bielefeld: transcript, 2012, pp. 7–21, see pp. 7–10.
6. See Hans Robert Jauss, Das Ende der Kunstperiode—Aspekte der literarischen Revolution bei Heine, Hugo und Stendhal', in *Literaturgeschichte als Provokation*, Frankfurt am Main: Suhrkamp, 1970, pp. 107–43, see p. 120 sq.; p. 141 sq.
7. See Gayatri Chakravorty Spivak, 'Crossing Borders', in: id. *Death of a Discipline*, New York: Columbia University Press, 2003, pp. 1–23.
8. See among others: Elke Sturm-Trigonakis, *Global playing in der Literatur: Ein Versuch über die neue Weltliteratur*, Würzburg: Königshausen & Neumann, 2007 (English translation: *Comparative Cultural Studies and the New Weltliteratur*, West Lafayette, Indiana: Purdue University Press, 2013); Christopher Prendergast, ed., *Debating World Literature*, London, New York: Verso, 2004; Manfred Koch, *Weimaraner Weltbewohner: Zur Genese von Goethes Begriff 'Weltliteratur'*, Tübingen: Max Niemeyer, 2002; Manfred Schmeling, ed., *Weltliteratur heute: Konzepte und Perspektiven*, Würzburg: Königshausen & Neumann, 1995.

9. 'Lassen Sie uns der eröffneten Kommunication immer freyer gebrauchen!' Letter to Thomas Carlyle of 8 August 1828. In: Großherzogin Sophie von Sachsen, ed., *Goethe*: *Werke*, Weimar, Böhlau, 1887–1919 = Weimarer Ausgabe IV, 44, p. 257 (Repr.: München, Deutscher Taschenbuch Verlag, 1987). One cannot help remembering Rimbaud's poem *Ce qu'on dit au poète à propos de fleurs*. A generation later, in 1871, the poet had a similar experience of a new modern velocity and, for the same reason, he calls for a new poetic language which can be read from Tréguier, a small town in the northern France, to Paramaribo, the capital of a Dutch colony in South-America at that time.
10. 'Bei allen Unterschieden im Grad der realen Ausdehnung und Verdichtung weltumspannender Kommunikation handelt es sich dennoch strukturell um *einen* Prozeß', Manfred Koch, *Weimarer Weltbewohner*, op. cit., p. 14.
11. 'So singt mein Mephistopheles ein Lied von Shakespeare, und warum sollte er das nicht? Warum sollte ich mir die Mühe geben, ein eigenes zu erfinden, wenn das von Shakespeare eben recht war und eben das sagte, was es sollte?' In: Johann Peter Eckermann, *Gespräche mit Goethe in den letzten Jahren seines Lebens: 1823–1832: Erster Teil*, Leipzig: Brockhaus, Zweite mit einem Register versehene Ausgabe 1837, p. 192.
12. 'Laßt uns doch vielseitig sein! Märkische Rübchen schmecken gut, am besten gemischt mit Kastanien, und diese beiden edlen Früchte wachsen weit auseinander'.
    'Erlaubt uns in unsern vermischten Schriften doch neben den abend—und nordländischen Formen auch die morgen—und südländischen!' Goethe. *Maximen und Reflexionen*, nos. 966, 967, in: Erich Trunz, ed., *Goethes Werke*, t. 12: *Schriften zur Kunst; Schriften zur Literatur; Maximen und Reflexionen*, Hamburg: Christian Wegner, 5th edn., 1963, p. 502.
13. 'Nur wiederholen wir, dass nicht die Rede sein könne, die Nationen sollen überein denken, sondern sie sollen nur einander gewahr werden, sich begreifen, und, wenn sie sich wechselseitig nicht lieben mögen, sich einander wenigstens dulden lernen'. *Goethes Schriften zur Literatur*, in: Erich Trunz, ed., *Goethes Werke* t. 12, op. cit., p. 363. See also: Hendrik Birus, 'Goethes Idee der Weltliteratur: Eine historische Vergegenwärtigung', in: Manfred Schmeling, ed., *Weltliteratur heute. Konzepte und Perspektiven*, Würzburg: Königshausen & Neumann, 1995, pp. 5–28, see p. 15.
14. Immanuel Kant, *Kritik der praktischen Vernunft* (1788).
15. 'Die Welt bleibt immer dieselbe, . . . , die Zustände wiederholen sich, das eine Volk lebt, liebt und empfindet wie das andere, warum sollte denn der eine Poet nicht wie der andere dichten? Die Situationen des Lebens sind sich gleich, warum sollten denn die Situationen der Gedichte sich nicht gleich seyn?' Johann Peter Eckermann, *Gespräche mit Goethe in den letzten Jahren seines Lebens*, op. cit., p. 190.
16. For a larger survey see: Sieghild Bogumil-Notz, 'Minority Discourse between question and response', Paper presented at the 1st International

Conference on Comparative Literature at the Central University of Rajasthan, Kishangar, Ajmer.

17. Quote in Edzard Obendieck, *Der lange Schatten des babylonischen Turmes: Das Fremde und der Fremde in der Literatur*, Göttingen: Vandenhoeck & Ruprecht, 2000, p. 42.
18. J.S. Mill. *On Liberty*, quoted by Homi K. Bhabha, *The Location of Culture*, London and New York: Routledge, 1994, p. 23.
19. After 200 years, there is a relief of the guard, Comparative Literature does not mainly deal with comparison anymore, but it is focussing on the questions of general literature, not in the sense of van Tieghem, whose definition, up to now, belongs to the comparative part of the discipline, but in a more theoretical and philosophical sense. See for a larger methodological discussion: Sieghild Bogumil-Notz, 'Comparative Literature: Methodology and Challenges in Europe with Special Reference to the French and German Context', in: Rizio Yohannan, ed., *Quest of a Disciplne: New Academic Directions for Comparative Literature*, New Delhi: CUP, 2012, pp. 29–48.
20. The pages following the quotes of the novel refer to the English translation: *If on a winter's night a traveller*, tr. William Weaver, London: Vintage Books, 1998. Epub ISBN: 9781446414330. Version 1.0 www.Randomhouse.co.uk.
21. «Le meilleur moyen pour apprendre à se connaître, c'est de chercher à comprendre autrui». André Gide, *Journal*, Nouvelle Revue Française, 10/02/1922, Paris: Gallimard, Pléiade, p. 730.
22. I would like to thank Gregor Rehmer for reviewing the initial English version of the chapter.

Editors and Contributors

DOROTHY M. FIGUEIRA is Distinguished Research Professor, Department of Comparative Literature, University of Georgia, and former President, ICLA. Her research interests include religion and literature, translation theory, exoticism, myth theory, and travel narratives. Her publications include *The Hermeneutics of Suspicion: Cross-Cultural Encounters with India* (2015); *Theatres in the Round: Multi-Ethnic, Indigenous, and Intertextual Dialogues in Drama* (2011, co-edited with Marc Maufort); and *Otherwise Occupied: Theories and Pedagogies of Alterity* (2008).

CHANDRA MOHAN is the General Secretary, Comparative Literature Association of India and an Advisor, International Higher Education, Central University of Gujarat, Gandhinagar. He is Chair ICLA Standing Committee for Research on South Asian Literatures and Cultures. His recent publications include *Gender and Diversity: India, Canada and Beyond,* co-edited (Rawat Publications, 2015); *Interdisciplinary Alternatives in Comparative Literature* (Sage Publications, 2013) co-edited with E.V. Ramakrishnan and Harish Trivedi.

SIEGHILD BOGUMLL-NÖTZ has been a Professor at Paris-Sorbonne Ill and Ruhr University of Bochuri, Germany. She has also been a co-opted member of the Department for Theatre Studies and Professor at the universities of Wuppertal and Kassel. She specialises in theory of poetry, history and poetics of French, German, and Spanish poetry of the 19th to 20th century especially poetics and poetry of Paul Celan, contemporary German and French theatre, European and Indian intercultural encounters, comparative literature. Her latest edited English publication is *Heroes Anywhere and Forever: From a German, Indian and American Perspective* (2015).

ASSUMPTA CAMPS is Professor of Literary Translation and Italian Contemporary Literature at the University of Barcelona (Spain),

Department of Modern Languages and Literatures and English Studies, Faculty of Philology. Her latest books are: *La traducción y recepción de Ia literatura italiana* and *Italia en Ia prensa periOdica durante el fran quismo* (2014) as well as *La traducción en Ia creación del canon poético* (2015).

IPSHITA CHANDA is Professor of Comparative Literature at Jadavpur University, Kolkata. She writes on Comparative Literature and Indian literatures in English, Hindi and Bengali. She also translates between Bengali, Hindi, Urdu and English. Her publications include: *Shaping the Discourse: Translations of Womens Writings from Bengali Periodicals 1864–1947, Stree Kolkata* (2013) "*Dhoraicharitmanas*" (2013). She has recently been elected to the Executive Board of International Comparative Literature Association.

INDRA NATH CHOUDHURI is the Chief Editor of the *Encyclopedia of Indian Literature* (revised version) of the National Academy of Letters (Sahitya Akademi) and also the Chief Editor of the *Laghu Hindi Viswakosh* of the Central Hindi Institute of the Ministry of Human Resource Development, New Delhi. He is the President of the Comparative Literature Association of India. His latest books include: *Medieval Indian Literature: Linguistic and Literary* (1912), *IGNCA and Hinduism: A Way of Life and a Mode of Thought* (1912). He has edited the 3rd Volume of the *Encyclopedia of Indian Literature* (2016) and also *Ta gore's Vision of the Contemporary World* (2016).

SISIR KUMAR DAS (1936–2003) was Tagore Professor at the Department of Modern Indian Languages and Literary Studies at the University of Delhi, Delhi. He was a poet, playwright and has also translated Aristotle's *Poetics* and a few Greek plays into Bengali. His publications include: *Comparative Literature: Theory and Practice* Co-Ed. (1989), *English Writings of Rabindranath Tagore* three volumes Ed. (1994, 1996), *A History of Indian Literature 1800–1910 Western Impact: Indian Response* (1991), *A History of Indian Literature 1911–1956 Struggle for Freedom: Triumph and Tragedy* (1995).

SAYANTAN DASGUPTA teaches Comparative Literature at Jadavpur University, Kolkata and is also Coordinator, Centre for Translation of Indian Literatures. His research areas include the history of Comparative Literature. He is author of *Indian English Literature: A Study in Historiography* and *Shyam Selvadurai: Texts and Contexts* and co-author of *Translation: Roles, Responsibilities and Boundaries*. He has edited *A South Asian Nationalism Readerand* several volumes of translations. He is currently co-editing annotated English translations of Rabindranath Tagore's *Prachin Sahitya* and *Buddhadeva*. He is currently Secretary of the Comparative Literature Association of India.

SUBHA CHAKRABORTY DASGUPTA is at present Visiting Professor in the Department of Modern Indian Languages and Literary Studies, University of Delhi. Earlier she was Professor and Coordinator, Centre of Advance Study, Department of Comparative Literature, Jadavpur University. She was an Editor of *Jadavpur Journal of Comparative Literature* from 2007–2012. She has been a Visiting Faculty at Tokyo University of Foreign Studies and also Secretary of Comparative Literature Association of India for two terms and part of a Research Team on Multilingualism in Literature of the International Comparative Literature Association. Her publications include: *Studies in Comparative Literature: Theory, Culture and Space Co-ed.* (2007). She also translates from English, French and Hindi into Bangla and into English from Bangla.

GANESH DEVY, formerly Professor of English at the MS. University of Baroda, is the founder of Bhasha Research and Publication Centre, Baroda and the Adivasi Academy at Tejgadh. His work combines cultural campagins for the conservation of threatened languages and human rights activism for Adivasis and nomadic communities in India. His publications include: *After Amnesia* (1992), *Of Many Heroes and Indian Literary Criticism* (1997) and *A Nomad Called Thief* (2007). He writes in Marathi, Gujarati and English.

EUGENE CHEN EOYANG has been a chair Professor of English at Lingrian University, Hong Kong, as well as Professor Emeritus of Comparative Literature and of East Asian Languages and Cultures, Indiana University. His research interests include translation and translation theory, Chinese literature, Literary theory, Oral literature and Multiculturalism. He has published *The Transparent Eye: Reflections on Translation, Chinese Literature and Comparative Poetics* (1993). He has also been a Vice President of FILLM and a member of the Executive Committee of the International Comparative Literature Association and also a fellow of the Royal Society for the Promotion of Arts, Manufactures and Commerce (FRSA).

D.W. FOKKEMA (1931–2011) was an Emeritus Professor of Comparative Literature at the University of Utrecht and was Director of the Research Institut for History and Culture in Utrecht from 1987–94. His most recent works include *Literary History, Modernism and Postmodernism* (1984). He co-authored with Elrud Ibsch, *Theories of Literature in the Twentieth Century*

(1977), *Modernist Conjectures* (1988) and *Knowledge and Commitment* (2000). He has been the President of International Comparative Literature Association.

GERALD E.P. GILLESPIE is Emeritus Professor at Stanford University and a former President of ICLA. His publications includes: *Echoland: Readings from Humanism to Postmodernism* (2006) and *Proust, Mann, Joyce in the Modernist Context* (2010). He has translated and edited *Ludwig Tieck's "Puss-in-Boots"and Theater of the Absurd* (2013) and *The Nightwatches of Bonaventura* (2014). He has also directed the collaborative ICLA volumes *Romantic Prose Fiction* (2008, with M. Engel and B. Dieterle), *Intersections, Interferences, Interdisciplines: Literature with Other Arts* (2014, with H.Saussy), and *Contextualizing World Literature* (2015, with Jean Bessière).

JASBIR JAIN has been Sahitya Akademi Writer in Residence at the University of Rajasthan, where she was also an Emeritus Fellow and a KK Birla Fellow in Comparative Literature. Recipient of the 2008 SALA Award and the 2003 Award of IACS for distinguished scholarship, Jam has worked across genres and written extensively on cultural and literary issues with a special focus on narratology, gender and Indian literatures. Her recent publications include *Indigenous Roots of Feminism: Culture, Subjectivity and Agency* (2011), *Theorizing Resistance* (2012), *The Diaspora Writes Home* (2015) and *Forgiveness: Between Memory and History* (2016).

SUKRITA PAUL KUMAR, currently holds the Aruna Asaf Ali Chair at University of Delhi. Formerly a Fellow of the Indian Institute of Advanced Study, Shimla, she is also a Fellow of the International Writing Programme, Iowa (USA) and Hong Kong Baptist University. Honorary faculty, Durrell Centre at Corfu (Greece), she has been a recipient of many prestigious fellowships and residencies. A well-known poet, translator and an artist, she has published several poetry collections and critical books such as *Narrating Partition* (2009), *Dream Catcher* (2015) and *Blind* (2016). She was also a guest editor of journal, *Manoa* (Hawaii).

MARC MAUFORT is Professor of English, American and Postcolonial Literatures at the Université Libre de Bruxelles, Belgium. He has written and co-edited several books on Eugene O'Neill as well as postcolonial and multi-ethnic drama. His most recent edited book is *New Territories, Theatre, Drama, and Performance in Post-apart heid South Africa* (2015). He is the current editor of *Recherche littéraire/Literary Research,* the bilingual publication of the International Association for Comparative Literature (ICLA).

ANISUR RAHMAN, formerly Professor of English at Jamia Millia Islamia, New Delhi, is currently Senior Advisor at Rekhta Foundation (www.rekhta.org). He works and publishes in the areas of postcolonial literature(s), comparative literature and theory and practice of literary translation. Some of his publications include: *Form and Value in the Poetry of Nissim Ezekiel* (1981), *Expressive Form in the Poetry of Kamala Das* (1981), *New Literatures in English* (1996). He has edited *Translation: Poetics and Practice* (2002) and co-edited *Translation/Representation* (2007), *Indian English Women Poets* (2009) and *Discoursing Minority: In-text and Co-text* (2014). Rahman has also published translations of poetry from Urdu into English and vice-versa. He is Secretary, Comparative Literature Association of India.

E.V. RAMAKRISHNAN is presently UGC Professor Emeritus at Central University of Gujarat, Gandhinagar. He is a bilingual writer and has published poetry and literary criticism in Malayalam and English. He is also a well-known translator. He has published three volumes of poetry in English: *Being Elsewhere in Myself* (1980), *A Python in a Snake Park* (1994) and *Terms of Seeing: New and Selected Poems* (2006). Among his critical books in English are: *Interdisciplinary Alternatives in Comparative Literature, Co-ed.* (2013). *Locating Indian Literature: Texts, Traditions and Translations* (2011) and *Making It New: Modernism in Malayalam, Marathi and Hind! Poetry* (1995). He has recently been elected to the Executive Board of the International Comparative Literature Association.

HAUN SAUSSY is University Professor in the University of Chicago, specializing in comparative literature, classical Chinese literature and social thought. His books include: *The Problem of a Chinese Aesthetic* (1993), *Great Walls of Discourse* (2001), *Comparative Literature in an Age of Globalization* (2006), *Partner to the Poor: A Paul Farmer Reader* (2010) and *The Ethnography of Rhythm* (2016). He is currently working on a study of translation in fourth-century China.

JÜRI TALVET has been a Chair Professor of World Literature at the University of 1rtu since 1992. He took his Ph.D. on the Spanish picaresque novel at Leningrad University in 1981. His main research areas are Comparative Poetics of Western Literature, Baroque poetics, 20th-century novel and poetry, Spanish and Latin- American literature, Estonian poetry and Intercultural studies. He has published nine books of essays in Estonian and nine collections of poetry. His recent publications in English translation are: *A Call for Cultural Symbiosis* (2005), *Estonian Elegy* (2008) and *Of Snow, of Soul* (2010).

ANNE TOMICHE, after holding positions in the United States (California, New York) and in various French universities, Anne Tomiche joined the University Paris-Sorbonne in 2010, where she is currently Professor of Comparative Literature. She has been the President of the French Comparative Literature Association (SFLGC) between 2005 and 2009, as well as a member of the ICLA Executive Council since 2010. She has recently published *La Naissance des avant-gardes* (2015) and *'Lintraduisible dont je suis fait' Artaud et les avant-gardes occidentales* (2012). She has also edited *Fictions du masculin dans les littératures occidentales* (2015) as well as *Comparative Literature as a Critical Approach/La Littérature comparée comme approche critique* (6 volumes of Proceedings of the 2013 ICLA Paris Congress) due for publication in 2017.

HARISH TRIVEDI, former Professor of English at the University of Delhi, was visiting professor at the universities of Chicago and London. He is the author of *Colonial Transactions: English Literature and India* (1995) and has co-edited *The Nation across the World: Postcolonial Literary Representations* (2007–2008) and *Postcolonial Translation: Theory and Practice* (1999). He contributed essays to the *Cambridge Companion* volumes on both Gandhi and Kipling (2011). Trivedi is currently one of the contributing editors of an international project based in Stockholm for writing a history of World Literature.

Index

www.ingramcontent.com/pod-product-compliance
Lightning Source LLC
Chambersburg PA
CBHW020937310726
48980CB00007B/807/J

* 9 7 8 9 3 8 4 0 9 2 7 3 3 *